The politics of expansion

MANCHESTER
1824

Manchester University Press

Contents

List of tables and figures

Tables

Figures

List of illustrations

Acknowledgements

This book owes its origins to my interest in exploring the impact of politics and policy change on education in Ireland. The work began as a Ph.D thesis with the History Department of Trinity College Dublin. As it developed the book sought to illuminate the interaction between the political system and the educational sector during an era of transformation in Irish education.

I should like to record my thanks firstly to Professor Eunan O'Halpin, my Ph.D supervisor, for his invaluable advice and assistance. I wish to pay a particular tribute to Professor John Horgan and Dr. Damian Murchan, who acted as examiners for the thesis and offered various constructive suggestions to improve the work. Thanks are also due to the administrative staff in the History Department, Jill Northridge, Jennifer Scholtz, Pamela Hilliard, Alan MacSimoin and Judith Lee.

I wish to thank the staff of the following libraries and archives for their assistance and co-operation: Trinity College Dublin Library, the National Library of Ireland, the National Archives, Representative Church Body Library, Braemor Park and UCD Archives Department. I wish to record my gratitude particularly to Dr. David Sheehy, Dublin Diocesan Archives, Dr. Liz Mullins, Irish Jesuit Archives, Karen Johnson, Christian Brothers' Archives, St. Mary's Province and Michelle Cooney, Christian Brothers' Archives, St. Helen's Province. The officers and staff of all three teaching unions were consistently helpful in providing available records and papers. I am particularly indebted to John MacGabhann of the TUI, Maura Leydon with the ASTI, and Ann McConnell and Aoife Doyle with the INTO. Bernadette Kinsella and Gráinne O'Neill of the Secretariat of Secondary Schools provided invaluable assistance in making available the records of the CMCSS and other private managerial bodies. I am also grateful for the assistance of the officials of the Records Management section of the Department of Education.

A special thanks to Manchester University Press for their hard work in preparing the manuscript for publication. I also wish to thank Helen Litton, who prepared the index to her usual high professional standard. Sara Smyth and Thomas Fayne of the National Photographic Archive gave indispensable help in unearthing the illustrations for the book; so too did Caroline Meleady in the Archives of Blackrock College.

Prof. John Coolahan, Prof. Áine Hyland and Dr. Séamas Ó Buachalla shared their valuable insights concerning the development of Irish education in the 1960s. Prof. Hyland also supplied me with important documentation relating to educational policy that was not available within the Department of Education. I wish to thank all the former elected representatives and officials, who gave generously of their time either through interviews or correspondence, including Dr. Patrick Hillery, Mr. Barry Desmond, Professor Martin O'Donoghue, Mr. Tony Ó Dálaigh and Mr. Thomas Leahy. I am particularly grateful to the late Mr. James Dukes, who responded to requests for information with unfailing courtesy and consideration. I am also indebted to fellow researchers who took note of material that was relevant to my work: Dr. Daithí Ò Corráin, Dr. Aoife Bhreathnach, Jim Cooke and Patrick Wall. I greatly appreciate the invaluable technical assistance provided by Dr. Mairéad de Róiste, who gave generously of her time and expertise on various issues. I owe a particular debt of gratitude to Dr. Shane Martin for proofreading various drafts of this study.

Finally friends and family members who helped and advised throughout the lengthy process of writing and rewriting deserve my profound gratitude. I wish to record my thanks especially to my parents, Maura and John Walsh, whose consistent help and encouragement has been essential to the successful completion of this work.

John Walsh
Trinity College Dublin

List of abbreviations

ASTI	Association of Secondary Teachers Ireland
CCSS	Conference of Catholic Secondary Schools
CEC	Central Executive Committee (teaching unions)
CHA	Catholic Headmasters' Association
CMCSS	Council of Managers of Catholic Secondary Schools
HEA	Higher Education Authority
IVEA	Irish Vocational Education Association
JMB	Joint Managerial Body
INTO	Irish National Teachers' Organisation
NESC	National Economic and Social Council
NIEC	National Industrial Economic Council
NPD	National Progressive Democrat Party
NUI	National University of Ireland
OECD	Organisation for Economic Co-operation and Development
RTC	Regional Technical College
RTÉ	Radio Telefís Éireann
SEC	Secondary Education Committee
TBA	Teaching Brothers' Association
TCD	Trinity College Dublin
TUI	Teachers' Union of Ireland
UCC	University College Cork
UCD	University College Dublin
UCG	University College Galway
VEC	Vocational Education Committee
VTA	Vocational Teachers' Association

Introduction

The transformation of the Irish educational system did not happen by accident; it was the outcome of deliberate policy decisions taken by representatives of the Irish state. It is generally acknowledged that a wide variety of significant changes in the educational system occurred in this period, but the transformation in the state's policy approach, which provided the essential context for these changes, has not received detailed historical analysis. The dramatic expansion of the educational sector in the 1960s cannot be adequately understood without considering the rapid and sweeping changes in education policy. The present study explores the far-reaching policy changes adopted by the state in this period and evaluates the impact of these changes on the Irish educational sector. It is not the intention of this work to suggest that any system of education can or should be regarded simply as a mechanism for the achievement of the state's policy objectives. But there is no doubt that the transformation of the Irish educational system was inextricably linked to the gradual evolution of the state's policy for educational expansion. It is essential to evaluate critically the role of the state and its interaction with other leading stakeholders within Irish education. This work investigates the origins and development of the profound changes in education policy between the late 1950s and early 1970s.

There is no doubt that the educational policy of the Irish state was transformed in this period. The state's timid and tentative approach to education in the 1950s was based on a conservative consensus, which was shared by politicians, senior officials and educational authorities. This consensus was based firmly on the assumption that the Irish state should play only a limited role in providing education or developing the educational sector. The Catholic and Protestant churches played a crucial part in providing both primary and second-level education: the vast majority of schools were owned and managed by religious authorities. The Catholic Church was the most powerful stakeholder in the Irish educational system throughout this period. The influence of the Catholic religious authorities was derived in part from the reality that the vast majority of the population was composed of practising Catholics and in part from the historical development of Irish education in a denominational direction during the nineteenth century. The Catholic Church had acquired a key position within the educational system before 1900 and its influence predated the foundation of the Irish state.[1] Following the achievement of independent statehood in 1922, Irish politicians and officials deferred extensively to the Catholic bishops in formulating educational policy and the Catholic Church occupied a uniquely powerful position within the educational system for a full generation. The Department of Education was reluctant to risk conflict with the Catholic Church and tended to leave the initiative in developing education to the private interests that dominated the system, notably the clerical managers and religious orders. Successive governments pursued limited and conservative objectives in education, focusing on modest initiatives to sustain primary education and on efforts to develop vocational education within the highly restrictive framework agreed between the new state and the Catholic bishops in 1930. Ministers tended to be preoccupied with the implementation of established policies, such as the attempt to revive the Irish language through the schools and with the cautious management of existing educational structures. The limited objectives and activity of the state in education reflected the prevailing cultural and political context of the time.

The department itself was perceived by many contemporaries as a barrier to educational reform. Professor John J. O'Meara of University College Dublin was by no means alone in his scathing critique of the department in March 1958: 'Hardly more than a ripple or two has come to disturb that stagnant pond which is the Department of Education since the State was founded - and it would seem that hardly a ripple ever will – for that department seems to share some of the qualities of the natural law: it seems to be immutable.'[2] While conservative attitudes on the part of many stakeholders within the system persisted throughout the 1960s, leading politicians and officials developed a proactive and interventionist policy for educational expansion. Indeed by the late 1960s the Department of Education was regarded by the secondary school managerial authorities as an aggressive and insensitive force for change in the educational sector.[3] Sr. Eileen Randles summarised the views of many secondary school managers when she argued in 1975 that the 'intemperate zeal of the Department of Education officials' aroused considerable resentment among the secondary school authorities in the previous decade.[4] These critical but strikingly divergent views of the department's approach underlined the fundamental transformation of the state's policy within the space of a single decade.

The evolution of a proactive, reforming approach by the state towards the educational sector began in the late 1950s. The changes in the educational objectives and policies of the state reflected wider changes in Irish society. The government's adoption of a programme of economic expansion in 1958 certainly encouraged the development of a more positive appreciation of the potential benefits of education for national economic development. The election of Seán Lemass as Taoiseach created a favourable political climate for the formulation of a coherent reforming policy in education. The appointment by Lemass of a succession of dynamic ministers, drawn from Fianna Fáil's younger generation, to head the Department of Education also enhanced the status of the department and heightened the profile of education as a political issue.[5] Domestic political and economic changes did not provide the sole impetus for educational advances. The international context for the policy changes should not be discounted, not least the Irish state's involvement in the Organisation for Economic Co-operation and Development (OECD). The OECD's zealous promotion of scientific education and technological development among its members exerted an important influence on the state's educational policy.

The government's educational policy initially evolved in a cautious and measured fashion under the direction of Dr. Patrick Hillery, Minister for Education between 1959 and 1965. Séamas Ó Buachalla indeed suggested that 'Hillery's main role was precursorial, preparing public and political opinion for the policy changes which were still in preparation.'[6] This view suggests that Hillery's term of office was important largely because it prepared the way for key policy changes made by others. But in fact the reforms initiated by Hillery involved significant policy changes, which were no less important than the more dramatic measures announced by his successors. The announcement by Hillery of the government's plan for post-primary education and the development of regional technological colleges on 20 May 1963 underlined that the transformation of the state's policy approach was already well advanced in the early 1960s. The steady advance in the role and influence of the state within the educational sector was reflected in the wide range of reforming initiatives undertaken by the department under Hillery. While Lemass's influence on the evolution of the state's policy was certainly significant, Hillery's own role in launching the process of educational reform has been underestimated. Hillery's contribution to the reform and expansion of the Irish educational sector in this period deserves a detailed reappraisal.

The increasing importance attached to education as a key element in economic development was reflected in the *Second Programme for Economic Expansion, Part II*, which gave considerable attention to the economic and social advantages of educational expansion.[7] Indeed it was alleged by various stakeholders within the educational system that the government's policy for educational reform was driven solely by economic objectives. It would be foolish to argue that the government's willingness to invest in education had nothing to do with its concern to sustain economic progress. But the commitment made by successive ministers to the principle of equality of educational opportunity in the 1960s is also relevant in analysing the various objectives which influenced the state's policy. The proactive policy approach adopted by the state was not developed solely by ministers or senior officials. It is widely recognised that *Investment in Education*, the report compiled by an Irish survey team between 1962 and 1965 under the auspices of the OECD and the Department of Education, greatly influenced the development of coherent educational planning by the department. The survey team's comprehensive analysis of the Irish educational system provided essential statistical data for educational planning and shaped the policies adopted by George Colley, during his relatively brief but influential term as Minister for Education (April 1965–July 1966).

Donogh O'Malley, who was the third reforming minister appointed by Lemass, secured political immortality with his dramatic announcement of the introduction of free post-primary education in September 1966. Any assessment of the initiative for free post-primary education has to consider not only O'Malley's undoubted personal commitment to the initiative, but also the influence of *Investment in Education*, the preparations within the Department of Education for some form of free education by 1970 and the role of Lemass in facilitating educational reform. O'Malley's influence should be reassessed in terms of his overall contribution to the transformation of the educational system, not simply on the basis of his dramatic initiative for free second-level education. O'Malley's key role in the expansion of higher technical education in the late 1960s has been obscured by the greater public drama of his announcement on free education. Moreover the Minister's achievements should be seen in the context of Lemass's commitment to give priority to educational expansion in the allocation of scarce national resources.

Education in Ireland has attracted considerable academic interest, but there has been no detailed historical analysis of the transformation of educational policy in the 1960s. Dr Séamas Ó Buachalla has provided a detailed examination of the policy process in his work *Education Policy in Twentieth Century Ireland* (Dublin, 1988). This work deals with the process of policy formulation and implementation in the first eight decades of the twentieth century and by its nature gives relatively little attention to the development of educational policy in the 1960s. Professor John Coolahan gives an excellent overview of educational change between 1960 and 1980 in his work, *Irish Education: Its History and Structure* (Dublin, 1981).[8] This is an informative commentary on the extent of the educational changes after 1960, which is not intended to deal in detail with the development of the state's policy for educational expansion. A more recent work by Eileen Doyle, *Leading the Way: Managing Voluntary Schools* (Dublin, 2000), focuses primarily on the development of the managerial bodies in secondary education.[9] All of these works provide valuable insights concerning the evolution of the Irish educational system in the twentieth century. There is a need, however, for a comprehensive historical analysis of the far-reaching changes in the educational sector in the 1960s.

This work is based principally on archival material, which was not previously available for research purposes or was not fully exploited with regard to education. My study draws on the records of the Department of Education, which are not yet publicly available. No policy files from the Department of Education after 1932 are available in the National Archives, but I was fortunate to gain access to the records held by the department itself. While all of the relevant material was not available within the department, the available material was extensive, particularly with regard to primary and post-primary education. The files of the Department of the Taoiseach in the National Archives also provided very full documentation on education, including extensive records of the Department of Education, which were unavailable elsewhere. The records of the Department of the Taoiseach had not been fully examined in this context previously and yielded much valuable information especially concerning the interaction between Lemass and successive ministers for Education. The records of the Department of Finance, especially its Economic Development Branch, also contained substantial material on education and on the Irish's state interaction with the OECD in the early 1960s. The work has also drawn upon the proceedings of the Public Accounts Committee, which have not previously been used in a study of educational policy.

The McQuaid Papers in the Dublin Diocesan Archives provided an invaluable source of information on relations between the Catholic Hierarchy and the Department of Education in this period. The archive of the Secretariat of Secondary Schools was a rich source for the papers of the Catholic managerial bodies. The book has drawn upon the records of the Irish Christian Brothers and the Irish Jesuit Archives: the records of the Jesuit order in particular contain papers and correspondence which have not previously been used in a study of education in this period. I also consulted the *Journal of the Proceedings of the General Synod of the Church of*

Ireland and the reports of the Secondary Education Committee (SEC), which illustrated the views of the Protestant churches and educational authorities on the process of educational expansion.

A wide range of additional archival and library material was consulted, including the records of all three teaching unions and the Irish Vocational Education Association (IVEA). The back issues of national and local newspapers in the National Library proved a valuable source for ministerial announcements and public reaction to educational initiatives. Personal papers are unfortunately not available for several prominent public figures in this period, including Seán Lemass, George Colley and Donogh O'Malley. My study has drawn upon the papers of other public figures, including General Richard Mulcahy and Cearbhall Ó Dálaigh, which are available in the Archives Department of University College Dublin. I have also undertaken a number of interviews with retired public figures, including politicians, officials of the Department of Education and academics who participated in the policy decisions of the period.

This study focuses on the expansion and development of the Irish educational system from primary to third-level education. I do not attempt to evaluate developments relating to the reformatory and industrial schools, which came formally under the remit of the Department of Education, although the policy issues affecting reformatory education and juvenile detention also involved the departments of Justice and Health. The area of reformatory education is not explored by this study as it remains a matter of contemporary controversy and much of the essential primary source material is still inaccessible. The attention given to some important areas of Irish education, such as the early development of special education and the limited official attempts to provide education for Travellers, is necessarily brief due to the character of this study. The work seeks to evaluate critically the influence exerted by the Irish state on the educational sector and to explore the impact of the policy changes in this period on the transformation of Irish education.

Notes

1 D.H. Akenson, *The Irish Education Experiment: The National System of Education in the Nineteenth Century* (London, 1970), pp. 275–315.
2 J.J. O'Meara, *Reform in Education* (Dublin, 1958), p. 6.
3 E. Randles, *Post-Primary Education in Ireland 1957–70* (Dublin, 1975), pp. 322–3.
4 Ibid.
5 S. Ó Buachalla, '*Investment in Education*: context, content and impact', *Administration*, vol. 44, no. 3 (Autumn 1996), pp. 10–20.

6 S. Ó Buachalla, *Education Policy in Twentieth Century Ireland* (Dublin, 1988), p. 290.

7 *Second Programme for Economic Expansion, Part II, laid by the Government before each House of the Oireachtas, July 1964* (Dublin, 1964), p. 193.

8 J. Coolahan, *Irish Education: Its History and Structure* (Dublin, 1981), pp. 131–40.

9 E. Doyle, *Leading the Way: Managing Voluntary Secondary Schools* (Dublin, 2000).

1

A conservative consensus: 1957–59

You have your teachers, your managers and your churches and I regard the position as Minister in the Department of Education as that of a kind of dungaree man, the plumber who will make satisfactory communications and streamline the forces and potentialities of the educational workers and educational management in this country. He will take the knock out of the pipes and will link up everything. I would be blind to my responsibility if I insisted on pontificating or lapsed into an easy acceptance of an imagined duty to philosophise here on educational matters.[1]

General Richard Mulcahy, Minister for Education in two inter-party governments, clearly expressed his view of the Irish educational system in his statement to the Dáil on 19 July 1956. The system was dominated by private interests, notably the Catholic and Protestant churches, especially at post-primary level. The Minister's statement was entirely consistent not only with the prevailing practice of the Department of Education but with the dominant political consensus concerning the state's limited role in the development of the educational system. Certainly Mulcahy's Fianna Fáil successor Jack Lynch gave no indication that the limited role of the state in managing or directing the educational system caused him any concern. Indeed he strongly defended the educational achievements of the Irish system in June 1958, claiming that 'misleading statements' made by left-wing politicians and critical commentators would undermine the reputation of Irish education abroad.[2] But while Lynch's public pronouncements paid homage to the conservative consensus of the previous generation, the new Minister proved willing to initiate incremental reforms, especially in primary education where his actions were least likely to involve conflict with established private interests.

The statement by Mulcahy, who served as Minister for Education for two terms, 1948–51 and 1954–57, accurately reflected the traditional policy approach followed by the Irish state. Mulcahy's minimalist conception of the role of the Minister for Education assumed that the management and direction of the educational system rested with private managers and the churches, with unspecified input from the teachers.[3] He effectively dis-

1 Jack Lynch, Minister for Education, and Birklum Shah, Ambassador of India, at the Italian reception in Lucan, 1959. Courtesy of the National Library of Ireland.

claimed all responsibility for the formulation of educational policy and indicated that the only viable role for the Minister was to facilitate the work of the private interests, which controlled the educational system. Mulcahy was a staunch defender of the educational system that had evolved in the independent Irish state. Mulcahy's highly restrictive definition of the state's role in education was a reflection of the consensus of the era. Seán O'Connor, a Principal Officer within the department from 1956, was personally appalled by Mulcahy's statement but commented that 'The sentiments he expressed, however, were in full accord with the senior officials of the Department.'[4] Similarly, James Dukes, who served as private secretary to Mulcahy, Jack Lynch and Patrick Hillery, believed that the senior officials regarded Education as a junior department, understaffed, under-resourced and unable to take on any additional responsibilities: 'they were up to their ears with work and it was very tight where money was concerned'.[5] Mulcahy had expressed openly the accepted position of the department.

The financial constraints imposed by the Department of Finance, especially pressure for cuts in the Education Estimates between 1955 and

1957, reinforced the prevailing official reluctance to take a proactive approach to the formulation of education policy. Dukes recalled: 'We were completely under the thumb of Finance.'[6] The Department of Education informed the Public Accounts Committee that no vacancies for the position of school inspector could be filled without seeking the permission of the Department of Finance. Moreover the Secretary was not allowed to take any measures to fill a vacancy until an actual retirement had occurred and even then vacancies could not be filled as they arose, as the department was obliged to wait until a number of vacancies could be filled en bloc.[7] Furthermore, efforts were made by the Department of Finance to curtail national school building, teacher salaries and schemes for the promotion of the Irish language during Mulcahy's second term as Minister. The Minister for Finance, Gerry Sweetman, proposed a series of stringent restrictions on educational expenditure in August 1954, including a reduction of future capital investment in vocational education.[8] Mulcahy firmly defended his departmental estimates and succeeded in blocking most of the cuts sought by the Department of Finance in the short term, although he was obliged to accept reductions in expenditure for secondary and vocational education in 1956.[9] Mulcahy had, however, little inclination to promote new policy initiatives. While Education, like other government departments, endured financial constraints in this period, it is evident that Mulcahy and his senior officials did not attempt to challenge the prevailing financial orthodoxy or expand the role of their department. Mulcahy himself was perceived by his officials as a decent and conscientious public figure but not a forceful or innovative minister.[10] He was not associated with any significant policy initiative during his second term as Minister for Education between 1954 and 1957. Mulcahy was deeply committed to the revival of the Irish language, but this commitment was expressed in his implementation of existing departmental policy. The programmes organised by the department to promote the Irish language, including special courses for teachers and funding for Irish publications, were maintained under Mulcahy's stewardship in the face of demands for severe reductions in such programmes by the Department of Finance.[11] Mulcahy's approach fully reflected the minimalist involvement of the Irish state in education, which was based upon the assumption that the policy initiative rested primarily with private, mainly clerical, interests.[12] The Department of Education did not challenge the predominant position held by clerical managers or religious orders within primary and secondary education until the 1960s.

Moreover a key feature of the Irish educational system up to the 1950s was the underdevelopment and neglect of vocational and technical education. Second-level education in Ireland was marked by a rigid division between the private secondary schools, which offered academic education and the vocational system, providing instruction in practical and technical subjects. The government's policy in the first generation of the new state perpetuated this division. Prof. John Marcus O'Sullivan, Minister for Education, gave comprehensive assurances to the Catholic Hierarchy in October 1930 that the vocational schools would provide continuation and technical education of a strictly practical character under the terms of the Vocational Education Act 1930: they would not provide general education, which would continue to be given in primary and secondary schools.[13] O'Sullivan specifically assured the bishops that a more universal system of post-primary education would not be achieved through the extension of the vocational system.[14] Successive governments since 1930 had maintained the vocational character of the sector, which was guaranteed by the Vocational Education Act and the Minister's assurances to the Hierarchy. Vocational school students were denied access to the Intermediate and Leaving Certificate examinations and restricted to a two-year second-level course for the Day Group Certificate. The restrictions imposed by the state helped to ensure that the status of the vocational system was always inferior to the prestige enjoyed by the private secondary schools.[15]

The deliberations of the Council of Education illustrated the conservative attitudes towards education and the role of the state, which prevailed among the educational authorities in this period. Mulcahy established the Council in April 1950 to undertake a review of the functions of primary, secondary and vocational education.[16] The Council was intended to advise the Minister 'upon such matters relating to educational theory and practice as it might think fit and upon any educational questions and problems referred to them by him'.[17] The Council was entirely dominated by established educational interests, especially representatives of the churches. The membership of the Council was drawn largely from the ranks of the educational authorities, excluding the teaching associations or formal representation by parents.[18] Indeed twenty-six of the twenty-nine members appointed by Mulcahy were professional educators and no less than eleven of the nominees were clergy of various denominations: the Council was chaired by two Catholic priests, first by Canon Denis O'Keeffe and then by Monsignor Martin Brenan.[19] The narrowly based membership of the Council underlined its status as a forum for powerful established interests, which had the largest stake in the existing structures of the educational sector.

The Council made its report on primary education to Mulcahy in September 1954. The report was generally conservative in its approach to educational problems. The Council clearly rejected the idea of a higher statutory school leaving age and saw no necessity to indicate any precise age for the end of primary education.[20] The report also strongly defended small one-teacher schools and regarded the transport of children to a central school, instead of keeping an existing school open, as 'an expedient of last resort'.[21] The Council's conclusions on the management of national schools reflected its hostility to state involvement in the educational system: the report expressed the fear that an unhealthy perception of state control could be created by the term 'National School' and recommended that the designation of 'Primary School' should be used instead, to indicate that the Irish schools were not in fact state schools.[22] It is difficult to dispute the dismissive verdict of Seán O'Connor, who described the report as 'that lacklustre and most conservative document'.[23]

The second report of the Council, which dealt with the secondary school programme, was even more dismissive of proposals for reform. The Council's deliberations were informed by no great sense of urgency: it started its analysis of the secondary school programme in 1954 and completed its report only in November 1960.[24] The report presented a deeply conservative analysis, which gave considerable emphasis to defending the distinctive character of secondary education in the Republic. The Council started from the premise that the central purpose of secondary schools was the inculcation of religious values: 'The ultimate purpose of secondary schools in Ireland is, in short, to prepare their pupils to be God-fearing and responsible citizens.'[25] The report drew a sharp distinction between secondary and vocational education, emphasising that the liberal education, involving the all-round formation of the individual, was the immediate objective of the secondary school. The Council proceeded to warn against the danger of giving excessive importance to science in secondary education at the expense of general moral and intellectual development: they argued that 'demands are being made which would subordinate the general education of the secondary school to specialised study and sacrifice the formation of the man in the interests of scientific progress'.[26]

The Council also showed a considerable suspicion of innovations that might involve increased state intervention in secondary education. The report noted with approval that the involvement of the state in secondary education was limited and defended the existing system, praising the co-operation between the department and the private school authorities. The Council emphatically opposed the idea of a formal system of vocational guidance operated by the state or indeed any public authority.[27] They also categorically rejected any general scheme of 'secondary education for all' on financial and educational grounds.[28] The Council dismissed the idea of free post-primary education as 'utopian', on the basis that the state could not sustain the financial burden.[29] Moreover they considered a universal scheme of free secondary education to be objectionable on the basis that it would reduce incentives for pupils and cause standards to fall. The Council instead argued that private initiative, supported by increased state grants and scholarships, provided the best means of extending the facilities for secondary education. The predominant attitude of the Council was not simply conservative and hostile to state intervention, but also elitist in its conception of secondary education. The report indicated that the managerial authorities represented on the Council were broadly satisfied with the key features of the existing system and were reluctant to contemplate significant changes.[30] The deeply conservative approach favoured by the Council ensured that its influence on educational policy was virtually nonexistent. The failure of the Council of Education to make any impact underlined the strength of the conservative consensus, which dominated the approach of the educational authorities in this period. The hostility of powerful educational interests to any significant policy change provided much of the rationale for the timid and tentative approach pursued by the state in the 1950s.

The replacement of General Mulcahy by Jack Lynch on 20 March 1957, following the election of a Fianna Fáil government led by Eamon de Valera, did not bring any immediate change in the state's minimalist approach to education. Lynch maintained cuts originally imposed by Mulcahy in secondary and vocational education, when he announced his first Estimates as Minister on 1 May 1957.[31] Lynch approved the Education Estimates, which had been prepared before Mulcahy's departure from office, without substantial amendment.[32] Mulcahy had imposed a cut of 10% in the capitation grants paid to secondary schools and a reduction of 6% in the annual state grants paid to the Vocational Education Committees (VECs). Lynch indicated that both cuts would be applied again in 1957–58 due to severe budgetary problems, although he promised to review the reductions and expressed particular regret that the cut affecting vocational education could not be reversed immediately.[33] Perhaps more significant than Lynch's endorsement of his predecessor's Estimates was the new Minister's commentary on the educational system in his speech on 1 May. He emphasised the importance of education, arguing that proper moral and social education was required to inculcate civic virtues and discourage emigration by young people.[34] He criticised unnecessary emigration, which was caused as much by 'a moral sickness' afflicting many Irish people as by material conditions: he regarded education as an essential means of overcoming this spiritual malaise and inculcating a strong national spirit.[35] The Minister argued too that Ireland enjoyed a sound educational system, which was not appreciated by critics of the system. While it was acknowledged that education in Ireland was faced with many problems, Lynch emphasised that such problems were not solely a matter for the state. The educational system was influenced by important private interests and the state could not simply take control of the educational structures to enforce drastic changes. He warned that a policy involving state control of education would undermine the autonomy of schools and infringe parental rights. In his first major parliamentary contribution as Minister, Lynch said little that was inconsistent with Mulcahy's approach and endorsed the traditional deference shown by the department to the clerical and religious managers. The new Minister had also indicated that the department shared responsibility with private educational interests for the formulation of future policy, suggesting that the Irish educational structure was a co-operative system in which the state was obliged to work closely with the relevant educational interests.[36] Lynch's statement, however, was cautious and conventional, rejecting criticism of educational provision as an unwarranted attempt to undermine the private managerial system.

Despite the conventional tone of his rhetoric, Lynch gave indications that he was ready to contemplate policy changes where reforms did not bring him into conflict with established educational interests. He initiated a proposal for an oral Irish test within the Leaving Certificate examination, announcing a feasibility study for such a test in his Estimates speech on 1 May.[37] Lynch also defended the established policy of reviving the Irish language, praising the effort made to revive Irish in the schools; he criticised Fine Gael TD Patrick O'Donnell on 10 June 1958 for adopting a 'defeatist view', in arguing that the language would fail unless priority was given to the Gaeltacht.[38] The Minister was able to tell critics of the policy that language revival was not simply a matter for the Department of Education, as de Valera had announced the establishment of a Commission on the Restoration of the Irish Language, which was to examine various means of achieving the revival of Irish.[39] The Taoiseach took the leading role in determining the terms of reference for the Commission, which was established in July 1958.[40] Lynch was, however, strongly committed to the introduction of an oral Irish test, believing that it would be greatly beneficial for the teaching of Irish. Following the completion of a favourable evaluation of the idea, the Secondary Education Branch began to plan for an oral test in Irish as part of the Leaving Certificate from 1960.[41] Lynch announced the introduction of the oral test in the Dáil on 22 May 1958. He strongly defended the decision to introduce the oral test for the Leaving Certificate rather than the Intermediate Certificate, arguing that the Leaving Certificate was the end-point of the Secondary school course and oral Irish would therefore feature on the entire Secondary course from the beginning.[42] Lynch's initiative was a significant curriculum innovation in the teaching of Irish, especially in the context of the public emphasis given by successive governments to the revival of the Irish language as a national objective.

First steps towards reform

The new Minister signalled another, more significant, policy change very early in his term. Lynch informed the Dáil on 1 May 1957 that he intended to review the ban on the employment of married women teachers in national schools.[43] Rule 72(1), which required women teachers to retire on marriage, had been maintained by the department since 1934 despite the vociferous opposition of the Irish National Teachers' Organisation (INTO).[44] Lynch described the ban as 'a great waste of teaching power'.[45] He made no secret of his disagreement with the marriage ban maintained by the department for over twenty-five years. Although his rhetoric remained cautious, the new Minister indicated early in his term of office that he was willing to reform traditional practices or policies, which were outmoded or even detrimental to educational development.

The reforms initiated by Lynch, with the important exception of the oral Irish test, involved primary education, the branch of the system in which the department exerted the greatest influence. The Minister soon acted upon his commitment to review the marriage ban, appointing a committee of six senior officials to examine the growing problem of untrained teachers in national schools. The department had introduced the rule from 1 October 1934, in the context of the world economic depression, a declining population and a surplus of teachers.[46] The situation was very different by the late 1950s, as the number of pupils in the national schools was steadily increasing, growing from an average enrolment of 472,536 in 1953–54 to 490,700 in 1957–58.[47] The gradual increase in the national school population meant that the output of trained teachers was insufficient to deal with the increased demand, although the teacher training colleges were fully subscribed. As the department recognised a category of untrained primary teachers, known as Junior Assistant Mistress, the marriage ban encouraged the employment of untrained teachers. National school managers tended to employ married women teachers on a temporary basis – no less than 235 married women teachers had been given temporary appointments by 1957–58.[48] But the shortage of trained teachers was an educational severe problem for the national schools: approximately 22% of all national schoolteachers were untrained in 1957–58.[49] The marriage ban was an educational liability, which was actively detrimental to the further development of primary education. Lynch had clearly recognised a compelling case for the removal of the marriage ban as early as May 1957. The committee of senior officials also favoured a reappraisal of the policy; they expressed grave concern at the employment of a substantial number of untrained teachers. Moreover a continuation of the rule meant that expenditure on training colleges for women teachers was increasingly unproductive, while

the withdrawal of the ban would allow the department to reclaim the marriage gratuity from married women teachers who returned to the teaching
service and phase out payment of the gratuity for the future.[50] The departmental committee also took into account 'present-day trends in relation to
the employment of married women', acknowledging that the employment
of married women was becoming part of 'the pattern of life in many countries'.[51] The senior officials of the department therefore perceived significant
advantages in the abolition of the rule not all related to education. James
Dukes recalled that 'they finally said, let's get rid of the ban, save money and
placate the Department of Finance, and provide trained teachers'.[52]

The review announced by Lynch led rapidly to the removal of the marriage ban. The Minister proposed the abolition of the rule to the government on 28 April 1958, emphasising that the policy change was dictated
by the necessity 'to alleviate the present untenable position in regard to
untrained and unqualified women teachers serving in national schools'.[53]
The Cabinet approved the removal of the marriage ban on 20 May.[54] The
Secretary then issued a circular to the national schools in June 1958,
which provided for its abolition. Rule 72(1) was revoked with effect from
1 July 1958.[55] All women teachers who had retired under the rule became
eligible for permanent employment in the national schools. Married women
teachers who held temporary appointments were recognised in a permanent and pensionable capacity from 1 July.[56] The conditions laid down
by the department provided for the restoration of such teachers to the
point on the salary scale which they had reached before their involuntary
retirement: married women teachers were obliged to refund their marriage
gratuity to obtain credit in respect of previous service for the purpose of
pension and retirement benefits. The circular also confirmed that no credit
for any purpose would be given to teachers for the period between their
retirement on marriage and their reappointment as recognised national
schoolteachers. Finally the department indicated that no women teachers
appointed after the removal of the ban would be eligible for a marriage
gratuity.[57] The senior officials had accepted the case for revoking the
marriage ban ostensibly to expand the supply of trained teachers. The
department's progress report for the second quarter of 1958 expressed
the hope that the removal of the Rule would 'help to relieve to some
extent the current shortage of trained teachers'.[58] The conditions laid
down for the re-entry of the married women teachers to permanent employment, however, indicated that the department also hoped to make savings
in the short term on the basis of the rule change.[59] The rapid progress of
the initiative to revoke the rule can be explained by official recognition that
it was financially prudent as well as educationally desirable to allow
married women teachers back into the permanent teaching service.

Lynch made the educational case for the decision when he announced the removal of the marriage ban in the Dáil on 22 May 1958. He noted with disapproval that a substantial proportion of the teachers in national schools were untrained, while at least 85 trained women teachers were being lost annually due to Rule 72(1).[60] He criticised the educational effects of the ban, arguing that married women teachers were being forced to retire from recognised teaching posts by the time they had reached an effective standard of teaching. The Minister declared that there was 'no reasonable alternative' to the removal of the ban, which would potentially provide between 400 and 500 married women teachers for permanent service in the national schools, including the trained temporary teachers already re-employed in the system.[61] The department had also estimated that approximately 85 additional teachers would be available annually for primary education as a consequence of the abolition of the ban. Lynch emphasised that the initiative would significantly expand the supply of trained teachers in the national schools and would facilitate an improvement in the pupil-teacher ratio.[62] The Minister placed the greatest emphasis on the genuine educational considerations, which demanded the removal of the marriage ban.

Lynch continued to defend the initiative as an essential reform dictated by educational considerations on 11 June 1958, when he outlined the specific terms of the decision to the Dáil. When Mulcahy questioned the social grounds for the decision, Lynch replied that the marriage ban was 'educationally indefensible' and reiterated that it represented a severe loss to the state of effective teaching capacity.[63] He asserted too that greater security of tenure for women teachers would encourage more effective and dedicated teaching. The Minister did not ignore social arguments which might support the decision, arguing that the employment of more married teachers was socially desirable, as emigration from both rural and urban areas could be reduced by encouraging married teachers to settle in their communities on a long-term basis. He firmly dismissed Mulcahy's concern about the propriety of mothers returning to the teaching force, arguing that 'a mother has the necessary poise and maturity' to deal with children.[64] But on the whole Lynch made the case that the initiative was based on unassailable educational grounds, informing Deputies that it was his duty to provide 'the highest form of education for all our children'.[65] Lynch's contention that the marriage ban was educationally wrong and damaging to primary education was essentially correct; perhaps for this reason, the opposition did not seriously challenge the decision. While Mulcahy expressed reservations about the reversal of a policy maintained by all parties for a quarter of a century, he did not vigorously oppose it, indicating that he did not wish to make it a matter of partisan controversy.

Brendan Corish TD, speaking for the Labour Party, argued that only improved conditions for teachers, not the removal of the marriage ban, would relieve the scarcity of trained teachers and regarded the removal of the rule as a bad precedent in the absence of any debate on the employment of female public servants in general.[66] But Corish referred only briefly to the ban and did not offer any suggestion that the Minister's proposal should be rejected. The Minister's initiative was also accepted without serious controversy by the most influential educational interest groups. The initiative satisfied a long-term demand of the INTO, which had strongly advocated the withdrawal of the rule since its introduction: the policy change marked a significant success for the national teachers' union.[67] More importantly, the most powerful stakeholder in the educational system, the Catholic Hierarchy, was essentially neutral towards the policy change. A memorandum from the Minister, indicating his reasons for removing the marriage ban, was simply noted without any further comment, by the general meeting of the Irish Hierarchy on 24 June 1958.[68] The department had introduced the rule and neither the Hierarchy nor the clerical managers showed any desire to defend it when the state moved to reverse its own long-term policy. The removal of the marriage ban was an initiative, which commanded widespread acquiescence if not active support among influential forces in Irish education.

The return of married women teachers to permanent employment in the national schools allowed the department to reduce its dependence on untrained teachers. The removal of the ban was followed by the Minister's decision to end the recruitment of untrained teachers. Lynch announced on 8 April 1959 that the competition for the category of Junior Assistant Mistress was being discontinued.[69] The indefinite suspension of recruitment for the position of Junior Assistant Mistress was facilitated by the return of approximately 250 married women teachers to the recognised teaching service in September 1958. Lynch estimated in April 1959 that the end of the marriage ban provided about 330 additional trained teachers in 1958–59.[70] The decision to stop the recruitment of Junior Assistant Mistresses did not end the practice of employing untrained teachers but it ensured that such appointments would be temporary and indicated a new commitment by the department to achieve a fully trained teaching service.[71] The removal of the marriage ban brought an end to the previous policy of recruiting a recognised category of untrained teachers. The rule change also paved the way for a modest improvement in the pupil-teacher ratio, which was announced by the Minister in April 1959. The unit figures, which governed the appointment of lay teachers, were reduced in national schools from 1 July 1959 to allow the appointment of a second teacher on the basis of lower average ratios.[72] While the improvement was marginal, it established a new element in educational policy. Lynch's improvement in the pupil-teacher ratio would be expanded by his successors.[73] The government made a definite commitment for the first time to achieve a gradual improvement of the pupil-teacher ratio. The removal of the marriage ban was not only an important policy change in its own right, but it also paved the way for new efforts by the state to minimise the dependence upon untrained teachers and to improve the pupil-teacher ratio in national schools. The policy change also underlined a new willingness on the part of the Minister and senior officials to reform traditional policies, which were damaging to the educational system and detrimental to the prospects for educational expansion.

The removal of Rule 72(1) was the most significant policy change introduced by Lynch. The decision was also the most important element in a process of incremental reform at primary level, which established a new framework for the employment and inspection of national teachers. The reform of the system of national school inspection was a more controversial policy change, which was vigorously promoted by Lynch and the Secretary of the department, Dr. Tarlach Ó Raifeartaigh. Lynch indicated on 22 May 1958 that he had launched a review of the system of inspection for national schoolteachers.[74] The review had been initiated at the request of the INTO; the national teachers' union was vocally critical of the system of inspection, which its leaders attacked as oppressive and dominated by the use of threats against national teachers.[75] The INTO particularly objected to the form of the inspector's report, which awarded 'merit marks' in each subject giving marks ranging from 'Very Satisfactory' to 'Not Satisfactory'.[76] Lynch and the senior officials were sympathetic to the national teachers' case. The Minister's objectives were illustrated by correspondence between Ó Raifeartaigh and Dr. James Fergus, Bishop of Achonry and joint secretary to the Hierarchy. Ó Raifeartaigh informed Fergus on 12 June 1957 that the Minister proposed to end annual inspections except for teachers on probation and teachers rated 'Not Satisfactory'.[77] Lynch was sympathetic to the INTO argument that the 'merit mark' could not adequately reflect the complexity of a teacher's work: the senior inspectors themselves had advised that the replacement of the 'merit mark' by a continuous narrative, outlining the work of the teacher, was educationally sound at least for satisfactory teachers. The Minister was seeking the Hierarchy's views before coming to a final decision, but Ó Raifeartaigh indicated that Lynch favoured the replacement of the 'merit mark' and a wide-ranging reform of the inspection system.[78]

Lynch hoped to improve relations between the department and the national teachers through a comprehensive reform of the system of inspection, which would remove a deeply held grievance held by the INTO. It was a sensible political move to conciliate the vocal and increasingly powerful INTO. But Lynch and his senior advisers were also influenced by educational considerations. Senior officials of the department no longer regarded the traditional inspection regime, which retained features of the system introduced by the British administration in Ireland at the beginning of the twentieth century, as reasonable or even viable in the late 1950s. Seán O'Connor, who served as a Principal Officer in the Primary Education Branch between 1956 and 1965, described the inspection system as 'intolerable to any professional body' because of the level of power given to the inspectors.[79] The department had little to gain by maintaining a system which was causing increasing tension between teachers and inspectors and so the Secretary took the lead in negotiations with the Catholic Hierarchy concerning the removal of the controversial 'merit mark'.[80]

While Lynch and the senior officials had resolved to achieve a comprehensive reform of the inspection system, they were obliged to seek the agreement of the school managers and the Catholic bishops. The agreement of the Hierarchy was not easily obtained. The bishops effectively rejected the Secretary's proposal at the general meeting of the Hierarchy on 25 June 1957.[81] Dr. James Staunton, Bishop of Ferns, accurately summarised the position reached by the majority of the Hierarchy: 'They approved a statement, which, though not absolutely insisting on the retention of the "merit mark", in its general tone did so insist'.[82] The opposition of the Hierarchy presented a formidable obstacle to the Minister's proposal. The Catholic national school managers took their lead from the bishops and were in any event unenthusiastic about the removal of the 'merit mark'. Lynch sought to overcome the Hierarchy's opposition by initiating negotiations directly with Dr. John Charles McQuaid, the long-serving Archbishop of Dublin. Ó Raifeartaigh addressed a detailed communication to McQuaid on 11 January 1958, arguing in favour of the replacement of the 'merit mark'.[83] Ó Raifeartaigh sought McQuaid's assistance in raising the issue with the bishops once more. The Archbishop was requested to propose the replacement of the 'merit mark' with a continuous narrative 'in the trust that their Lordships will on further consideration see their way to modify their view in the matter.'[84] The Secretary had asked McQuaid, politely but clearly, to induce the bishops to change their minds and support the Minister's plans.

McQuaid responded favourably to the Secretary's overture: he immediately agreed to communicate the views of the Minister to the bishops.[85] McQuaid's intervention transformed the position of the Hierarchy. The bishops agreed, at their general meeting on 24 June 1958, to the proposal for the replacement of the 'merit mark' by a narrative report, 'in deference to the wishes of the Minister for Education'.[86] They stipulated that the new narrative report should make an assessment on the teacher's work which would fulfil a similar function to the previous procedure: this condition was set by McQuaid and accepted by the Minister.[87] Lynch himself acknowledged the importance of McQuaid's intervention. Following the Hierarchy's formal acceptance of the reform, Lynch warmly thanked McQuaid in a letter to the Archbishop on 3 July 1958. The Minister acknowledged that he had been greatly concerned to win the agreement of the bishops for the reform of the inspection system and he believed that the Hierarchy's decision had been made at McQuaid's instigation.[88] While the Hierarchy had claimed to be acting in deference to the wishes of the Minister, their change of course was a mark of deference to the Archbishop of Dublin. The interaction between the department and the Hierarchy concerning the abolition of the 'merit mark' underlined Lynch's tenacity in pursuing the reform of the inspection system despite the initial opposition of the bishops. The episode also illustrated the power of the Catholic Hierarchy in the Irish educational system. The Minister was able to proceed rapidly once the agreement of the Catholic bishops had been achieved. The new directives for national inspection were announced in a letter to the INTO and the school managers by Ó Raifeartaigh on 23 July 1958.[89] The 'merit mark' was replaced with a continuous narrative on the work of the teacher, for all teachers except those on probation or with the rating 'Not Satisfactory'. Likewise the practice of obligatory general inspections every year was ended for all teachers except those in the same categories.[90] The reform of the inspection system was welcomed by the INTO general secretary, D.J. Kelleher: the union's former general secretary T.J. O'Connell commented, 'A new and enlightened system of inspection had come into being.'[91] Certainly the reformed system was much more acceptable to the primary teachers, who were no longer subject to close and critical assessment by the inspectors as a result of the changes in the regulations.

The Minister, advised by the senior officials, had done much to eliminate long-term grievances pursued by the INTO over the previous two decades. The reforms were primarily rule changes, which were by no means radical in character, with the important exception of the removal of the marriage ban. But the incremental reforms reflected Lynch's desire to adopt a more activist approach than his predecessors in confronting educational problems at primary level. The implementation of moderate reforming measures by Lynch not only brought constructive advances in primary education but also helped to pave the way for more radical initiatives by his successors, as Lynch's proactive approach marked a break with the traditional pattern of ministerial inertia in education.

Reversing the cuts

Shortly after taking up office, Lynch had expressed his view that state investment in the Irish educational system was inadequate. He had argued in presenting the first Estimates for his term on 1 May 1957 that Irish education suffered especially from the allocation of insufficient resources.[92] The Minister did not, however, have the resources available to him to initiate major changes in the educational system. There was little evidence of increased investment in education for most of Lynch's term. The government's spending on primary, post-primary and higher education in 1958–59 revealed only a very modest increase from the previous year: indeed the state's expenditure on the secondary sector even showed a marginal decline.[93] Lynch indicated on 22 May 1958 that he was still unable to restore the cut in the capitation grants to secondary schools and gave no time frame for the reversal of the cut.[94] The retention of the 10% cut in the capitation grants underlined that secondary education continued to suffer a decline in state support in real terms. The vocational sector fared better than secondary education. Lynch secured the approval of the Cabinet on 17 December 1957 for the restoration of the 6% cut in the annual grants to the VECs for 1958–59.[95] But with the exception of the restoration of the cut affecting vocational education, the financial stringency imposed upon the Department of Education during Mulcahy's second term was largely retained until 1959. The Department of Finance successfully opposed the withdrawal of the cut in the capitation grants for 1958–59.[96] The Department of Education submitted the question to the government on 7 December 1957, but Lynch failed to get the agreement of the government to reverse the cut. The Minister and his officials tried again on 15 November 1958, when they resubmitted their case for the withdrawal of the cut to the Department of Finance. On this occasion the Department of Finance proved more amenable and the restoration of the cut was agreed by the government on 1 April 1959.[97] The cuts that Lynch was obliged to impose in 1957, due to the pressure of the Department of Finance in an unfavourable economic climate, were not fully removed until April 1959, only three months before the end of his term. Lynch's freedom of action was severely limited by financial constraints for most of his term as Minister for Education.

The undoubted financial constraints contributed to Lynch's caution in discussing the government's education policy, which remained ill-defined throughout his term. While Lynch's initiatives brought modest practical advances in primary education, the Minister remained wary of articulating a definite policy approach that went beyond piecemeal improvements. He certainly emphasised the importance of improving the pupil-teacher ratio and increasing the supply of trained teachers, but he did not articulate a clear vision of the future for Irish education. He was criticised on 8 April 1959 by various Opposition TDs, including Mulcahy and Dr. Noel Browne, for failing to outline a definite policy in the debate on the Education Estimates.[98] Lynch acknowledged that he had made minimal general reference to educational policy and the future educational programme of the government: 'I did not prognosticate on what would happen in the future.'[99] He drew attention instead to practical improvements introduced during his term, including the removal of the marriage ban and the modest reduction in the pupil-teacher ratio in the national schools. While these initiatives were clearly beneficial, Lynch's piecemeal reforms almost exclusively benefited primary education. The Minister was particularly wary of outlining a definite policy approach for the expansion of post-primary education. Certainly he restored the cut in funding for the VECs. But no attempt was made to mitigate the disadvantages imposed by the state, in agreement with the Catholic Church, upon vocational education. Lynch recognised the widespread perception that vocational schools offered only second-class education. When he announced the restoration of the cut in the grants to the VECs on 22 May 1958, the Minister praised the work of the vocational schools and suggested that the public had not yet fully appreciated the advantages of vocational education.[100] His statement was scathingly described by O'Connor as 'an effort to blame the parents for the failure of the system to attract pupils to its schools despite the energy and drive of its administrators and teachers and the enthusiasms of politicians'.[101] Certainly Lynch offered no indication of any constructive move by the government to enhance the status of vocational education. While the Minister was concerned that parents were not using the vocational system in sufficient numbers, he did not propose to take any action to remove the restrictions imposed by the state upon the vocational schools. Any such initiative would risk incurring the hostility of the Hierarchy, by undermining O'Sullivan's assurances that vocational schools would never seek to offer a broad curriculum going beyond practical instruction or to compete with secondary schools in providing academic education.[102] Lynch was content in 1958 to restore the cut in the annual VEC grants, showing no inclination to propose changes which might raise the status of vocational education.

The Minister's statements, however, underlined an increasing official concern with the development of vocational education. Lynch again emphasised the importance of vocational education in the Dáil on 8 April 1959, arguing that many vocational courses provided for the well-being of the country.[103] Likewise *Economic Development*, composed by T.K. Whitaker and other officials of the Department of Finance, which was published in November 1958, drew attention to the potential of vocational education to contribute to national development.[104] The report, which formed the basis of the first programme for economic expansion, envisaged that rural vocational schools could play a significant part in agricultural training, due to the flexibility of the vocational system and the enthusiasm of the vocational teachers.[105] The growing emphasis among politicians and senior officials on the development of vocational education was reflected in state expenditure. The department made available additional funding for vocational school building: Lynch announced that it had been decided to initiate the building of sixteen new vocational schools in 1959–60 at a cost of £480,000, while £155,000 would be spent on improvements to fifteen existing schools.[106] Lynch and the senior officials of his department regarded the expansion of vocational education as an important objective. But the Minister made no attempt to remove the disadvantages previously imposed by the state on vocational education, which restricted the development of the vocational system and greatly limited the potential contribution of the vocational schools to a general expansion of post-primary education.

The Minister also avoided any real intervention at all in the secondary school system. Indeed Sr. Eileen Randles, who later served as a member of the executive of the Conference of Catholic Secondary Schools (CCSS), recorded a contemporary view that 'he virtually ignored Secondary Education'.[107] Lynch followed the example of his predecessors in pursuing a minimalist approach, as the department traditionally acknowledged the managerial autonomy of the private secondary schools, subject to the department's control of the curriculum. Moreover the Council of Education was still considering the curriculum of the secondary school. As the Council's report was submitted only to Lynch's successor, Patrick Hillery, the Minister could undertake initiatives at secondary level only by pre-empting its views.[108] It is evident also that the Minister and senior officials identified other priorities, which could be pursued with less risk of conflict with powerful educational interests.[109] It was more pragmatic for Lynch to initiate reforms in primary education, where the role of the department was most clearly established and even to encourage the development of vocational education within traditional constraints, than to risk confrontation with the private educational interests, which controlled the secondary schools. The progress reports of the Department of Education, which were undertaken on a quarterly basis for submission to the Department of the Taoiseach, illustrated the low priority given to secondary education between 1957 and 1959.[110] The Secondary Education Branch submitted no entry at all for five of the twelve progress reports compiled by the department between January 1957 and December 1959.[111] The Branch submitted no material for the department's quarterly reports covering the final quarter of 1957 and the second quarter of 1958. In response to requests from the department's Headquarters Section for material relating to the quarter ended on 31 December 1958 and the quarter ended on 30 June 1959, an official of the Secondary Education Branch replied: 'Níl aon rud le tuairisciú' – 'there is nothing to report'.[112] The same reply was given for the quarter ended on 31 December 1959.[113] When the Branch did submit material for the progress reports, the entry for secondary education usually consisted only of the number of schools applying for recognition from the department and the number of new schools accorded recognition, sometimes with a summary of the training courses provided by the department for teachers.[114] No ministerial or departmental initiative at all affecting secondary education was recorded in the progress reports between 1957 and 1959. The Secondary Education Branch was largely left to its own devices in this period, without any substantial ministerial intervention. The minimalist approach maintained by the Secondary Branch reflected the absence of any coherent state policy for the development of post-primary education.

The lack of a clearly defined government policy on post-primary education was underlined by Lynch's response to demands by Opposition TDs for an extension of the statutory school leaving age. Dr. Noel Browne asked a parliamentary question on 19 February 1958, enquiring whether the Minister intended to raise the compulsory school leaving age from fourteen to fifteen or sixteen years.[115] Lynch responded that he did not propose to consider an extension of the school leaving age, arguing that the number of pupils was increasing in conjunction with increased facilities.[116] The Minister made no commitment to the provision of increased educational facilities, but instead sought repeatedly to refute arguments made by Browne in the Dáil and by educational commentators in the national newspapers, that a large majority of Irish children received no education at all after the age of fourteen. Lynch urged TDs on 10 June 1958 to reject ill-informed criticism of the Irish educational system, arguing that almost two-thirds of Irish children between the ages of fourteen and sixteen received full-time education: 78,000 children out of a total of 125,000 in the relevant age category were attending full-time school courses in 1956–57.[117] These statistics, however, included 18,000 pupils who were still attending primary schools, including schoolchildren in the Secondary Tops attached to national schools. This meant that approximately 60,000 children were receiving full-time education in post-primary schools.[118] About half of the cohort aged between fourteen and sixteen did not receive full-time post-primary education in the secondary or vocational sector. Browne had overstated his case, but Lynch's defence was equally dubious and the scale of the challenge facing the government if its members wished to promote wider participation in post-primary education was clear.

Lynch did not clarify the intentions of the government with regard to post-primary education. He indicated in response to parliamentary questions by Declan Costello TD on 25 November 1958 that he was not convinced that the extension of the school leaving age was appropriate. He argued instead that it appeared to be 'rather a matter of providing increased educational facilities' than of extending the age for compulsory attendance.[119] The Minister also indicated that the government had not made any assessment of how such facilities might be provided or about what form of education would be appropriate if pupils were required to attend full-time courses for a longer period.[120] So the necessity for additional facilities to expand participation was acknowledged, but no indication was given of the appropriate methods to achieve this end. The government's approach concerning post-primary education remained shrouded in ambiguity. The Minister and the senior officials of the department had no clear idea in the late 1950s of how to manage and facilitate the expansion of post-primary education. The secondary system was enjoying a steady expansion in this period, absorbing an annual increase of approximately 3,000 students. The department received applications for recognition from forty new schools between September 1957 and September 1959: twenty-one new secondary schools were recognised between January 1958 and March 1959.[121] Private secondary education was, however, beyond the means of a majority of Irish parents.[122] Moreover while the Minister hoped to see a greater development of vocational education, the vocational system laboured under restrictions concerning the provision of general education imposed by the state itself. The dilemma that faced the Minister and the department in the late 1950s was neatly summarised by O'Connor: 'Nobody doubted the need for additional facilities: the question was where to site them.'[123] Both the secondary schools and the vocational system in different ways presented significant obstacles to a serious effort by the state to promote the expansion of post-primary education. The extension of the school leaving age posed intractable problems, due to the divided structure of post-primary education in the Republic, to which the Minister and senior officials had as yet no clear answers.[124] Moreover Eamon de Valera, in his final term as Taoiseach, made no attempt to encourage a proactive approach by the state to the development of the educational sector. De Valera displayed no inclination to encourage Lynch to take potentially risky or controversial policy initiatives, which might provoke conflict with established educational interests. Lynch's decision to avoid any commitment to raising the statutory school leaving age reflected the realities of the educational system and the absence of any definite government policy to overcome traditional divisions in second level education.

The lack of a coherent government policy on post-primary education did not prevent the allocation of greater resources to the educational system. The Estimates for 1959–60, which were proposed by Lynch on 8 April 1959, provided an early indication of the growing importance attached to education by politicians and senior officials. The state's net expenditure on primary education increased by about 12% from the previous year.[125] Secondary education was by no means neglected, as Lynch secured the necessary resources to reverse the 10% cut in the capitation grants to secondary schools. Moreover the Exchequer's spending on vocational education showed a significant increase of almost 10%.[126] While Lynch particularly praised the work of the VECs, the educational system as a whole benefited from a higher level of state expenditure. Significantly Lynch argued that vocational education brought important benefits to the nation, underlining that education could make a major contribution to national progress.[127] This ministerial acknowledgement that education could contribute to the social and economic development of the nation provided the first real indication of changing official attitudes towards education, which would lead to the allocation of greater resources to the expansion of the educational system. The development of a viable policy to ensure the effective use of the increasing resources available for education was, however, a challenge inherited by Lynch's successor, Dr. Patrick Hillery.

The move to Belfield

If the government's policy approach towards education was generally ill-defined in the late 1950s, it was almost non-existent with regard to third-level education. Higher education presented a special category in many respects, not least because the universities and Colleges of Technology had been under the jurisdiction of the Department of Finance until 1957 and were not part of the traditional remit of the Department of Education. The responsibility for universities and colleges was transferred to the Department of Education in 1957, at the instigation of T.K. Whitaker.[128] The reaction to the transfer within the Department of Education itself was initially unfavourable. James Dukes, who was given a share of responsibility for the third-level sector as a newly appointed Assistant Principal Officer in 1960, believed that he was one of the few officials willing to have anything to do with third-level education.[129] Certainly the financial constraints on the department in the late 1950s did not encourage the senior officials to welcome any new responsibilities, especially as the Department of

Finance agreed to give Education only a single additional post – the position filled by James Dukes – to deal with the new responsibility.[130] Dukes himself recalled 'mine was the only job we got out of taking over the Universities. It was typical of Finance – they gave us one post – one post!'[131] Dukes's acerbic view of Finance's actions was undoubtedly shared by the senior officials, who were obliged to assume responsibility for the third-level sector with only a very modest increase in available staff resources.

The department also assumed responsibility for higher education at a time when the third-level sector was struggling with a severe accommodation crisis. The number of students in the National University of Ireland (NUI) had approximately doubled from 2,684 in 1930–31 to 5,980 in 1957–58.[132] While this represented a very limited expansion in the proportion of the population involved in third-level education, the increase had occurred over three decades in which there had been no significant capital development in the university sector. The colleges were heavily overcrowded, unable to cope with any further expansion and facing arrears of building work, which they lacked the funding to undertake.[133] De Valera responded to an appeal for assistance from the authorities of the National University by proposing the establishment of a Commission to consider the accommodation needs of the NUI.[134] The Cabinet approved on 20 August 1957 the establishment of the Commission, which was intended to 'inquire into the accommodation needs of the Constituent Colleges of the National University and to advise as to how in the present circumstances these needs could best be met'.[135] Cearbhall Ó Dálaigh, then a judge of the Supreme Court, chaired the Commission: Séamus Ó Cathail of the Department of Finance acted as its secretary.[136] Lynch addressed the first meeting of the Commission on 15 October 1957. He urged the members to examine the urgent accommodation problems in the three university colleges of the NUI and to relate these problems to 'the national need'.[137] The government delegated to the Commission the responsibility for evaluating the accommodation requirements of the largest segment of the third-level sector, encouraging the members to make a case for state investment in the NUI in terms of its value to national development.

The government had no definite policy at all towards higher education in 1957 and delegated much of the planning required for the development of the university sector to the Commission. Trinity College Dublin was not included in the terms of reference of the Commission, as the government was responding primarily to representations from the authorities of the NUI to resolve its accommodation problems and was not seeking to initiate any wide-ranging review of third-level education. The authorities in University College Dublin (UCD) were particularly concerned to secure the endorsement of the government for the transfer of the college from

Earlsfort Terrace to a new site at Belfield in south Dublin. The move to Belfield was vigorously promoted by the President of UCD, Dr. Michael Tierney, and had been supported by the governing body of the college since November 1951.[138] But the proposed transfer of UCD to Belfield was highly contentious even among the college's academic staff. A form of amalgamation between the two universities in Dublin was proposed by John J. O'Meara, Professor of Classical Languages at UCD, in a lecture entitled 'Reform in Education', on 27 March 1958.[139] He argued that 'Dublin would have one of the greatest universities in the English-speaking world, if to the old and great tradition of Trinity College were joined the traditions of Newman's Catholic University.'[140] O'Meara urged a close association between UCD and Trinity College, involving a pooling of resources and a joint approach in acquiring funding and property from the government and private sources.[141] While O'Meara did not regard a full merger between the two colleges as practical in the short term, his call for a considerable measure of amalgamation between Trinity and UCD underlined that the academic staff of UCD were by no means united in favour of the transfer to Belfield.

Aodhogán O'Rahilly, a member of the Commission who favoured the integration of Trinity College with UCD, soon sought to have the option of amalgamation considered. Ó Dálaigh asked Lynch on 5 March 1958 to clarify whether the Commission was permitted to make a recommendation concerning the integration of the two institutions.[142] The government rapidly closed off this option, resolving on 14 March that the terms of reference for the Commission could not be interpreted in this way and that they would not be amended to allow for a recommendation on amalgamation.[143] O'Rahilly threatened to resign from the Commission when it became obvious that integration was not a practical option, but was persuaded to remain a member by the Taoiseach.[144] De Valera, who maintained regular contact with Dr. Tierney, was concerned to facilitate the plans for expansion on the new site made by the college authorities.[145] It was therefore not surprising that the Commission was constrained by restrictive terms of reference approved by the government.

Lynch had expressed the hope, in appointing the Commission, that the group would make their report as soon as possible. The Commission did indeed complete their work rapidly. The group produced interim reports on the accommodation needs of UCD by 14 June 1958 and on the building requirements of University College Cork (UCC) by 18 October. The final report, incorporating a section on University College Galway (UCG) and general considerations for future university development, was completed by 1 May 1959.[146] The Commission made a compelling case for investment by the state in higher education, arguing that 'The well-being of university education and of the country are closely linked.'[147] The report indicated that accommodation problems were already so severe in all the colleges that 'break-down point has almost been reached' and recommended an ambitious building programme, which would cost £8 million over a ten-year period. The Commission laid down general principles for university development, including the maintenance of the physical unity of each institution, the accommodation of the sciences in new buildings, the importance of flexible site planning and the building of accommodation open to adaptation.[148] These general considerations had a clear relevance not only for the NUI but also for all future developments in third-level institutions. The Commission's analysis also drew attention to the consequences for university education of state underfunding for a generation.

The Commission made specific recommendations for each university college of the NUI. They endorsed the view of the authorities in UCD that the accommodation available to the college in Earlsfort Terrace was completely inadequate and recommended the transfer of the entire college to a new site at an estimated cost to the state of £6,700,000. The Commission concluded that the site at Belfield would deliver 'a final and satisfactory solution to the College's accommodation problems'.[149] This definite endorsement of the transfer of UCD to Belfield was made by the majority of the Commission, despite a vigorous dissent by O'Rahilly, who argued for the amalgamation of UCD and Trinity College.[150] The Commission's recommendation proved highly influential. Lynch proposed on 23 April 1959 that the government should give its approval in principle to the transfer of the entire college to the new site. The Minister also sought the establishment of an inter-departmental committee to consider whether it was feasible to construct a new building accommodating science departments at Belfield in advance of any comprehensive site planning.[151] The Minister and senior officials of his department had accepted the Commission's recommendations concerning UCD even before they received its final report. The proposal did not command universal support within the government. The Minister for Health and Social Welfare, Seán MacEntee, strongly objected to the proposed transfer and argued that the government should consider the amalgamation of the two universities in Dublin. MacEntee firmly endorsed O'Rahilly's dissenting opinion, warning that the transfer of UCD could only be accomplished 'at an enormous capital cost'.[152]

The Department of Education rejected the arguments of MacEntee and O'Rahilly. A submission by the department to the government on 20 May ruled out amalgamation on the basis that it would contravene the ban on the attendance of Catholics at Trinity College maintained by the Hierarchy and deny Catholics their legitimate right to denominational education at university level.[153] This argument was given additional force by a recent intervention in the debate on the part of Cardinal John D'Alton, the Catholic Archbishop of Armagh. D'Alton had issued a public warning against any merger of the existing universities on 23 June 1958, at a prize-giving ceremony in Maynooth: he hoped that there would not be 'any ill-considered experiment in the education field' and described a merger between Trinity College and UCD as 'a union of incompatibles'.[154] The Cardinal's statement underlined that any proposal for amalgamation carried the risk of serious conflict with the Catholic Hierarchy. Moreover the Department of Education's proposal enjoyed the crucial support of the Taoiseach. De Valera fully agreed with the proposed transfer of UCD to the new site. He stipulated only that such a decision in principle would require the approval of the Dáil.[155] The government soon adopted de Valera's approach. The Cabinet approved in principle the transfer of UCD to the Belfield site, subject to the agreement of the Dáil, on 26 May 1959. They agreed that a supplementary estimate for a token amount would be presented to the Dáil at an early stage to secure parliamentary approval for the proposal.[156] The government also approved the establishment of an inter-departmental committee to assess whether a new science building should be provided at Belfield in the short term.[157] Although the Dáil did not consider the transfer of UCD until March 1960, the government's decision marked a decisive commitment to the development of the new campus at Belfield.

The Commission also indicated that the existing accommodation for UCC and UCG was inadequate. While their accommodation needs could be met on the main college sites, it was recommended that open ground adjoining the institutions should be reserved for third-level development, if necessary by legislation. The report concluded that the necessary building projects for the two colleges should be funded by the state.[158] A University Development Committee was proposed not only to supervise the extensive building programme recommended by the Commission but to serve as a liaison mechanism between the colleges and the government and perhaps also to advise on long-term plans for development.[159] While the government did not immediately implement this recommendation, the establishment of the Higher Education Authority in 1968 created an institution fulfilling the functions proposed by the Commission. The report of the Commission not only provided a comprehensive building programme for the colleges of the NUI, but also made an eloquent appeal for public investment in third-level education as a national priority.

The Commission's report was completed shortly before the end of Lynch's term of office. Although the final report was not received before the Estimates for 1959–60 were finalised, the enhanced allocation for higher education underlined Lynch appreciated the message of the

Commission. The net expenditure for Universities and Colleges in 1959–
60 amounted to £948,560, which marked an increase of 37% from the
previous year.[160] The improved level of state support represented a more
substantial advance in a single year than the total net increase enjoyed by
higher education between 1954 and 1959.[161] Lynch indicated in his comments on the Estimates that the university sector had taken on great
importance, especially in the teaching of the sciences. He announced that
the government was acting to increase the grants to each institution: this
additional funding was designed to meet the current spending of each
college. Lynch also noted that the final report of the Commission was
expected soon and indicated that increased capital grants would be provided in the meantime to fulfil the most urgent accommodation requirements of the universities.[162] The compelling case made by the Commission
exerted considerable influence even before its final report was presented to
the Minister. Lynch was already aware of the interim reports on UCD and
UCC and could not have been ignorant of the likely conclusions of the
Commission. Certainly Lynch's Estimates speech gave a clear indication
that the development of higher education had become a priority for the
government. A new commitment had been made by the state to capital
investment in third-level education. While politicians and officials had not
yet formulated any definite policy for the development of higher education,
the government had accepted the principle that the universities should
receive significantly greater state support, especially in terms of capital
development.

Changing attitudes

Lynch's term drew to a close less than three months after the approval by
the Dáil of the Estimates for 1959–60, which gave an early indication of
the changing attitudes towards education by politicians and senior officials
at the end of the 1950s. Following the election of de Valera as President of
Ireland in June 1959, the new Taoiseach, Seán Lemass, appointed Lynch
as Minister for Industry and Commerce. Dr. Patrick Hillery, who was
appointed to the government for the first time by Lemass, succeeded Lynch
as Minister for Education.

Educational policy in the 1950s was dominated by a conservative consensus, shaped by deference to private, mainly clerical educational interests and by severe financial constraints. Lynch's term of office saw the first
tentative indications of policy change in education. The new Minister
adopted a cautious reforming approach, which reflected his lack of sympathy with the traditional consensus on the role of the state in Irish education. Lynch undertook reforming initiatives in primary education, including

the removal of the marriage ban and the first tentative measures to improve the pupil-teacher ratio in national schools. The revision of the system of national school inspection illustrated Lynch's approach as an incremental reformer who worked effectively within the traditional constraints of the educational system. The Minister adopted a more active approach to the resolution of educational problems than his predecessors, especially in primary education, while taking care to avoid conflict with established educational interests. He promoted piecemeal reforms of considerable importance but avoided any new general statement of educational policy. The policy of the government concerning the expansion of post-primary education remained uncertain and indeed incoherent. Although de Valera took an active interest in the development of higher education, he did not attempt to formulate a definite policy for educational expansion or encourage his Minister to undertake any proactive measures to facilitate the growing expansion of post-primary education. But it was in the late 1950s that the first indications emerged of a new conviction among politicians and senior officials that education could play an important part in the social and economic development of the nation. The new commitment by the government to give a higher priority to education was illustrated by the establishment of the Commission on accommodation needs in the colleges of the NUI and by the Minister's endorsement of greater public investment to develop third-level education. While Lynch's initiatives were by no means radical, the first hesitant indications of the state's policy of educational expansion in the 1960s can be found in Lynch's term of office during the previous decade.

Notes

1 *Dáil Debates*, vol. 159, col. 1494, 19 July 1956.
2 Ibid., col. 1489–503.
3 Ibid., Ó Buachalla, *Education Policy*, p. 274; see Introduction, p. 2.
4 S. O'Connor, *A Troubled Sky: Reflections on the Irish Educational Scene 1957–68* (Dublin, 1986), p. 2.
5 Interview with James Dukes, 28 April 2003.
6 Interview with James Dukes, 4 December 2000.
7 *Committee of Public Accounts, Appropriation Accounts 1948–49* (Dublin, 1951), p. 65.
8 Archives Department, University College Dublin (UCDA), *The Mulcahy Papers*, P7/C/154, G. Sweetman to R. Mulcahy, 18 August 1954.
9 *The Mulcahy Papers*, P7/C/154, Mulcahy to Sweetman, 30 September 1954, T. Ó Raifeartaigh to the Secretary, Department of Finance, 6 October 1954.
10 Interview with James Dukes, 4 December 2000, Ó Buachalla, *Education Policy*, p. 275.

11 UCDA, *The Mulcahy Papers*, P7/C/154, G. Sweetman to R. Mulcahy, 18 August 1954.

12 O'Connor, *A Troubled Sky*, pp. 11–12.

13 Letter from J.M. O'Sullivan TD, Minister for Education, to Dr. D. Keane, Bishop of Limerick, on the Vocational Education Act 1930, 31 October 1930, A. Hyland and K. Milne (eds), *Irish Educational Documents*, vol. 2 (Dublin, 1992), pp. 219–22.

14 A. Hyland, 'The curriculum of vocational education 1930–1966', in J. Logan (ed.), *Teachers' Union: The TUI and its Forerunners in Irish Education 1899–1994* (Dublin, 1999), pp. 133–4.

15 O'Connor, *A Troubled Sky*, pp. 28–9, Randles, *Post-Primary Education*, p. 27.

16 Ó Buachalla, *Education Policy*, pp. 273–4.

17 Council of Education, *(2) The Curriculum of the Secondary School* (Dublin, 1962), iv–v.

18 Ó Buachalla, *Education Policy*, pp. 67–8.

19 Council of Education, *(2) Curriculum of Secondary School*, ii.

20 Council of Education, *(1) The Function of the Primary School (2) The Curriculum to be Pursued in the Primary School* (Dublin, 1954), pp. 266–8.

21 Ibid., p. 290.

22 Ibid.

23 O'Connor, *A Troubled Sky*, p. 37.

24 Council of Education, *(2) Curriculum of Secondary School*, p. 282.

25 Ibid., p. 256.

26 Ibid., p. 184.

27 Ibid., p. 256.

28 Ibid., pp. 280–2.

29 Ibid., p. 252.

30 O'Connor, *A Troubled Sky*, p. 69, Hyland, 'The curriculum', in Logan, *Teachers' Union*, p. 149.

31 Randles, *Post-Primary Education*, pp. 22–3.

32 *Dáil Debates*, vol. 161, col. 494, 1 May 1957.

33 Ibid., col. 494–503.

34 Ibid., Randles, *Post-Primary Education*, pp. 22–3.

35 *Dáil Debates*, vol. 161, col. 494–503, 1 May 1957.

36 Ibid.

37 Ibid., Ó Buachalla, *Education Policy*, p. 277.

38 *Dáil Debates*, vol. 168, col. 1510, 10 June 1958.

39 Ibid., CAB 2/18, G.C.8/75, Cabinet Minutes, 24 January 1958, pp. 1–2.

40 CAB 2/18, G.C.8/97, Cabinet Minutes, 22 April 1958, p. 2.

41 W26/30, M80/1, C.O. 704 (ii), *Progress Report for the Quarter ended 31 March 1958*, Department of Education.

42 *Dáil Debates*, vol. 168, col. 644–5, 22 May 1958.

43 *Dáil Debates*, vol. 161, col. 696–707, 1 May 1957.

44 O'Connor, *A Troubled Sky*, p. 33.

45 *Dáil Debates*, vol. 161, col. 696–707, 1 May 1957.

46 NA D/T 6231C, *Memorandum to the Government, Untrained and Unqualified Teachers in National Schools, Removal of Ban on Married Women*, 28 April 1958, pp. 1–3.

47 *Tuarascáil, An Roinn Oideachais, 1957–58* (Dublin, 1959), p. 57.

48 *Dáil Debates*, vol. 168, col. 638–40, 22 May 1958.

49 J. Coolahan, 'Educational policy for national schools 1960–1985', in D.G. Mulcahy and D. O'Sullivan (eds), *Irish Educational Policy: Process and Substance* (Dublin, 1989), p. 28.

50 NA D/T 6231C, *Memorandum to the Government, Removal of Ban on Married Women*, 28 April 1958, pp. 1–3.

51 Ibid., *Appendix A*, p. 1.

52 Interview with James Dukes, 13 November 2002.

53 NA D/T 6231C, *Memorandum to the Government, Removal of Ban on Married Women*, 28 April 1958, p. 3.

54 CAB 2/18, G.C.8/104, Cabinet Minutes, 20 May 1958, pp. 2–3.

55 Circular 11/58, Department of Education, June 1958.

56 *Dáil Debates*, vol. 168, col. 1498–502, 11 June 1958.

57 Circular 11/58, Department of Education, June 1958.

58 W26/30, M80/1, C.O. 704 (ii), *Progress Report for the Quarter ended 30 June 1958*, Department of Education, p. 1.

59 NA D/T 6231C, *Memorandum to the Government, Removal of Ban on Married Women*, 28 April 1958, p. 3.

60 *Dáil Debates*, vol. 168, col. 638–40, 22 May 1958.

61 Ibid.

62 Ibid.

63 *Dáil Debates*, vol. 168, col. 1498–502, 11 June 1958.

64 Ibid.

65 Ibid.

66 Ibid.

67 T.J. O'Connell, *A History of the INTO 1868–1968* (Dublin, 1969), p. 284.

68 Dublin Diocesan Archives (DDA) AB8/B/XV/b/04, *Papers of Dr. John Charles McQuaid, Archbishop of Dublin*, Minutes of the Irish Hierarchy, 24 June 1958.

69 *Dáil Debates*, vol. 174, col. 57–8, 8 April 1959.

70 W26/30, M80/1, C.O. 704 (ii), *Progress Report for the Quarter ended 30 September 1958*, Department of Education, *Dáil Debates*, vol. 174, col. 57–8, 8 April 1959.

71 O'Connor, *A Troubled Sky*, p. 35.

72 Coolahan, 'National schools 1960–1985', in Mulcahy and O'Sullivan, *Irish Educational Policy*, p. 31.

73 O'Connor, *A Troubled Sky*, p. 34.

74 *Dáil Debates* vol. 168, col. 641, 22 May 1958.

75 O'Connell, *History of the INTO*, pp. 422–5.

76 Ibid., O'Connor, *A Troubled Sky*, p. 35.

77 DDA AB8/B/XVIII/18, *McQuaid Papers*, T. Ó Raifeartaigh to J. Fergus, 12 June 1957.

78 Ibid.

79 O'Connor, *A Troubled Sky*, p. 35.

80 DDA AB8/B/XVIII/18, *McQuaid Papers*, Ó Raifeartaigh to Fergus, 12 June 1957, Ó Raifeartaigh to McQuaid, 11 January 1958.

81 DDA AB8/XV/b/03, *McQuaid Papers*, Minutes, General Meeting of the Hierarchy, 25 June 1957.

82 DDA AB8/B/XVIII/18, *McQuaid Papers*, J. Staunton to McQuaid, 21 January 1958.

83 Ó Raifeartaigh to McQuaid, 11 January 1958.

84 Ibid.

85 McQuaid to Ó Raifeartaigh, 11 January 1958.

86 Minutes, General Meeting of the Hierarchy, 24 June 1958.

87 Minutes, General Meeting of the Hierarchy, 14 October 1958.

88 Lynch to McQuaid, 3 July 1958.

89 Circular 16/59, Department of Education, July 1958, O'Connell, *History of the INTO*, pp. 422–5.

90 Circular 16/59, Department of Education, July 1958, pp. 1–4.

91 O'Connell, *History of the INTO*, p. 420.

92 *Dáil Debates*, vol. 161, col. 503, 1 May 1957.

93 See Appendix 1, Table 1, p. 328.

94 *Dáil Debates*, vol. 168, col. 643–4, 22 May 1958.

95 CAB 2/18, G.C.8/67, Cabinet Minutes, 17 December 1957, pp. 2–3.

96 M 300/2, *Memorandum, 10% Cut in Capitation and Bilingual Grants*, Secondary Education Branch, Department of Education, 16 December 1966.

97 Ibid.

98 *Dáil Debates*, vol. 174, col. 73–84, 8 April 1959, Randles, *Post-Primary Education*, p. 34.

99 *Dáil Debates*, vol. 174, col. 210–22, 8 April 1959.

100 *Dáil Debates*, vol. 168, col. 649, 22 May 1958.

101 O'Connor, *A Troubled Sky*, pp. 28–9.

102 Letter from J.M. O'Sullivan TD, Minister for Education, to Dr. D. Keane, Bishop of Limerick, on the Vocational Education Act 1930, 31 October 1930, Hyland and Milne, *Irish Educational Documents* 2, pp. 219–22.

103 *Dáil Debates*, vol. 174, col. 67, 8 April 1959.

104 T.K. Whitaker, *Economic Development* (Dublin, 1958), pp. 112–13.

105 Ibid., p. 112.

106 *Dáil Debates*, vol. 174, col. 62, 8 April 1959.

107 Randles, *Post-Primary Education*, p. 24.

108 Ibid.

109 O'Connor, *A Troubled Sky*, p. 37.

110 W26/30, M80/1, C.O. 704 (ii), *Progress Reports 1957–65*, Department of Education.

111 Ibid.

112 W26/30, M80/1, M. Ó Flathartaigh to L. Ó Laidhin, October 1958, W26/30, M80/1, *Tuairisc ar dhul chun cinn na Roinne don ráithe dár chríoch 30 Meitheamh 1959*, Secondary Education Branch, Department of Education.

113 W26/30, M80/1, *Tuairisc ar dhul chun cinn na Roinne don ráithe dár chríoch 31 Nollaig 1959*, Secondary Education Branch, Department of Education.

114 W26/30, M80/1, C.O. 704 (ii), *Progress Reports 1957–65*, Department of Education.

115 *Dáil Debates*, vol. 165, col. 372–3, 19 February 1958.

116 Ibid.

117 *Dáil Debates*, vol. 168, col. 1512–13, 10 June 1958.

118 Ibid.

119 *Dáil Debates*, vol. 171, col. 800–1, 25 November 1958.

120 *Dáil Debates*, vol. 168, col. 1512–13, 10 June 1958.

121 W26/30, M80/1, C.O. 704 (ii), *Progress Reports 1957–65*, Department of Education.

122 Randles, *Post-Primary Education*, p. 25.

123 O'Connor, *A Troubled Sky*, p. 34.

124 Ibid.

125 *Committee of Public Accounts, Appropriation Accounts 1959–60, Summary* (Dublin, 1962), p. 100; Appendix 1, Table 1, p. 328.

126 Ibid.; Appendix 1, Table 1, p. 328.

127 *Dáil Debates*, vol. 174, col. 62, 8 April 1959.

128 *Committee of Public Accounts, Appropriation Accounts 1956–57* (Dublin, 1958), p. 5.

129 Interview with James Dukes, 28 April 2003.

130 *Thom's Directory of Ireland 1961* (Dublin, 1961), pp. 17–19.

131 Interview with James Dukes, 28 April 2003.

132 *Report of the Commission on Accommodation Needs of the Constituent Colleges of the National University of Ireland* (Dublin, 1959), p. 128.

133 Ibid.

134 Ibid., p. 1.

135 CAB 2/18, G.C.8/38, Cabinet Minutes, 20 August 1957, pp. 2–3.

136 NA D/T S.16289, *Irish Press*, 'Commission on NUI Named', 28 September 1957.

137 *Commission on Accommodation Needs*, p. 1.

138 NA D/T S.16289, M. Tierney to Eamon de Valera, 13 April 1959, O'Connor, *A Troubled Sky*, p. 46.

139 O'Meara, *Reform in Education*, pp. 18–19.

140 NA D/T S.16448, *Irish Times*, ' "Some Union" between TCD and UCD Urged: Welding of Tradition', 28 March 1958.

141 *Irish Times*, 'The NUI: Outline of a New Approach', 5 December 1958, *Irish Independent*, 'Why not Combine Dublin's Two Universities?', 30 July 1959.

142 NA D/T S.16289, C. Ó Dálaigh to J. Lynch, 5 March 1958.

143 NA D/T S.16289, Decision slip, *Cruinniú Rialtais, Commission on Accommodation Needs of University Colleges: Terms of Reference*, 14 March 1958.

144 NA D/T S.16289, A. O'Rahilly to de Valera, 13 March 1958.
145 NA D/T S.16289, Tierney to de Valera, 13 April 1959, *Note by official of the Department of the Taoiseach concerning meeting between Eamon de Valera and Michael Tierney*, 16 May 1959.
146 *Commission on Accommodation Needs*, p. 124.
147 Ibid., p. 128.
148 Ibid., pp. 127–8.
149 Ibid., p. 44.
150 Ibid., pp. 47–8.
151 NA D/T S.16289, C.O.911, *Memorandum for the Government, Interim Reports of the Commission on Accommodation Needs of the Constituent Colleges of the NUI*, 23 April 1959, pp. 1–4.
152 NA D/T S.16289, C.O.911, *Memorandum for the Government*, 20 May 1959, p. 12.
153 Ibid., pp. 14–15.
154 *Irish Press*, 'Cardinal's Warning on Education: Should Not Merge Universities', 24 June 1958.
155 NA D/T S.16289, M. Moynihan to Ó Raifeartaigh, 29 April 1959.
156 NA D/T S.16289, *Statement by the Government Information Bureau on behalf of the Department of Education*, 2 June 1959.
157 CAB 2/19, G.C.8/191, Cabinet Minutes, 26 May 1959, pp. 2–3.
158 *Commission on Accommodation Needs*, p. 125.
159 Ibid., p. 128.
160 *Committee of Public Accounts, Appropriation Accounts 1959–60*, p. 100.
161 Ibid.; see Appendix 1, Table 1, p. 328.
162 *Dáil Debates*, vol. 174, col. 72–3, 8 April 1959.

2

A cautious beginning: 1959–61

The importance of initiatives taken by ministers and officials early in the process of educational expansion has been underestimated. Dr. Patrick Hillery was characterised by Ó Buachalla as a conscientious minister who was cautious and tentative in formulating and expressing his policy objectives, although he delivered desirable practical improvements in the educational system.[1] This interpretation was shared by influential contemporaries especially with regard to Hillery's first term as minister between June 1959 and September 1961. Sr. Eileen Randles regarded the Minister on the basis of his early pronouncements as 'an ardent champion of the existing educational system'.[2] Seán O'Connor believed that he showed 'no evidence of any intention to exert change' in his first two years as a minister.[3] While this interpretation of Hillery's approach is by no means entirely inaccurate, it does not adequately consider the importance of the initiatives promoted by the Minister and senior officials of the department during Hillery's first term.

Hillery was initially cautious in pursuing policy changes and generally tended to avoid announcing his policy approach through public speeches or press conferences early on in his ministerial career. But even as a new minister, Hillery initiated important incremental advances in primary and post-primary education. He undertook also a general reappraisal of the traditional approach employed by the department to promote the revival of the Irish language through the schools. An activist approach by the state to educational problems was gradually developed by Hillery, although the government still remained wary of conflict with established private interests. The department under Hillery began to implement a definite policy for the expansion of post-primary education for the first time. While the state allocated greater resources to the development of the universities, a Commission on Higher Education was established to chart the future development of third-level education. The department under Hillery began to intervene more effectively and consistently to address long-term problems within the educational system.

Hillery and Lemass clarified the policy of the government towards education in October 1959, in a debate on a motion proposed by Dr. Noel Browne and Jack McQuillan, the two members of the left-wing National Progressive Democrat party (NPD), calling for the extension of the statutory school leaving age to at least fifteen years. Hillery defended the educational system against criticisms by Browne: in the course of the debate on the motion he declared that there was nothing to prevent 'expansion or adjustments to allow our system to cater for all our needs and it is on that basis that I would approach the motion'.[4] But the new Minister also indicated that it was his 'earnest wish' to enable all children to continue in post-primary education at least up to the age of fifteen, arguing that the most effective way to achieve this objective was to provide the necessary facilities for post-primary education.[5] Hillery also promised to extend the scholarships scheme to create wider opportunities of post-primary and university education for talented pupils. He had given the first real indication of a definite policy approach for the gradual expansion of post-primary education.

The new policy was clarified and given the full support of the government through a statement made by the new Taoiseach. Lemass intervened personally on 28 October 1959 in the debate on the Dáil motion put forward by Browne and McQuillan.[6] Lemass made a commitment that 'The aim of Government policy is to bring about a situation in which all children will continue their schooling until they are at least fifteen years of age.'[7] The Taoiseach informed the Dáil that the government fully agreed with the aim of the motion, but disagreed with the method proposed by the Opposition TDs, namely the extension of compulsory attendance at schools up to the age of fifteen years.[8] Lemass pledged to achieve this objective as soon as possible, without immediately extending compulsory attendance on a statutory basis up to fifteen years of age. He summarised the government policy as a commitment to the gradual extension of post-primary educational facilities, combined with the expansion of scholarship schemes.[9] The government's approach was based on the assumption that the expansion of the facilities for post-primary education would deliver their objective within a reasonable time frame. Lemass and Hillery had outlined a policy based on a measured expansion of post-primary facilities and scholarships. It was not at all the radical approach sought by Browne, which involved the introduction of free and compulsory education up to the age of fifteen; but Lemass's policy statement provided a definite gradualist approach by the state for the expansion of post-primary education.[10] Moreover the Taoiseach's intervention in the debate, only four months after his election, underlined the increasing priority that would be accorded to education under his leadership. Lemass's statement not only established a new policy commitment by the government to educational expansion, but also indicated that the new Taoiseach would not hesitate to intervene directly to clarify or promote a policy for which one of his younger ministers had responsibility. Lemass and Hillery inaugurated in October 1959 a cautious but definite policy approach by the state, which was designed to achieve a gradual expansion of the educational system, while avoiding any short-term commitment to the extension of the statutory school leaving age.

Incremental reform: primary education

This gradualist approach to educational expansion provided for important practical improvements in the primary school system. The department under Hillery promoted a range of reforming measures to deal with the most obvious flaws in the system. Hillery extended the incremental reforming approach in the primary sector, which had been initiated by Lynch. The programme for the building was accelerated, due to a substantially increased state investment in the programme by 1961–62. The allocation for the building programme almost doubled in this period.[11] The enhanced allocation for primary school building reflected the government's concern to expand the physical capacity of the system. Hillery also introduced new state grants for national schools and acted to improve the pupil-teacher ratio. The Minister announced on 24 May 1961 a new scheme providing funding for the painting and decoration of national schools.[12] The scheme made state grants available from 1 April 1962 towards the cost of painting national schools externally every four years and for internal decoration every eight years.[13] While the maintenance of the schools remained a local responsibility, the department usually provided a grant of two-thirds of the expenditure incurred on painting the building. Hillery and Ó Raifeartaigh believed that regular painting of the buildings would reduce the number of national schools which required replacement: the Secretary urged school managers to co-operate with the scheme to avoid the 'premature reconstruction' of national schools.[14] While the scheme was a relatively modest improvement based partly on pragmatic official calculations designed to save money in the long term, it was the first state programme which directly funded the decoration and upkeep of national schools.

Hillery also extended the marginal improvement made by Lynch in the pupil-teacher ratio in primary schools: the Minister reduced the pupil quotas required for the appointment and retention of lay teachers in national schools from 1 July 1960.[15] The improvement in the pupil-teacher ratio was by no means dramatic: but the second revision of the pupil quotas in two years reflected the department's willingness to expand the teaching resources available to the primary schools. The department's concern to improve staffing levels in national schools increasingly bene-fited lay teachers, as it became clear to the officials that the expanding needs of the educational system could not be met primarily through the traditional sources of the religious orders and diocesan clergy.[16] Lay national teachers benefited from efforts by the department to improve pro-motional opportunities. Hillery announced in April and May 1961 the creation of special posts of responsibility for national teachers and the introduction of additional posts for lay teachers serving in national schools controlled by religious orders.[17] The department under Hillery pursued a strategy of gradual expansion in primary education, involving a wide range of modest incremental changes, which were generally designed to increase the physical capacity and teaching resources of the educational system.

Changing direction: the Irish language

The practical reforming measures taken in this period were not limited to an expansion of the physical capacity of the system. The department also promoted significant developments in the primary and secondary school curriculum. The first major curriculum reform introduced during Hillery's term was the oral test in Irish. The oral test had been initiated by Lynch and was implemented for the first time as part of the Leaving Certificate examination in 1960.[18] The new Minister introduced the oral test without any detailed consultation with the associations of school managers, pro-voking a protest from the Catholic Headmasters' Association (CHA).[19] While this initiative was inherited from Lynch, Hillery did not hesitate to introduce significant policy changes in the department's traditional approach to the revival of the Irish language. He approved Circular 11/60 on the teaching of Irish, which was issued to the primary school authori-ties in January 1960.[20] The managers and principal teachers of national schools were informed that inspectors would in future give greater impor-tance to oral Irish than written Irish in assessing the work of teachers. Moreover teachers of junior classes, where teaching through the medium of Irish was previously the norm, were allowed to change 'the emphasis from teaching through Irish to the teaching of Irish Conversation', if they considered that greater progress would be made in oral Irish.[21] While the circular appeared to give greater freedom to teachers to determine their teaching methods only on the basis that the standard of oral Irish would improve, the department had effectively abandoned the traditional policy of teaching through the medium of Irish in national schools.[22] Circular

11/60 marked a subtle but vital policy shift by the Minister for Education. The change of emphasis from teaching through Irish to the teaching of oral Irish formed part of a more general reassessment of the language policy in education by the department.

The official reappraisal of the traditional approach to the revival of Irish was most obvious in the reform of national teacher training announced by Hillery in 1960. The system of training for national schoolteachers was built to a large extent around the Preparatory Colleges during the first generation of the independent Irish state. The colleges were state secondary schools, which provided education through Irish for candidates who gave a commitment to enter the teaching profession.[23] The five Preparatory Colleges for Catholic students included Coláiste Íde in Dingle, Coláiste Muire, Tourmakeady, Coláiste Íosagáin, Ballyvourney, Coláiste Bríde in Falcarragh and Coláiste Éinde in Galway. Coláiste Moibhí, in Shankill, Dublin, was the sole Protestant Preparatory College.[24] The Preparatory Colleges had been established between 1926 and 1929 by the newly independent Irish state to ensure that a significant proportion of native Irish speakers from the Gaeltacht became national teachers and that other young people who were candidates for the training colleges received a thorough grounding in Irish.[25] The students from the Preparatory Colleges received access to the training colleges for national schoolteachers on a preferential basis, as 25% of all places were reserved for them and such students were allowed entry to the training colleges without further competition, provided they fulfilled the minimum Leaving Certificate requirements for entry. The system was intended to promote the revival of the Irish language in the national schools at a time when the state faced difficulties in obtaining candidates for the teaching profession with the required knowledge of Irish.[26] The colleges had been criticised by the INTO and by the Catholic bishops. The senior officials of the department itself increasingly regarded the system as a liability: it was costly to run six secondary schools and the academic quality of the colleges was difficult to defend, as the standard of the Preparatory College students at the Leaving Certificate was lower than the level reached by successful candidates in the open competition for the training colleges.[27] Hillery put a proposal to the Cabinet on 9 November 1959 for the closure of the Preparatory Colleges and the establishment of an extended scholarship scheme for Gaeltacht students.[28] The memorandum submitted to the government made a strong case for abolition of the colleges, arguing that they were no longer necessary and that there were 'fundamental objections' to the system.[29] The most important objections identified by Hillery and the senior officials were the undesirable segregation of future teachers from other students and the unfair pressure placed on pupils aged only thirteen to decide their future careers at such an early age: the department also expressed reservations about the considerable expenditure of state funds in achieving objectives which could be attained by other means at less cost. Hillery argued that an extended scheme of scholarships for Gaeltacht pupils would advance the cause of Irish more effectively by giving greater impetus to the oral Irish scheme in secondary schools and would also deliver greater educational opportunities for native Irish speakers. The Minister proposed to close the five colleges serving Catholic pupils, while allowing the sole Protestant college to continue in operation, as the department considered that the Protestant secondary schools were still unable to provide candidates for the teaching profession with a sufficient knowledge of Irish.[30] The Cabinet approved Hillery's initiative over two meetings on 13 November and 15 December 1959.[31] The Minister then consulted with the bishops of the relevant dioceses, proposing that the clergy or religious orders, which had conducted the colleges, would take over the buildings for use as Class A secondary schools, in which the courses would be given entirely through Irish.[32] Arrangements were made for the sale of four of the five colleges to the relevant diocesan clergy or religious communities, while Coláiste Bríde in Falcarragh was transferred to the Board of Public Works. Hillery announced on 24 May 1960 the abolition of the Preparatory College system as a means of recruitment for Catholic teachers.[33] Although Coláiste Moibhí continued to operate, the courses in the other five colleges were discontinued at the end of the school year on 31 July 1961.

The department announced a revised scheme of scholarships for Gaeltacht pupils to replace the Preparatory Colleges in accordance with Hillery's proposal.[34] The extended scholarship scheme provided for an increase in the number of secondary school scholarships awarded annually by the department to Gaeltacht pupils from eighteen to eighty. Similarly, the number of university scholarships for Gaeltacht students increased from five to fifteen.[35] As an average of fifty Gaeltacht students had secured places in the Preparatory Colleges between 1957 and 1959, in addition to the eighteen scholarships awarded on the basis of a competitive examination, the extended scheme of scholarships was a moderate improvement in the educational opportunities offered by the state to native speakers of Irish.[36] The introduction of a revised scholarships' scheme as an alternative to the Preparatory Colleges reflected Hillery's emphasis on the extension of scholarships as an essential means towards the expansion of educational opportunity.

The abolition of the state secondary schools for Catholic pupils transformed the system of recruitment for primary teachers, which would in future be based upon open competition for entry to the training colleges. The initiative also marked a significant revision of the state's policy for the revival of the Irish language. Hillery's announcement had removed an important element of the Irish language policy in the national schools. The traditional language revival methods employed in the schools required a regular supply of teachers using Irish as their vernacular: the abolition of the Preparatory Colleges terminated the sole official process for supplying such teachers.[37] Hillery's willingness to modify the traditional language policy was also underlined by the abolition of the Teastas Dhá-Theangach; the bilingual certificate, which testified to the ability of primary teachers to teach through the medium of Irish as well as English, was a required qualification for all teachers since the late 1920s.[38] Hillery announced the abolition of the Teastas Dhá-Theangach on 24 May 1961, replacing it with an oral Irish test and providing grants of £15 to training college students to assist them in learning Irish.[39] The Minister had abandoned or modified the most important elements of the traditional policy for the revival of Irish in primary education. It was a policy change of considerable importance, achieved with almost no opposition or even public attention.

Seán O'Connor, who disagreed with the abolition of the Preparatory Colleges, believed that: 'By the issuing of the January Circular on the teaching of Irish and the closing of the Preparatory Colleges, Dr. Hillery ensured the disestablishment of the Irish language.'[40] O'Connor's sweeping assertion exaggerated the extent of the changes. The requirements for Irish to be taken as a compulsory subject for the award of the Intermediate and Leaving Certificate examinations remained in place. Moreover O'Connor himself acknowledged that there was no deliberate attempt by the Minister to dismantle the Irish language revival in the schools.[41] But Hillery certainly abandoned the mechanisms employed by the department to implement the revival of Irish in primary education for the previous generation. The Minister sought instead to promote the teaching of oral Irish, while the traditional approach which had underpinned the language policy in primary education – teaching through the medium of Irish – was quietly dropped. The senior officials of the department believed with considerable justice that the teaching methods employed to achieve the revival of Irish in the schools had proved ineffective. But the reappraisal of the language policy early in Hillery's term also reflected a more significant change in the approach of the Department of Education, which had been closely associated with the national objective of language revival since the 1920s. Hillery himself remarked that: 'It was important that the revival of the Irish language was not the purpose of the Department of Education primarily.'[42] The Minister was clearly sceptical of the traditional policy of restoring the Irish language through the schools and was concerned that his department should not be treated simply as the agency for language revival.[43] James Dukes, who was Hillery's first private secretary in 1959, commented that 'He tried to bring a bit of sense into it.'[44] Hillery curtailed or abolished many of the initiatives which gave precedence to Irish in national schools and preferential treatment to native Irish speakers in the recruitment of national teachers. While the established policy objective of language revival was maintained, the traditional policy of primacy for Irish in primary education was substantially diluted by the department under Hillery.

A gradualist approach

While Hillery's freedom of action in post-primary education was much more limited, especially with the regard to the private secondary schools, he proved capable of delivering incremental advances, especially in vocational education. One of the earliest initiatives taken by the department was designed to extend the system of vocational education and enable vocational schools in rural areas to contribute to the development of the agricultural sector. *Economic Development* had made recommendations for additional educational opportunities for those working in agriculture and closer collaboration between the vocational authorities and the Department of Agriculture.[45] In accordance with recommendations made by the report, an inter-departmental committee consisting of four senior officials from the departments of Education and Agriculture was established on 13 February 1959 to co-ordinate the activity of the rural vocational schools and the Agricultural Advisory Service.[46] The inter-departmental group set out to establish a joint programme involving a part-time agricultural course in the vocational schools. The main product of this inter-departmental collaboration was the Winter Farm Schools Scheme, which was launched in November 1959.[47] The scheme involved part-time education during the winter months for young farmers aged between eighteen and twenty-five. The scheme, which was organised by the VECs in co-operation with the two departments, saw the establishment of thirty-seven part-time courses throughout the country in the winter of 1959.[48] The reaction to the scheme was not, however, universally positive. McQuaid reported to the Hierarchy in October 1959 about 'an objectionable feature' of the original scheme, namely the suggestion that officials of the department were to select suitable candidates to lecture on social ethics. The Archbishop's concerns were met when it was arranged for local clergy to conduct the relevant course.[49] The collaborative venture between the VECs and the departments of Education and Agriculture was highly successful, drawing an attendance of over eight hundred farmers to the part-time courses in 1959–60.[50] The successful implementation of the joint initiative reflected the growing concern on the part of politicians and senior officials to exploit the potential contribution of vocational education to economic development.

The official conviction of the importance of education in preparing qualified workers for employment was also underlined by the reform of the regulations for apprenticeship. A new national board responsible for the regulation of apprenticeship, An Chéard Chomhairle, was established on 11 April 1960, under the terms of the Apprenticeship Act, 1958.[51] The new legislation, which was piloted through the Oireachtas by Jack Lynch as Minister for Industry and Commerce in 1959, replaced the Apprenticeship Act of 1931. The existing Act was clearly inadequate as a regulatory measure, as it had applied only to craft trades, which voluntarily put themselves within the scope of the legislation.[52] The new legislation provided for the establishment of An Chéard Chomhairle, which was empowered to set down the minimum age for apprenticeship and the educational qualifications necessary for apprentices.[53] The new board also enjoyed the power to regulate the education and examination of apprentices, in conjunction with the Department of Education. The new initiative was strongly influenced by trade union and employer interests. Indeed a joint committee representing the trade unions and employers had recommended the establishment of An Chéard Chomhairle and its membership included five nominees of the employers and five union representatives, as well as three nominees of the VECs.[54] The new apprenticeship board was intended to establish effective regulation of the conditions for apprenticeship and to prevent abuses, such as the exploitation of apprentices for cheap labour by employers who failed to provide opportunities for training.[55] The new approach had immediate implications for technical education, as apprenticeship committees established by An Chéard Chomhairle were empowered to require the attendance of apprentices at technical courses and to compel employers to release apprentices for such courses without loss of earnings. The establishment of An Chéard Chomhairle led to the creation of a new regulatory framework for the recruitment and education of apprentices.[56]

This new approach to the regulation of apprenticeship required close co-operation between An Chéard Chomhairle and the Department of Education. The new board placed considerable emphasis on the achievement of proper educational qualifications by candidates for apprenticeship and required the collaboration of the department to establish the new regulatory framework for apprentices. The Board established a minimum age for entry into apprenticeship of fifteen years and required minimum educational qualifications for all potential apprentices after 1 September 1963.[57] The new minimum qualifications laid down by An Chéard Chomhairle

required young people seeking an apprenticeship to secure a pass in specified subjects in either the Day Group Certificate examination for vocational
schools or the Intermediate Certificate examination: an equivalent educational qualification was also acceptable. John Agnew, chair of An Chéard
Chomhairle, outlined the new minimum qualifications in March 1961: a
public letter addressed by Agnew to the parents of national school pupils
in sixth class was circulated by the Department of Education to all national
schools. Agnew advised parents to ensure that children seeking apprenticeship in craft trades were enrolled in the appropriate vocational or
secondary school courses in September 1961, so that they would have
the opportunity to secure the minimum educational qualifications.[58] The
department fully supported the new initiative. Ó Raifeartaigh issued a circular to the national school managers, indicating that Hillery was concerned to have the letter from An Chéard Chomhairle circulated to all
parents or guardians of boys in the sixth class.[59] The impetus for the effective regulation of conditions of apprenticeship did not come from the
department, but the Minister supported the initiative when it was launched
by the new National Apprenticeship Board. An Chéard Chomhairle broke
new ground in requiring minimum educational standards for apprenticeship. The regulations established by the new National Apprenticeship
Board were certainly designed to prevent the exploitation of apprentices
by unscrupulous employers. But it was evident too that post-primary educational qualifications, in either vocational or secondary school courses,
were now considered the appropriate gateway to apprenticeship in craft
trades. The new regulations underlined that the representatives of the
employers and the trade unions, as well as politicians and senior officials,
shared a consensus that education was an essential prerequisite to productive employment.

    The Department of Education had traditionally given considerable
attention to vocational education, while secondary education was essentially controlled and run by private, mainly clerical, interests with minimal
intervention by the officials.[60] Secondary education was expanding rapidly
at the beginning of the 1960s. The department gave recognition to sixteen
new secondary schools in 1959–60 and to a further fifteen in 1960–61.[61]
Recognition was an act of practical significance, which facilitated the
expansion of secondary education, as the department paid the incremental
salary of secondary teachers in recognised schools. The department was
more active between 1959 and 1961 than previously in its approach
to secondary education, even if its initiatives were usually small-scale.
A new scheme was introduced providing a non-pensionable allowance of
£200 annually from 1 August 1961 for 'probationer' teachers, namely
teachers who had secured the necessary academic qualifications and were

undertaking the teaching service required for registration. Another new scheme enabled lay secondary school teachers to gain credit on the incremental salary scale for teaching service in developing countries in Africa.[62] The Minister made no attempt to direct the expansion of the secondary schools, which remained dominated by private interests. But while the role of the state in secondary education was still very limited, the department at the beginning of the 1960s started to promote incremental reforms at post-primary level to overcome the most obvious shortcomings in the educational system.

Few shortcomings were more evident than the inadequacy of the local authorities' scholarship scheme. Local authorities throughout the state awarded only 582 scholarships for post-primary schools in 1958. This total increased hardly at all in the following years, with 619 scholarships being awarded by 1960.[63] The level of support for university scholarships was even more limited. Local authorities awarded only 117 university scholarships nationally in 1958 and 155 in 1961.[64] The overall provision for the scheme on a national basis was minimal, not least because there was no contribution from the Exchequer. While the Department of Education provided scholarship schemes for pupils from the Gaeltacht and third-level students who were willing to pursue their university courses through Irish, the local authorities provided the only general scheme of scholarships.

Legislation introduced by Hillery transformed the local authorities' scholarship scheme. The Local Authorities Scholarships (Amendment) Bill, which was published on 4 July 1961, was designed to establish a greatly expanded scholarship scheme.[65] Hillery outlined the terms of the Bill to the Dáil on 25 July, describing the minimal provision for scholarships awarded by the local authorities as 'a serious defect' in the educational system.[66] The new measure was intended not to provide direct state scholarships on a general basis but to increase and supplement the funding provided by the local authorities. The purpose of the Bill was to provide additional funding of approximately £300,000 from the national government for the local authority scholarships over four years. The new legislation was also intended to encourage local councils to increase their contribution to the scholarship scheme by raising additional funding on the rates. The Minister aimed to secure an increase of £90,000 in the overall contribution made by the local authorities.[67] The state contribution was designed to increase steadily in proportion to the funding raised by the local authority to achieve a five to four ratio between state and local contributions after four years. It was envisaged that four years after the establishment of the new scheme the total allocation for scholarships would roughly be quadrupled, rising from £150,000 provided by the local

authorities alone in 1960–61 to £540,000 under the new scheme by
1965–66.[68] The scholarships would be awarded on the basis of a competitive examination at national level set by the department: up to a quarter
of the scholarships would be awarded on merit alone without any means
test. The new legislation was shaped by the idea of greater educational
opportunity for the talented child. Hillery argued on 25 July that the individual talent of the Irish people was an invaluable resource and that the
aim of the Bill was 'to bring forward for the benefit of the nation as a whole,
the country's best talent, wherever it is to be found'.[69] He summarised his
objective in extending the scholarship scheme in the Dáil on 1 August
1961: 'The principle is that if there are brains in the country, we should
get them through the full course of education as far as we can afford to do
so and that they should earn their way on merit.'[70] Hillery emphasised the
need to enable talented children from all social categories to progress up
the educational ladder, presenting the extension of scholarships as a social
and educational necessity. The initiative was not a manifesto for equality
in education, but a pragmatic attempt to help talented children.

The highest priority under the new scheme was given to post-primary
scholarships. The legislation stipulated that two-thirds of the total scholarship funding was to be allocated to second-level education, while one-third
was reserved for university education.[71] Hillery was concerned to channel
greater state funding to second-level education, strongly defending the
priority given to the post-primary scholarships during the debate on
the Bill.[72] The most significant innovation of the Scholarships Bill was the
introduction of direct payments by the national government towards
the cost of local authority scholarships. While the department already
provided limited scholarship programmes, mainly for the promotion of the
Irish language, the legislation signalled a new approach by the state,
which provided funding for a general scheme of scholarships for the first
time. The legislation also enabled the Minister to sanction the terms of
the local authority schemes, giving the department significant influence
over the terms and value of the scholarships.[73] The Bill established a
new framework for the award of scholarships by the local authorities and
transformed the financial provision for post-primary and university
scholarships.

The obvious advantages of the legislation guaranteed it an easy passage
through the Dáil, despite some criticism of its terms by Opposition TDs.
Mulcahy complained about the terms relating to university scholarships,
while Noel Browne attacked the Bill as a pre-election manoeuvre by the
government.[74] The Bill was, however, approved without a division at any
stage on 2 August 1961, within a month of its introduction.[75] As the Dáil
was dissolved on 1 September for a general election, Browne's suspicions

about the timing of the Bill were well founded, but the importance of the new legislation transcended pre-election politics. The legislation marked the first real attempt by the state to widen educational opportunity, especially with regard to post-primary education. The new Scholarships Act immediately contributed to a major increase in the number of scholarship candidates. In 1962 5,622 candidates took the post-primary scholarship examinations, compared to only 3,122 in 1961. The Department of Education was providing £60,000 in a single year towards the cost of local authority scholarships by 1963–64.[76] Hillery had urged local authorities in July 1961 to secure the increased level of funding by taking advantage of the terms of the Act. The local councils required little encouragement. The number of scholarships for post-primary schools more than doubled between 1961 and 1962, rising from 831 to 1,927. The university scholarships saw a more moderate increase from 155 in 1961 to 254 in 1962.[77] The direct support for scholarships from the national government promoted a rapid expansion in the scholarship scheme, especially at post-primary level.

The incremental reforming approach pursued by Hillery offered reasonable short-term measures to alleviate persistent educational problems, which had been neglected by previous governments. The gradualist policy adopted by Lemass gave priority to the expansion of educational facilities and scholarships in the first instance. This approach certainly had substantial limitations: it did little to overcome underlying faults in the system such as the underdevelopment of vocational education and was only beginning to have some impact at post-primary level by 1961. But whatever the shortcomings of their initial approach, Lemass and Hillery had initiated a viable policy for the expansion of second-level education.

A tale of two commissions

If the state was beginning to implement a workable policy for the expansion of post-primary education during Hillery's first term as Minister for Education, its approach to the development of higher education remained ill-defined. Hillery inherited the report of the Commission on Accommodation Needs for the colleges of the NUI.[78] The government had accepted the Commission's recommendation for the transfer of UCD from Earlsfort Terrace to the new site at Belfield shortly before Hillery's appointment. The department under Hillery vigorously promoted the transfer of UCD to the new site. Máirtín Ó Flathartaigh of the Department of Education chaired the inter-departmental committee, including representatives of the Department of Finance and the Commissioners of Public Works, which was established by the Cabinet in May 1959 to examine the urgent accommodation needs of the college's science faculty.[79] The committee endorsed the immediate development of science facilities on the new site in November 1959. This verdict was not entirely unanimous. John Mooney, the representative of the Department of Finance, signed the report 'with some misgivings', expressing serious reservations about the college's plans for the development of the site at Belfield.[80] Hillery and the officials of his department did not share such reservations. The Minister presented a proposal to the government on 22 February 1960, advocating the immediate development of accommodation for the college's science departments at Belfield.[81] The Cabinet duly agreed on 1 March to provide state funding for the construction of a new science building at Belfield, which would be available for use by October 1961.[82] Hillery then proposed a supplementary Estimate in the Dáil on 23 March 1960 providing for a token allocation of £10.[83] The token Vote was designed to secure the approval in principle of the Dáil for the transfer of the college to Belfield. While the full allocation for the development of the new site would not be authorised in the short term, Hillery announced the government's decision to provide immediately for a new science building on the Belfield site, at a total cost of £250,000. As the college authorities were able to raise £100,000 for the new building, the state would provide the remainder of the funding. The Minister commented that the transfer of the college as a whole could well require a period of twenty years.[84] While only the funding for the new science building was being provided initially, the government had made a long-term commitment to the establishment of a new campus at Belfield.

The Minister's opening speech to the debate made the case for the transfer of UCD, relying heavily on the conclusions of the Commission on Accommodation Needs. The Commission had concluded that Earlsfort Terrace was hopelessly overcrowded and that any attempt to extend it would be inadequate and impractical.[85] Hillery therefore emphasised the unsuitable nature of the Earlsfort Terrace site and ruled out any high-rise development to expand the accommodation.[86] The option of redeveloping Earlsfort Terrace through extensive use of compulsory acquisition was rejected both by the Commission and by the Minister, who argued that the property rights of householders and institutions in the area deserved respect.[87] He also suggested that the cost of compulsory acquisition in the centre of Dublin could prove greater than the cost of funding the new campus, referring to the Commission's assessment that the redevelopment of Earlsfort Terrace could require an allocation of almost £8,000,000.[88] Hillery and the senior officials accepted without reservation the conclusions of the Commission on the redevelopment of Earlsfort Terrace. James

Dukes, who shared responsibility for the building programme in the universities as an Assistant Principal Officer, commented on the favourable attitude of the senior officials to the Belfield development: 'They were convinced that you couldn't stay in Earlsfort Terrace, it was too small.'[89] Moreover the Minister was clearly concerned to avoid the expense and possible conflict with private interests involved in a process of compulsory acquisition.

Another alternative to the development of the site at Belfield, namely the amalgamation of UCD with Trinity College Dublin, had been strongly advocated by Aodhogán O'Rahilly in a Reservation to the report of the Commission.[90] But with the exception of the dissenting voice of O'Rahilly, the Commission had not given any consideration to the possibility of merger, as their terms of reference excluded Trinity College. Moreover merger did not appear a practical proposition due to the ban on the attendance of Catholics at Trinity College maintained by the Hierarchy. Hillery too rejected the possibility of amalgamation on 23 March, largely on the basis that such a solution would undermine the fundamental rights of parents to guarantee the denominational education of their children.[91] He noted that Article 42 of the Constitution required the state to respect the lawful preference of parents not to send their children to any educational institution designated by the state in violation of their conscience. Hillery argued that he was obliged to respect the consciences of all Irish citizens, Catholic or Protestant, in considering the question of university amalgamation. He asserted that the basic principle of 'the non-forcing of conscience' would be the decisive factor in considering any redistribution or amalgamation of faculties at university level.[92] Hillery not only rejected the idea of merger between Trinity College and UCD but also asserted that any combination of faculties had to be acceptable to parents of each denomination. The Minister's statement had less to do with the rights of parents than with the collective view of the Catholic bishops. The Hierarchy regarded the colleges of the NUI as acceptable institutions for the education of Catholics, but was deeply hostile to Trinity College not simply on the basis of its Protestant tradition but because it was considered to be a repository of anti-Catholic and atheist influences.[93] Hillery emphasised that all four universities, including Trinity College, had their own part to play in educational development and national life. But his statement implied that the religious acceptability of proposals for reform in higher education, as defined by the Catholic Hierarchy, would have to be the guiding principle in any debate on university integration.

Hillery's statement on higher education was heavily influenced by his senior officials, especially Ó Raifeartaigh.[94] Significantly McQuaid wrote to both the Minister and the Secretary of the department on 24 March 1960, to offer his congratulations on Hillery's statement in the Dáil. The Archbishop, who vehemently opposed any suggestion of merger between Trinity College and UCD, thanked Hillery for his courage in guaranteeing Catholics the right to their own university education.[95] McQuaid, however, also warmly praised Ó Raifeartaigh for the excellence of the Minister's speech and commented: 'For your share in securing our right to Catholic education, I am very grateful.'[96] The Secretary replied on the same day in terms which left no doubt of his influential role in drafting the Minister's speech. He assured McQuaid that it was an extraordinary privilege for him to play a part in securing the future of Catholic higher education: as a result of the Minister's statement, he believed that the right of Catholics to university education had now been fully recognised. The Secretary, in a revealing passage, also thanked McQuaid for his 'inspiration and guidance throughout'.[97] The Minister's statement, with its emphasis on the importance of denominational principles in determining the future of higher education, owed much to Ó Raifeartaigh, his most senior adviser. The Secretary had engaged in close consultation with McQuaid on the future development of higher education, including the proposal to transfer UCD to Belfield. There is no doubt that such official consultation occurred with Hillery's full approval. The Minister's affirmation that any reform of university education had to be acceptable to all religious denominations underlined not only the influence of Ó Raifeartaigh, but also Hillery's concern to avoid any conflict with the Catholic bishops over the future of UCD.

The Minister's commitment to the development of the Belfield site cannot, however, be attributed solely to the influence of the Department of Education or even the Archbishop of Dublin. The project for a new campus had acquired considerable momentum by the late 1950s, not least due to the determination of the UCD authorities to bring about the transfer. O'Connor believed that it was too late to stop the move to Belfield as early as 1957.[98] Certainly the options available to the Minister were severely restricted by 1960, in the aftermath of the government's decision to support the development of Belfield. The Commission had rejected an extensive redevelopment of the Earlsfort Terrace site. Any attempt to promote amalgamation between the two universities in Dublin would certainly have involved the Minister in conflict with the Catholic Hierarchy and the UCD authorities. The development of the Belfield site represented a satisfactory solution for a government that had no desire for conflict with the educational or ecclesiastical authorities.

The debate in the Dáil on Hillery's token Estimate underlined that Fine Gael's parliamentary party was solidly supportive of the proposal. The leader of Fine Gael James Dillon and former Finance Minister Patrick McGilligan both warmly endorsed Hillery's approach.[99] Patrick O'Donnell, who concluded the debate on behalf of the main opposition party, assured the Minister of Fine Gael's collective support for the proposal to establish a new campus for UCD.[100] Fianna Fáil's parliamentary party was much more divided. Several Fianna Fáil TDs, including former Justice Minister Gerry Boland and backbench Deputy Lionel Booth, expressed strong reservations about the transfer of UCD to Belfield.[101] But a majority of the Fianna Fáil deputies who spoke in the debate either agreed with Hillery's proposal or argued that the Minister had no real alternative. Donogh O'Malley, who had previously advocated an amalgamation between Trinity College and UCD (and would do so again), declared that the Minister had no alternative but to act on the basis of the Commission's recommendations at this stage.[102] The strongest case against the proposal was made by Noel Browne and Jack McQuillan of the NPD. Browne attacked the transfer as 'the decision of old men' who lacked appreciation of the needs of the modern world and he called for some form of amalgamation as an alternative to the removal of UCD from the centre of the city.[103] The two NPD members sought a free vote on the token Estimate, hoping to exploit Fianna Fáil's divisions on the issue. But Hillery won the day without much difficulty. There was no vote at all, although Browne recorded his dissent from the decision: the Dáil passed the Estimate without a division on 31 March 1960.[104] The relative ease with which Hillery secured the agreement of the Dáil to the development of the new campus at Belfield illustrated the pragmatic case for the government's decision. Any attempt to promote university amalgamation would have encountered much fiercer resistance. The government's commitment to the new campus was a pragmatic response to the prevailing political and educational realities.

The debate on the token Vote for Belfield offered the first indications of the Minister's approach to the development of third-level education. Hillery announced his intention on 23 March to establish a new Commission of Inquiry on Higher Education.[105] While the government would provide capital funding to deal with the accommodation problems of the universities in the short term, the new Commission would evaluate a wide variety of issues related to the long-term development of higher education. Hillery did not outline fully the terms of reference for the new group, but indicated that the method of allocation for annual grants to the colleges and the demand made by the Limerick University Project Committee for a new university would certainly fall within the remit of the Commission. The Minister also intended the Commission to recommend ways of avoiding 'needless duplication' between professional courses in universities and courses in higher technical schools which both received state funding.[106]

Hillery later informed the Dáil that the process for university appointments would also be included in the remit for the Commission.[107] This commitment was made following a controversy concerning academic appointments made by the governing body of UCD. The government established a Board of Visitors to conduct an investigation and the Visitors concluded in February 1960 that the governing body had no authority to make the disputed appointments.[108] Hillery responded by securing the approval of the Dáil for special legislation to validate the appointments and allow the governing body to maintain its previous practice on a temporary basis: he also included university appointments in the terms of reference for the new Commission.[109]

The establishment of a new Commission was an implicit acknowledgement by Hillery of the necessity for a comprehensive long-term approach to the development of higher education. The Minister provided wide-ranging terms of reference for the new Commission, when it was formally established on 4 October 1960. Hillery requested the Commission to inquire into and make recommendations in relation to university, professional, technological and higher education generally.[110] The Commission was requested to give special attention to the general organisation of education, the nature and extent of the provision to be made for such education and the procedures for making academic and administrative appointments in the universities. The new group was also asked to examine the provision of courses of higher education through Irish.[111] The Commission was given a broad remit encompassing all third-level institutions. The comprehensive terms of reference provided by Hillery underlined that the Commission on Higher Education was intended to conduct a wide-ranging review of the third-level sector and make recommendations for the future organisation of third-level education in the Irish state. The only restriction imposed on the new group by Hillery initially was that its recommendations had to conform to the basic principles outlined in his statement to the Dáil on 23 March 1960. The Minister subsequently informed the Commission that the transfer of UCD to Belfield did not come within its terms of reference, as the government and the Dáil had approved the proposal for the transfer of the college to the new site.[112] The government appointed Justice Cearbhall Ó Dálaigh, who had previously headed the Commission on Accommodation Needs, as chairman of the Commission on Higher Education. Its membership included eminent academics from the universities, Catholic and Protestant clergy and representatives of business and the public service.[113] The Commission was the first committee of inquiry appointed by an independent Irish government on higher education. The Commission's deliberations proved lengthy and its report was not submitted until 1967, considerably later than Hillery had hoped and over two years after the end of his term as Minister for Education. The decision to appoint a Commission with a wide remit and comprehensive terms of reference reflected Hillery's recognition that coherent educational planning was required for the future development of higher education. Yet the delay in marking its report severely limited the influence of the Commission and ensured that the evolution of a long-term policy for the expansion of higher education was deferred indefinitely.

The gradual approach to educational expansion enunciated by Lemass and pursued by Hillery showed a realistic political caution, but was not tentative or hesitant at least with regard to the development of primary and post-primary education. The department under Hillery initiated a range of measures in primary education, which were intended to expand the physical capacity and teaching resources of the system. The modification of the Irish language policy in education, illustrated by the closure of the Catholic Preparatory Colleges, was a significant policy change, which diluted the primacy traditionally given to Irish in the national schools. The extent of the incremental changes announced by Hillery at post-primary level testified to a more active and assertive approach by the Department of Education. The Winter Farm Schools initiative underlined the increasing importance given to vocational education in promoting economic development. An Chéard Chomhairle, in collaboration with the Department of Education, established education as a necessary prerequisite for apprenticeship. Moreover the extension of the scholarship schemes also signalled a greater readiness to intervene in second-level education by the national government. The reforming initiatives introduced by Hillery marked the cautious beginning of a sustained process of state intervention in education.

Hillery was at his most cautious in dealing with university institutions, relying on his senior officials and taking care to avoid conflict with the established educational interests. But the beginning of the 1960s saw an increased commitment by the state to capital funding for the universities. The government's decision to finance the development of the Belfield campus for UCD marked an important long-term commitment by the state, which was made in advance of any attempt to plan the future development of higher education as a whole. The establishment of a new Commission on Higher Education marked the first real attempt by the state to promote a comprehensive review of third-level education. Hillery pursued a cautious but definite policy for educational expansion, which was given the full support of the government by Lemass. Perhaps the most significant legacy of Hillery's first term as Minister for Education was not any particular initiative but the evolution of a viable policy for a gradual expansion of second-level education.

Notes

1 Ó Buachalla, *Education Policy*, pp. 277–85.
2 Randles, *Post-Primary Education*, p. 39.
3 O'Connor, *A Troubled Sky*, p. 60.
4 *Dáil Debates*, vol. 177, col. 200, 21 October 1959.
5 Ibid., col. 202.
6 *Dáil Debates*, vol. 177, col. 470, 28 October 1959.
7 Ibid.
8 Ibid., Ó Buachalla, *Education Policy*, p. 73.
9 *Dáil Debates*, vol. 177, col. 470–1, 28 October 1959.
10 Ó Buachalla, *Education Policy*, p. 307.
11 T.J. McElligott, *Education in Ireland* (Dublin, 1966), p. 50; Appendix 1, Table 3, p. 329.
12 *Dáil Debates*, vol. 189, col. 842, 24 May 1961.
13 Circular 22/61, Department of Education, October 1961.
14 Ibid.
15 Circular 22/60, Department of Education, June 1960.
16 Interview with James Dukes, 4 December 2000.
17 Circular 16/61, Department of Education, April 1961, *Dáil Debates*, vol. 189, col. 842, 24 May 1961.
18 *Dáil Debates*, vol. 182, col. 75, 24 May 1960.
19 W26/13, M94/4, *Minutes of meeting between the Catholic Headmasters' Association and the Minister for Education*, Department of Education, 2 March 1962.
20 Circular 11/60, Department of Education, January 1960.
21 Ibid.
22 Ibid., O'Connor, *A Troubled Sky*, p. 44.
23 W26/2, M2001/5, *Memorandum to the Government, Department of Education*, 9 November 1959.
24 *Committee of Public Accounts, Appropriation Accounts 1960–61* (Dublin, 1962), p. 84.
25 W26/2, M2001/5, *Memorandum to the Government, Department of Education*, November 1959.
26 Ibid., Randles, *Post-Primary Education*, p. 29.
27 O'Connor, *A Troubled Sky*, pp. 52–4.
28 W26/2, M2001/5, *Memorandum to the Government, Department of Education*, 9 November 1959.
29 Ibid.
30 Ibid., V. Jones, 'Coláiste Moibhí: the last Preparatory College', *Irish Educational Studies*, vol. 15, 1996, p. 109.
31 CAB 2/20, G.C.99/28, Cabinet Minutes, 13 November 1959, pp. 3–4, CAB 2/20, G.C. 9/36, Cabinet Minutes, 15 December 1959, pp. 3–4.
32 DDA AB8/XV/b/04, *McQuaid Papers*, Minutes, General Meeting of the Hierarchy, 21 June 1960.
33 *Dáil Debates*, vol. 182, col. 72–3, 24 May 1960.

34 Circular M19/60, Department of Education, November 1960.
35 W26/30, M80/1, *Progress Report for the Quarter ended 30 June 1960*, Department of Education, W26/30, M2001/5, *Memorandum, Additional Gaeltacht Scholarships to be made available*, 15 July 1960.
36 W26/30, M2001/5, *Memorandum, Additional Gaeltacht Scholarships to be made available*, 15 July 1960.
37 O'Connor, *A Troubled Sky*, p. 54.
38 Ibid., pp. 56–7.
39 *Dáil Debates*, vol. 189, col. 842, 24 May 1961.
40 O'Connor, *A Troubled Sky*, p. 54.
41 Ibid., pp. 54–5.
42 Interview with Dr. Patrick Hillery, 25 February 2002.
43 Interview with Dr. Hillery, 25 February 2002.
44 Interview with James Dukes, 28 April 2003.
45 Whitaker, *Economic Development*, p. 113.
46 NA D/T S.12891C, *Memorandum by the Department of Agriculture*, 9 March 1959.
47 W26/30, M80/1, *Progress Report for the Quarter ended 30 September 1959*, Department of Education.
48 Ibid.
49 DDA AB8/B/XV/b/04, *McQuaid Papers*, Minutes, General Meeting of the Hierarchy, 13 October 1959, p. 2.
50 O'Connor, *A Troubled Sky*, p. 51.
51 Randles, *Post-Primary Education*, p. 42.
52 *Dáil Debates*, vol. 177, col. 77, 21 October 1959, *Dáil Debates*, vol. 177, col. 377, 28 October 1959.
53 NA D/T S.16808, *The Apprenticeship Act 1958, as passed by both Houses of the Oireachtas*, 9 December 1959, pp. 12–13.
54 Ibid., p. 5.
55 Ibid., p. 3, *Dáil Debates*, vol. 177, col. 77–130, 21 October 1959.
56 Hyland and Milne, *Irish Educational Documents 2*, pp. 238–9.
57 Circular 12/61, Department of Education, March 1961.
58 DDA AB8/B/XVIII/18, *McQuaid Papers*, Letter by J. Agnew to all National School parents, March 1961.
59 Circular 12/61, Department of Education, March 1961.
60 W26/30, M80/1, *Progress Reports 1957–1959*, Department of Education.
61 W26/30, M80/1, *Progress Report for the Quarter ended 31 March 1960*, Department of Education, *Progress Report for the Quarter ended 31 March 1961*, Department of Education.
62 W26/30, M80/1, *Progress Report for the Quarter ended 30 June 1961*, Department of Education.
63 *Dáil Debates*, vol. 191, col. 517–20, 11 July 1961.
64 W26/4, M2014/58, *University Scholarships Awarded By County Or County Borough Councils 1958–59*, Department of Education, *Dáil Debates*, vol. 191, col. 521–4, 11 July 1961.

65 *Dáil Debates*, vol. 191, col. 15, 4 July 1961, Coolahan, *Irish Education*, p. 139.
66 *Dáil Debates*, vol. 191, col. 1683, 25 July 1961.
67 Ibid.
68 Ibid., col. 1737–44.
69 Ibid., col. 1684–6.
70 *Dáil Debates*, vol. 191, col. 2342, 1 August 1961.
71 Ibid., col. 2325–40.
72 Ibid., col. 2354–60.
73 Ibid., col. 2342–9.
74 *Dáil Debates*, vol. 191, col. 1688–709, 25 July 1961.
75 *Dáil Debates*, vol. 191, col. 2423–5, 2 August 1961.
76 *Dáil Debates*, vol. 206, col. 1083–6, 11 December 1963.
77 *Dáil Debates*, vol. 203, col. 384, 29 May 1963.
78 *Commission on Accommodation Needs*, p. 124.
79 NA D/T S.16803A, *Report of Inter-Departmental Committee on Accommodation for the Faculty of Science, UCD*, 13 November 1959, p. 1.
80 Ibid., pp. 11–12, *Reservation by Mr. J. Mooney*, pp. 13–14.
81 NA D/T S.16803A, C.O.911, *Memorandum for the Government, Office of the Minister for Education*, 22 February 1960, pp. 1–10.
82 CAB 2/20, G.C.9/52, Cabinet Minutes, 1 March 1960, pp. 2–3.
83 *Dáil Debates*, vol. 180, col. 926–7, 23 March 1960.
84 Ibid., col. 945–8.
85 *Commission on Accommodation Needs*, p. 44.
86 *Dáil Debates*, vol. 180, col. 943–4, 23 March 1960.
87 Ibid., *Commission on Accommodation Needs*, p. 44.
88 *Dáil Debates*, vol. 180, col. 944, 23 March 1960, *Commission on Accommodation Needs*, p. 44.
89 Interview with James Dukes, 28 April 2003.
90 *Commission on Accommodation Needs*, pp. 47–8.
91 *Dáil Debates*, vol. 180, col. 940–1, 23 March 1960.
92 Ibid.
93 MFS 8223, L10.4, *Minutes, Commission on Higher Education*, 26 May 1961, pp. 141–61.
94 O'Connor, *A Troubled Sky*, p. 91.
95 DDA AB8/B/XVIII/18, *McQuaid Papers*, McQuaid to Dr. P.J. Hillery, 24 March 1960.
96 McQuaid to Ó Raifeartaigh, 24 March 1960.
97 Ó Raifeartaigh to McQuaid, 24 March 1960.
98 O'Connor, *A Troubled Sky*, p. 45.
99 *Dáil Debates*, vol. 180, col. 955–1172, 23 March 1960.
100 *Dáil Debates*, vol. 180, col. 1502–4, 31 March 1960.
101 Ibid., col. 1479–500.
102 *Dáil Debates*, vol. 180, col. 966–78, 23 March 1960.
103 *Dáil Debates*, vol. 180, col. 1260–8, col. 1360–85, 31 March 1960.

104 Ibid., col. 1507.
105 *Dáil Debates*, vol. 180, col. 952–3, 23 March 1960.
106 *Dáil Debates*, vol. 180, col. 1505, 31 March 1960.
107 *Dáil Debates*, vol. 181, col. 299, 28 April 1960.
108 NA D/T 16644, J. Kenny to M. Moynihan, 29 May 1959, *Report of the Board of Visitors, UCD*, February 1960, pp. 4–8.
109 *Dáil Debates*, vol. 181, col. 1620–3, 19 May 1960.
110 CAB 2/20, G.C.9/90, Cabinet Minutes, 16 August 1960, pp. 3–4.
111 Ibid.
112 *Report of the Commission on Higher Education 1960–67, vol. 1: Presentation and Summary of Report* (Dublin, 1967), pp. 1–2.
113 CAB 2/20, G.C.9/94, Cabinet Minutes, 13 September 1960, pp. 3–4.

3

Educational reform: 1961–65

'To do what is possible is my job and not to have the whole matter upset because of some supposed principle or ideal.'[1] Patrick Hillery's pragmatic defence of his policy approach on 11 June 1963 appeared to identify him as a cautious piecemeal reformer, who was wary of radical innovation. Certainly Hillery steadfastly refused to endorse the ideal of free post-primary education and rarely enunciated an overall vision for the future of Irish education. But Hillery's second term between 1961 and 1965 brought a series of incremental reforms in most areas of Irish education. More significantly, useful piecemeal reforms were no longer the summit of the department's ambitions: Hillery's term of office saw the beginning of coherent educational planning by the state for the first time. A survey of the state's long-term educational needs, to be conducted in conjunction with the OECD, was announced by Hillery in June 1962. The department also took important measures to address long-term problems in primary education. The Minister significantly enhanced the financial resources available to vocational education and introduced reforms designed to alleviate traditional shortcomings in the secondary system, especially by promoting the teaching of science and modern languages. The state also extended its financial support for the capital development of the universities. While Hillery consistently enunciated a policy of gradual expansion, his policy approach evolved with time and came to include ambitious policy initiatives, notably the comprehensive schools proposal in May 1963. Moreover education was explicitly recognised by the government as a vital national priority, which required an increasing investment of national resources in an era of economic expansion.

The OECD pilot study

Perhaps the most influential initiative of Hillery's tenure as Minister for Education was taken at the outset of his second term. Hillery and the senior officials of the department were increasingly influenced by policy ideas

2 Roddy Connolly, Dr. Maeve Hillery, Liam Cosgrave and Dr. Patrick Hillery (left to right) at the opening of the new extension to Blackrock College. Courtesy of Blackrock College.

promoted by the Organisation for Economic Co-operation and Development (OECD), especially its advocacy for coherent planning of educational needs. The international organisation, which began its official existence as the Organisation for European Economic Co-operation (OEEC) in 1948, expanded its membership to include the United States of America and Canada in 1961, when it was restructured as the OECD.[2] The Governing Committee for Scientific and Technical Personnel, which had been established within the international organisation in 1958, identified the development of education and scientific research as an essential element in the achievement of economic growth.[3] The Committee's programme for 1961–62 emphasised that education and science should be treated as priority areas for the allocation of resources by its member states. The organisation's approach was profoundly influenced by the international rivalry between the West and the Soviet Union at the height of the Cold War. The OEEC programme envisaged that the success of the competing systems in achieving social progress and economic development 'will undoubtedly affect their respective influence in the world at large and particularly in the underdeveloped countries'.[4] The Committee considered that educational and scientific investment could play a significant part in 'the world competition' between the OEEC states and the Communist bloc.[5]

The newly reconstituted OECD, which came into existence on 30 September 1961, vigorously promoted the Committee's view that education should be regarded as a key factor in economic development. The OECD officials were greatly influenced by human capital theory, which held that investment in people produced a greater return of investment than investment in physical capital. Human capital theory emerged as a major strand of economic thinking in the early 1960s, due especially to the work of Gary Becker and Theodore Schultz.[6] The OECD's first major event was a policy conference on 'Economic Growth and Investment in Education', which was held in Washington between 16 and 20 October 1961.[7] Two Irish representatives attended the conference, Seán MacGearailt, Assistant Secretary of the Department of Education and John F. McInerney, Deputy Assistant Secretary of the Department of Finance.[8] The Directorate of Scientific Affairs of the OECD issued a proposal shortly before the conference for the establishment of pilot studies on long-term educational needs in developed countries.[9] The Directorate asserted that an increased supply of skilled technical workers was widely acknowledged as an essential requirement for economic growth in most member states, while a greater policy emphasis on the achievement of 'social aims' also demanded the expansion of educational facilities. The OECD proposal placed a high value on state investment in human resources, on the basis that the full development of individual potential brought substantial benefits to society: 'Both economic and non-economic aims therefore point to the conclusion that increased investment in human resources must play a vital role in national politics in the 1960s.'[10] The OECD believed that investment in education was increasingly recognised as one of the main instruments in the achievement of social and economic progress.

The Directorate of Scientific Affairs played the leading role in the establishment of the Mediterranean Regional Project, which involved six southern European states, Greece, Italy, Spain, Portugal, Yugoslavia and Turkey, in the early 1960s. The OECD assisted national teams in undertaking studies on the long-term requirements for skilled labour and needs for educational resources in each state.[11] The Directorate in October 1961 proposed similar pilot studies by European states with more developed economies. The Washington conference agreed an international initiative, the *Education Investment and Planning Programme* (EIPP), which was based on the Directorate's proposal.[12] Keill Eide, Principal Administrator of the Directorate, then approached the Irish representatives, suggesting that they should advise the Irish government to undertake the proposed pilot study.[13] The Irish officials immediately agreed to recommend co-operation with the pilot study to the relevant ministers. The delegations of Ireland and Austria were the initial volunteers for co-operation with the project, although the EIPP was subsequently joined by other European states.[14]

The willing acceptance of the OECD initiative by McInerney and Mac-Gearailt, which was subsequently approved by Hillery, proved a decision with far-reaching implications for Irish education.

Leading officials in the departments of Education and Finance favoured the OECD study. The project was discussed at a meeting on 31 October 1961 involving the two Irish representatives to the conference, as well as Ó Raifeartaigh and T.K. Whitaker. McInerney, who was a strong proponent of the study, found general agreement among the officials that the OECD initiative offered a valuable opportunity.[15] Ó Raifeartaigh raised the OECD proposal, indicating that his department favoured the project. Whitaker agreed that such a pilot survey was necessary to allow the state to plan for an adequate supply of scientific and technical manpower, which was essential in sustaining economic expansion. He also commented that the guidance of the OECD would be helpful in conducting the project. The officials agreed that Ó Raifeartaigh would write formally to Whitaker, who would then take up the proposed project with other relevant departments.[16] Ó Raifeartaigh proceeded to outline the case for the study to Whitaker on 8 November 1961. Ó Raifeartaigh indicated that his department favoured such a study to ascertain the educational requirements and targets, which would form part of economic planning for the next five years.[17] He pointed out that 'the emphasis everywhere at present appears to be on investment in education as a necessary prerequisite for economic growth'.[18] The Irish officials at the Washington conference reported that long-term planning in education was already being undertaken by other developed states and the Secretary acknowledged that Ireland was joining 'an international consensus' on the need for coherent planning of educational expansion. Ó Raifeartaigh sought a firm decision on the project at an early date. Whitaker lost no time in seeking agreement for the proposal from the departments of Industry and Commerce, Agriculture and External Affairs, as well as the Central Statistics Office. He also informed Nicholas Nolan, Secretary to the government, that the Department of Finance favoured the adoption of the pilot study.[19] Whitaker quickly secured general agreement from the other departments for the proposed study, telling Ó Raifeartaigh on 15 December that they should now proceed with the project.[20] The Department of Education made a formal application to participate in the OECD programme in February 1962 and the Council of the OECD approved the Irish application on 21 June.[21] The rapid official decision to go ahead meant that Ireland became the first OECD member state to volunteer for participation in the project.

The OECD's initiative was taken up with enthusiasm by Lemass and Hillery. The political context was very favourable for the initiation of the pilot study. The government, which was beginning the preparation of the *Second Programme for Economic Expansion*, regarded a survey of long-term educational needs as an essential element in a process of national economic planning. Lemass informed Cearbhall Ó Dálaigh, chair of the Commission on Higher Education, on 21 June 1962 that the government was undertaking the pilot study in part because the OECD approach heavily emphasised economic planning. Moreover the Taoiseach cited Ireland's application to join the European Economic Community (EEC) as another important element influencing the government's support for the study. He considered that the government's acceptance of the OECD initiative 'could have a very important bearing on our future relations with the European Economic Community'.[22] Hillery announced the initiation of the pilot study, which was to be implemented by a national survey team in conjunction with the OECD, on 22 June 1962 at a Labour/Management conference in Shannon Airport.[23] The OECD undertook to cover 50% of the running costs of the educational survey over a period of two years. The survey team, which was appointed by Hillery on 29 July 1962, was headed by Patrick Lynch, Professor of Economics at UCD. The national team also included William Hyland of the United Nations Statistics Office, Pádraig Ó Nualláin, Inspector of Secondary Schools and Martin O'Donoghue, lecturer in Economics at Trinity College Dublin, while Cathal MacGabhann of the Department of Education acted as secretary to the group.[24] The work of the survey team was overseen by a National Steering Committee appointed by the Minister, which was chaired by Seán MacGearailt. Hillery secured the approval of the government for the appointment of a broad-based Committee, which included representatives of the departments of Education, Finance, Agriculture and Industry and Commerce, the Economic Research Institute and the Central Statistics Office, as well as the universities, agricultural interests, employers and the Irish Congress of Trade Unions.[25] The broad-based character of the Steering Committee contrasted sharply with the composition of previous committees of inquiry relating to education, especially the Council of Education, which had been dominated by clergy and professional educators. The inclusion of representatives of the trade unions and employers on the Committee marked an important break with the past and underlined the government's concern to link education with wider economic development.[26]

The terms of reference for the project were announced by Hillery in the Dáil on 3 July 1962. The national team would undertake a comprehensive survey of the state's long-term needs for educational resources. The terms of reference for the pilot study included:

- an evaluation of the existing position in relation to skilled manpower;
- the framing of educational targets, including provision for research, in relation to the assessments to be made of overall needs for skilled

manpower according to field of study and level of skill, for the next 10–15 years – alternative estimates, made according to different basic assumptions, were intended to take into account trends in economic and demographic factors, and also the experience of other countries;
- the assessment, on the basis of alternative estimates, of future essential demand for educational facilities at different levels based on present trends and international experience;
- estimates of future enrolments at different levels of education based on the alternative assumptions devised by the survey team;
- an assessment of the necessary expansion of educational resources, namely the teachers, buildings and equipment required by future educational expansion;
- evaluations of the expenditure entailed by the various alternatives for the expansion of educational resources – the evaluations were to be expressed in relation to macro-economic data, such as GNP;
- consideration of arrangements necessary to ensure the review of educational needs at regular intervals, with particular regard to the nature and extent of the additional statistical data which should be collected and the method and frequency of such collections;
- an evaluation of the extent to which the assessments of the survey might be influenced by providing educational facilities in Ireland for students from other countries and by offering educational aid in the form of teachers and other trained personnel for service in developing countries.[27]

The department drew the terms of reference almost entirely from the proposal for the pilot studies in developed countries issued by the Directorate of Scientific Affairs on 12 October 1961.[28] The sole element not derived from the OECD proposal was the proposed evaluation of the implications of providing educational aid to developing countries. While the OECD had raised the possibility of providing educational facilities in Ireland to students from other countries, the inclusion of aid to developing countries in the survey team's terms of reference reflected the Irish tradition of missionary and educational work in Africa, especially by the religious orders.[29] Although the Directorate of Scientific Affairs affirmed that the responsibility for the pilot survey rested with teams appointed by the national authorities, the OECD exerted a pervasive influence over the objectives and parameters of the new study. The Minister and his senior officials were content to adopt the OECD blueprint for the pilot study almost without amendment. The terms of reference were definite and specific, requiring the team to evaluate the educational system in the context of existing policies and to undertake a detailed assessment of the workings of the system on the basis of relevant statistical data.[30] While specific policy recommendations were not envisaged by the terms of reference, the survey team was asked to undertake a full evaluation of long-term educational needs, particularly with regard to the future requirements of the economy for skilled manpower. The team was required also to assess the implications of future levels of enrolment, based on alternative estimates of demand for education for the expansion of educational resources and the level of state expenditure in education.[31] The new study was intended to provide a comprehensive analysis of future educational needs and a coherent approach for the effective allocation of resources to education.

The Taoiseach underlined the importance of the study of long-term educational needs even before the survey team started its work. Lemass drew attention to the new project on 8 July 1962 in a speech given to the Marist Brothers' Centenary celebrations in Sligo. The Taoiseach indicated that his government was well aware of the many inadequacies in the educational system and was seeking to plan for the future. Lemass declared that the new study was designed 'to frame a development programme and set the educational targets which must be realised if our facilities are to be kept in proper relation to our requirements as a progressive national community'.[32] He emphasised the importance of education in supplying the country's growing need for qualified scientific and technical personnel: 'It is in the growth and improvement of our education system that the foundations of our future prosperity must be firmly based.'[33] Lemass firmly asserted the government's commitment to the expansion of the educational system, not least because education would contribute to the economic development of the state. He was careful to assure his Marist audience that Irish educational aims would not be restricted to the production of a steady supply of technicians and scientists; he commented that the most important educational aim of all was to turn out well-rounded individuals who were fully prepared to cope with the pressures of a materialistic world.[34] But Lemass's concern to relate the planning of future educational developments to wider economic and social needs was evident.

Lemass's portrayal of educational expansion as a factor in economic prosperity was reiterated by Hillery, when he addressed the inaugural meeting of the Steering Committee in October 1962. The Minister argued that the role of education in promoting economic development had been given too little attention in the past; but he emphasised that 'Education is now accepted as an investment of national resources' and it was recognised as a major factor in economic development.[35] His comments underlined that the government had fully accepted the OECD's analysis of the importance of investment in education. Hillery, like the Taoiseach, stressed that the needs of the economy did not provide the sole imperative for the study, asserting that the survey team would take account of the wider aims of education. Indeed there should be no conflict between the educational needs of society and individual aspiration: investment by the state in education facilitated the aspirations of individuals and served the social and economic needs of the country. Hillery asserted that economic expansion and the full development of the potential of individual citizens both depended on the delivery of the necessary educational resources. He commented that: 'A country that allows its "human capital" to lie fallow will, if I may mix my metaphors, be left behind culturally as well as economically.'[36] The new study was designed to evaluate the educational needs of an expanding economy, but also the economic implications of the increasing demand for education.[37] Hillery rapidly adopted the ideas and rhetoric of the OECD, which had made a compelling case for investment in education by its member states.

The launch of the study of long-term educational needs in June 1962 reflected a definite policy commitment by the Irish government to coherent planning of educational needs, in the wider context of economic and social development. Hillery referred frequently to the work of the survey team as a means of achieving proper planning of educational provision. He declared in the Dáil on 27 May 1964 that future state provision for educational needs would be based upon the assessments of the survey team, especially their estimates of manpower needs. Hillery believed correctly that the analysis of the educational problems to be provided by the survey team would demand vastly increased expenditure, but emphasised that 'it will be expenditure on a studied plan and not just the lashing out of money in a haphazard fashion'.[38] He not only advocated proper educational planning but also emphasised the necessity for the adaptation of the educational system to provide for the social and economic needs of the time. The activity of the survey team marked the first real attempt by the independent Irish state to initiate a far-reaching reform of the educational system. The work of the national team paved the way for coherent educational planning based upon accurate statistical information. The adoption of the pilot survey by Hillery was a key policy decision in the reform and expansion of the Irish educational sector. The establishment of the *Investment in Education* study marked the first explicit acknowledgement by any Irish government of the need for a comprehensive reappraisal of the educational system, which would go far beyond the incremental reforms already initiated by the Minister for Education.

The launch of the OECD project, combined with the statements by Lemass and Hillery, indicated that the government was willing to allocate significantly increased resources to education, on the basis of rational planning of educational requirements. The launch of the pilot study coincided with the preparations for the *Second Programme for Economic Expansion*, which led the Department of Education to produce a general outline of its priorities for the following five years. The outline, entitled *Forecast of Developments in Educational Services During the 5-Year Period 1963–68*, was produced in response to a request from the Department of Finance for material concerning education for the Second Programme.[39] The *Forecast*, which was sent by Ó Raifeartaigh to the Department of Finance on 6 January 1962, was not itself an attempt to set educational targets on a coherent basis but a wide-ranging summary of the projects and initiatives, which the department aimed to undertake in the course of the Second Programme. The *Forecast* provided a concise outline of the department's priorities, as perceived by the senior officials. The summary was most detailed and ambitious in its discussion of primary and vocational education. The department sought an investment of between £1.5 and £2 million annually by the state in the primary school building programme to sustain an adequate rate of replacement of unsatisfactory school buildings. The *Forecast* emphasised the need to improve the pupil-teacher ratio in national schools by providing 900 additional teaching posts over five years.[40] The *Forecast*'s assessment of the necessary measures to provide better schools and more teachers at primary level demanded substantial investment by the state.

The department showed greater ambition in proposing an extensive restructuring of vocational education. The *Forecast* put forward several important reforms of the vocational system. It was proposed to extend the two-year day course in vocational schools, which culminated in the Day Group Certificate, by adding a third year to the existing course. The department also hoped to introduce new courses in technical education leading to a Technical Schools Leaving Certificate.[41] The creation of this additional element in the system was intended to supply 'the missing rung in our educational ladder', by enabling vocational school students to proceed to a further educational level and achieve a comparable educational standard to secondary school pupils taking Leaving Certificate courses.[42] The department noted that the establishment by An Chéard Chomhairle of new minimum educational standards for apprenticeship had brought a substantial increase in the enrolment of boys in day courses provided by vocational schools; this expansion in enrolment required additional teachers and accommodation.[43] The department's plans for vocational education were wide-ranging and innovative, even if they did not yet amount to a fully formulated or costed programme. Senior officials believed that the vocational schools offered considerable scope for reform and expansion of the educational system at post-primary level.

The *Forecast* was more tentative in its discussion of secondary education, although key priorities for educational policy were identified, notably
the extension of the teaching of science and modern languages. The
department emphasised the importance of curriculum reform to modernise the programmes in maths and science, drawing attention to the
need for appropriate state schemes to alleviate the shortage of qualified
teachers in these subjects. The officials also aimed to ensure that secondary
schools in future would provide a wider curriculum, which gave adequate
attention to the teaching of science and modern continental languages.[44]
Significantly the *Forecast* raised the possibility of providing comprehensive
schools, delivering a broad programme of subjects, in rural areas where
existing provision for secondary education was non-existent or limited in
the scope of its curriculum.[45] The department tentatively floated the idea
of comprehensive schools as a solution to the problem of educational
underdevelopment in remote rural areas, but gave no firm details on the
nature of the comprehensive school or the possible costs of such a project.
It was proposed only to initiate consultation with the appropriate authorities, which in practical terms meant the Catholic bishops. The vagueness
of the *Forecast* was understandable, as no coherent plan had been
formulated concerning post-primary education by January 1962. The
department, however, had given a tentative endorsement to the idea
of comprehensive schools. Moreover the *Forecast* also argued for the
introduction of a subsidised system of transport for pupils attending larger
secondary schools, on the basis that such a system would facilitate 'some
degree of planning of the steps to be taken to bring about an adequate
system of secondary education over the country as a whole'.[46] The senior
officials accepted the necessity by early 1962 for coherent planning of
educational expansion and aimed to intervene directly in shaping the
development of the secondary system, which had traditionally been the
preserve of private interests. While the department's plans remained
largely tentative and cautious, the policy ideas proposed by the *Forecast*
underlined a new willingness on the part of the Minister and senior officials
to consider innovative and potentially radical reforms in post-primary
education.

The *Forecast* made no policy proposals for university education. The
department merely noted that as the Commission on Higher Education
was continuing its deliberations, no definite forecast could be made
concerning the long-term development of university education.[47] It was
acknowledged that the state was committed to funding extensive building
programmes for the universities, especially the transfer of UCD to Belfield,
but otherwise the *Forecast* had little to say about higher education. The
Forecast as a whole was a mixture of incremental initiatives, similar to the

measures taken by Hillery between 1959 and 1961, and tentative proposals for more radical change. The *Forecast* reflected the department's
new-found commitment to more wide-ranging and effective intervention
by the state in expanding the educational system, as well as a considerable
degree of uncertainty about the form that such intervention would take.

Intervening in primary education

The *Forecast* certainly provided an accurate outline of the department's
initiatives in primary education between 1962 and 1965. The state's
approach to the expansion of primary education showed considerable continuity with the incremental measures adopted since 1959 to increase the
physical capacity of the system. The grants allocated to the Commissioners
of Public Works for primary school building increased substantially, delivering a steady expansion in the primary school building programme.[48] The
department under Hillery gave a high priority to the replacement of unsuitable school buildings and the upgrading of the physical resources of the
system. The Minister also placed considerable emphasis on the improvement of the pupil-teacher ratio. The average enrolment ratios governing
the appointment and retention of teachers were reduced in July 1962 and
again in October 1964.[49] Hillery also sought to increase the supply of
trained teachers to the national schools. The Minister authorised state
funding for the reconstruction and extension of St. Patrick's Training
College, Drumcondra, to provide accommodation for more than 300 students overall, allowing the college to train approximately 100 additional
students as national schoolteachers.[50] The department secured a bank
loan of £750,000 for the college, which was to be repaid annually by the
Minister over a period of thirty-five years. The remainder of the cost, which
was initially estimated at £2,500,000, was provided directly by the state
in capital grants.[51] But despite the department's efforts to provide an
increased supply of trained teachers, the pupil-teacher ratio remained
stubbornly high, especially in Dublin where 737 primary school classes in
1964 contained fifty or more pupils.[52]

A survey of national schools in the Dublin area was undertaken by the
department in 1964, with the objective of reducing large classes to a more
manageable size. The department sought to reduce class sizes firstly by the
reorganisation of existing classes, but where this proved impractical the
Minister resorted to the provision of prefabricated classrooms. The use of
prefabricated structures became an important element of the department's
strategy to reduce the pupil-teacher ratio. Official approval was given for
the supply of 112 prefabricated classrooms and the appointment of 104

additional teachers in the Dublin area between June and September 1964.[53] These measures reflected the scale of the overcrowding problem in urban primary schools and the recognition by the department that effective short-term remedies were urgently required. Hillery reinforced the practical measures to reduce class sizes by requiring all national schools in Dublin to establish a maximum class size of fifty pupils in all infants' classes from 1 July 1964. Circular 16/64 required the national school managers to limit the admission of new infant pupils to a maximum of fifty per class.[54] Hillery promoted a range of incremental measures to deal with the most obvious flaws in the system.

The Minister's efforts to enhance the physical and academic resources of the primary education system were not restricted to the increased supply of accommodation and teachers. The *Forecast* had anticipated the introduction of a scheme to establish reference libraries in national schools. Hillery initiated the scheme in November 1963, making grants available for the establishment of school libraries in five counties initially, namely Laois, Leitrim, Monaghan, Limerick and Waterford (excluding the cities of Limerick and Waterford).[55] The department arranged to supply reference works to all national schools in these areas, at a cost of £20,000, between January and March 1964. Hillery indicated that the scheme was being introduced on a phased basis and that the department would support the establishment of reference libraries in all national schools at a cost of £150,000.[56] The scheme was gradually extended to the entire country between 1964 and 1968.[57] The new scheme was the first public initiative to provide for permanent libraries in national schools and marked a significant advance in the academic resources provided by the state for primary education.

The initiatives taken by the department between 1961 and 1965 were much more effective and wide-ranging than the previous cautious measures of improvement. The advances were certainly due in part to increased state investment in education. But the department also took a more proactive and innovative approach in reducing class sizes and providing reference libraries on a national basis for the first time. The Minister and senior officials intervened effectively and with increasing confidence to direct the process of expansion in primary education.

A new era: special education

The department under Hillery also took an innovative approach to the development of special education. Although primary schools for blind and deaf pupils had existed since the nineteenth century, the department gave formal recognition to special education as a distinctive sector for the first time in the early 1960s. Special training for teachers of pupils with disabilities was provided for the first time in 1961, when a training course for such teachers was initiated in St. Patrick's Training College.[58] Schools for blind or partially sighted children became special schools in a real sense in 1962, when the department authorised a special teacher-pupil ratio of 1:15 and a grant for specialised equipment for such schools.[59] This initiative was an important landmark in the development of special education and it was soon followed by the introduction of special staffing measures for schools for pupils with impaired hearing. The department had already recognised the first schools for mentally handicapped pupils in 1955: special education in this area began to expand significantly in the early 1960s, as official recognition was given to special schools for students suffering from moderate mental disabilities and behavioural problems.[60] Hillery's term saw the first meaningful attempt by the Irish government to develop an area which had previously been neglected by the state.[61] The department's initiatives represented only a modest beginning in the area of special education. Nevertheless the first coherent attempts by the Irish state to support and develop special education occurred in this period and the initiatives taken by Hillery reflected the department's newly proactive and reforming approach in dealing with various educational problems by the early 1960s.

Incremental reform at second level

Hillery influenced the development of post-primary education more effectively than his predecessors, seeking particularly to facilitate the expansion of vocational education. The state considerably extended the vocational school building programme in this period: the establishment of thirty-nine new vocational or technical schools between 1960–61 and 1964–65 underlined the rapid expansion of vocational education.[62] Additional state investment in vocational education was facilitated by new legislation, which was initiated by Hillery to raise the legal ceiling for the grants made by local authorities to the VECs. The Vocational Education Acts fixed the maximum local rate that could be raised for vocational education at 15d in the pound for most authorities and 17d or 18d for a small number of urban councils, including the city of Dublin.[63] Contributions up to the maximum local rate had already been taken up by a number of committees by 1961–62; at least ten of the VECs faced insolvency without further aid.[64] The existing legislation also imposed ceilings on the annual increase in the local rate that could be secured by the VECs from the local authority. Hillery proposed new legislation in February 1962 to establish a maximum local rate of 24d in the pound for all VECs. He also aimed to ensure that the VEC would be able to secure an annual increase of 2d in the pound on demand from the local authority and up to 4d by prior agreement.[65] The legislation was designed to ensure a significant increase in the grants paid to the VECs by the Exchequer, as these grants were determined in relation to the committees' income from the local rates; the department provided a grant for vocational education, which matched or doubled the amount contributed by the local authorities.[66] The Department of Education's submission to the government made a strong case, however, that a substantial proportion of the cost of vocational education should be contributed from the local rates, as it was essentially a local service.[67]

The proposal faced opposition within the government. Neil Blaney, the Minister for Local Government, vehemently objected to the proposed legislation, opposing any increase in the local rate for vocational education. Blaney's department argued that education should be a national service and displayed a marked lack of enthusiasm for vocational education: 'local authorities do not have to pay for primary, secondary or university education and it is anomalous that they should be saddled with vocational education'.[68] Blaney's standpoint was entirely hostile to the reforming approach recently adopted by the Department of Education, which was based on the view that both local and national government had an obligation to support vocational education. The Cabinet was obliged to adjudicate the sharp divergence between the two ministers in April 1962. Hillery secured authorisation to proceed with the Bill on the basis of his original proposal. The revised limits for increases in the local rate were set at 1d in the pound available on demand by the VEC and 3d in the pound subject to prior agreement by the local authority.[69] While the revised ceilings were lower than Hillery had wished, the draft Bill contained most of the terms sought by the Department of Education. The Bill raised the maximum local rate for vocational education to 24d in the pound for all areas.[70] The Cabinet approved the legislation on 22 June and the Dáil passed the Bill without a vote in November 1962.[71]

The Vocational Education (Amendment) Act, 1962, significantly improved the level of state funding for vocational education, although the VECs still frequently required supplementary grants from the Exchequer to maintain solvency. The Minister had already allocated special grants to the VECs for Donegal and Leitrim in 1960 and 1961. Hillery later secured the agreement of the Department of Finance to make special grants to the sixteen committees, which were showing a substantial deficit by 1962–63.[72] The special grants to the VECs were maintained and extended by the department, even after the new legislation came into effect. Seán

MacGearailt informed the Public Accounts Committee on 6 March 1969 that all the VECs received special state grants to maintain their solvency by 1967–68.[73] The allocation of special grants to all the VECs reflected the steady expansion in the central state funding for vocational education. The enforcement by An Chéard Chomhairle of minimum educational standards for apprenticeship certainly increased the demand for vocational training and contributed to the expansion of vocational education.[74] But the development of the vocational system was underpinned by enhanced state investment, initiated primarily by Hillery and the Department of Education.

The state faced a more complex challenge in secondary education, which was dominated by private educational interests, especially the churches. While the powers of the Minister of Education in secondary education were still largely restricted to the regulation of teachers' salaries and the revision of the curriculum, the department began to use its established powers to promote new policies. The extension of the restricted curriculum in many secondary schools to include science and modern languages emerged as a key policy priority for the department. The senior officials were well aware of the low priority given to science subjects and modern languages in many secondary schools, which traditionally gave considerable attention instead to classical subjects and the Irish language.[75] The department's approach was also influenced by the OECD's concern to promote scientific studies and overcome the classical and academic bias of the secondary school curriculum.[76] The Minister acted to promote more general teaching of science by introducing curriculum reforms and special subsidies for schools.[77] Revised courses for the Leaving Certificate in physics and chemistry were introduced in 1962–63.[78] Likewise the mathematics curriculum was revised and notified to school managers in 1964, on the basis that the Leaving Certificate examination in 1966 would follow the revised courses.[79] A new scheme of grants was provided from August 1961 to finance the cost of equipping science laboratories in new secondary schools and those schools in which science was not previously available. More significantly, the Minister introduced a new scheme in 1964 to encourage secondary schools to employ qualified science teachers. The scheme involved the payment of an additional grant of £150 annually to schools for every qualified teacher, who held a university degree in science and was teaching the subject on a weekly basis.[80] The science grant was designed to promote the recruitment of highly qualified science teachers and to expand the teaching of science subjects in the secondary schools.[81] The traditional powers of the Minister in regulating teachers' salaries were employed to encourage new academic practices at secondary level.

The official concern to promote science in the secondary schools also led to the introduction of an educational television service for the first time. The department began a pilot scheme in February 1964, in conjunction with RTÉ, to provide school television programmes on physics courses to selected schools.[82] A full scheme was then introduced to enable secondary schools to use the new service 'Telefís Scoile', which showed programmes for science and mathematics. The state covered up to 75% of the cost incurred by schools in purchasing televisions to deliver the new service for an experimental period of two years.[83] The department proved willing to introduce imaginative reforming measures in an attempt to overcome the bias against science in the traditional secondary school system.

Hillery also sought to use ministerial influence over teacher salaries to promote the teaching of modern continental languages. Recognised teachers of modern continental languages who had given service in schools on the Continent were allowed to receive credit on the salary scales for such service from 1961.[84] Additional allowances for foreign language teachers in second-level education were introduced in 1962.[85] Hillery also announced the establishment in 1964 of a new language centre for teachers in the Franciscan College, Gormanston, in co-operation with Fr. Colmán Ó hUallacháin O.F.M., who acted as the department's adviser on language teaching. The new centre was employed by the department for research on teaching methods and for training teachers in the latest audio-visual techniques for language teaching.[86] The department sought to combine curriculum reform with additional grants and allowances, which provided a financial inducement to schools to broaden their curriculum.

The department's initiatives in the early 1960s reflected an implicit acknowledgement by Hillery and the officials of severe limitations in the school curriculum at secondary level. Their initiatives enjoyed a qualified success. The proportion of secondary schools which included science on their curriculum increased from 67% in 1961–62 to 73% in 1964–65.[87] This moderate expansion in the teaching of science by the middle of the decade did not fully satisfy the officials themselves. The department achieved more rapid success in its efforts to promote modern language teaching. The number of pupils studying French showed a substantial increase from 32,000 in 1958–59 to 52,000 in 1963–64.[88] Hillery readily embraced incremental reforms designed to alleviate traditional shortcomings in the secondary system, especially academic limitations with the potential to curtail the education of the workers of the future.

The Minister, however, was initially wary of offering a definitive statement of the government's policy or a full-scale critique of the flaws of the educational system. Hillery was criticised especially by Opposition politicians for failing to offer a coherent programme of reform for the system as a whole. On 23 May 1962 the leader of Fine Gael, James Dillon, attacked Hillery's failure to offer 'a comprehensive review' of the system and a plan for the future.[89] In the same Dáil debate Noel Browne criticised the Minister for failing to deliver fundamental reform of an unequal and inefficient system. He ridiculed Hillery as 'a sort of political castrate in charge of this tremendously important Department'.[90] Hillery responded by strongly defending the government's policy of gradual expansion. He reminded the Dáil on 6 June 1962 of the underdeveloped and underfunded system that he had inherited, bluntly criticising certain aspects of the system: 'we had a 50 year backlog of bad schools'.[91] The Minister made such comments to underline the extent of the problems that confronted him and to justify his measured approach. He hoped that his speech 'will explain to Deputies why my statements are sober. We have to wait not only for the finance but also for the time.'[92] He strongly advocated the need for a gradual and orderly approach to educational expansion. He pointed with some justice to the 'silent progress' of his own term. But while Hillery defended the gradualist policy of the government, he also pledged to bring forward plans for the expansion of second-level education 'in the near future'. Hillery's commitment to a significant initiative at post-primary level foreshadowed the launch of the groundbreaking proposal for comprehensive schools in 1963.

'A revolutionary step': comprehensive schools

The development of the Minister's initiative was encouraged by public criticism of the existing educational system, which was expressed by activist groups within civil society as well as by opposition parties. The case for educational reform was made most forcefully by Tuairim, a political research society founded in 1954 to provide a platform for members of the post-Treaty generation. The London Branch of Tuairim discussed a paper on the Irish educational system in April 1961, which was issued as a pamphlet entitled *Irish Education* in October 1962. The pamphlet presented a scathing critique of the traditional educational structures. The Tuairim research group argued that Irish educational attitudes were Victorian and criticised the 'political paralysis' which had traditionally permeated the Department of Education.[93] The pamphlet made various constructive recommendations for improving the educational system, not least the recognition by the state of teaching service in Britain on the incremental salary scales.[94] The study group argued that the proliferation of small schools at all levels of the educational system was educationally and economically unsound. Tuairim proposed the integration of educational facilities and the establishment of a national scheme of subsidised school transport.[95] The ideas of the research group were too radical to secure acceptance in 1962, but the proposals for the rationalisation of educational facilities would become the official policy of the Irish state within four years.

Tuairim also played an important role in stimulating public debate on education. The Dublin Branch of Tuairim held a study weekend in Greystones in November 1961, which considered a paper produced by the Branch entitled *Educating Towards A United Europe*.[96] The Tuairim pamphlet argued that the prospect of Ireland's accession to the EEC demanded 'fundamental adjustments' in a stagnant educational system if the Irish people were to make an effective contribution to the development of a united Europe.[97] The study weekend involved a wide-ranging discussion of weaknesses in Irish education, which included contributions by a prominent trade unionist, Charles McCarthy, general secretary of the Vocational Teachers' Association (VTA) and a leading educator, Thomas Kilroy, principal of Stratford College, Rathgar.[98] Tuairim provided a forum for critical discussion of the numerous deficiencies in the educational system and persistently drew public attention to the case for policy changes. The activity of the research group encouraged greater public interest in education and helped to place educational reform firmly on the political agenda.

The government also faced increasing political pressure for educational reform from its opponents. The Labour Party issued a policy document, entitled *Challenge and Change in Education*, in March 1963, which called for far-reaching changes in Irish educational structures.[99] The Labour policy document, which was composed mainly by Barry Desmond and Catherine McGuinness, was a manifesto for a radical reform of the educational system. The Labour Party endorsed the raising of the school leaving age, initially to fifteen but later to sixteen years and sought the establishment of a National Planning Branch within the department to implement rational planning of educational needs.[100] The document sought the introduction of free post-primary education for all children as 'a social and economic necessity of the first importance'.[101] The Labour policy also envisaged a radical restructuring of secondary education to provide larger central schools, which would be served by a central transport scheme funded by the state. *Challenge and Change* identified the extension and development of vocational education as an urgent educational necessity, emphasising that economic progress would require a highly educated and adaptable labour force.[102] The Labour Party's reforming approach mirrored many of the sentiments expressed by Hillery and Lemass, although Labour advocated more rapid and sweeping changes than the government was willing to endorse in 1963. The launch of Labour's education policy also intensified the political pressure on Hillery to bring forward his own initiative. Ó Raifeartaigh privately informed the Catholic bishops in February 1963 that the Minister wished to make a public statement on his plans for education in the short term, as the Labour Party was about to publish its policy document and 'he wants to forestall them'.[103] While Hillery was already considering a new initiative for post-primary education before the publication of the Labour policy, he was certainly concerned to limit the political impact of *Challenge and Change*. The launch of Labour's policy influenced the timing of Hillery's initiative in May 1963, providing an additional incentive for an early announcement of the Minister's plans for post-primary education.

The department's *Forecast* in January 1962 had raised the possibility of establishing comprehensive schools in areas not well served by traditional post-primary education.[104] Hillery made an initial proposal for a new type of post-primary school in a memorandum to the Department of the Taoiseach on 7 July 1962, following the report of an Inter-Departmental Committee on the Problems of Small Western Farms.[105] As his department had not been represented on the Committee, Hillery took the opportunity to comment on the educational problems in the relevant areas. The memorandum noted that post-primary education was often not available at all in the western small farm areas; even where post-primary schools were available the facilities were completely inadequate. Hillery proposed the establishment of several new post-primary schools, offering a comprehensive course of three years for pupils aged from twelve to fifteen; the curriculum of these schools should be broad-based but maintain 'a very definite practical bias'.[106] The new schools would be sufficiently large to provide a broad-based three-year course and a subsequent course of two years involving greater specialisation. This concept envisaged central schools serving a wide area, which would require transport services to bring in all pupils outside a three-mile radius of the school. The department proposed that the Exchequer should meet the capital cost of providing the school buildings, while two-thirds of the cost of the transport service would also be subsidised by the state.[107] Hillery sought to secure the agreement of the Cabinet Committee dealing with the report on small farm areas for the principle that the state would provide a new type of post-primary school. If this principle was accepted, then the Department of Education would prepare a definite proposal for the implementation of a pilot scheme in the areas with the most pressing educational needs.[108]

Tadgh Ó Cearbhaill, Assistant Secretary of the Department of the Taoiseach, forwarded this preliminary proposal to all the relevant ministers on 9 July. The Taoiseach then intervened to support Hillery's initiative. Lemass asked the ministers to indicate whether they would agree to the inclusion of a reference to such an educational initiative in the Taoiseach's forthcoming public statement, on the implementation of the report by the government.[109] Hillery's initiative received support from several ministers, including his predecessor, Jack Lynch, as Minister for Industry and Commerce.[110] The initiative was, however, strongly opposed by the Department of Finance. Whitaker criticised the proposal in a lengthy reply to Nicholas Nolan on 18 July.[111] He drew attention to the extensive costs involved in the proposed initiative and sought a thorough review of its financial implications. He argued that full consultation with educational interests, including the churches, school managers and teaching unions, would be necessary before any commitment was made by the government. Moreover Whitaker issued a clear warning on behalf of the Minister for Finance, Dr. Jim Ryan: 'In the circumstances the Minister is strongly of the opinion that any announcement made at this stage in connection with these proposals should be limited to a general statement to the effect that special attention is being given to the question of improving post-primary educational facilities in the western rural areas.'[112] Whitaker not only expressed strong reservations about the proposed initiative but categorically rejected Hillery's attempt to secure agreement in principle for the proposal from relevant ministers.

Ryan reiterated Whitaker's views in an official reply to Ó Cearbhaill's note on 23 July. The Minister expressed 'no objection in principle' to the proposed pilot scheme but urged that any public reference to it should consist only of a general indication of the government's intention to improve post-primary facilities in the relevant areas.[113] Ryan indicated that no commitment should be made to the principle of the proposal before the scheme was fully evaluated in terms of the cost, mode of implementation and implications for existing educational services.[114] While the tone of the Minister's response was more diplomatic than Whitaker's comments, the message conveyed to other departments was identical. The Department of Finance was entirely opposed to any endorsement of the proposal at least until the full implications of the scheme were fully evaluated. Moreover Whitaker had grave reservations about the initiative on financial and educational grounds.

Hillery, however, was not deterred by the Department of Finance's negative response. The Minister issued an uncompromising defence of his original proposal on 26 July, strongly refuting the criticisms made by the Department of Finance. The Minister's response dismissed Whitaker's concern about consultation with the religious authorities and other educational interests, with a pointed reminder that such consultation was appropriately left to the Department of Education, which would initiate the necessary consultation at the appropriate time. The official reply approved by Hillery argued that a general reference to a potential extension of existing facilities in the Taoiseach's statement would 'in many ways be worse than making no reference at all to education in any statement that may be issued'.[115] The Minister pointed out that private interests had already failed to provide secondary education in the western small farm areas and were most unlikely to do so in the future; the relevant areas were too thinly populated to make the running of a secondary school a viable proposition. He also argued that nothing had been proposed in his department's original memorandum that had not already been adopted by other European states, which took a progressive approach to education. Hillery believed that any reference to education in Lemass's statement should not only acknowledge the special problems concerning the under-development of second-level education in the western small farm areas but also contain 'a firm statement of intention to take special measures in order to cater for them'.[116]

Lemass essentially resolved the dispute in Hillery's favour. Lemass included a short but positive reference to the proposal in his public statement on the report at Muintir na Tíre Rural Week; the speech was delivered on his behalf by Charles Haughey, Minister for Justice, on 14 August 1962.[117] The Taoiseach's statement acknowledged that special problems existed with regard to post-primary education in the western small farm areas and indicated that Hillery was preparing proposals to remedy these deficiencies.[118] Significantly Lemass's statement also announced that 'the Minister's ideas, which have not yet been fully developed, envisage a new type of post-primary school with a curriculum which, although broad-based, would also have a definite practical bias'.[119] While Lemass avoided giving a definite commitment to these ideas, his statement was firmly based on the Department of Education's original proposal. The Taoiseach gave a firm indication that a new initiative was being prepared by the government to overcome deficiencies in post-primary education in specific areas.[120] Lemass also publicly introduced the idea of a new type of post-primary school, provided by the state, as a solution to the underdevelopment of second-level education in thinly populated rural areas. The section of Lemass's statement on education attracted little public attention in August 1962.[121] The Taoiseach had, however, signalled a new departure in educational policy, indicating that the government was considering an important initiative for the expansion of post-primary education.

An important impetus to reform in vocational and technical education was given, shortly after Lemass's address, by a review of technician training in Ireland, conducted by examiners operating under the auspices of the Department of Education and the OECD. The OECD examiners were invited by the department to undertake a review of technical education in the context of economic development, with special emphasis on the position of the technician.[122] The examiners, Prof. Alan Peacock and Dr. Werner Rasmussen, undertook a visit to Ireland in September 1962, accompanied by Dr. Petr Ter-Davtian of the OECD Directorate of Scientific Affairs. They identified a number of deficiencies in technical education in Ireland, including the absence of an adequate preparatory course for entrants to the Colleges of Technology in Dublin. The examiners drew attention to the 'strong classical and linguistic bias' of the secondary schools, which gave inadequate attention to science and mathematics. They also commented on a general lack of flexibility in the Irish educational system, which was particularly evident in the lack of any educational ladder from the vocational school to university education.[123]

The report of the examiners was considered at a 'confrontation' meeting organised by the OECD in Paris on 29 January 1963, which was attended by Hillery, Ó Raifeartaigh, Patrick Lynch, Michael O'Flanagan, Chief Inspector of the department's Technical Instruction Branch and Prof. J.P. O'Donnell, of the Chemical Engineering Department in UCD.[124] The examiners, especially Dr. Rasmussen, raised the concern that there seemed to be a lack of awareness in Ireland of the general need for scientific and technician education. They recommended that expenditure on education should be regarded as one of the most productive forms of long-term national investment and that broadly designed courses of technical education were required to provide training relevant to all modern economic activities.[125] In response to the examiners' comments, Hillery confirmed that 'it is our Government's policy to make a substantial investment in education'.[126] He assured the OECD experts that his department was committed to making changes in the educational system and would welcome advice on the form that such changes might take. Hillery acknowledged that the state's approach to the development of vocational and higher technical education was still tentative and welcomed input from the OECD on future policy measures.

The expert advisers made several key recommendations that were endorsed by the Irish delegation. The examiners recommended the introduction of regional technical education in southern and western areas of the country, which lacked access to post-primary or higher technical education. They emphasised the need for an adequate regional distribution of post-primary technical courses, which could serve as a ladder to higher technical education. Michael O'Flanagan agreed that such technical courses were desirable and indicated that the department was considering plans for the development of technical education, for students around the age of sixteen, in urban areas in western and southern Ireland.[127] The proposal by the examiners for a senior cycle technical course leading to a Technical Schools Leaving Certificate was endorsed by the department, which had raised a similar idea in its *Forecast* in January 1962.[128] A recommendation by the OECD experts for the establishment of a permanent statistical and development unit in the Department of Education was also accepted by the Irish delegation.[129] The examiners drew renewed attention to existing deficiencies in vocational and higher technical education, placing greater pressure on the Minister to act on some of the reforming ideas under consideration by the department. The experts proposed specific improvements, which were generally accepted as desirable by the Irish delegation. Yet Hillery did not attempt to implement specific reforms pinpointed by the OECD in isolation from the wider problems of second-level education. The ideas of the OECD experts were instead incorporated in the initiative for the reform of post-primary education, which had been under consideration by the department since the summer of 1962.

The first detailed proposal for the reform of second-level education was drafted by the officials of the department, on the basis of an outline submitted by Hillery.[130] A committee was established in June 1962 by Ó Raifeartaigh, to advise the Minister on future educational needs in post-primary education. The committee, which was chaired by Dr. Maurice Duggan, also included Dr. Finbar O'Callaghan, Tomás Ó Floinn, Liam Ó Maolchatha and Micheál Ó Súilleabháin.[131] The committee produced an interim report on 8 December 1962, which argued that a minimum period of post-primary education was a national necessity. The committee recommended free and compulsory second-level education for all children up to the age of fifteen.[132] The report also rejected the idea of large comprehensive schools modelled on the English system as impractical and proposed instead a comprehensive post-primary course for junior cycle pupils in secondary and vocational schools.[133] Hillery and the senior officials did not, however, adopt all the recommendations of the internal report. The department's initiative, entitled *Proposal for Comprehensive Post-Primary Education: Pilot Scheme related to Small Farm Areas*, used certain elements of the report by Duggan's committee, such as its arguments for a common post-primary course for all pupils aged twelve to fifteen.[134] But the official proposal also included a definite recommendation for several comprehensive schools of between 150 and 400 pupils and it entirely ignored the committee's suggestion of free post-primary education for all children up to the age of fifteen.[135] Hillery had no intention of proposing free education as part of the new scheme – he believed that the opposition generated by such a proposal would wreck the initiative. 'It wasn't about free education. The whole thing would have collapsed due to the opposition.'[136] Imelda Bonel-Elliott suggested that the report by Duggan's committee was an important element in the formulation of the major reforms at post-primary level in the 1960s.[137] But the report, which was not distributed within the department, was more important in supporting the case for major changes in second-level education than as a direct influence on Hillery's plans. The department had already formulated initial proposals for the extension of the vocational school programme and for the introduction of comprehensive education in its *Forecast of Developments*.[138] The report by Duggan's committee was significant mainly as an indication of new thinking about educational policy among the officials of the department.

The department's proposal clearly identified key problems in post-primary education. Most importantly the provision of secondary education depended entirely on private initiative, implying that more remote regions were unlikely ever to have a secondary school as no incentive existed for the private sector to build a school for very few pupils. The most striking defect of the system was summarised bluntly: a large residue of pupils would never receive post-primary education 'under the present system of private enterprise'.[139] Moreover the department's paper identified further problems flowing from this 'fundamental structural defect' in the educational system.[140] Many rural secondary schools were too small, employing inadequate numbers of staff and therefore providing only a limited curriculum, giving little or no attention to continental languages or science. The departmental proposal also described private schools under one-man management as 'inherently unstable'.[141] This was a revealing comment, which gave some indication of dissatisfaction among senior officials with the tight control of schools by individual clergy. The department also expressed grave concern at the rigid separation between secondary and vocational education, noting that the two strands of the post-primary system operated in 'separate watertight compartments'.[142] The solution was the establishment by the state of comprehensive post-primary schools, which were initially described as Junior Secondary Schools.[143] This proposal formed the basis of the policy announcement made by Hillery in May 1963.

The department's proposal made rapid progress through the administrative and political obstacles that could have blocked its path, due to Hillery's effective advocacy and the support of the Taoiseach. The proposal was first submitted to the Department of Finance and was rejected.[144] Hillery then appealed directly to the Taoiseach, making the case for comprehensive schools to Lemass on 9 January 1963.[145] The Minister made a strong argument for a pilot scheme involving comprehensive schools in the western small farm areas. Hillery noted that private interests had failed in the relevant areas to provide for education and so could not credibly object to state action. He hoped that the pilot scheme would provide a model of post-primary education, which could later be extended to the whole country. Hillery acknowledged both the considerable expense of the plan and the possible opposition of private interests, including the Catholic Hierarchy, but urged that it was necessary and probably inevitable. The Minister even argued that the comprehensive schools plan might well prove to be the only opportunity to introduce a 'really satisfactory system of post-primary education'.[146]

Only four months elapsed before the Department of Education's proposal became, in a modified form, the publicly acknowledged policy of the government. Lemass played a crucial role in the rapid evolution of government policy on education. Hillery had suggested that his department's proposal should be forwarded to the Cabinet Committee on Small Farms. The Taoiseach found a more effective means of promoting Hillery's initiative. Lemass withheld the proposal from the Cabinet Committee, instead arranging a meeting involving only Hillery, the Taoiseach himself and Jim Ryan.[147] Hillery elaborated on his department's proposal in a further letter to Lemass on 12 January, indicating that he hoped to achieve 'one system of post-primary education which would have a number of streams'.[148] The Minister emphasised his determination to achieve equality of opportunity for all according to talent. Hillery's message secured a rapid and positive response from Lemass. The Taoiseach explicitly endorsed the new initiative in his response on 14 January, although he also noted his own lack of knowledge about the cost of the plan and other practical problems.[149] He warned the Minister that public confusion about the government's policy would persist until Hillery's plan was announced. Lemass gave Hillery clear directions on the procedure to be followed in the meeting with the Minister for Finance. Indeed the Taoiseach warned Hillery to 'come to this meeting with the nature of the decisions you desire very clear in your mind' – Lemass even sought in advance a draft of the decisions as Hillery wished to have them recorded.[150] Lemass also indicated that Ryan could not be expected to give full approval to the proposal at the first meeting. But the Taoiseach's commitment to Hillery's proposal and his determination to fast track it through the normal procedures of the government were evident.

The summary of the decisions requested by Lemass was drafted by Hillery's officials and contained three main elements.[151] The draft summary envisaged a new system of post-primary education based on comprehensive courses and where necessary comprehensive schools. A pilot scheme would be introduced in more remote rural areas as a first step in this direction.[152] The Minister also sought authorisation to consult with the Catholic bishop in each relevant area to give effect to the proposal, as it was envisaged that the pilot scheme would involve only Catholic schools.[153] Hillery secured agreement from Jim Ryan for the plan by following the procedure recommended by Lemass, despite some delay caused by the Department of Finance. Ó Cearbhaill composed a handwritten memo on 8 March noting that Seán MacGearailt was pressing for an early decision on the comprehensive schools proposal, which was then still being considered by the Department of Finance.[154] The memorandum was intended for the attention of the Taoiseach and the Department of Finance. Lemass's reaction is not recorded but Hillery soon secured Ryan's agreement for the comprehensive schools initiative.[155] The Taoiseach then told Hillery to launch the scheme publicly without bringing it back to the Cabinet for formal approval, telling the Minister bluntly: 'You'll never get it through the Government.'[156] So the scheme for comprehensive schools was launched by Hillery at a press conference on 20 May 1963. Lemass had not only played a crucial role in steering the initiative successfully past the procedural obstacles that might have frustrated it, he had also given Hillery the authority to go ahead without formal Cabinet approval.

Hillery's policy announcement on 20 May identified major weaknesses in the existing second-level sector, which provided the rationale for the comprehensive schools proposal. These flaws included the failure of the system to provide post-primary education for a substantial segment of the population and the complete absence of co-ordination between secondary and vocational schools.[157] Hillery declared that a third of Irish children received no post-primary education. These children were 'today's Third Estate, whose voice amid the babel of competing claims from the more privileged, has hitherto scarcely been heard.'[158] The Minister clearly endorsed the concept of equality of opportunity as a guiding principle of state policy. He announced that the state would take the initiative in resolving these problems by providing a number of new post-primary schools catering in the first instance for specific regions. Hillery proposed a comprehensive post-primary day school, providing a three-year course leading to the Intermediate Certificate examination.[159] The new comprehensive school would provide for at least 150 students and would be open to all within a ten mile radius of the school; pupils would enter the comprehensive school after the sixth standard in primary school.[160] The comprehensive school would offer a wide range of subjects to pupils, including all those available in the secondary and vocational schools. Hillery specifically rejected selection at an early age, ruling out any system similar to the eleven-plus examination prevalent in Britain and instead aimed to provide a comprehensive curriculum for children in the twelve to sixteen age group.[161] The school buildings would be financed largely by the state, while the running costs would be funded through annual grants from the department and the VECs. The salaries of the teachers would be paid by the department.[162] Hillery's announcement marked a fundamental policy change from the practice of successive governments since the foundation of the Irish state. The national government would intervene directly to provide broadly based post-primary education for the first time.

Hillery offered a clear vision of the role of comprehensive schools and their place in the educational system. He considered that specialisation was appropriate following the three-year comprehensive course. His proposal envisaged that pupils of the comprehensive schools would move into secondary or technical education at the age of fifteen or sixteen. Hillery hoped that local technical schools would function as a 'senior storey' of the comprehensive school or as a separate institution for comprehensive students.[163] More significantly, the Minister proposed a radical new departure in technical education to accommodate pupils who did not intend to proceed with academic education after the age of fifteen. Hillery announced his intention to establish Regional Technological Colleges, in conjunction with the VECs; the regional colleges would provide courses for a new public examination, the Technical Schools Leaving Certificate.[164] The objective of the new examination was to enable technical students to achieve a standard of education comparable in status with the academic standard delivered by the secondary schools. The Technical Schools Leaving Certificate was intended to qualify students for entry to third-level education or to employment training for skilled technical and management positions. The regional colleges were designed to accommodate not only pupils from the new comprehensive schools but any students who displayed 'practical aptitudes'.[165] The existing vocational schools were intended to provide many of the recruits for the new colleges. The Regional Technological Colleges were originally intended as a bridge to third-level education or skilled technical employment for students with technical aptitudes. The proposal marked the beginning of a dramatic development of higher technical education, which would lead to the foundation of the first Regional Technical Colleges (RTCs) as an element of the third-level sector in 1969.[166] Hillery's proposal was a serious attempt to widen educational opportunity for students with technical aptitudes.

The wide-ranging initiative also sought to improve co-ordination between the secondary school system and the vocational schools by introducing a common standard of evaluation. Hillery announced the extension of the two-year day course in vocational schools to make it a three-year course.[167] This paved the way for vocational students to take the Intermediate Certificate examination in a number of subjects by 1966. The Minister also announced the revision of the Intermediate Certificate to provide a broadly common examination for students from the secondary and vocational sectors. Hillery claimed with considerable justice that the measure, which was intended to achieve parity in standards and evaluation between the different systems, was an important educational reform.[168]

Hillery's policy initiative of 20 May 1963 aimed to promote equality of educational opportunity and to improve the co-ordination between the very different strands of the educational system. The initiative deserves to be evaluated not only with regard to its specific achievements but also in the context of the underdeveloped Irish educational system in the early 1960s. The comprehensive schools proposal was initially implemented as a pilot project involving only three schools, in Cootehill, Co. Cavan, Shannon, Co. Clare and Carraroe, Co. Galway, which opened in September 1966.[169] But Hillery's announcement marked the first major initiative by the Irish state to provide for second-level education, outside the specific ambit of technical instruction. The direct intervention of the national government to establish a new form of post-primary school was unprecedented.

Hillery's proposal was significant too because it owed much to economic imperatives as well as social and educational demands. He himself hoped that the reforms would 'give the country a systematic supply of youth with a sufficient technical education' to meet the needs of the economy.[170] The proposed regional colleges were clearly intended to provide a supply of skilled technical workers to meet the demands of an expanding economy. It was, however, the educational potential of the regional colleges which made this innovation one of the most radical announced by Hillery. While the first Regional Technical Colleges were not established until 1969, they became an integral part of the third-level system in the following decade.[171] Certainly the RTCs performed very different functions from the role initially envisaged by Hillery, not least because the proposal for separate second-level courses leading to a Technical Schools Leaving Certificate was shelved by Hillery's successors.[172] But the foundation of the regional colleges was a significant extension of educational opportunity, even if the implementation of the initiative was a long way off in 1963. The policy announcement as a whole marked the first serious attempt by the Irish state to deliver second-level education for the children of all its citizens.

The Minister's initiative also involved a sustained effort to raise the quality and status of technical education, which was reflected not only in the plan for the Regional Technological Colleges but also in the proposed reform of the examination system to guarantee parity of standards and assessment between the widely diverging sectors. Hillery initiated a revision of the Intermediate Certificate examination to provide a common system of assessment for all post-primary schools in the junior cycle. A curriculum committee was established within the department, chaired by Tomás Ó Floinn, which drafted the revised programme for the

Intermediate Certificate and drew up the curriculum for the comprehensive schools.[173] The Minister's hope that the common examination at Intermediate Certificate level would ensure a similar standard of work in all post-primary schools was, however, certainly too optimistic. It was always unlikely that the deeply entrenched division between vocational and secondary education could be overcome simply by a common examination. But the revised state examination at least provided a greater degree of co-ordination between two systems, which had previously operated on an entirely separate basis. Certainly the revised examination system marked the first real effort by the state to co-ordinate the activity of the vocational sector and the private secondary schools. Hillery's announcement on 20 May 1963 was a far-reaching reforming initiative, which heralded a radical policy departure in second-level education. The initiative was the first of the major reforming measures which transformed the Irish educational system in the era of expansion.

The proposals unveiled by Hillery secured a positive reception in the media. The *Irish Press* gave a highly favourable response to the announcement, describing the plan on 22 May 1963 as 'revolutionary' and 'a welcome move to streamline the system and bring [it] into line with modern needs'.[174] Such a response was perhaps not surprising, in the context of the newspaper's long-standing connections with Fianna Fáil. But the *Irish Times* was almost equally effusive; an editorial on 21 May welcomed Hillery's plan and praised the comprehensive model adopted by the Minister.[175] The initiative received a less positive response from the teaching unions, as the union representatives were angered by the lack of any consultation with them before the policy announcement. The INTO joined with the associations representing secondary and vocational teachers, the ASTI and the VTA, to issue a joint statement on 25 May protesting at the lack of ministerial consultation.[176] But the teaching unions broadly welcomed many of the specific proposals announced by Hillery. The INTO treasurer, Senator Seán Brosnahan, welcomed the Minister's rejection of the eleven-plus method of selection, while calling for the early raising of the school leaving age. Charles McCarthy welcomed the extension of the vocational school courses and the announcement of the Regional Technological Colleges, although he also expressed great disappointment at the Minister's failure to consult vocational teachers.[177] There was little public reaction, however, from the church authorities, especially the Catholic Hierarchy, which made no immediate response to the initiative.

The implications of Hillery's proposals for the churches were not clear at the outset. Hillery did not define the desired management structure during his press conference on 20 May, as agreement had not been reached with the Catholic Hierarchy at that stage.[178] While the pilot scheme consisted entirely of Catholic schools, the Minister indicated that the department would welcome a future proposal for a Protestant comprehensive school by the appropriate educational authorities.[179] Hillery's cautious rhetoric on the management structure reflected the sensitive nature of church–state relations on education.[180] Hillery informally consulted the Hierarchy on the proposal at an early stage, discussing the idea with Dr. William Conway, the newly appointed Archbishop of Armagh, without reaching agreement.[181] The initial reaction of the Hierarchy to the proposal was hostile. The bishops agreed to oppose any attempt to establish state secondary schools at their general meeting on 1 October 1962.[182] The Bishop of Elphin, Dr. Vincent Hanly, who called personally to the department on 12 December 1962 to seek information about the initiative, was told by senior officials that the scheme would in due course apply to the entire country.[183] This information heightened the fears of several bishops, including Hanly himself and McQuaid. McQuaid told Hanly on 5 January 1963 that the proposed scheme was gravely objectionable, as the department was proposing to establish state secondary schools, which would be non-denominational and co-educational.[184] The Standing Committee of the Hierarchy on 8 January instructed Hanly and Fergus to ensure that no scheme was published before the bishops had the opportunity to approve the proposal.[185]

The Secretary of the department attempted unsuccessfully to reassure the bishops, briefing Hanly and Fergus in February 1963, at the Bishop of Achonry's house in Ballaghadereen, on the key elements of the Minister's policy announcement. Ó Raifeartaigh assured the two bishops that the new schools would be vested in trustees appointed by the local bishop. He also informed them that Hillery's public announcement on the scheme would not be definitive, as no final scheme would be published until it was agreed with the bishops.[186] While the bishops did not object to a general statement by the Minister on post-primary education, they were concerned that no detailed announcement should be made in the short term and expressed particular opposition to the proposal allowing vocational school students to undertake the Intermediate Certificate course.[187] The Hierarchy's representatives were seriously alarmed by the specific content of the initiative. Hillery later commented that 'The Hierarchy were totally against it.'[188] Hanly warned Fergus and McQuaid that 'Since our meeting with Dr. Ó Raifeartaigh on Friday I cannot help feeling that we are on the edge of an educational crisis.'[189] He believed that the comprehensive schools plan would cause the conversion of vocational schools into state secondary schools, which would compete successfully with the voluntary secondary schools. McQuaid took up the bishops' concerns about the plan with the Secretary of the department. Ó Raifeartaigh gave assurances to the

Archbishop that the comprehensive schools would be denominational and under the management of the parish clergy. Following his discussions with the Secretary, McQuaid assured Fergus on 2 March 1963 that the church's voluntary secondary schools had nothing to fear from the department's initiative. He commented that, regardless of the state's policies, parents would continue to see 'a certain social distinction' between the secondary schools and either comprehensive or vocational schools.[190] McQuaid told the secretary to the Hierarchy that 'We cannot change the heart of man', asserting that the social prestige of the secondary schools would maintain their attraction to parents even if the comprehensive schools offered virtually free education.[191] McQuaid was willing to accept a scheme for comprehensive schools, if the Minister ruled out co-education and gave firm guarantees concerning the denominational character and management of the schools. McQuaid's pragmatic assessment of the limited consequences of the initiative for secondary education contrasted with Hanly's suspicion that Hillery was acting to undermine private denominational education.

Hanly's suspicion was certainly unfounded. Hillery pledged at the press conference on 20 May that the comprehensive schools would be denominational and under the control of boards of management that would safeguard Catholic interests.[192] The Hierarchy as a whole remained suspicious, however, of the state's unprecedented intervention in post-primary education. The bishops agreed at their general meeting on 25 June 1963 that the initiative was 'a revolutionary step'; the Minister would be allowed to establish post-primary schools, while vocational education would be transformed.[193] The Hierarchy sought clarification from the department concerning the management of the new schools, the implications for existing secondary schools and co-education. The bishops were concerned that a clerical Manager, appointed by the local bishop, should control any new school with the power to appoint staff and determine the curriculum in accordance with Catholic teaching. They also sought assurances that there would be no co-education and that the new schools would not adversely affect existing secondary schools.[194] The Hierarchy did not reject the scheme in principle, but sought to reshape the proposal to meet their concerns.

Hillery, accompanied by Ó Raifeartaigh and MacGearailt, began the negotiations with the bishops by meeting Hanly and Fergus to discuss the new scheme on 28 June 1963.[195] The bishops argued that the entry of the state into the field of general post-primary education was a revolutionary measure. They were dissatisfied with the proposed reform of vocational schools and the lack of any clarity in Hillery's statement concerning the possibility of co-education. Hillery replied that his press statement 'was not intended as a blue-print but a pointer', acknowledging the ambiguity of his proposal on some aspects of the new scheme.[196] But he also emphasised that private education had failed to provide for certain regions of the country and therefore intervention by the state was necessary. The meeting was inconclusive and revealed considerable differences between the department and the Hierarchy on the management of the new schools. The department proposed boards of management for the comprehensive schools which included a nominee of the local bishop acting as chair, a nominee of the Minister and the Chief Executive Officer of the local VEC.[197] The Hierarchy's representatives asserted that the Bishop's nominee, as chair of the board, should be entitled to appoint the teaching staff and claimed that Hillery had accepted this arrangement on 28 June.[198] But the senior officials firmly rejected this interpretation, which the bishops incorporated in their record of the meeting. Seán MacGearailt informed the bishops on 26 July that all appointments in the comprehensive schools were subject to the approval of the Minister: the chair of the board of management would be entitled to veto the nomination of any candidate on religious or moral grounds but the ultimate power of appointment remained with the Minister.[199] The two bishops described MacGearailt's intervention as 'slightly tendentious' in their report to the Hierarchy but conceded that it represented Hillery's view.[200] The dispute reflected the difficulties that confronted politicians and officials in establishing a new form of post-primary education in uneasy collaboration with established vested interests.

The lack of progress in the negotiations was underlined when the Hierarchy decided to request further clarification from the department on the scheme. James Fergus communicated the persistent reservations of the Hierarchy to the Minister on 29 October. He warned Hillery that, due to a principle of Canon Law, individual bishops were precluded from accepting the proposal until the Irish Hierarchy had made a collective decision.[201] The secretary to the Hierarchy sought clarification on a wide range of issues, including the functions of the board of management and the provision for the teaching of religion in the new schools; he also requested definite assurances that the department was not proposing co-educational schools.[202] Fergus reiterated the Hierarchy's fear that the reform of the vocational system would place private secondary schools at a financial disadvantage, as they would be obliged to compete with state-funded vocational schools, which would now offer a similar type of education. The Hierarchy strongly urged the Minister to provide substantial financial assistance to secondary schools to cover their capital costs. The bishops argued too that as the character of the vocational schools would be transformed by the new initiative, the arrangements for the teaching of religion in secondary schools should be extended to the vocational system.[203] The Hierarchy took an uncompromising position in defending denominational education and the voluntary secondary schools, while they were also concerned to prevent co-education in the new comprehensive schools.

Hillery replied in a conciliatory fashion to the Hierarchy's letter. He clarified that the board of management would operate in a similar way to the national school managers; appointments would be made by the board of management subject to the approval of the Minister.[204] He promised the Hierarchy that he would facilitate training in the teaching of religion for all teachers and endorsed the bishops' view of the need for systematic religious instruction in the vocational schools. While Hillery indicated that single-sex schools would be preferable, he carefully did not rule out mixed schools in areas with a widely dispersed population. He made no commitment to capital grants for secondary education, but pledged that the government was considering an increase in the existing grants to the secondary schools.[205] While the Minister's assurances did not fully overcome their reservations about the scheme, the bishops were now more concerned to secure specific concessions than to dispute the principle of the scheme. Hillery received another episcopal deputation, led by William Conway, on 5 December 1963. The bishops sought to obtain assurances concerning financial aid to existing secondary schools, the teaching of religion in post-primary education and arrangements for the Deeds of Trust for comprehensive schools, which safeguarded denominational education.[206] Hillery, who was supported by Ó Raifeartaigh and MacGearailt, sought to accommodate fully the concerns of the bishops. He reiterated that Christian doctrine would be taught as part of the syllabus in all post-primary schools. The Minister was flexible on the terms for the Deed of Trust, readily accepting input from the bishops; indeed Hillery was willing to allow the local bishop to nominate all three trustees for each comprehensive school.[207] Although he declined to give any immediate commitment to provide direct capital grants for secondary schools, Hillery assured the delegation on a confidential basis that he hoped to introduce a new scheme, which would deliver the financial support required by the schools.[208] It was not surprising that the bishops were asked to keep this information to themselves, as no new scheme for grants to secondary schools had yet been formulated by the department. The bishops were nevertheless satisfied with the outcome of the negotiations. The Standing Committee of the Hierarchy agreed on 7 January 1964 that, in view of the assurances given by the Minister and his officials, the relevant bishops should be authorised to hold discussions with the department for the establishment of comprehensive schools.[209] Hillery had secured the Hierarchy's agreement, in general terms, to the comprehensive schools scheme. It would require difficult and sometimes tense negotiations over the following year before individual bishops agreed to co-operate with the pilot scheme. Yet Hillery's success should not be underestimated: the bishops had implicitly accepted the direct intervention of the state to provide broadly based post-primary education, which had been denounced as revolutionary in June 1963.

Hillery's negotiations with the Hierarchy on the comprehensive schools plan injected greater urgency into the department's efforts to facilitate the expansion of secondary education. The private secondary school system was expanding rapidly in the early 1960s. The total number of pupils enrolled in secondary schools increased from 80,400 in 1961–62 to 92,989 in 1964–65. The secondary school population was expanding by over 3,500 annually in this period.[210] The rapid expansion of secondary education fuelled an increasing demand for state assistance by the secondary school managers, who were obliged to finance extensive building programmes. The Catholic bishops left Hillery in no doubt that they saw an urgent need for the extension of state assistance to meet the building costs of secondary schools. Fergus informed the Minister on 29 October 1963 that 'in the context of the present proposed reorganisation of post-primary education, the Bishops attach the utmost importance to this matter'.[211] Moreover Hillery was concerned by persistent criticisms of post-primary education made by Fine Gael: Declan Costello TD called for 'urgent and immediate reform' of the educational system in the Dáil on 12 December 1963, drawing attention to the lack of state building grants for secondary schools.[212] Hillery therefore recommended to the Taoiseach on 4 February 1964 that a scheme of capital grants should be established to provide state assistance in financing the secondary school building programme.[213] Hillery enclosed for Lemass's attention a highly critical article entitled 'Eire's educational plight', which appeared in the *Belfast Telegraph* on 17 January 1964. The article made a scathing analysis of education in the Republic, which was described as antiquated, underfunded and inefficient; the absence of state aid in building or maintaining secondary schools was one of the many flaws identified in the Republic's educational system.[214] Hillery pointedly commented to Lemass: 'The tragedy about this article is that we could not attempt to refute it, because we lag so far behind the Six Counties in provision for education.'[215] It was no coincidence that the three bishops who met Hillery on 5 December 1963 had declared that they were 'at the end of their tether' in raising capital for secondary school building programmes in the Republic.[216] The bishops had also commented on the more favourable treatment accorded to voluntary secondary schools in Northern Ireland, where 65% of the capital costs were covered by the state.[217] The proposed introduction of capital grants was designed to satisfy the Hierarchy, whose co-operation was required by the department in establishing the comprehensive schools. The new measure was also desirable to discredit Fine Gael's criticism of the government's educational policy. Hillery warned the Taoiseach that the government would be damaged if the Opposition appeared to take the initiative on educational matters. He advised that the government could no longer avoid introducing building grants and it would be political folly to delay the measure.[218] Hillery urged that the new initiative should be taken immediately and requested Lemass to arrange an urgent meeting with the Minister for Finance to discuss the proposal.

Lemass fully supported Hillery's initiative. The Taoiseach indicated to Jim Ryan on 5 February 1964 that Hillery had outlined the necessity for a system of grants for the building and reconstruction of secondary schools.[219] Lemass arranged a meeting to discuss the issue on 10 February, which was attended by Hillery, Ryan and the Taoiseach himself. The principle of the scheme was agreed by the Taoiseach and the two ministers at this meeting.[220] Lemass was determined to arrange for the announcement of the new initiative as quickly as possible, although the details of the scheme had not yet been developed. Lemass's urgency was explained by the imminence of two by-elections, to be held on 19 February in Kildare and Cork, which would determine his ability to retain power without calling a general election. It was hardly surprising that Lemass announced the new initiative on 13 February 1964, only nine days after it had first been proposed by Hillery. The Taoiseach declared that the government would initiate 'a new departure' for secondary education in the course of his response to a lecture given by Dr. John Vaizey, lecturer in Economics at Oxford, on 'The Economics of Education', at St. Patrick's Training College, Drumcondra.[221] Lemass indicated that Hillery would soon introduce a scheme of direct building grants to secondary schools, which would enable them to play their part in the government's plans for the expansion of post-primary education. The Taoiseach made only a brief announcement concerning the new scheme and its timing was clearly dictated by the forthcoming by-elections. The announcement was, however, welcomed by William Conway, who congratulated Lemass and Hillery for acting to relieve some of the financial burdens shouldered by clerical schools and religious congregations.[222] The *Irish Independent*, meanwhile, commented upon 'a quite historic announcement' by the Taoiseach, which was also 'almost historic in its brevity'.[223] Despite its highly political timing, Lemass's announcement on 13 February 1964 marked a significant policy departure from the traditional approach followed by the Irish state, which had left capital support for secondary education entirely to private interests.

The Department of Education publicised the details of the new scheme for capital grants to the secondary schools in April 1964. The scheme, which came into effect from May 1964, provided for grants to the secondary school authorities that would cover up to 60% of the costs incurred in building or extending eligible secondary schools.[224] The scheme, which usually applied only to secondary schools with at least 150 pupils, operated on the basis that the authorities raised the necessary capital for the building programmes, while the state financed up to 60% of the annual debt service charges incurred by the schools.[225] The secondary school authorities were deeply dissatisfied with the conditions imposed on the scheme, especially the imposition of a reduction, amounting to 5% of the building grant, in the capitation grant for all schools receiving the capital funding.[226] But the building grants were rapidly taken up by the secondary school managers; sixty-five schools applied for assistance under the scheme by the end of 1964.[227] Hillery also announced on 20 February 1964 that the capitation grant to secondary schools would be increased by 20% from the current school year.[228] The government acted to retain the political initiative on education, which was the object of increasing policy competition between the major parties. Although the measure was certainly dictated by political expediency, the scheme of building grants introduced direct state aid in the establishment of secondary schools for the first time.

Lemass's speech on 13 February 1964 drew public attention primarily due to the announcement of the scheme of building grants. But the implications for educational policy of the *Second Programme for Economic Expansion* provided the major theme of the Taoiseach's address. The *Second Programme, Part I*, which was published by the government in August 1963, indicated that 'special attention' would be given to education, training and other forms of human investment.[229] The *Second Programme* identified educational expansion as a key national priority, asserting that better education and training would stimulate continued economic expansion. The government's programme for economic development confidently asserted that 'Even the economic returns from investment in education are likely to be as high in the long-run as those from investment in physical capital.'[230] Lemass's address on 13 February 1964 fully reflected the approach to educational expansion outlined by the *Second Programme*, expressing with the utmost clarity the government's rationale for investment in education. He commented that education was 'both a cause of economic growth and a product of such growth': education enhanced the general earning power of the nation, while increased production would provide the resources for educational advances.[231] He hoped that by the end of the decade education would become 'a growth industry' in Ireland.[232]

Lemass echoed the language of the *Second Programme*, reiterating that the development of physical capital without corresponding investment in education would be 'a futile undertaking, perhaps even an impossible one'.[233] He affirmed that education should be provided as an end in itself because it developed human potential, but educational policy also had far-reaching social and economic implications. The Taoiseach emphasised that the government aimed to formulate a long-term educational policy on the basis of the reports of the *Investment in Education* survey team and of the Commission on Higher Education. It was his contention that economic planning made no sense unless it was accompanied by educational planning. The government had therefore decided, in the *Second Programme*, that improvements in social services, including education, 'must go hand in hand with economic progress'.[234] Lemass's speech illustrated the extent to which economic progress and educational expansion had become inextricably linked in the government's approach to national development. The Taoiseach's address underlined too the importance which he attached to an innovative educational policy in creating the conditions for sustained economic and social progress.

A detailed overview of the state's objectives and initiatives in education was provided by the *Second Programme, Part II*, which was issued by the government in July 1964 to elaborate on the principles outlined by the earlier document. The second part of the programme, which included a chapter on education, emphasised that social and economic considerations reinforced the case for the allocation of 'an increasing share of expanding national resources to education'.[235] The programme reiterated that expenditure on education was an investment that would deliver increasing returns in terms of economic progress: moreover the expansion of educational facilities helped to 'equalise opportunities' by enabling a greater proportion of the population to secure a higher standard of living.[236] The *Second Programme, Part II*, also established several ambitious objectives for the future development of Irish education. Annual targets were set for national school building, which included the completion of 100 new schools and 50 major enlargement schemes each year. The programme emphasised the importance of educational research; a commitment was given to support the establishment of an educational research unit, which would undertake research on teaching methods and other educational issues, in St. Patrick's Training College, Drumcondra. The staffing recommendations of the Council of Education, which envisaged the recruitment of about 2,000 additional teachers in primary schools, were rejected; instead it was proposed to increase the number of trained teachers in national schools by about 1,000 between 1965 and 1970.[237]

The government's plans for post-primary education included the comprehensive schools scheme announced by Hillery and a major expansion of secondary school accommodation, to provide for the extension of the school leaving age.[238] Significantly, the government indicated that the school leaving age would be raised to fifteen years before the end of the Second Programme, describing the statutory extension as 'a pre-condition of further progress'.[239] The programme made a definite commitment to proceed with the extension of the school leaving age, although the time frame for the decision depended on continuing prosperity. The government aimed to provide technical education to meet the demands of industry through new second-level technical courses and the Regional Technological Colleges.[240] The concern of the Department of Education about inadequate liaison between employers and the VECs was noted by the government, which urged closer co-operation between employers and vocational education authorities.[241] The *Second Programme for Economic Expansion* established or publicly reaffirmed a variety of ambitious objectives for the expansion of the educational system.

The development of more definite policy objectives in the programme formed part of an ongoing evolution of the state's educational policy. Hillery made a detailed policy statement dealing with second-level education on 18 February 1965 in the course of a Dáil debate on the government's financial strategy.[242] The Minister defended his measured approach, warning that educational progress demanded substantial investment over a considerable period of time: 'It is not just a matter of saying, "We will raise the school leaving age". These slogans are meaningless.'[243] He confirmed, however, the government's intention to raise the school leaving age to fifteen years by 1970, on the basis of a gradual expansion of the facilities and teaching resources of the educational system. The Minister's comments reflected the priorities set out by the *Second Programme*, which emphasised that the raising of the school leaving age demanded long-term planning to provide the additional school accommodation and teachers by 1970.[244] Hillery also dismissed the possibility of free post-primary education, claiming: 'Exaggerated slogans such as "Free Education For All" are not possible.'[245] He clearly expressed his conviction that free education was impractical, while arguing that it was essential to achieve greater educational opportunity by providing some post-primary education to all children.[246] Hillery's statement that the government's central priority was to ensure some level of post-primary education for all implied a large-scale expansion and restructuring of second-level education. Despite Hillery's cautious rhetoric, the government was pursuing coherent and ambitious policy objectives for the expansion of post-primary education by 1965.

University expansion

The government's policy on higher education, however, remained incomplete and ill-defined. The *Second Programme* noted that all detailed policy decisions would have to await the report of the Commission on Higher Education.[247] But the government provided substantial funding in the interim to deal with the severe accommodation problems faced by the universities. The number of full-time students in Irish universities increased from 7,601 in 1952–53 to 13,017 in 1962–63, causing serious over-crowding in most colleges, but especially in UCD.[248] The transfer of UCD to the Belfield site was regarded by the Department of Education as the most urgent priority in the university sector. The department's *Forecast* proclaimed that: 'The university project of transcending importance in relation to economic development in the 1963–68 period will be the provision of the new Science Block in University College Dublin.'[249] The contract for the construction of the new science building at Belfield was signed by the department on 18 April 1962 at a cost to the state of £1,940,195; the new building was formally opened in September 1964.[250] The demands of the other universities within the NUI were not neglected. Hillery sought approval from the government in May 1962 for substantial public investment in UCC and UCG, in line with the recommendations made by the Commission on Accommodation Needs. The Cabinet approved in principle the recommendations concerning the two colleges on 22 May 1962.[251] A more specific proposal for the construction of a new science building in UCC, at an estimated cost of £900,000, was put by Hillery to the Cabinet on 25 February 1964.[252] The government duly approved the proposal, which provided accommodation for the departments of Chemistry, Physics and Mathematical Sciences, as well as a new science library for the college.[253] The department under Hillery gave a high priority to the development and expansion of science faculties at higher level in higher education.

The state's capital investment in higher education was not devoted entirely to the funding of enhanced science facilities. The government also agreed in March 1963 to provide funding for an arts and administration block for UCD at Belfield, in accordance with the commitment made by the state in 1960 to finance the transfer of the college to the new site.[254] In addition, the department undertook to provide half of the necessary funding for the extension of the Library in Trinity College Dublin, up to a total cost of £736,000.[255] The government undertook large-scale capital investment in higher education in this period, which was designed to meet the immediate accommodation needs of the universities. The state's capital funding of higher education was primarily but not exclusively devoted to the establishment of adequate facilities for scientific education.

This intervention by the state to facilitate the expansion of the universities occurred despite the absence of any definite long-term policy for the development of higher education. The department declined to give any firm forecast for the long-term development of university education in January 1962 when its officials were preparing relevant material for the *Second Programme*, on the basis that such policy development formed part of the remit of the Commission on Higher Education.[256] As the Commission did not complete its study of higher education until 1967, the department's officials simply pressed ahead with the capital development of university education in a pragmatic fashion, paying little attention to long-term policy issues. The government similarly operated on the basis that interim measures were being taken to relieve the immediate accommodation problems in the universities, pending the completion of the Commission's report.[257] James Dukes, the official who held responsibility for the universities between 1960 and 1963, commented on the frustrations caused by the situation for the department itself and for Séamus Ó Cathail, the secretary to the Commission: 'The Commission didn't help us very much. Poor old Jim Cahill was there; he was meant to produce a report. Every time he picked up a paper, we [the department] were doing something else.'[258] The department's activism in providing the necessary resources for the expansion of higher education was driven by the urgency of the universities' accommodation needs and their obvious inability to finance the necessary development on their own. James Dukes recalled: 'I said to Jim [Cahill], we have to do it, otherwise it won't be done.'[259] The department's practical support exerted a much greater influence on the development of higher education in the 1960s than the prolonged deliberations of the Commission. The extensive capital investment by the state, delivered largely at the instigation of the Department of Education, provided the financial underpinning for the expansion of the universities. Meanwhile the deliberations of the Commission remained marginal to the ongoing development of higher education.

Diluting the language revival

The department under Hillery did not initiate any further policy changes in its approach to the teaching of Irish after 1961, but the Minister took care to avoid any new commitments to the revival of Irish through the schools, which were sought by the Commission on the Restoration of the Irish Language. The final report of the Commission, which was published in January 1964, devoted considerable attention to education, recommending that the state should maintain and extend its initiatives for the revival of Irish within the educational system.[260] The government set out its decisions on the recommendations of the Commission in the *White Paper on the Restoration of the Irish Language*, which was published in January 1965. The *White Paper* affirmed that 'the national aim is to restore the Irish language as a general medium of communication'.[261] While the policy document acknowledged that all sections of the community had to play their part in the realisation of this aim, the government also emphasised that the 'special position' of Irish in the schools should be maintained and indeed reinforced.[262] The Department of Education, which drafted the section of the *White Paper* dealing with education, generally endorsed the Commission's approach, but argued that many of its specific recommendations concerning the teaching of Irish were already being implemented.[263] Moreover Hillery rejected several important recommendations made by the Commission. The Minister rejected the Commission's proposal for the publication of a general plan of action to secure the teaching of some subjects through Irish in all primary schools. Hillery considered that further investigation of the effects of teaching through a language other than the home language of the child was required before any attempt was made to extend the use of Irish as a teaching medium.[264] Hillery and the senior officials were already sceptical of the benefits of employing Irish as a teaching medium even before the Commission's report was published. The officials were well aware that a study conducted in 1961 by Dr. John Macnamara, a lecturer in St. Patrick's College, Drumcondra, had identified negative educational consequences arising directly from the policy of language revival in the schools.[265] Macnamara's study, which was published in 1966, found that the general policy of giving precedence to Irish in primary schools had a significant negative impact on attainment in English among native speakers of English in Ireland, namely the vast majority of national school children.[266] While the officials did not accept many of Macnamara's conclusions, they had no intention of endorsing the further extension of a policy, which already appeared distinctly problematic and unsuccessful.

The Minister also refused to accept the Commission's recommendation for an extension of the two-year training period for national teachers to provide courses in modern methods of language teaching.[267] The senior officials considered that the training course would have to be extended by one year anyway to accommodate the existing workload imposed on the students.[268] The *White Paper* rejected too the proposal that all candidates for entry to secondary teaching should be obliged to pass a new formal examination in written and oral Irish, rather than an oral test.[269] The Commission exerted little influence on the policy pursued by the department under Hillery, who promoted a dilution of the traditional policy rather than an intensification of efforts to revive the language. O'Connor recalled that the recommendations endorsed by the Minister were essentially exhortations by the Commission, while 'those with any real bite were not accepted'.[270]

The evolution of the Irish language policy was certainly influenced by the increasing public criticism of the traditional approach, which helped to shape the government's cautious defence of the policy for language revival. Fine Gael made the radical revision of the traditional policy an important plank of its programme in successive general elections in 1961 and 1965, when the party pledged to end 'compulsory Irish' in the schools if elected to office.[271] Moreover other opponents of the strong element of compulsion in the state's policy towards the teaching of Irish became more organised and vocal by the middle of the decade. The Language Freedom Movement was established in the autumn of 1965, as a pressure group seeking the abolition of compulsory instruction in Irish.[272] There was therefore a sound political rationale for the Minister's position that he was taking all reasonable measures that could be expected to revive the Irish language. O'Connor acknowledged that 'There were many who said that he was doing much more than he ought.'[273] But the Minister's sceptical response to the initiatives proposed by the Commission was not simply dictated by political expediency. Hillery did not accept that the language could be revived mainly through the schools and he rejected any recommendations that appeared to follow this approach. Hillery's reaction to the report of the Commission reflected not simply an understandable political caution, but a realistic appraisal that the traditional policy of reviving the Irish language through the schools was flawed and unworkable.

Hillery's legacy: reformer not precursor

The Department of Education under Hillery played an influential and proactive role in developing a gradual expansion of the educational system between 1961 and 1965. The appointment of the survey team in 1962 underlined the government's commitment to state intervention in the educational sector on a planned and coherent basis. Lemass and Hillery rapidly adopted the policy ideas of the OECD concerning the value of education as an investment in human resources. The department intervened effectively to manage and extend the process of expansion in primary education. Hillery made an invaluable contribution to the development of special education; his department's initiatives, which accorded official recognition to special programmes for children with various disabilities for the first time, marked the beginning of a new era in special education. The Minister also gave a high priority to the expansion of vocational education, securing the passage of the Vocational Education (Amendment) Act, 1962, in the face of significant opposition within the government. The announcement of the comprehensive schools pilot project and the regional technological colleges on 20 May 1963 initiated the first of a series of radical reforming measures, which transformed the Irish educational system. Hillery's policy announcement was a landmark in an increasingly rapid process of educational expansion and reflected a new commitment by the Irish state to broad-based second-level education. The *Second Programme* identified educational progress as a key national priority, which was essential to future economic development. While long-term policy decisions on third-level education were deferred pending the report of the Commission on Higher Education, large-scale capital investment by the state underpinned the expansion of the university sector.

The development of more intense political competition on education policy between the government and the main opposition parties tended to accelerate the pace of educational reform. But the activism shown by the state at all levels of the educational system is best explained in the context of Lemass's interest in education. The Taoiseach played a central part in taking education almost from the bottom of the heap to the top of the political agenda. The successful launch of the comprehensive schools initiative owed much to Lemass's skilful promotion of the plan within the government. The Minister benefited greatly from Lemass's policy activism; Hillery took full advantage of the Taoiseach's support to pursue effectively a gradualist policy of reform, which began the transformation of the Irish educational system. Hillery's term of office brought the development of sustained and proactive intervention by the state in the educational system as a whole, as well as the initiation of policy themes that would be pursued by his immediate successors. Hillery's advocacy of educational planning, improved co-ordination between the different branches of the system and equality of opportunity all implied further government action to expand the educational system. But Hillery did not simply prepare the way for the more dramatic and far-reaching initiatives of his successors; his proactive reforming approach marked a decisive break with the conservative consensus of the previous generation and delivered lasting changes in the state's educational policy.

Notes

1 *Dáil Debates*, vol. 203, col. 684, 11 June 1963.
2 NA D/FIN 2001/3/546, D500/2/62, OECD *Press Statement*, 5 October 1961.

3 NA D/FIN 2001/3/546, D500/2/62, Governing Committee for Scientific and Technical Personnel, *STP/GC (61) 1, Outline Programme For Scientific And Technical Personnel 1961–62*, 30 January 1961, pp. 3–4.

4 Ibid., p. 4.

5 Ibid., p. 4.

6 D. O'Sullivan, *Cultural Politics and Irish Education since the 1950s* (Dublin, 2005), p. 143.

7 NA D/FIN 2001/3/546, D500/2/62, Governing Committee for Scientific and Technical Personnel, *STP/GC (61) 13, Policy Conference on Economic Growth and the Role of Investment in Education and Science: Project STP-24*, 22 February 1961, pp. 1–3.

8 S. MacGearailt to M. Breathnach, 15 August 1961.

9 NA D/T S.12891D/1/62, OECD, *STP 62 (1), Pilot Studies on Long-Term Needs for Educational Resources in Economically Developed Countries*, 12 October 1961, p. 1.

10 Ibid.

11 Ibid., p. 2.

12 Ibid., pp. 2–3, Ó Buachalla, '*Investment in Education*', pp. 10–20.

13 NA D/FIN 2001/3/546, D500/2/62, John F. McInerney, Note of meeting, 31 October 1961, p. 1.

14 Ibid., Ó Buachalla, '*Investment in Education*', pp. 10–20.

15 NA D/FIN 2001/3/546, D500/2/62, McInerney, Note of meeting, 31 October 1961, pp. 1–2.

16 Ibid., p. 2.

17 NA D/T S.12891D/1/62, Ó Raifeartaigh to Whitaker, 8 November 1961, p. 1.

18 Ibid., p. 4.

19 NA D/FIN 2001/3/775, D500/8/63, Whitaker to J.C. Nagle, J.C.B. McCarthy and C. Cremin, 9 November 1961; Whitaker to N.S. Ó Nualláin, 20 November 1961.

20 Whitaker to Ó Raifeartaigh, 15 December 1961.

21 Ó Raifeartaigh to Whitaker, 30 April 1962, Whitaker to M. Cullen, the Ford Foundation, 4 July 1962.

22 NA D/T 97/6/437, S.17913, N.S. Ó Nualláin to C. Ó Dálaigh, Chief Justice, 21 June 1962.

23 NA D/T 97/6/437, S.17913, *Address by Dr. P.J. Hillery TD, Minister for Education, on the occasion of his opening the Labour/Management Conference at Shannon Airport*, 22 June 1962, pp. 1–6.

24 NA D/T S.12891D/1/62, *Irish Press*, 'Long-Term Educational Needs will be Investigated', 30 July 1962.

25 NA D/T 97/6/437, S.17913, *Note of Government meeting*, 26 June 1962.

26 Ó Buachalla, '*Investment in Education*', pp. 10–20.

27 *Dáil Debates*, vol. 196, col. 1303–4, 3 July 1962.

28 NA D/T S.12891D/1/62, OECD, *STP 62 (1), Terms of Reference, Pilot Studies on Long-Term Needs for Educational Resources in Developed Countries*, 12 October 1961, pp. 4–5.

29 *Dáil Debates*, vol. 196, col. 1303–4, 3 July 1962.
30 Ó Buachalla, '*Investment in Education*', pp. 10–20.
31 *Dáil Debates*, vol. 196, col. 1303–4, 3 July 1962.
32 NA D/T S.12891D/1/62, *Speech by Seán Lemass TD, Taoiseach, at the Marist Brothers' Centenary celebrations*, 8 July 1962, p. 1.
33 Ibid., p. 2.
34 Ibid.
35 *Speech by Dr. Hillery to the inaugural meeting of the Steering Committee, October 1962*, Hyland and Milne, *Irish Educational Documents* 2, pp. 30–1.
36 Ibid.
37 Ibid.
38 *Dáil Debates*, vol. 210, col. 287, 27 May 1964.
39 NA D/T S.12891D/1/62, *Forecast of Developments in Educational Services During the 5-Year Period 1963–68*, Department of Education, 6 January 1962, pp. 1–9.
40 Ibid., pp. 1–2.
41 Ibid., p. 5.
42 *Forecast, Appendix A*, 6 January 1962, p. 1.
43 *Forecast*, 6 January 1962, p. 6.
44 Ibid., p. 2.
45 Ibid., p. 4.
46 Ibid., p. 4.
47 Ibid., p. 7.
48 See Appendix 1, Table 3, p. 329; *Tuarascáil, An Roinn Oideachais 1961–62* (Dublin, 1964), p. 88, *Tuarascáil, Táblaí Staitistic, An Roinn Oideachais 1964–65* (Dublin, 1966), p. 8.
49 W26/30, M80/1, C.O. 704 (3), *Progress Report for the Quarter ended 30 September 1962*, Department of Education, 13 October 1962, p. 1, Circular 20/64, Department of Education, June 1964, p. 1.
50 NA D/T S.12891D/1/62, *Forecast*, 6 January 1962, p. 1.
51 *Committee of Public Accounts, Appropriation Accounts 1962–63* (Dublin, 1964), pp. 100–6, *Committee of Public Accounts, Appropriation Accounts 1965–66* (Dublin, 1967), p. 117.
52 *Dáil Debates*, vol. 210, col. 333, 14 May 1964.
53 W26/30, M80/1, C.O. 704 (3), *Progress Report for the Quarter ended 30 September 1964*, Department of Education, 30 October 1964, p. 1.
54 Circular 16/64, Department of Education, May 1964.
55 Circular 21/63, Department of Education, November 1963.
56 W26/30, M80/1, C.O. 704 (3), *Progress Report for the Quarter ended 31 March 1964*, Department of Education, 14 April 1964, p. 1.
57 *Committee of Public Accounts, Appropriation Accounts 1965–66*, p. 118.
58 *Investment in Education, Part 2: Annexes and Appendices to the Report of the Survey Team appointed by the Minister for Education in October 1962* (Dublin, 1965), pp. 35–6.
59 T.A. Ó Cuilleanáin, 'Special education in Ireland', *Oideas*, no. 1 (Autumn 1968), pp. 5–17.

60 Ibid.; J. Coolahan, 'Dr. P.J. Hillery – Minister for Education: 1959–1965', *Journal for ASTI Convention*, Easter 1990, pp. 15–19.

61 J. Coolahan, 'Dr. P.J. Hillery – Minister for Education: 1959–1965', *Journal for ASTI Convention*, Easter 1990, pp. 15–19; see Chapter 4, pp. 153–4.

62 *Tuarascáil, An Roinn Oideachais 1960–61* (Dublin, 1963), p. 93, *Tuarascáil, An Roinn Oideachais 1964–65*, p. 3.

63 NA D/T S.17238/62, *Summary of Memorandum to the Government, Proposal for a Bill to amend the Vocational Education Acts 1930 to 1953, Appendix*, 7 February 1962.

64 *Summary of Memorandum to the Government*, 7 February 1962, p. 9.

65 Ibid., p. 3.

66 *Committee of Public Accounts, Appropriation Accounts 1960–61* (Dublin, 1962), p. 84.

67 NA D/T S.17238/62, *Summary of Memorandum to the Government*, 7 February 1962, pp. 6–7.

68 NA D/T S.17238/62, *Vocational Education Amendment Bill 1962, Department of Local Government*, 13 April 1962, p. 1.

69 CAB 2/22, G.C.10/31, Cabinet Minutes, 13 April 1962, pp. 2–3.

70 NA D/T S.17238/62, G.O.1/62, *Memorandum for the Government, Vocational Education (Amendment) Bill*, 21 June 1962, p. 1.

71 CAB 2/22, G.C.10/43, Cabinet Minutes, 22 June 1962, p. 2, *Dáil Debates*, vol. 197, col. 770–800, 8 November 1962.

72 NA D/T S.17238/62, *Memorandum to the Government*, 7 February 1962, pp. 5–9.

73 *Committee of Public Accounts, Appropriation Accounts 1967–68* (Dublin, 1969), p. 123.

74 NA D/T S.17238/62, *Memorandum to the Government*, 7 February 1962, p. 5.

75 *Investment in Education, Part 1, Report of the Survey Team appointed by the Minister for Education in October 1962* (Dublin, 1965), pp. 278–81.

76 See p. 83.

77 Ó Buachalla, *Education Policy*, p. 281.

78 Circular M22/62, Department of Education, August 1962.

79 Circular M3/65, Department of Education, January 1965, W26/30, M80/1, *Progress Report for the Quarter ended 31 December 1964*, Department of Education, p. 1.

80 W26/30, M80/1, *Progress Report for the Quarter ended 7 September 1963*, Department of Education, p. 1.

81 M.E.1, *Scheme in aid of the Employment of Graduate Science Teachers*, Department of Education, July 1963.

82 W26/30, M80/1, C.O. 704 (3), *Progress Report for the Quarter ended 31 March 1964*, Department of Education, 14 April 1964, p. 2.

83 NA D/FIN 2001/3/1073, D2/14/65, *First Progress report on the Second Programme for Economic Expansion*, Department of Education, 7 April 1965, p. 3.

84 Circular M17/61, Department of Education, June 1961.

85 *Dáil Debates*, vol. 195, col. 1383, 23 May 1962.

86 Ibid., p. 4.

87 NA D/FIN 2001/3/1073, D2/14/65, Ó Raifeartaigh to Whitaker, 11 February 1965, *Draft of First Progress report for the Second Programme for Economic Expansion*, Department of Education, p. 3.

88 NA D/FIN 2001/3/1073, D2/14/65, *First Progress report on the Second Programme*, 7 April 1965, p. 4.

89 *Dáil Debates*, vol. 195, col. 1471–93, 23 May 1962.

90 Ibid., col. 1493–514.

91 *Dáil Debates*, vol. 195, col. 2184, 6 June 1962.

92 Ibid., col. 2189.

93 Tuairim, *Irish Education* (London, 1962), pp. 2–5.

94 Ibid., p. 12.

95 Ibid., pp. 16–18, Randles, *Post-Primary Education*, p. 67.

96 NA D/T S.12891D/1/62, *Hibernia*, 'Educating Towards A United Europe', February 1962.

97 Tuairim, *Educating Towards A United Europe* (Dublin, 1961), p. 6.

98 NA D/T S.12891D/1/61, *Irish Press*, 'Headmaster Lists Weaknesses in Irish education', 27 November 1961.

99 Labour Party, *Challenge and Change in Education* (Dublin, 1963).

100 Ibid., pp. 2–3.

101 Ibid., p. 10.

102 Ibid., pp. 12–18.

103 DDA AB8/B/XV/b/05, *McQuaid Papers*, Minutes of the Irish Hierarchy, Fergus to McQuaid, 20 February 1963.

104 NA D/T S.12891D/1/62, *Forecast*, 6 January 1962, pp. 3–4.

105 NA D/T S.12891D/2/62, *Memorandum from the Minister for Education concerning the Small Farms report, 'Post-Primary Education in the Areas Concerned'*, 7 July 1962, p. 1.

106 Ibid.

107 Ibid., p. 2.

108 Ibid., p. 3.

109 T. Ó Cearbhaill to Ministers on the Inter-Departmental Committee on the Problems of Small Western Farms, 9 July 1962.

110 E. Childers to Ó Cearbhaill, 11 July 1962, K. Boland to T. Ó Cearbhaill, 13 July 1962, Private Secretary to Lynch to Ó Cearbhaill, 14 July 1962.

111 Whitaker to Ó Nualláin, 18 July 1962.

112 Ibid.

113 M. Ó Sealbhaigh to Ó Cearbhaill, 23 July 1962.

114 Ibid.

115 T. Leahy to Ó Cearbhaill, 26 July 1962, pp. 1–2.

116 Ibid.

117 Ó Cearbhaill to Lemass, 26 July 1962, Randles, *Post-Primary Education*, p. 107.

118 NA D/T S.12891D/2/62, *Outline of Statement of Government Policy on Suggestions in Report of the Inter-Departmental Committee on the Problems of Small Western Farms*, 1 August 1962, p. 8.
119 Ibid.
120 Ibid.
121 Randles, *Post-Primary Education*, p. 107.
122 OECD, *OECD Reviews of National Policies For Science and Education: Training of Technicians in Ireland* (Paris, 1964), p. 81.
123 Ibid., pp. 88–9.
124 Ibid., p. 95.
125 Ibid., p. 101.
126 Ibid., p. 102.
127 Ibid., p. 106.
128 Ibid., p. 108.
129 Ibid., pp. 105–6.
130 Interview with Dr. Hillery, 25 February 2002.
131 I. Bonel-Elliott, 'The role of the Duggan report (1962) in the reform of the Irish education system', *Administration*, vol. 44, no. 3 (Autumn 1996), pp. 42–60.
132 Departmental Committee, *Tuarascáil Shealadach ón Choiste a Cuireadh I mbun Scrúdú a Dheánamh ar Oideachas Iarbhunscoile*, December 1962, pp. 5–6.
133 Ibid., pp. 10–12.
134 NA D/T 17405 C/63, *Proposal for Comprehensive Post-Primary Education: Pilot Scheme related to Small Farm Areas*, Department of Education, 9 January 1963.
135 Ibid.
136 Interview with Dr. Hillery, 25 February 2002.
137 Bonel-Elliott, 'The role of the Duggan report (1962)', *Administration*, vol. 44, no. 3, p. 43.
138 NA D/T S.12891D/1/62, *Forecast*, 6 January 1962, pp. 1–9.
139 NA D/T 17405 C/63, *Proposal for Comprehensive Post-Primary Education*, 9 January 1963.
140 Ibid.
141 Ibid.
142 Ibid.
143 Ibid.
144 Whitaker to Ó Nualláin, 18 July 1962, Interview with Dr. Hillery, 25 February 2002.
145 NA D/T 17405 C/63, Hillery to Lemass, 9 January 1963.
146 Ibid.
147 Lemass to Hillery, 11 January 1963.
148 Hillery to Lemass, 12 January 1963.
149 Lemass to Hillery, 14 January 1963.
150 Ibid.

151 NA D/T 17405 C/63, *Memorandum from the Department of Education, Proposals relating to comprehensive post-primary education*, January 1963.
152 Ibid.
153 Ibid.
154 NA D/T 17405 C/63, *Proposals relating to comprehensive post-primary education*, 8 March 1963.
155 Interview with Dr. Hillery, 25 February 2002.
156 Interview with Dr. Hillery, 25 February 2002.
157 NA D/T 17405 C/63, *Statement by Dr. P.J. Hillery T.D., Minister for Education, in relation to Post-Primary Education*, 20 May 1963, p. 6.
158 Ibid., p. 5.
159 Ibid., pp. 7–8.
160 Ibid., pp. 8–10.
161 Ibid., p. 7.
162 Ibid., pp. 9–10.
163 Ibid., pp. 8–9.
164 Ibid., p. 11.
165 Ibid., pp. 12–13.
166 Coolahan, *Irish Education*, p. 139.
167 NA D/T 17405 C/63, *Statement by Dr. P.J. Hillery T.D., Minister for Education, in relation to Post-Primary Education*, 20 May 1963, p. 13.
168 Ibid., p. 14.
169 *Committee of Public Accounts, Appropriation Accounts 1965–66*, pp. 117–18.
170 NA D/T 17405 C/63, *Statement by Dr. P.J. Hillery T.D., Minister for Education, in relation to Post-Primary Education*, 20 May 1963, p. 14.
171 Coolahan, *Irish Education*, p. 139.
172 Chapter 6, p. 227.
173 W26/30, M80/1, *Draft Progress report on secondary education for Second Programme*, Department of Education, February 1965, p. 1.
174 *Irish Press*, 'Dr. Hillery Plan is Hailed', 22 May 1963, *Irish Press*, 'New Deal in Education', 22 May 1963.
175 *Irish Times*, Editorial, 21 May 1963.
176 *Irish Times*, 'Teachers' Organisation Not Consulted on New Plans', 21 May 1963, I. Bonel-Elliott, 'La Politique de l'enseignement du second degré en république d'Irlande 1963–93' (Ph.D thesis, Sorbonne, 1994), p. 311.
177 *Irish Press*, 'Dr. Hillery Plan is Hailed', 22 May 1963.
178 Interview with Dr. Hillery, 25 February 2002.
179 *Irish Press*, 'Dr. Hillery Plan is Hailed', 22 May 1963.
180 See Introduction, p. 2.
181 Interview with Dr. Hillery, 25 February 2002.
182 DDA AB8/B/XV/b/05, *McQuaid Papers*, Minutes, General Meeting of the Hierarchy, 1 October 1962, p. 1.
183 Dr. V. Hanly to McQuaid, 31 December 1962.
184 McQuaid to Hanly, 5 January 1963.

185 Minutes, Standing Committee of the Hierarchy, 8 January 1963, p. 1.
186 Fergus to McQuaid, 20 February 1963.
187 Ibid.
188 Interview with Dr. Hillery, 25 February 2002.
189 DDA AB8/B/XV/b/05, *McQuaid Papers*, Hanly to Fergus, 18 February 1963.
190 McQuaid to Fergus, 2 March 1963.
191 Ibid.
192 NA D/T 17405 C/63, *Statement by Dr. P.J. Hillery T.D., Minister for Education, in relation to Post-Primary Education*, 20 May 1963, p. 7.
193 DDA AB8/B/XV/b/05, *McQuaid Papers*, Minutes, General Meeting of the Hierarchy, 25 June 1963, p. 3.
194 Ibid.
195 DDA AB8/B/XV/b/05, *McQuaid Papers*, *First Memorandum by the Bishops of Elphin and Achonry, The New Post-Primary Schools Scheme*, 28 June 1963.
196 Ibid.
197 NA D/T 17405 C/63, *Proposal for Comprehensive Post-Primary Education*, 9 January 1963.
198 DDA AB8/B/XV/b/05, *McQuaid Papers*, *First Memorandum by the Bishops of Elphin and Achonry, The New Post-Primary Schools Scheme*, 28 June 1963.
199 *Second Memorandum by the Bishops of Elphin and Achonry, The New Post-Primary Schools Scheme*, 26 July 1963.
200 Ibid.
201 Fergus to Hillery, 29 October 1963, p. 1.
202 Ibid.
203 Ibid., p. 2.
204 Hillery to Fergus, November 1963, p. 1.
205 Ibid., pp. 1–2.
206 DDA AB8/B/XV/b/05, *Memorandum, The Hillery Scheme*, 5 December 1963.
207 Ibid.
208 Ibid.
209 Minutes, Standing Committee of the Hierarchy, 7 January 1964, p. 1.
210 *Tuarascáil, An Roinn Oideachais 1961–62*, p. 87, *Turascáil, An Roinn Oideachais 1964–65*.
211 DDA AB8/B/XV/b/05, *McQuaid Papers*, Fergus to Hillery, 29 October 1963, p. 2.
212 *Dáil Debates*, vol. 206, col. 1186, 12 December 1963.
213 NA D/T S.17592/95, Hillery to Lemass, 4 February 1964, p. 1.
214 *Belfast Telegraph*, 'Eire's Educational Plight', 17 January 1964.
215 NA D/T S.17592/95, Hillery to Lemass, 4 February 1964, p. 1.
216 Ibid.
217 Ibid.
218 Ibid., p. 2.
219 Lemass to Ryan, 5 February 1964.

220 NA D/T S.17592/95, *Internal memorandum, Department of the Taoiseach*, 10 February 1964.

221 NA D/T S.12891E/95, *Speech by Seán Lemass TD, Taoiseach, following address by John Vaizey on 'The Economics of Education', St. Patrick's Training College, Drumcondra*, 13 February 1964, p. 2.

222 NA D/T S.17592/95, Conway to Lemass, 17 February 1964.

223 *Irish Independent*, 'Grant for Schools', 14 February 1964.

224 Circular M15/64, Department of Education, April 1964.

225 D/FIN 2001/3/1073, D2/14/65, *First Progress report on Second Programme*, 7 April 1965, p. 2.

226 Randles, *Post-Primary Education*, p. 149.

227 D/FIN 2001/3/1073, D2/14/65, *First Progress report on Second Programme*, 7 April 1965, p. 2.

228 *Dáil Debates*, vol. 207, col. 1379, 20 February 1964.

229 *Second Programme for Economic Expansion, Part I, laid by the Government before each House of the Oireachtas, August 1963* (Dublin, 1963), p. 17.

230 Ibid., p. 13.

231 NA D/T S.12891E/95, *Speech by Seán Lemass TD, Taoiseach, following address by John Vaizey on 'The Economics of Education', St. Patrick's Training College, Drumcondra*, 13 February 1964, pp. 1–2.

232 Ibid.

233 Ibid.

234 Ibid., p. 3, *Second Programme, Part I*, p. 15.

235 *Second Programme, Part II*, p. 193.

236 Ibid.

237 Ibid., pp. 194–6.

238 Ibid., pp. 200–2.

239 Ibid., p. 198.

240 Ibid., pp. 203–5.

241 Ibid., p. 205.

242 *Dáil Debates*, vol. 214, col. 710–21, 18 February 1965.

243 Ibid.

244 *Second Programme, Part II*, p. 198.

245 *Dáil Debates*, vol. 214, col. 710–21, 18 February 1965.

246 Ibid.

247 *Second Programme, Part II*, p. 198.

248 Ibid.

249 NA D/T S.12891D/1/62, *Forecast*, 6 January 1962, p. 7.

250 W26/30, M80/1, C.O. 704 (3), *Progress Report for the Quarter ended 30 June 1962*, Department of Education, p. 2, *Progress Report for the Quarter ended 30 September 1964*, Department of Education, p. 3.

251 CAB 2/22, G.C.10/37, Cabinet Minutes, 22 May 1962, p. 7.

252 CAB 2/22, G.C.10/143, Cabinet Minutes, 25 February 1964, pp. 2–3.

253 Ibid., W26/30, M80/1, C.O. 704 (3), *Progress Report for the Quarter ended 31 March 1964*, Department of Education, p. 2.

254 CAB 2/22, G.C.10/89, Cabinet Minutes, 22 March 1964, pp. 3–4.
255 *Second Programme, Part II*, p. 206.
256 NA D/T S.12891D/1/62, *Forecast*, 6 January 1962, p. 7.
257 *Second Programme, Part II*, p. 206.
258 Interview with James Dukes, 28 April 2003.
259 Ibid.
260 *Final Report of the Commission on the Restoration of the Irish Language* (Dublin, 1964), pp. 416–32.
261 *White Paper on the Restoration of the Irish Language, laid by the Government before each House of the Oireachtas, January 1965* (Dublin, 1965), p. 4.
262 Ibid., p. 98.
263 Ibid., pp. 100–8.
264 Ibid., p. 106.
265 J. Macnamara, *Bilingualism and Primary Education: A Study of the Irish Experience* (Edinburgh, 1966), p. 134, O'Connor, *A Troubled Sky*, p. 89.
266 Macnamara, *Bilingualism*, pp. 135–8.
267 *White Paper on the Restoration of the Irish Language*, p. 100.
268 O'Connor, *A Troubled Sky*, p. 89.
269 *White Paper on the Restoration of the Irish Language*, p. 118.
270 O'Connor, *A Troubled Sky*, p. 89.
271 J. Horgan, *Seán Lemass: The Enigmatic Patriot* (Dublin, 1997), pp. 304–9.
272 O'Connor, *A Troubled Sky*, p. 106.
273 Ibid., p. 89.

4

The impact of *Investment in Education*: 1965–66

'There were no real ideas until the OECD project': this was Hillery's verdict on the study conducted by the Irish survey team under the auspices of the OECD and the Department of Education.[1] While the department certainly adopted new policy ideas before the completion of the project, the pilot study profoundly influenced the state's policy for educational reform and expansion in the second half of the decade. The report of the survey team, appropriately entitled *Investment in Education*, contributed greatly to the transformation of the Irish educational system. The completion of the pilot study coincided with George Colley's appointment as Minister for Education. Colley's policy activism was greatly influenced by *Investment* and he acted to introduce wide-ranging reforms based on the conclusions of the report. The initiation by Colley of the amalgama-tion of small national schools was a radical reform with profound long-term implications for primary education. The Minister also promoted a new approach for the expansion of post-primary education, based on co-operation and the pooling of resources between secondary and vocational schools. Colley, who enjoyed the staunch support of the Taoiseach, gave a firm direction to the state's efforts to expand and reform the educational system. Colley also established long-term educational planning as an integral part of the government's policy of expansion.

George Colley had displayed considerable interest in education long before his elevation to ministerial office. He was a regular contributor to Dáil debates on education as a backbench TD.[2] Moreover Colley enjoyed friendly connections with senior officials of the Department of Education, notably Seán O'Connor, before his appointment as a Minister.[3] Following the general election in April 1965, Colley, who had previously served as Parliamentary Secretary to the Minister for Lands, was given his first Cabinet portfolio as Minister for Education. The Taoiseach's decision to appoint another young and ambitious politician to the education portfolio underlined the increasing political status of the Department of Education, which had been regarded as a relatively junior department at least until the late 1950s.[4] Education had become an important first stage in the ministerial careers of younger Fianna Fáil politicians under the leadership of Lemass. Colley's two predecessors were also promoted by the Taoiseach in April 1965: Jack Lynch became Minister for Finance, while Patrick Hillery was appointed as Minister for Industry and Commerce. Moreover the central importance attached by the Taoiseach to educational expansion as a key element of national development was underlined by his comments to the monthly periodical *Open* on 29 January 1965: 'The day of the unskilled worker, at any social level, is passing and with the development of modern science and technology, the future belongs to those who have trained themselves to meet its specific requirements in knowledge and skill.'[5] Lemass reaffirmed that educational expansion was an indispensable element in the economic development of the nation. Lemass's commitment to the expansion of the educational system provided a favourable political context for the reforms initiated by Colley.

The new Minister introduced the first Estimates of his term to the Dáil on 16 June 1965. The overall allocation for education announced by Colley for 1965–66 amounted to over £30 million, which was an increase in a single year of over 6%.[6] Colley's term saw a further substantial increase in educational expenditure, which had been growing rapidly throughout Hillery's second term. Current spending on primary education alone in 1965–66 exceeded the total current expenditure by the Exchequer on education in 1961–62: capital expenditure roughly trebled in the same period.[7] The rapid increase in state expenditure on education underlined the considerable cost of the incremental reforms already undertaken by the government. The additional expenditure announced by Colley was due in part to the implementation of measures introduced by Hillery, including the expansion of the scholarships scheme, which was fully implemented by 1965–66. Colley also inherited a range of reforming proposals, which had been initiated by Hillery but not yet implemented, notably the plan for comprehensive schools. The new Minister announced the allocation of funding for the building of the first four comprehensive schools. He confirmed too that a common Intermediate Certificate for secondary and vocational schools would be introduced in September 1966.[8] Colley also reaffirmed the government's intention to proceed with the establishment of eight new Regional Technical Colleges.[9] Colley's speech on 16 June displayed considerable continuity with the policy approach pursued by Hillery and Lemass since 1959.

Colley, however, did not simply recite increased financial allocations or affirm his commitment to existing policies. The new Minister also outlined his priorities in a wide-ranging address to the Dáil. He identified the

extension of the statutory school leaving age as a key reform to be implemented by the government. It was, however, a reform that involved almost
every kind of educational problem, from providing adequate accommodation and sufficient teachers to the revision of courses and the assessment
of pupils' aptitudes. But despite these difficulties, Colley declared that the
initiative had to be implemented in the short term to ensure equality of
educational opportunity for all Irish children. He emphasised the urgent
necessity for the initiation of detailed educational planning, if the objective
of raising the school leaving age was to be achieved by the end of the
decade: 'By 1970 there will be few European countries in which the school
leaving age will be less than fifteen. If we are to achieve that position with
the rest, the time to start planning for it is not 1969, but now.'[10] The
raising of the school leaving age entailed a wide range of educational
changes. Colley appealed for close co-operation between the state and
private educational interests in achieving such reforms. Colley aimed not
only to improve communication between the department and the private
educational authorities but also to secure broad support for important
educational changes and to involve the private interests in the implementation of the state's reforming objectives.

Colley's appeal for co-operation between the state and the private educational authorities was motivated at least in part by his concern to secure
support for the various initiatives announced or contemplated by the government. He indicated on 16 June that the department was considering a
reorganisation of primary education. The Minister told the Dáil that he
wished to change the pattern of primary school building to ensure the
establishment of larger national schools in future.[11] Colley commented
that he was most concerned to achieve a solution which made the best
possible use of teachers for the benefit of all pupils.[12] He evidently regarded
the continued building of small schools in general as an inefficient and
wasteful use of educational resources. Colley signalled on 16 June that he
was considering the introduction of a new policy involving the amalgamation of small national schools.

The Minister also sought to clarify the government's policy towards
post-primary education. He discussed the role of the comprehensive
schools, noting that various fears had been expressed by private school
managers about the new initiative. Colley assured TDs that comprehensive
schools were never intended to replace secondary and vocational schools.
The new scheme was designed to extend post-primary education, by establishing comprehensive schools in areas that previously lacked adequate
educational facilities. But it was not the sole purpose of the new scheme
simply to fill gaps in educational facilities. Colley hoped that the comprehensive schools would act as 'a kind of pace-setter in post-primary

education generally'.[13] The Minister and senior officials envisaged that the comprehensive schools would give direction and leadership in post-primary education by providing a comprehensive curriculum, which would link the secondary schools and the vocational system. A system of vocational guidance, to be provided by the department's new psychological service in conjunction with teachers, would be introduced for the first time in the new schools. Colley also advocated close collaboration between secondary and vocational schools, including the sharing of resources between the two separate systems.[14] Colley's comments foreshadowed his sustained attempt in the following year to promote a co-operative approach between the secondary school authorities and the VECs, with the intention of reducing duplication in the use of educational resources.

Colley's wide-ranging address on 16 June, which set out his key priorities as Minister for Education, was itself a new departure. Most previous ministers had avoided any detailed policy statements which might cause conflict with powerful educational interests. Even Hillery, who risked conflict with established private interests by extending state intervention in post-primary education, was generally reluctant to outline an overall policy approach. Hillery came closest to providing a definitive statement of the government's education policy to the Dáil only in February 1965, shortly before the end of his term as Minister for Education. Colley, however, had no hesitation in enunciating his vision of the future for the Irish educational system. The new Minister delivered a detailed policy statement within two months of his appointment. Moreover he provided an early indication of important policy changes which were to be initiated during his term of office.

The influence of *Investment*

The new Minister anticipated the publication of the *Investment in Education* study in the course of his address, drawing attention to its importance in guiding future educational planning.[15] The report was available to Colley when he took office, although it was not formally submitted to him until November 1965.[16] The Minister was certainly aware of the general conclusions of the report well in advance of its publication, as Seán MacGearailt chaired the Steering Committee which supervised the work of the survey team. *Investment* made only one formal recommendation, the creation of a development unit in the Department of Education: the new unit was intended to take responsibility for the collection of educational statistics and to undertake long-term planning for future educational needs.[17] The survey team recommended that the new development unit should be headed by an Assistant Secretary and staffed by professional personnel, including a statistician, a sociologist and a full-time economist.[18] The national team generally avoided formal recommendations, as they might be vulnerable to criticism by established interests. The language employed by the team was cautious and judicious, seeking to avoid any implication of excessive policy activism.[19] Martin O'Donoghue recalled that 'specific recommendations might be shot down; you could get the wrong minister and the Department of Education might then lapse back into inaction'.[20]

While the report made only a single formal recommendation, the general conclusions of the pilot study made an impressive case for far-reaching educational reform. The survey team presented a wide-ranging and highly critical analysis of the educational system, based on the accumulation for the first time of comprehensive statistical data about education in the Irish state. The study identified severe deficiencies in the educational sector. The report's analysis revealed a substantial gap between the projected output of qualified school-leavers and the requirements of the economy for quali-fied manpower. It was estimated that a shortfall of 76,000 would arise between the labour force demand for employees with a junior post-primary certificate by 1971 and the actual supply of school leavers with such a qualification.[21] The report concluded that the educational system was failing to meet the minimum needs of the Irish economy especially with regard to the demand for an increased flow of skilled employees.

The conclusions of *Investment* were not, however, restricted to the economic implications of educational inadequacies. The survey team also drew attention to 'significant disparities' in educational participation, which involved considerable inequalities between different socio-economic categories and regions of the country.[22] The report noted that 11,000 pupils, approximately one-fifth of all the children who finished primary education each year, left full-time education without securing any educa-tional qualification, including even the Primary Certificate.[23] The study identified 'a marked association between participation and social group', drawing attention to the low rate of participation in post-primary educa-tion by pupils drawn from the unskilled and semi-skilled occupational categories, as well as the unemployed.[24] A commentary on *Investment* by the National Industrial Economic Council (NIEC) in January 1966 noted that the participation rate in post-primary education, among individuals aged fifteen to nineteen in 1961, was four to five times greater for pupils drawn from the higher salaried and farming categories than for the children of unskilled and semi-skilled manual workers.[25] *Investment* also illustrated a massive disparity in participation between social groups at university level, where the survey team found that 'the strong association between university entrance and social group is unmistakable'.[26] Indeed

65% of university entrants who undertook the Leaving Certificate in 1963 were the children of professionals, employers and higher white-collar employees. Only 2% of university students were drawn from the unskilled and semi-skilled manual category, while 4% were the children of the unemployed or widows.[27] The strikingly low level of university participation by the children of unskilled blue-collar workers was clearly influenced by the high proportion of such children who left second-level education prematurely, without any post-primary qualification. The severe inequalities in educational participation at post-primary and university level also reflected broader factors linked to social class. The material costs of continuing school attendance after the compulsory phase were simply beyond the means of unskilled blue-collar workers, who were most likely to face poverty and periodic unemployment even in a time of relative prosperity. The opportunity costs of educational participation were also much greater for low-income families, who could not easily forgo the additional income generated by getting a young member into the workforce as soon as possible. The report did not only focus on inequalities linked to social class but also highlighted wide regional variations in educational participation at post-primary level. Most counties in Munster showed a relatively high level of participation in second-level education, with between 40% and 60% of the relevant age cohort attending post-primary schools. But all three Ulster counties in the Republic fared relatively badly in terms of educational participation, as did three Leinster counties, Laois, Meath and Kildare, where the proportion of the age group receiving second-level education fell below 40%.[28] The survey team warned of the need for public policy 'to concern itself with these anomalies'.[29]

Perhaps the most influential element of the report's analysis was its assessment of the efficiency of the educational system. The survey team identified significant efficiency gaps in the use of existing educational resources, caused by an unplanned and haphazard pattern of historical development.[30] The report noted that there were 736 one-teacher national schools in 1962–63. Of all national schools, 76% taught less than 100 pupils.[31] The small schools incurred greater costs per pupil than larger schools and certainly provided no greater educational benefit to pupils.[32] Indeed the report produced substantial evidence that pupils in small schools were at a disadvantage relative to their compatriots in large schools. The smaller national schools offered a more restricted curriculum than their larger counterparts, as optional subjects were more likely to be curtailed. These restrictions were explained in part by the inferior facilities provided by small schools: 65% of one-teacher schools were based in nineteenth-century buildings, while many small schools were poorly equipped with educational facilities. Most one to three-teacher schools lacked central heating, while over 2,000 small schools did not have drinking water. *Investment* concluded that the physical facilities of smaller schools were 'very much inferior' to the facilities provided by larger schools.[33] Moreover the report suggested that small schools, defined as one to three-teacher schools, had a higher incidence of pupils whose progress through the classes was delayed by two or more years.[34] The survey team's analysis provided a damning indictment of the haphazard allocation of educational resources in primary education. The small national schools were not only expensive to maintain, but relatively high users of teaching resources. The small schools contained 50.4% of all national schoolteachers but only 38% of all pupils.[35] The pupil-teacher ratios were therefore much higher in larger schools, which experienced severe problems due to high class sizes. This imbalance in the distribution of teachers helped to create a situation in which 84% of the pupils in large schools were to be found in classes of forty or more.[36] The survey team understandably questioned whether 'the present distribution of schools is the most suitable, satisfactory or economical method of providing primary education'.[37] The report advised the department to consider an alternative approach, which might achieve the same ends more efficiently. *Investment* concluded that the department should examine the possibility of reducing the number of very small schools, by introducing appropriate transport services: a reduction in the number of small schools would produce considerable savings and secure important benefits through the delivery of better educational services.[38] The survey team's analysis provided a compelling rationale for the reorganisation of primary education, which was to be rapidly taken up by Colley.

The report indicated that the efficiency gaps in the educational system as a whole were widespread enough to prevent any solution to the problems of manpower shortages or inequalities in educational participation. The survey team argued that an unplanned expansion of primary and post-primary education would 'merely multiply the existing structure' and rapidly exhaust available resources.[39] The report suggested the adoption of an alternative strategy, based on coherent planning of educational needs, which might achieve the same ends more efficiently than the traditional haphazard approach to the distribution of educational resources. The report's conclusions not only illuminated the failures of educational policy in the past, but also charted a way forward for constructive development in the future. *Investment* was a devastating analysis of the Irish educational system, and made a compelling case for radical reform.

The report of the survey team was a landmark of the greatest importance in the transformation of the Irish educational system. The importance of the report was widely recognised by contemporaries, not least the senior officials of the department. O'Connor commented that: 'The importance of the report to the Department of Education cannot be overemphasised. The public were now aware of the deficiencies and inequalities of the system and remedial action could no longer be postponed.'[40] The department's officials were well aware of the faults of the system by 1965, but they had traditionally taken a cautious, low-key approach, which was ineffective in resolving long-standing educational problems. Such caution was no longer a practical option following the comprehensive and scathing analysis of the educational system provided by *Investment*. O'Connor later argued that the publication of an independent report of such range and quality left the Minister with a stark choice: 'to devise policies consistent with the facts produced by the report or to do nothing at all. It was reasonable to presume that the Minister would not adopt the second option.'[41] *Investment* illustrated the deficiencies of the educational system in such a definitive fashion that the department was obliged to confront the fundamental problems which plagued Irish education. The report also provided the statistical data and policy analysis to underpin state action, which could address the problems fully chronicled by the survey team. *Investment* outlined an invaluable rationale and blueprint for the transformation of the Irish educational system.

The conclusions of the report received a favourable response from ministers and senior officials at least in part due to the official conviction that education was an important element in economic expansion. The analysis presented by the survey team was greatly influenced by the assumption that education was a key factor in economic development. The report asserted: 'It is not necessary to be able to measure precisely the contribution of education to economic growth in order to recognise the significance of education to economic development.'[42] The survey team's analysis emphasised that educational planning had to be related to economic planning: this approach had been promoted by Lemass since 1962 and was included in the *Second Programme*.[43] The Taoiseach fully recognised the importance of *Investment* and had no hesitation in publicising its critical analysis of the educational system. Lemass wrote to Colley immediately after receiving the report on 27 November 1965, noting the Minister's view that *Investment* would be difficult to summarise effectively. Lemass told Colley that an effort had to be made to summarise the report and urged him to publish an official commentary on *Investment*, to underline the key points of the report.[44] Colley immediately assured the Taoiseach that he would arrange the publication of a commentary summarising the conclusions of the report.[45] The report was published on 23 December 1965, along with a detailed press release drafted by the department, which highlighted the report's conclusions concerning the failings of the educational system.[46] Lemass clearly perceived the potential for significant change in the survey team's critical evaluation of Irish education and was determined that the government would take up the issues raised by the report in a proactive fashion.

The report's critical analysis of educational realities became an integral part of government policy even before it was published. Lemass and Colley fully accepted the survey team's conclusion that effective long-term planning was essential to overcome the substantial deficiencies within the educational system. The department implemented the recommendation for the creation of a development unit before the report was presented to the Minister in November 1965. Colley announced the formation of a new Development Branch within the Department of Education in his address on 16 June. The Development Branch would take responsibility for the collection of educational statistics and would undertake long-term planning for educational expansion. Colley indicated that the Branch would aim 'to plan, consult, stimulate, set out a programme of measures and see to the implementation of educational improvements and reform'.[47] Hillery had initiated the establishment of the Development Branch early in 1965, but it was Colley who publicly announced the formation of the new unit, indicating that he envisaged a central role for the Branch in the future reorganisation of Irish education.[48] A third position of Assistant Secretary was created within the department, which was filled by Seán O'Connor as head of the Development Branch. The Minister also appointed William Hyland of the OECD survey team as the senior statistician in the new Branch, although the department lacked the funding to provide for the full staffing of the unit initially. The new Branch undertook, as one of its first duties, a comprehensive survey of available post-primary educational facilities and of future requirements for post-primary education.[49] The Minister and senior officials acted to initiate coherent planning of educational needs even before the report was published.

Amalgamation

The Minister for Education rapidly adopted the report's proposal for a comprehensive reorganisation of the distribution of national schools. Colley announced a radical new initiative in educational policy, which was largely inspired by *Investment in Education*, in July 1965. Colley informed the Dáil on 21 July 1965 that he intended, where feasible, to replace small one-teacher and two-teacher national schools with larger central schools, served by school transport schemes financed by the state.[50] He told the Dáil that 'It seems quite clear to me that we have to take a very firm decision on this matter of small schools.'[51] Colley argued, on the basis of the analysis made by *Investment*, that educational attainment on the part of pupils in small national schools was significantly inferior to the level reached by pupils in larger schools: school facilities and teaching aids were also far inferior in small schools. He believed that one-teacher schools were particularly problematic, as a single teacher could not effectively cover all the classes in a school. Colley indicated that when the question of replacing a teacher in a small school or providing a new building for such a school arose, the department would investigate whether the establishment of a new central school was feasible.[52] He promised that each case would be examined on its merits and that the amalgamation of small national schools would be combined with the provision of a school transport service, which would be fully funded by the state. Colley appealed to the opposition parties to support the policy of amalgamation, urging opposition politicians not to lend support to local agitation against the new approach.[53] It appeared that Colley's hopes for cross-party support were well founded, as amalgamation initially commanded considerable support among leading opposition politicians. James Tully TD of the Labour Party fully agreed with Colley on 21 July about the deficiencies of one-teacher schools and the Labour Party was generally supportive of amalgamation during the subsequent controversy. Moreover, influential Fine Gael figures also favoured the reorganisation of primary education. James Dillon, who had recently retired as leader of Fine Gael, was an advocate of larger national schools while Patrick O'Donnell, who served as the party's spokesman on education until April 1965, strongly supported the new policy. O'Donnell indeed told Colley in the Dáil on 21 July that amalgamation had been demanded previously by Fine Gael: 'This is what Fine Gael have advocated on many occasions, as the Minister has pointed out.'[54] Significantly Denis Jones TD, who had succeeded O'Donnell as Fine Gael's spokesman on education, did not endorse the new initiative, although he did not indicate any opposition to amalgamation on 21 July.[55] Colley's announcement of the new policy, which involved a radical reorganisation of primary education, met with virtually no opposition in the Dáil initially.

The new initiative was, however, strongly opposed by local interests in many areas and by several Catholic bishops, especially Dr. Michael Browne, Bishop of Galway. Browne vehemently attacked amalgamation on 2 September 1965 at the opening of a new two-teacher school at St. Brigid's Well, Liscannor, Co. Clare.[56] He asserted that the policy would cause great damage to rural Ireland and condemned the decision to close two-teacher schools, demanding: 'Are they all to be abolished and merged just as it is proposed to merge the small farms?'[57] The Minister replied forcefully to Browne's criticisms of amalgamation, in a speech at Galway on 11 September. Colley described Browne's comments as 'distressingly inaccurate and intemperate', asserting that the Bishop's views did not represent the unanimous opinion of the Catholic Hierarchy.[58] Colley had not formally sought the opinion of the Hierarchy on the new policy, but he privately consulted Cardinal Conway about the initiative, receiving a favourable response. Indeed Colley reported to Lemass on 24 September that Conway 'agreed in principle with the policy' and had even suggested an area of his archdiocese where an amalgamation might be viable.[59] The Minister's suggestion that the Catholic bishops were not united in their approach to amalgamation was essentially correct, although the Hierarchy did not formally discuss the new initiative until October 1965.

Following the beginning of public controversy about the initiative, Colley outlined a comprehensive rationale for the policy of amalgamation to Lemass on 24 September 1965. The Minister told Lemass that there were about 730 one-teacher schools, frequently staffed by untrained teachers, who were obliged to cope with all classes in such schools.[60] Many of these schools were left without any teacher for considerable periods each year, in part because it was extremely difficult for one-teacher schools to attract and retain teachers. Colley made the case for amalgamation by referring to the conclusions of *Investment*. He told Lemass that a general survey of pupils in one-teacher schools had disclosed that 'they are educationally about two years behind pupils being taught in larger schools'.[61] Similar considerations applied to two-teacher schools, although the disadvantages were not as great as those experienced by one-teacher schools. Colley indicated that the department had initiated an assessment of all proposals for new two-teacher schools, with the intention of creating new central schools, which would enjoy an increased number of teachers. The Minister believed that the reorganisation of primary education was essential on educational and social grounds. He considered that efforts should be made to have one teacher for each class in any school, although this objective was not always attainable. He also emphasised the social benefits of amalgamation for rural communities, arguing that parents would no longer be willing to live in areas which failed to provide adequate educational opportunity for their children.[62] Colley outlined a compelling rationale for the policy of amalgamation: he was clearly concerned to maintain Lemass's support for an initiative that was already highly controversial.

Lemass replied immediately to Colley's memorandum on 25 September, fully supporting the case for amalgamation. He assured Colley that 'I think the arguments in favour of your policy in this regard, as set out in the Memorandum, will be seen to be very convincing by all reasonable people.'[63] But Lemass also told the Minister that the case for larger central schools had not yet been 'sufficiently publicised', warning Colley to make a series of speeches in the near future to promote public understanding of the new policy.[64] Lemass was concerned to promote public support for a radical and controversial educational reform. Colley readily agreed on 27 September that it was vital to publicise the case for amalgamation, indicating that he intended to make speeches promoting the new policy in the short term.[65] The Minister outlined his strategy for the implementation of the policy: he had communicated the new approach in the first instance to the educational authorities and other interests closely involved with the administration of the national schools. Colley concentrated initially on communicating the new policy to the Board of Works, the parish priests who served as national school managers and Cardinal Conway. The Minister had also maintained close contact with Fianna Fáil TDs representing constituencies in which local protests against the policy had occurred.[66] Colley's comments on his initial efforts to implement the new initiative illustrated the political sensitivity of the issue. The Minister was concerned not only to communicate his new approach to the relevant authorities and agencies, but to contain and forestall opposition to amalgamation by persuading the government's backbenchers of the merits of the initiative.

The Minister's initial efforts to secure the co-operation of the school managers in the process of amalgamation had a mixed outcome. The Catholic Clerical Managers' Association did not openly oppose the Minister's policy, but privately expressed severe reservations to the department about the closure of two-teacher schools and the introduction of transport services to new central schools, especially for younger children.[67] Colley complained to the Taoiseach on 27 September that Catholic clerical managers in some dioceses were willing to consider new arrangements for school transport but then 'got orders from their Bishop not to agree to the arrangements'.[68] While the Minister believed that such local problems would be overcome in due course, he conceded that there could be 'some awkward situations arising in the meantime'.[69] Colley was well aware of the considerable strength of local and in some cases clerical opposition to the policy but was determined to press ahead with amalgamation. The Minister's private consultation with Cardinal Conway underlined his concern to avoid a full-scale conflict with the Catholic bishops, which might well obstruct the implementation of the new policy. The Hierarchy considered the Minister's initiative at its general meeting on 12 October 1965 largely on the basis of newspaper reports, as Colley made no formal attempt to ascertain the opinion of the bishops.[70] The bishops expressed 'their deep concern and anxiety, as Trustees and Patrons of primary schools, that a general policy of such far-reaching consequences should be suddenly introduced'.[71] The Hierarchy was seriously dissatisfied by

Colley's rapid and decisive announcement of such an important policy change, in the absence of formal consultation with established educational interests. The bishops expressed reservations about the policy of amalgamation, arguing that educationalists were divided in their views on the quality of small schools. But they also acknowledged that the closure of small schools might well be unavoidable in certain cases.[72] The bishops informed the Minister on 17 October that it was 'the unanimous opinion of the Hierarchy' that the case of each school should be decided on its merits, following full consultation with the parents and the managerial authorities.[73] The Hierarchy did not express opposition in principle to the policy of amalgamation. While the collective opinion of the bishops was critical of the Minister's approach, the Hierarchy did not endorse Browne's categorical opposition to amalgamation. It appears that Colley's private communication with Cardinal Conway helped to influence the initial response of the bishops to the initiative.

A conflict between the state and the Catholic bishops concerning the policy change was avoided because Colley was willing to accommodate the specific concerns of the Hierarchy while steadfastly maintaining the essential principle of amalgamation. Colley and three senior officials met the Episcopal Commission for Primary Education on 10 January 1966 to discuss the concerns of the bishops.[74] The Minister emphasised his determination to proceed with the amalgamation of one and two-teacher schools. He politely acknowledged an argument made by the bishops that social considerations were also relevant but clarified that he had no intention of changing his approach. The Minister guaranteed, however, that the department would fully consult the managers and if possible the relevant parents in each case. He also assured the bishops that no parish would be left without a primary school as a result of amalgamation. The bishops were most concerned about the proposed transport scheme, raising 'many difficulties concerning the whole matter of transport'.[75] Colley indicated that the department would take full responsibility for the cost of the transport service if necessary, although the manager would be able to make a nominal voluntary contribution. The officials asserted that the organisation of the transport scheme could be undertaken without serious difficulties. Colley also commented pointedly that many managers were willing to collaborate with the new policy, but would not agree any arrangements with the department, as they believed that the bishops were opposed to amalgamation.[76] The discussion underlined the Hierarchy's considerable reservations about the new policy, especially concerning the establishment of the transport service. The bishops were sufficiently concerned to seek legal advice on the powers of the Minister to close state-aided schools vested in private trustees. The Standing Committee of the Hierarchy recommended on 11 January 1966 that each bishop should instruct the school managers in his diocese to report upon any proposed amalgamation and to ensure that the parents were fully consulted in all cases.[77] The Hierarchy did not, however, offer support to local groups opposed to amalgamation. The department proved willing to consult with the local bishop and school managers concerning proposals for amalgamation, which satisfied the Hierarchy's concern to avoid the imposition of changes in the educational structure of the parish without the involvement of the bishop.[78]

The bishops as a whole were much more concerned by early 1966 with the implications of the proposed transport service than with the principle of amalgamation. The Standing Committee insisted that the responsibility for the transport service should rest entirely with the state.[79] The Hierarchy also expressed various reservations about the provision of a new transport service to central schools at their general meeting in June 1966. The bishops were concerned that the managers should not have to bear the financial cost of the service or risk assuming liability for accidents involving pupils. They also perceived a 'moral danger' to the welfare of schoolchildren if they were to avail of the transport service without adequate supervision.[80] The Hierarchy was determined that the managers should not take responsibility in any way for a school transport service. The bishops advised the managers to ensure that their role with regard to school transport was as limited as possible: any agreement with the department should maintain only a formal role for the manager in approving the contract for the transport service, with the department itself taking full responsibility for the cost and administration of the service. Despite their grave reservations about the new transport service, the bishops agreed to allow the managers to work out appropriate arrangements for school transport with the department, on the basis that any agreement would be referred to the Hierarchy before it was finalised.[81] Colley's conviction that the bishops determined the approach of the managers towards amalgamation was essentially correct. Significantly, however, the Hierarchy proved willing to allow the clerical managers to co-operate with the state's policy, on the condition that the school transport service was fully administered and financed by the department. This approach did not present a great obstacle to the government's policy, as Colley had consistently promised a free transport service funded by the state for central schools. While most bishops had considerable reservations about the new policy, especially the school transport service, they did not oppose amalgamation in principle or make any collective attempt to obstruct the state's policy. Although the Minister could not avert clashes with individual bishops, Colley and the senior officials certainly succeeded in avoiding a conflict

between the state and the Hierarchy as a whole concerning the reorganisation of primary education.

The Minister also acted decisively to reassure the INTO that amalgamation would not undermine the employment and conditions of primary teachers. Colley discussed the new policy with representatives of the
Central Executive Committee (CEC) of the INTO on 10 September 1965.[82]
The Minister gave the INTO delegation a categorical assurance concerning
the employment of the primary teachers affected by the change: 'No teacher
serving in a permanent capacity would lose his position as a result of this
policy of amalgamation.'[83] The INTO representatives initially indicated
that they had 'no fixed policy' on amalgamation until they secured more
detailed information and investigated the consequences of the abolition of
small schools.[84] Colley publicised his assurances to the INTO in the Dáil on
17 February 1966, informing TDs that any national schoolteachers
affected by the plan would not only remain in employment but would
retain their full salary and allowances.[85] The CEC was concerned about the
impact of amalgamation not only on the employment of their members,
but also on the prospects for promotion for primary teachers, as the closure
of small schools would extinguish the posts of principal teacher in such
schools. But the INTO Executive expressed no objection in principle to
amalgamation, seeking instead to secure specific guarantees from the
Minister to protect the position of the teachers concerned.[86] The CEC representatives raised a series of concerns with Colley at a further meeting on
24 February 1966. They emphasised that schools should not be amalgamated 'without due consideration of all the local factors', seeking close
consultation by the officials with the local teachers.[87] They also sought
assurances that there would be no loss of employment and argued that
amalgamation was causing a suspension of essential maintenance work
in old schools, forcing teachers to work under appalling conditions. Finally
the CEC representatives made the case for compensation to the primary
teaching profession, through the creation of new avenues for promotion,
to offset the posts due to be eliminated as a result of amalgamation. Colley
dealt with the INTO's concerns in a conciliatory fashion. He fully accepted
the union's position that local factors should be considered and indicated
that the department was willing to include the teachers concerned in discussions on the future of their schools. Moreover the Minister again gave
a firm assurance to the delegation that the teachers affected by the policy
would be employed in an amalgamated school. He also undertook to
resolve the problems concerning the maintenance of old schools, pledging
that any necessary temporary repairs would be authorised immediately.
Colley gave a more cautious response to the INTO's proposals with regard
to promotion, agreeing only to consider a memorandum from the union

on new posts and increments for the teaching profession.[88] While Colley avoided any commitment to the INTO's proposals for financial compensation, he provided definite assurances which satisfied the union's core concerns on most aspects of amalgamation.

The Minister's assurances proved sufficient to satisfy the CEC, which adopted a cautiously favourable approach to amalgamation. The CEC recommended acceptance of amalgamation in principle, on a conditional basis, to the annual Congress of the INTO in April 1966. The CEC identified adequate local discussion on amalgamation, no loss of employment for the relevant teachers and the development of new promotional opportunities, as the union's key requirements if the policy was to be accepted.[89] The INTO congress on 12–15 April broadly supported the CEC's position, passing a motion which approved in principle of the policy of amalgamation and mandated the CEC to deliver several conditions which protected the position of primary teachers.[90] The Congress endorsed most of the requirements laid down by the CEC and also demanded that no rural school should be amalgamated with an urban school. The motion stipulated too that 'under no circumstances should any lay school be amalgamated with a school run by a religious order'.[91] The final demand was of considerable importance to the INTO, which had previously engaged in a bitter dispute with the Marist order over the transfer of a primary school in Ballina to the control of the order. Colley had already indicated his willingness to accept most of the INTO's conditions. He had assured the INTO as early as September 1965 that he did not wish, in general, to promote the amalgamation of lay and religious schools. The Minister also informed the union that he did not envisage any amalgamations between urban and rural schools.[92] Despite some opposition to amalgamation among INTO branches, the CEC took a constructive approach to the policy, accepting the reorganisation of primary education in principle but securing specific concessions to protect the position of teachers affected by amalgamation. Colley consulted the primary teachers' union extensively and sought with considerable success to meet the concerns of the INTO leadership about amalgamation. The Minister's conciliatory approach proved effective in winning the conditional support of the INTO for the new policy.

Colley concentrated initially on private negotiations with the INTO, the managers and the Hierarchy, seeking to secure the support of important stakeholders in the educational system for amalgamation. But he soon followed Lemass's advice to make a strong public case for the new policy. Colley vigorously promoted the amalgamation of small national schools in a speech delivered at Ballinrobe, Co. Mayo, on 11 November 1965.[93] He pointed out that one and two-teacher schools did not provide the educational facilities offered by larger schools, while the proposed central schools would deliver a more extensive syllabus with a greater emphasis on subjects relevant to pupils in rural areas. Colley presented amalgamation as an important element in resolving the perennial problem of rural depopulation. He argued that larger central schools would encourage parents to remain in their native parish and would reduce emigration.[94] Colley also emphasised the educational and social benefits of the new policy in the Dáil, when parliamentary critics of the policy argued that amalgamation would devastate rural communities. When Oliver J. Flanagan, the Fine Gael TD for Laois-Offaly, challenged Colley to clarify the details of the initiative on 21 October 1965, the Minister provided a definitive statement of the government's policy.[95] Colley reiterated that one and two-teacher schools would be gradually replaced by larger central schools, served by school transport schemes provided by the state. Colley drew attention particularly to the wasteful and inefficient use of teachers which had been identified by *Investment*, warning the Dáil that the existing distribution of national schools wasted scarce teaching resources: 'A proliferation of small schools means that in relation to the instruction he can give the teacher is serving in conditions where his services are least effective.'[96] The Minister also assured TDs that there was 'no blanket decision' to abolish all two-teacher schools: decisions to amalgamate such schools were taken only on the merits of each case. Colley's firm defence of the policy did not deter Flanagan, who criticised amalgamation on the basis that the small school was a centre of community activity in a rural area. Flanagan warned the Minister to defer the implementation of the new approach and take account of the opposition to amalgamation: 'The Minister should not go too far on it. I beg of him not to go too far.'[97] The colourful Fine Gael Deputy soon emerged as the most vociferous opponent of amalgamation in the Dáil, but he was by no means alone in opposing the policy. Fine Gael's spokesman on education, Denis Jones, was also critical of the closure of small schools. Jones announced on 15 February 1966 Fine Gael's opposition to the closure of any two-teacher schools without a local public inquiry.[98] Fine Gael moved to a firmly sceptical position on amalgamation by early 1966. Colley's vigorous defence of the policy underlined, however, that the opposition of Flanagan and other Fine Gael TDs had little influence on the government's approach. Colley and Lemass were convinced of the long-term educational and social benefits of the policy, which outweighed the short-term discontent with the government caused by amalgamation in some rural areas.

It was not the parliamentary critics of amalgamation who presented the most severe challenge to the Minister's policy. Although the Hierarchy did not oppose amalgamation in principle, Michael Browne soon emerged as the principal spokesman of the opposition to the new policy. Colley's efforts to promote the policy change ignited a storm of controversy, which culminated in a public clash between the Minister and Browne in February 1966. Colley addressed a meeting composed of NUI graduates in Galway on 5 February 1966, defending the right of the Minister for Education to make and implement educational policy.[99] While Colley emphasised the importance of consultation and co-operation between the department and private educational interests, he firmly asserted the predominant role of the Minister in the formulation of educational policy: 'this was where a Minister stood apart, and alone'.[100] Following Colley's address, Browne immediately replied to the Minister's speech and roundly denounced the policy of amalgamation as 'a catastrophe – a major calamity for our Irish countryside'.[101] He argued that the Minister meant to close half the primary schools in the state: Colley's policy would intensify rural depopulation and inflict a disastrous blow on rural Ireland. The Bishop declared that the Minister's attempt to close small national schools was 'illegal and unconstitutional'.[102] Browne claimed that the closure of small schools was a violation of the constitutional right of parents to freedom of education and an unwarranted attempt by the state to undermine the authority of the clerical managers. He considered that the state's intervention was illegal, as national schools were vested in clerical trustees and the Minister was unilaterally breaching the Deeds of Trust which had been agreed by the department with the clerical trustees: 'National schools are not State property, like police barracks.'[103] The Bishop was attacking not only the amalgamation of small schools but also the intervention of the state in the organisation of primary education. He accused Colley of undermining the liberties achieved by the sacrifices of previous generations, invoking the memory of Pearse and the leaders of the 1916 Rising: Browne declared that Pearse had died for national freedom, not to enable a Minister 'to impose autocracy or dictatorship on the people of Ireland and especially not in education – for he was a teacher, founder of a secondary school'.[104] The Bishop denounced Colley as an urban politician who knew nothing of rural education and was enforcing his policy in a dictatorial fashion: 'There is one role that does not belong to a Minister for Education in this country: it is the role of a dictator.'[105] Browne's vitriolic response to Colley's address on 5 February was certainly the most dramatic moment of the agitation against the policy of amalgamation. But Browne's speech was much more than a denunciation of amalgamation. The Bishop not only made a fierce attack on the Minister's policy, but also directly challenged the legitimacy of effective state intervention to reform the educational system.

Colley took up Browne's challenge without hesitation. Tony Ó Dálaigh, the Minister's private secretary, commented that 'he was straight and direct: he was not a man to run from Bishops'.[106] Browne left the meeting abruptly immediately after delivering his criticisms of the Minister.[107] Colley responded forcefully to the Bishop's onslaught, seeking to rebut Browne's criticisms and defending the right of the Minister for Education to initiate policy reform.[108] The Minister strongly disputed Browne's allegation that amalgamation was disastrous for rural Ireland, arguing that it was inadequate educational provision which would cause greater emigration and rural depopulation: 'I think if we do not give our children a chance of a decent education, they will fly faster from the country.'[109] He challenged the Bishop's assertion that the policy was unconstitutional, questioning why Browne had not tested his claim through the courts if he was convinced of the unconstitutionality of amalgamation. Colley pointed out that the policy would not lead to the amalgamation of all two-teacher schools and would produce more three-teacher schools, instead of bringing the closure of all small schools, as the Bishop had suggested. Colley categorically rejected Browne's denunciation of the increasing power of the state and particularly the Minister for Education. He emphasised that the Minister was accountable to the Dáil and that his power had clear limits. Colley, however, bluntly reasserted his conviction that the Minister was primarily responsible for the initiation and management of educational reform: 'the only one who was in a position to achieve educational advance on a nation-wide scale was the Minister for Education'.[110] He acknowledged that the Minister required goodwill and co-operation to achieve policy objectives but warned that a few individuals would not be allowed to obstruct necessary educational reforms by withholding such co-operation.[111] Browne had issued an unusually direct and public challenge to the Minister for Education. Colley not only rejected the Bishop's criticisms but also forcefully asserted the right of the Minister to make policy and implement educational reforms.

Colley followed up his initial reply to Browne by issuing a letter to the *Irish Press* on 8 February 1966, which gave a more comprehensive and elaborate rebuttal of the Bishop's criticisms.[112] The *Irish Press* provided extensive coverage on 7 and 8 February of Colley's response and also gave considerable attention to Browne's abrupt departure from the meeting.[113] O'Connor, who believed that the Bishop did not stage a deliberate 'walk-out' but left the meeting to keep a later appointment, commented that Browne might well have secured greater public support for his case if he had not added to the public sensation by leaving so abruptly: 'While the points he made were extensively quoted in the news press, so also, was the fact that he had walked out.'[114] Browne refused to explain the apparent 'walk-out' and indeed declined to give any further comment on the matter to the media, leaving the Minister greater scope to present his case.[115]

Colley was able to use the public clash to promote the policy of amalgamation through the national media, especially the sympathetic *Irish Press*.

The public controversy generated by Browne's clash with the Minister was not, however, entirely favourable to Colley. The *Irish Independent*, which devoted an editorial entitled 'Clash at Galway' to the dispute on 7 February, argued that Browne's tactics and his 'occasionally militant language' were not the most important aspects of the debate.[116] The editorial asserted that Browne's argument on the social value of small primary schools deserved consideration and that the future shape of rural education should be decided only after all relevant interests had been fully considered.[117] The editorial position of the *Irish Independent* was broadly the same as the approach adopted by Fine Gael immediately after the clash between Colley and Browne. While Colley succeeded in promoting his policy effectively following the Bishop's criticisms, the public dispute also encouraged the parliamentary opposition to amalgamation in the short term. The Minister took care to reassure the Fianna Fáil parliamentary party concerning the viability of the policy following his public dispute with Browne. He told a meeting of the parliamentary party on 9 February that Browne's views were not shared by the majority of the bishops or even by many clerical managers in his own diocese.[118] While several backbench TDs raised concerns about amalgamation, there was no serious challenge to the Minister's approach within his own party. But Browne's intervention certainly encouraged Fine Gael to take a definite stand against amalgamation. When the Minister introduced a supplementary Estimate to the Dáil on 15 February 1966, Denis Jones announced Fine Gael's opposition to any early amalgamation of small national schools.[119] Jones delivered a wide-ranging critique of the proposed reorganisation of primary education. He regretted the early closure of one-teacher schools but emphasised especially Fine Gael's opposition to the amalgamation of any two-teacher school, in the absence of a full local public inquiry involving parents and all other educational interests.[120] Jones argued that the Minister was proceeding with amalgamation too quickly: 'I feel that the Minister has moved too far, too fast.'[121] The Fine Gael proposal envisaged the indefinite suspension of the policy of amalgamation. Moreover Jones attacked not only amalgamation but also the influence of *Investment* on the government's policy. The Fine Gael spokesman criticised the economic orientation of the OECD study, arguing that the survey team had failed to take into account that 'education is a social service', which could not be measured simply in economic terms.[122] He warned that economic factors, derived from the report, were taking precedence over social and community needs.[123]

Jones's criticisms of the Minister's policy were supported by several other Fine Gael TDs, including Oliver J. Flanagan, who went considerably further than most of his party in attacking amalgamation. He denounced Colley's policy as the first step towards the abolition of the managerial system and the establishment of centralised state control over education.[124] Flanagan welcomed Browne's intervention in the debate and called on the Hierarchy to advise the government that the state was acting beyond its legitimate authority. He even raised the dreaded spectre of Communism as a result of excessive state intervention: 'Most certainly this is what we would expect as a Communist step.'[125] Flanagan's extravagant denunciation of amalgamation and his wild allegations against Colley were not endorsed by other Fine Gael representatives. Jones had, however, firmly established Fine Gael's opposition to the radical reorganisation of primary education. Despite O'Donnell's initial support for amalgamation in July 1965, Fine Gael was seeking the indefinite deferral of the policy by February 1966. The Opposition parties were divided on the initiative, as the Labour Party proved more consistent than Fine Gael in its approach to amalgamation. The Labour spokesperson on education, Eileen Desmond TD, indicated on 15 February that the Party generally agreed with the Minister's policy.[126] Desmond noted that the Labour Party's policy document *Challenge and Change in Education* advocated the amalgamation of small primary schools.[127] She commented that the Party saw a strong case for the closure of a significant number of small schools, although she also urged the Minister to examine each case on its merits. Desmond sought clarification only that free transport would be provided by the state for all pupils affected by amalgamation: Colley immediately intervened in the debate to confirm that the transport service would be free for pupils affected by the policy.[128] The Labour spokesperson showed no enthusiasm for Fine Gael's alternative proposal of a special public inquiry. The Labour Party's general endorsement of amalgamation underlined that the initiative commanded the support of a substantial majority in the Dáil and facilitated the Minister's efforts to present Fine Gael's opposition to the policy as short-term political opportunism.

Colley gave no ground to critics of amalgamation in his reply to the debate on 16–17 February 1966. He firstly denounced Flanagan's attack on the policy as 'mischievous, of evil intent and utterly irresponsible'.[129] The Minister dismissed contemptuously Flanagan's allegation that the government was seeking insidiously to undermine the managerial system. Colley also made a scathing attack on Fine Gael, accusing the largest opposition party of changing course on amalgamation in response to pressure from reactionary local interests. He derided Jones' proposal of a local public inquiry for each case of amalgamation as 'a gimmick'.[130] Colley was unequivocal in his defence of amalgamation, which he regarded as an essential prerequisite for the effective allocation of teaching resources and the achievement of a high standard of education for all pupils. He would not countenance the continued proliferation of small schools, which placed pupils at a relative educational disadvantage: 'This would condemn many more generations of our children to an education which we believe is not as good as what we can give them. I could not feel justified in condemning generations of our children to that.'[131] He maintained that amalgamation had to be implemented as a matter of urgency to provide adequate educational opportunity for all, as appropriate educational opportunities were not available to pupils in small schools: 'I am not prepared to condemn these children to these conditions in order to pacify the most reactionary elements of the community.'[132] He also sought to rebut the social arguments used by most critics of his policy, emphasising that the introduction of adequate educational services in rural areas was socially desirable: while the policy was also economically sensible, this was merely 'a subsidiary reason' for amalgamation.[133] The Minister asserted that the case for amalgamation was clearly established and it remained for him to implement the policy as a matter of urgency. The reorganisation of primary education would be pursued by the state even in the face of considerable public and parliamentary opposition.

Colley also strongly defended *Investment* against criticisms that it was dominated by economic considerations. He pointed out that the report provided an analysis of the slower rate of progression achieved by pupils in small schools, as well as a description of the severe deficiencies in facilities, which characterised such schools. Although the survey team's terms of reference were derived from economics, Colley was certainly correct in highlighting that the study had ranged far beyond economic considerations in its rigorous analysis of the Irish educational system.[134] Colley's restatement of the policy on amalgamation reflected the influence exerted by *Investment*. The Minister's firm defence of the radical reorganisation of primary education relied explicitly on the analysis and data provided by the report. Although Colley's fervent personal commitment to the controversial initiative was evident, *Investment* provided the essential basis for the policy of amalgamation.

The government remained firmly committed to the reorganisation of primary education, despite the storm of controversy early in 1966. The Minister took the leading role in establishing and promoting the new policy in the face of substantial opposition. Colley vigorously defended the policy against influential critics of amalgamation within the Catholic Hierarchy and Fine Gael. He was entirely committed to the implementation of the controversial initiative, which he regarded as an indispensable means of achieving equal educational opportunity for all primary school pupils. The policy of amalgamation could not have been implemented without the unqualified support of the Taoiseach. Lemass fully endorsed the Minister's initiative and correctly advised Colley to secure wider public support for the policy. The amalgamation of small national schools proceeded rapidly under Colley's successors. The department closed over 900 small schools as part of the ongoing policy of amalgamation by 1972.[135] The effective implementation of the policy ensured that between 1966 and 1973 the number of one and two-teacher schools was reduced by about 1,100, or over a third of the original total.[136] The policy of amalgamation delivered a radical reorganisation of primary education within a decade of its introduction.

The implementation of amalgamation and the public clash between the Minister and the Bishop of Galway illustrated the extent of the transformation in the state's educational policy within a single decade. The Minister not only successfully promoted a radical reorganisation of primary education but also confronted influential opponents of his policy publicly. Perhaps the most significant aspect of the public dispute was that it happened at all. Such a clash between the Minister for Education and a senior Catholic prelate would have been inconceivable even a decade earlier. The dispute was not the prelude to a full-scale conflict between the state and the most powerful stakeholder in the educational system, the Catholic Church, as the Hierarchy did not adopt Browne's position of intransigent opposition to the state's policy. But the clash at Galway marked the first open conflict between the Minister for Education and a Catholic bishop concerning the reform and expansion of the educational system. Moreover the public dispute on the state's educational policy underlined the contrast between Colley's definite and authoritative approach to policy formulation and the timid, conservative practice followed by successive ministers until the late 1950s.

Integration

Colley and the senior officials of the department envisaged a central role for the state in planning and co-ordinating the expansion of post-primary education. The Minister sought to achieve greater collaboration between the secondary school authorities and the VECs to facilitate the development of second-level education. Colley clarified his policy approach in public speeches and meetings with educational interest groups during the final three months of 1965. He outlined the government's objectives for the expansion of post-primary education in his address to mark the opening of Clonmel Vocational School on 7 October 1965.[137] He aimed to ensure that the secondary and vocational schools would no longer operate separately in 'watertight compartments': each system would provide courses traditionally associated with the other.[138] This sentiment very much echoed Hillery's policy announcement in May 1963. But Colley's address went considerably further than previous ministerial statements and signalled a significant development of the government's policy towards post-primary education.

The Minister identified the achievement of equality of educational opportunity for all as his most important objective; 'my ideal is for all our children, whatever type of school they attend, to have equality of educational opportunity'.[139] He believed that the achievement of parity of standard and 'parity of esteem' between the two diverse strands of post-primary education was the first step towards equality of educational opportunity.[140] Colley considered that such parity between the two systems was best achieved by ensuring that all pupils shared the same public examination: he announced that the introduction of a three-year course of post-primary education for all children, involving a broad post-primary course leading to a common Intermediate Certificate examination, was an integral part of the government's policy. Significantly he drew attention to recent economic development, which provided the context for the government's approach. Colley commented that an increasing proportion of available employment in Ireland was of a type 'which demands a higher level of education than is possible of attainment in a two years post-primary course'.[141] The government regarded the expansion of post-primary education as an essential advance, which would provide an increased supply of skilled employees for the economy as well as a desirable extension of educational opportunity.

Colley acknowledged at Clonmel that the introduction of a three-year course at post-primary level would present significant problems, especially in providing adequate accommodation and sufficient teachers. The scale of the challenge demanded close collaboration between the secondary and vocational school authorities. Colley appealed to the school authorities to consider second-level education as a single unit: 'all post-primary school authorities should see our education system as a unit, as one system rather than two, and should accordingly, collaborate and co-operate as far as they can in the provision of the necessary facilities in connection with the Intermediate Certificate course'.[142] The achievement of a high level of collaboration between the two separate post-primary systems was an essential part of the Minister's approach. He confirmed that the state would act, in accordance with Hillery's policy announcement in May 1963, to overturn the limitations imposed on vocational education by agreement between the Minister and the Catholic bishops in 1930. Colley was, however, not setting out simply to implement his predecessor's policies. He aimed not only to provide 'parity of esteem' for vocational schools but also to break down the traditional barriers between academic and vocational education.[143] He also affirmed that equality of educational opportunity for all would be a key objective of the state's policy and emphasised that the government regarded the introduction of a three-year post-primary course for all pupils as an urgent economic and social necessity.

The Minister's policy was designed to ensure that the expansion of post-primary education was based on effective co-ordination of available resources and rational planning for educational needs. He informed the officers of the ASTI on 8 October 1965 that it was essential to make the best possible use of all available resources, including post-primary school buildings and teachers.[144] He commented bluntly that 'no new schools would be built haphazardly but would be sited having regard to the information which would be made available from the investigation now proceeding regarding the future demand for post-primary education'.[145] The survey of current post-primary facilities and future requirements, being undertaken by the Development Branch, was designed to provide for long-term planning of the future expansion of second-level education.[146] Colley was unwilling to sanction the building of new schools in the traditional haphazard fashion. He imposed short-term restrictions on the building of post-primary schools in October 1965, suspending any action by the department to sanction the construction of new second-level schools until the survey of educational needs in each area was completed.[147] Colley was not simply relying on ministerial exhortation to achieve his objectives, but was willing to assert the authority of the state over the development of post-primary education to secure effective long-term planning.

Colley's concern to achieve a planned expansion of educational facilities clearly demanded extensive intervention by the state to co-ordinate the separate systems of post-primary education. Colley made the case for effective co-ordination by the state of the development of second-level education, in his address on 'Changes in Irish Education', to the Cork Branch of Tuairim on 19 November 1965.[148] He argued that the traditional unplanned approach to the building of post-primary schools was acceptable in the past, as there was plenty of room for expansion: but as the state contained approximately 900 post-primary schools by 1965, the educational facilities currently available could provide almost enough accommodation to give some post-primary education to all children. The haphazard building of secondary and vocational schools could not continue indefinitely.[149] Colley asserted that the Minister for Education alone had the necessary authority to direct the expansion of post-primary education, as neither the secondary school managers nor the VECs could be expected to stop the unplanned expansion: 'The point has arrived accordingly where the only existing central administrative authority, the State, must step in.'[150] Colley clarified the rationale for his decision to restrict further unplanned development of secondary and vocational education and established that the state would take the central role in directing educational expansion. He correctly identified an institutional fragmentation in post-primary education, which was caused by the division between the secondary schools and the vocational system, combined with the considerable autonomy enjoyed by the private secondary schools themselves. Colley was convinced that the Minister and the Department of Education provided the only central authority, which could direct the necessary changes in second-level education.[151] It was Colley who established in unequivocal terms the central role of the Minister for Education in formulating and implementing policy changes at post-primary level. While Hillery had certainly established the right of the Minister to initiate important policy changes by 1963, he had usually acted in a cautious and understated fashion, seeking to avoid public clashes with private educational interests. Colley, however, zealously promoted the state's reforming approach through frequent public speeches and articles in the national media. He had done much to clarify and develop the government's policy for the expansion of post-primary education, in a series of parliamentary statements and public speeches, since his appointment in April 1965.[152]

The Minister's efforts to achieve rational planning of post-primary educational needs underlined the influence of *Investment* on the government's policy. Colley echoed the survey team in drawing attention to the necessity to end the haphazard pattern of expansion and plan the further development of post-primary education.[153] The department's efforts to evolve a planning programme, through the surveys undertaken by the Development Branch, clearly owed much to the report. Moreover Colley's conviction that only the effective co-ordination of the secondary and vocational systems offered the prospect of post-primary education for all was shaped by the survey team's conclusion that social inequalities in participation would not be overcome without achieving a more efficient use of educational resources.[154]

Colley aimed to achieve a more effective use of resources in post-primary education by securing close co-operation between the secondary school authorities and the VECs. Colley's policy for the expansion of second-level education was outlined most fully in his letter to the secondary school managers and the Chief Executive Officers of the VECs on 4 January 1966.[155] He reiterated that the government's primary objective was the achievement of equality of educational opportunity for all: in practical terms this meant providing post-primary education for all the children of the state. Colley also confirmed the government's intention to raise the statutory school leaving age to fifteen by 1970.[156] These ambitious policy objectives, particularly the raising of the school leaving age, created a significant challenge for the Department of Education in delivering the necessary facilities and teaching resources by 1970. Colley emphasised that immediate action was required to prepare for the raising of the school leaving age: while the data secured by the Development Branch's national survey of post-primary facilities would be invaluable for future planning, the survey had not been fully completed by the Branch in January 1966 and the Minister wished to take immediate measures to bring about the full use of existing post-primary facilities. Colley therefore appealed to the school authorities to ensure that the secondary schools and the vocational system became a single educational unit. He urged that the institutional barriers between the two systems should be overcome, not least because the rigidity of the division denied many pupils an education which reflected their aptitudes. Significantly he also stressed the necessity for greater collaboration in second-level education to promote national economic development. Colley argued that the effective use of all available educational resources, to achieve greater educational opportunity, would contribute to national economic salvation: 'our national survival demands the full use of all the talents of our citizens'.[157] The Minister made a compelling case that the elimination of traditional barriers in post-primary education was not only essential on educational grounds but an economic and social imperative.

Colley proposed the pooling of available resources between secondary and vocational schools, which should retain their distinctive character but would collaborate closely together to provide a common curriculum. 'What I have in mind is that there should be a pooling of forces so that the shortcoming of one will be met from the resources of the other, thus making available to the student in either school the post-primary education best suited to him.'[158] Colley recommended an extensive sharing of facilities and an interchange of teachers between secondary and vocational schools. The department envisaged that vocational schools might provide facilities for the teaching of woodwork in secondary schools, while the secondary school authorities might make available resources for the teaching of science to vocational school pupils. The pooling of resources was designed to facilitate the delivery of a broad curriculum by both secondary and vocational schools. The revised Intermediate Certificate course was intended by the department to establish a common standard for all post-primary schools. Colley informed the school authorities that the common Intermediate Certificate examination would be taken by both vocational and secondary school pupils for the first time in 1969. The department also intended to retain the Day Group Certificate examination, which would be available to pupils who wished to take up apprenticeship training before completing the Intermediate Certificate course.[159] The establishment of the common Intermediate Certificate examination, which was designed to create a broad post-primary curriculum, provided much of the rationale for the intensive pooling of resources proposed by the Minister. Colley and the senior officials were well aware that a broad curriculum, including academic and vocational elements, could be achieved only through collaboration between the secondary and vocational systems.

The Minister's concern to bring the separate systems together within a single educational unit was underlined by his comments on the role of comprehensive schools. Hillery had announced in May 1963 that the comprehensive schools were intended to provide post-primary education in local areas which had previously lacked adequate educational facilities.[160] Colley referred to this rationale for the establishment of the new schools in his letter, but he also drew attention to the importance of the comprehensive schools as a model for an integrated post-primary system: 'Apart from their local importance these schools are of general significance because they will signpost the way to an integrated post-primary system of education.'[161] Colley told the school authorities that the number of public comprehensive schools would not be very considerable. He aimed instead to secure the establishment of a comprehensive system in each region, which would be achieved by the exchange of facilities and other forms of collaboration between secondary and vocational schools. It was envisaged that such institutional collaboration would gradually make a comprehensive curriculum available to all post-primary pupils and would lay the foundations of an integrated post-primary system.[162]

Colley did not simply outline his policy approach, but proposed specific measures to achieve the pooling of resources sought by the department. The Minister requested the secondary school authorities and representatives of the vocational system to formulate, through mutual consultation, proposals for the full use of existing facilities and the provision of additional facilities where necessary.[163] The school authorities were informed that meetings should be convened in each county, which would be attended by the secondary and vocational school authorities, as well as an inspector of the department. The inspector would assist the post-primary school authorities in considering the issues raised by the Minister and would transmit any proposed arrangements for collaboration to the department.[164] Colley envisaged that a pooling of resources would be achieved through the local meetings, which would consider the results of the national survey of post-primary education undertaken by the

Development Branch.[165] A constructive process of local consultation was a vital element in Colley's approach to educational planning. Colley requested the local conferences to give a detailed opinion on the need for additional facilities in their area and the way in which such facilities could be provided most effectively. He wished to ascertain whether temporary arrangements to share existing accommodation could be made between secondary and vocational schools.[166] The Minister also sought to promote the exchange of teachers between secondary and vocational schools. He asked the school authorities to explore the possibility of an interchange of teachers, which could facilitate the introduction of subjects to schools where they had not previously been taught and promote the establishment of a comprehensive curriculum. The conferences were requested to evaluate whether the teaching resources in their area were being utilised most effectively: if additional teachers were required, the authorities were asked to give their views on the appointment of extra teachers to serve all the post-primary schools in their area.[167] Colley also raised the possibility of an interchange of pupils, suggesting the formation of common classes, composed of pupils from both systems, for subjects which would not otherwise be provided in either secondary or vocational schools. Finally the conferences were asked to consider how obstacles to the pooling of resources should be overcome. Colley sought effective collaboration between the post-primary school authorities on the basis that such co-operation offered the best prospect of providing increased educational opportunity for all post-primary pupils.[168]

Although Colley's appeal for general collaboration between the secondary and vocational school authorities appeared sensible and uncontroversial, his initiative marked a radical policy departure in the context of the rigidly segregated pattern of post-primary education in 1966. The Minister was seeking to break down traditional institutional barriers in second-level education, which had been firmly established for a generation. Moreover Colley demanded not simply a new co-operative approach by the school authorities, but the effective co-ordination of educational resources at post-primary level to overcome the efficiency gaps in the system identified by *Investment*. The Minister's policy demanded substantial organisational and curriculum changes on the part of secondary and vocational schools to provide for the establishment of a comprehensive system. The pooling of resources sought by Colley was an essential element in the gradual integration of post-primary education, which was a key objective of the department. While Colley emphasised that secondary and vocational schools would retain their distinctive character, he clearly proposed the integration in practical terms of the secondary and vocational systems. Colley's initiative on 4 January 1966 envisaged nothing less than a sweeping reform and reorganisation of post-primary education. The Minister's letter to the school authorities was as much an unequivocal statement of the government's policy as an appeal for collaboration. Colley's proposal for wide-ranging collaboration between the secondary and vocational schools was one of the most radical educational initiatives undertaken by any Minister since the foundation of the state.

Colley's initiative at first secured a mildly positive response from most school authorities. The Minister's intention to extend educational opportunity was supported in principle by the VECs and the religious orders involved in secondary education.[169] But the department soon discovered that the existence of general goodwill towards the Minister's objectives did not necessarily translate into co-operation with the state's policy. Colley told the Dáil on 16 February 1966 that he was 'very heartened' by the positive reaction of secondary school managers and the VECs to his letter.[170] He expressed confidence that there was a genuine desire for co-operation at local level by the school authorities. Colley was, however, much too optimistic about the prospects for collaboration in the short term.[171] Vocational school authorities and teachers were willing to contemplate various forms of co-operation, as the sharing of teachers and facilities would help them to provide the common Intermediate Certificate course in vocational schools from September 1966. The Irish Vocational Education Association (IVEA), which represented the interests of the VECs, broadly supported Colley's policy. The IVEA President, Canon John McCarthy, declared in June 1966 that the VECs endorsed many aspects of the government's approach, including the extension of the school leaving age and the establishment of technical colleges.[172] He pledged that the IVEA would respond constructively to Colley's proposals, as the VECs wished to co-operate fully with the upgrading of the post-primary educational system.[173] The VTA gave the most enthusiastic response to the Minister's approach. Charles McCarthy commented in January 1966 that Colley's initiative was 'extraordinarily significant'.[174] McCarthy fully endorsed co-operation between the secondary and vocational authorities at local level and urged the Minister to promote 'a partnership of institutions' between primary, secondary and vocational schools.[175]

But Colley's vision of an integrated post-primary system received a generally cautious response from established educational interests at secondary level. Secondary school managers who enjoyed considerable autonomy tended to be sceptical of the Minister's initiative.[176] The Standing Committee of the CCSS agreed on 18 February 1966 that the principle of co-operation was excellent but identified 'enormous difficulties to be cleared before what the Minister seems to envisage can be a reality'.[177] Likewise the Education Committee of the Teaching Brothers' Association (TBA), which represented the male teaching orders, welcomed Colley's initiative in principle on 29 January, but warned the Minister that the sharing of facilities at post-primary level involved grave managerial and administrative problems.[178] Colley's inclusive approach did not secure the acceptance by most managerial authorities of educational planning. The school authorities in many areas took a tentative approach to the initiation of the local meetings and Colley soon appointed inspectors of the department to convene the meetings.[179] The department faced considerable difficulties in achieving collaboration between secondary and vocational school authorities, not least the reservations of the Catholic Hierarchy, which maintained close connections with the Catholic managerial bodies.

The Standing Committee of the Hierarchy expressed disquiet at the implications of Colley's policy for post-primary education as early as 11 January 1966. The bishops were sceptical about the policy of collaboration, recommending that Catholic secondary schools should agree to co-operate with the Minister's request 'insofar as it was feasible'.[180] The Standing Committee advised each bishop to instruct the headmasters of the secondary schools in his diocese to initiate informal consultation with local vocational authorities concerning possible forms of co-operation. But the bishops emphasised that such consultation would involve no formal commitment by the secondary schools and should be undertaken primarily to forestall the intervention of the department in restructuring post-primary education: 'This consultation should take place before any Inspector of the Department arrived to take a hand in the matter.'[181] While the bishops did not object to some collaboration between secondary and vocational schools, they advised the Catholic school managers to co-operate with the Minister's policy only where they considered his approach to be feasible. Moreover the Hierarchy was alarmed by the prospect of extensive state intervention in the organisation of secondary education. The cautious approach recommended by the bishops to the Catholic managers underlined that the participation of the secondary school authorities in the process of consultation gave no guarantee of a constructive attitude on their part to educational planning.

The Protestant educational authorities took a very different approach to the proposed integration of post-primary education. The General Synod of the Church of Ireland decided to seek the reorganisation of secondary education well before Colley's appeal to the school authorities. The General Synod established in May 1962 an Advisory Committee on Secondary Education in the Republic of Ireland, chaired by Dr. R.G. Perdue, Bishop of Cork: Dr. Kenneth Milne, the secretary of the Church of Ireland Board of Education from February 1963, also served as secretary to the new Committee.[182] The Advisory Committee undertook a detailed analysis of

Protestant secondary schools in the Republic and made its report to the General Synod in May 1965.[183] The Committee recommended that educational standards could be maintained and improved only through the creation of fewer and larger schools. The report favoured the establishment of a smaller number of large schools for the Protestant community to provide for adequate facilities and staffing resources within the secondary schools. The Advisory Committee made a strong case for a root-and-branch reorganisation of Protestant secondary education: 'We therefore consider that there must be a substantial planned reduction in the number of schools.'[184] The General Synod in May 1965 accepted the basic principles of the report and adopted the Committee's proposal for the creation of a new group, composed of representatives of all the Protestant denominations, which would formulate a common policy for Protestant secondary education in the Republic.[185] The Secondary Education Committee (SEC), which was established in 1965, consisted of representatives of the Church of Ireland, the Presbyterian Church, the Methodist Church and the Religious Society of Friends. The SEC was authorised to develop a common approach for the reform of Protestant secondary education in the Republic and to undertake negotiations with the Minister and other authorities for the implementation of this policy.[186]

The new Committee's priorities complemented the policy objectives of the state. The SEC agreed that its most vital task was 'to secure that the best possible educational opportunity is available to every child'.[187] The Committee set out to impress upon the Protestant school authorities the necessity to plan effectively for the future in accordance with changing educational requirements and drew attention to the importance of co-operation between Protestant schools. The SEC's commitment to improved educational opportunity for Protestant pupils and its concern to achieve a radical reorganisation of Protestant secondary education dovetailed neatly with the state's policy. The SEC's approach was entirely consistent with Colley's appeal to the post-primary school authorities for effective collaboration to ensure the coherent planning of educational needs. The first report of the Committee to the General Synod in May 1966 explicitly acknowledged the common ground shared by the Minister and the SEC: 'We are in sympathy with the general thinking of the Minister for Education, Mr. George Colley, and his predecessor, Dr. Hillery, as regards the development of post-primary education.'[188] The SEC not only endorsed Colley's general approach but also aimed to encourage specific mergers and amalgamations by Protestant secondary schools in the short term.[189] The Protestant educational authorities took a proactive approach to educational reform, initiating the reorganisation of their secondary schools for the benefit of the Protestant community. The Protestant churches, especially the authorities of the Church of Ireland, made a definite commitment to the reorganisation of post-primary education in the Republic, even before the Department of Education itself.

The more numerous and influential Catholic educational authorities, however, showed little inclination to support a wide-ranging reform of post-primary education. The managers of the Catholic secondary schools were willing to participate in the meetings organised by the department, but often used the process as a forum to express their concerns about the Minister's policy. The TBA urged Colley on 20 February 1966 to adopt 'a go-slow policy' towards collaboration, warning that any attempt to proceed rapidly with the initiative would be counter-productive: 'Over hastiness, we fear, may only lead to greater confusion and dissatisfaction.'[190] The CCSS, the largest Catholic managerial body, feared that the department was seeking to undermine the autonomy of the private secondary schools.[191] The planning meetings, which were initiated following Colley's letter, generally proved unproductive as a result of practical and political problems that obstructed collaboration. Certainly practical difficulties, such as the distance between vocational and secondary schools in many areas, impeded the development of the pooling of resources proposed by the Minister.[192] But secondary school managers, who were accustomed to administrative freedom and autonomy from the state, were willing to use practical problems as a means of delaying any significant changes. Sr. Randles, who was familiar with the attitudes of the Catholic managerial bodies as a member of the CCSS, commented: 'There was an unspoken feeling that if it could be shown that the Minister's proposals were not feasible on practical grounds, the alarming prospect of great changes in the educational structures would recede.'[193] The ASTI was also suspicious of the state's policy, not least because the association was not initially given representation at the planning meetings. The ASTI convention on 13–14 April 1966 passed a resolution demanding that the association should 'guard zealously the rights of secondary teachers and of secondary education in general in view of the Minister's policy of integration'.[194] The association's leadership was mandated to oppose any arrangement which would compel a secondary teacher to teach in a different type of school. The ASTI delegates were concerned to protect secondary teachers against compulsory redeployment. But the ASTI Convention also pledged to oppose any arrangement sought by the department 'which might later be used to undermine the secondary teachers' independence of state control'.[195] The ASTI aimed to preserve an exclusive status for secondary teaching in relation to other segments of the teaching profession and to retain the autonomy from state control traditionally enjoyed by secondary schools. The ASTI later secured representation at the local planning meetings but remained hostile to the state's efforts to create an integrated system of post-primary education.[196] The ASTI shared the reluctance of the Catholic secondary school authorities to co-operate with the reshaping of post-primary education proposed by the Minister.

Colley's initiative therefore made little progress in the short term, due to real practical difficulties and to the reluctance of most established educational interests in the secondary system to promote the extensive collaboration sought by the department. Colley conceded to the Dáil on 16 February that co-operation between secondary and vocational schools was 'at a preliminary stage', noting that further local meetings would be necessary.[197] The achievement of the local collaboration sought by the Minister proved highly problematic. The managerial authorities were reluctant to make any definite decisions at the initial meetings on the pooling of educational resources.[198] Indeed when the ASTI sought information from the managerial bodies on the local meetings, the association was effectively told by the CHA that there was nothing to report. The CHA informed the ASTI officers in May 1966 that secondary school managers had engaged in consultation with vocational school representatives at local level, but that 'nothing positive has so far emerged'.[199] It was a revealing admission by the influential Catholic association that no tangible progress towards collaboration had been achieved. Senior officials of the department echoed this judgment. Seán O'Connor gave a bleak assessment of the situation to the Minister in May 1966, advising Colley that the initiative would fail unless the department acted immediately to finance collaborative efforts in areas where co-operation was attainable.[200] O'Connor was pessimistic about the prospects for the policy of integration in the short term, even if the department secured additional funding to support local initiatives: 'The difficulties were daunting and the advantages doubtful.'[201] The scepticism of the powerful Catholic managerial bodies and the Catholic Hierarchy presented a formidable challenge to Colley's initiative. The Catholic secondary school associations did not openly oppose the Minister's policy, but they were reluctant to collaborate with the integration of the educational system, which would curtail their traditional autonomy. The Minister's unprecedented initiative did not succeed in achieving a general pooling of resources between secondary and vocational schools. But his initiative made the integration of the divided systems of post-primary education a core element of the state's educational policy. The objective of collaboration would not be abandoned by his successors, although different methods would be necessary. While the practical results of his policy were very limited in the short term, Colley brought the integration of the secondary and vocational systems to the forefront of the government's agenda in education.

Colley was more successful in pursuing other strands of the policy to achieve an integrated system of post-primary education. He acted decisively to complete the revision of the junior cycle post-primary curriculum, which was designed to ensure the introduction of the common Intermediate Certificate course for all post-primary pupils in September 1966. While the department had drafted revised courses for the Intermediate Certificate examination by 1965, there had been minimal consultation with the managerial bodies and teaching unions on the new curriculum. Colley was determined to involve the educational interest groups fully in the process of curriculum reform. The department convened a preliminary meeting between the managerial bodies, the ASTI and departmental officials concerning the revised Intermediate Certificate in May 1965, shortly after Colley's appointment as Minister for Education.[202] A joint meeting between the department's officials and all the secondary educational associations was held on 3 June: the officials sought mainly to reassure the managers that the revised Intermediate Certificate would not adversely affect the secondary schools.[203] All the post-primary educational associations were invited to participate fully in the revision of the Intermediate Certificate course. The department informed the managerial authorities and the teaching associations on 24 September that a series of subject committees would be convened to discuss the proposed syllabuses for the common examination. Colley decided that each subject committee would include representatives of the secondary managerial bodies, the VECs, the ASTI and the VTA, as well as relevant inspectors of the department.[204] The introduction of subject committees including representatives of all the educational associations was a significant innovation, which facilitated the participation of the private stakeholders in the reform of the curriculum. The department established fourteen subject committees to finalise the revised courses, which included not only the traditional academic subjects for the Intermediate Certificate, but also practical courses such as manual training: civics was also included on the post-primary school programme for the first time.[205] The department ensured that the managerial bodies and teaching associations were involved in the development of a comprehensive curriculum for post-primary education.

The work of the subject committees began in December 1965 and was completed by May 1966, although the approval of some courses was delayed due to disagreement between officials and representatives of the associations on the course content. The department concluded the consultative process by arranging a general meeting with the school associations to agree the revised courses on 1 April 1966. Although the meeting did not resolve all the outstanding issues, most of the revised courses received general agreement by May.[206] The department, which was concerned to implement the revised programmes by September 1966, brushed aside any remaining reservations on the part of the school associations. The ASTI expressed its opposition to the format of the revised Higher Course in English on 24 June 1966, but the department dismissed the union's objections and brought the course into effect.[207] The Minister provided for extensive consultation with the post-primary school associations, but had no intention of abdicating the department's power to set the curriculum.

The department succeeded in establishing a broad-based junior cycle curriculum from September 1966. Ó Raifeartaigh issued Circular M27/66, which provided for the introduction of the revised Intermediate Certificate examination, to the school authorities in June 1966.[208] The Secretary announced that the scope and content of the courses at junior cycle had been revised, in the context of Hillery's policy announcement in May 1963, to establish a common public examination for all pupils undertaking post-primary education. The revised curriculum would come into effect in September 1966, opening the way for the implementation of the common examination in 1969. The department provided a revised list of no less than twenty-five possible examination subjects, which included all the academic subjects taught in secondary schools and vocational courses in woodwork, metalwork and mechanical drawing.[209] Civics was included for the first time as a compulsory subject in secondary schools, although it was not to be examined for the Intermediate Certificate.[210] The department outlined the new syllabuses for most subjects and established revised conditions for the common examination. Recognised pupils in all post-primary schools and approved 'secondary tops' of national schools were eligible to take the examination.[211] The pupils were required, in accordance with Colley's commitment to provide a minimum course of post-primary education for all, to follow the second-level programme set by the department for three years before undertaking the public exam. Circular M27/66 ushered in a common Intermediate Certificate examination and provided the basis for a comprehensive curriculum embracing all post-primary schools. The wide range of the revised courses undermined the previously rigid separation between the academic curriculum of the secondary schools and the practical approach of the vocational system. The revised Intermediate Certificate programme offered secondary and vocational schools an opportunity to provide a comprehensive curriculum for their pupils. The department under Colley secured the implementation of a wide-ranging reform of the junior cycle curriculum, which effectively promoted the government's objective of a comprehensive post-primary system.

Colley also took effective measures to establish the first group of comprehensive schools. The department initiated the construction of the first three comprehensive schools in 1965. The Minister secured an additional allocation of £90,000 for the new schools, as part of the supplementary Estimate approved by the Dáil in February 1966, because the construction process was proceeding more rapidly than the senior officials had initially anticipated.[212] The Minister, however, faced greater difficulties in establishing the new schools than he was willing to acknowledge publicly. The Catholic Hierarchy, which had reluctantly accepted the introduction of comprehensive education in 1964, raised renewed objections in 1966 concerning the management and ownership of the new schools. The Standing Committee of the Hierarchy expressed dissatisfaction on 11 January 1966 with a list of draft regulations issued by Colley for the management of the comprehensive schools.[213] The bishops were dissatisfied that the regulations provided for the appointment of the board of management by the Minister and made no provision for the appointment of trustees for the schools. The bishops had hoped that the department would allow clerical trustees to purchase the school sites so that the new schools would not be owned directly by the state. The Standing Committee also objected to the clause giving the board of management the power to appoint teachers, arguing that the bishops' nominee, as chair of the board, should have the right to appoint the teachers, subject to ministerial approval.[214] The Standing Committee instructed the three bishops concerned to withhold their acceptance of the regulations and postpone the nomination of a representative to the board of management of each school, until the Hierarchy secured a satisfactory clarification from the Minister.[215] The revival of the Hierarchy's reservations about the new schools was potentially a serious obstacle to the implementation of the initiative.

Colley acted to overcome the objections of the bishops by providing assurances on the management of the new schools. He confirmed that the local bishop would appoint the chair of the board of management for each comprehensive school. The regulations gave the bishop's nominee the right to veto any candidate for appointment as a teacher on grounds of faith and morals, although the Minister did not concede any additional powers to the clerical nominee over the appointment of teachers.[216] Colley, however, provided the bishops with a draft of the Form of Agreement, which would govern the relationship between the board and the teachers. He also proposed that the school premises should be vested in trustees appointed by the local bishop, although the role of the trustees would be essentially nominal, as they would have no other function than holding the premises. The bishops, at their general meeting on 21–22 June 1966, were 'reasonably satisfied' with the Minister's assurances concerning the management and staffing arrangements for the comprehensive schools.[217] The Hierarchy was still concerned about the nominal role of the trustees, as the department declined to allow clerical trustees to purchase the sites for the schools.[218] While the bishops' complaint about the position of the trustees was not fully resolved, the Hierarchy was satisfied enough with the Minister's assurances that no further obstacles were placed in the way of the new scheme. The first group of the new schools, including St. Aidan's Comprehensive school in Cootehill, Scoil Chuimsitheach Naomh Ciarán, Carraroe and St. Patrick's Comprehensive school in Shannon, opened their doors to pupils in September 1966.[219] While the facilities for the first comprehensive schools were not completed by 1966, the department proceeded with the opening of the new schools, aiming to complete the necessary building work by 1968.[220] Colley acted decisively to ensure that the comprehensive schools' pilot project was implemented. While Hillery made the initial policy announcement, Colley publicly identified the introduction of comprehensive education as an essential priority for the government and secured the funding for the scheme. The Minister also avoided a serious conflict with the Hierarchy, which would have delayed or perhaps even derailed the implementation of the scheme.

The establishment of the first three comprehensive schools in September 1966 saw the creation of a new hybrid element within the Irish educational system. The introduction of comprehensive education, which combined the academic and vocational streams, underlined that the traditional division between secondary and vocational education was being effectively undermined. The initiative led to the establishment of only a relatively small number of comprehensive schools: only fifteen comprehensive schools were established in the Republic by 1977 and the building of comprehensive schools gradually ceased with the emergence of community schools in the 1970s.[221] But the department under Colley's direction implemented the first tangible measures to erode the traditional barriers between secondary and vocational education. Moreover the establishment of comprehensive schools, even on a pilot basis, made direct intervention by the state in the provision of post-primary education a reality for the first time.

Colley enjoyed considerable success in converting the reforming ideals announced by his predecessor into reality. He was sometimes less successful in implementing innovative proposals of his own, not least because he was the Minister for Education for barely fifteen months. But Colley did not simply implement policy ideas inherited from Hillery or manage the government's reforming policies. O'Connor was essentially correct when he commented that Colley 'was determined to refashion second level education in its structures and in its content'.[222] He sought to apply the analysis of *Investment* to the expansion of the post-primary sector and proposed a radical reform of second-level education, which was designed to co-ordinate the use of available resources in secondary and vocational education. The Minister gave a central role to the Development Branch in planning the future expansion of second-level education. The adoption of long-term educational planning by the department under Colley brought extensive intervention by the state in directing educational expansion. While he did not achieve his most ambitious objectives, Colley certainly established coherent planning for educational needs as an integral part of the government's policy at post-primary level.

Higher education

Colley's commitment to long-term planning of educational needs did not produce any great change in the state's approach towards higher education. The formulation of a definitive policy for the development of higher education had been deferred by the government since 1960, pending the completion of the report of the Commission on Higher Education. The Commission continued its lengthy deliberations throughout Colley's term. The Minister was obliged to defend the slow pace of the Commission's work in the Dáil on 21 October 1965, in response to a critical query from Patrick O'Donnell. Colley assured the House that there was 'no avoidable delay' in the presentation of the report: the Commission was drafting its recommendations as quickly as possible and he expected that the report would be completed within six months.[223] Colley's optimism proved sadly misplaced. The Commission did not present its report to the government until February 1967, over seven months after Colley ceased to be Minister for Education. He made no attempt to clarify the state's approach to the development of higher education in the meantime, maintaining the position adopted by Hillery that the government was obliged to consider the report of the Commission before articulating a more definite policy.

The lack of a well-defined policy approach towards higher education did not prevent the allocation of substantial public funding to meet the urgent accommodation needs of the universities. The Minister secured additional capital investment by the state in higher education, at a time when the government was moving to restrict capital expenditure. The Cabinet on 3 December 1965 instructed ministers to achieve reductions in capital expenditure for 1965–66, which were required by the White Paper on Capital Expenditure. Moreover it was decided that expenditure on the Public Capital Programme for 1966–67 would have to remain within limits specified by the Cabinet, as recommended by the Department of Finance.[224] The concern of the Department of Finance to limit capital spending did not prevent the allocation of additional resources to the university building programmes. Colley gained the agreement of the government on 13 July 1965 for additional state investment in the building programme for UCC. The Cabinet approved a proposal drafted by the Department of Education, which provided for an increase from £900,000 to £1,143,000 in the estimated cost of the new science building for UCC.[225] Colley successfully made the case that the initial allocation for the new building should be increased to provide more extensive facilities for science teaching and research. The government's readiness to authorise further capital expenditure for higher education brought even greater benefits for UCD. The Minister submitted a proposal to the Cabinet on 27 August 1965, which recommended that the college authorities should be authorised to proceed with the construction of a new arts and administration block at Belfield, at an estimated cost of £2,500,000.[226] Colley obtained the approval of the Cabinet for the proposal in principle on 7 September 1965, on the basis that the UCD authorities would not be informed of the decision without the prior agreement of the Minister for Finance.[227] The UCD authorities were subsequently authorised to proceed with the new project, which was funded by the state.[228] The department under Colley enjoyed considerable success in securing additional capital funding for the universities, despite the concerns of the Minister for Finance to limit capital spending.

The government maintained the commitment, enunciated by the *Second Programme*, to provide the necessary funding to deal with the accommodation requirements of the universities.[229] Colley also announced in June 1965 the allocation of increased state funding to most universities and the Dublin Institute for Advanced Studies to provide mainly for the employment of additional staff.[230] The government fulfilled its specific commitment to assist the universities in overcoming pressing accommodation problems, but did not attempt to outline a more general policy for the development of higher education. The government's pragmatic approach and the failure of the Commission on Higher Education to report more promptly ensured that the state lacked any coherent policy for the long-term development of higher education for most of the decade. But the extensive capital funding provided by the state to support the expansion of higher education underlined the importance attached to educational expansion at all levels by the government under Lemass.

Developing special education

The department under Colley and his successor, Donogh O'Malley, also played a significant part in developing the state's policy for the expansion of special education, which had started to receive effective assistance from the government only in the early 1960s. The report of the Commission on Mental Handicap, which was completed in March 1965, exerted considerable influence on the state's approach to the education of disabled children.[231] Colley welcomed the Commission's report on 16 June 1965 and indicated that an inter-departmental committee, which included officials from the departments of Education and Health, was examining the implementation of its recommendations.[232] Colley's department soon accepted the Commission's recommendation that the education of pupils with a mild mental disability, who were generally unable to benefit from education in ordinary classes, should be entirely separate from facilities provided for pupils with a more serious intellectual disability. The senior officials also agreed with the Commission's view that the term 'mental handicap' should not be used in the official designation of special schools serving pupils with a mild mental disability.[233] The department sought to provide additional opportunities for the education of such pupils in accordance with the recommendations of the Commission, by giving official recognition and financial support to new special primary schools.[234] The additional educational facilities for such pupils were provided almost entirely through the establishment of special day schools.[235] New day schools for pupils with a mild mental disability were established with the assistance of voluntary committees in Castlebar, Navan and Kilkenny between 1966 and 1968.[236] The department under Colley and O'Malley achieved considerable success in developing improved facilities for pupils with a mental disability. The overall number of special schools for such pupils expanded rapidly from twelve in 1962 to thirty-two in 1967, with an increase in the total enrolment from 880 to 2,637.[237] The department made real progress in expanding the very limited educational opportunities available to pupils suffering from a mental disability, although its success was restricted to primary education, as most of these pupils left school at the age of fourteen. In 1968, T.A. Ó Cuilleanáin, the inspector of the Primary Branch who held responsibility for special education in the late 1960s, acknowledged in the department's own educational journal, *Oideas*, that: 'The initial steps have been taken to tackle this problem but a great deal remains to be done.'[238]

Ó Cuilleanáin's conclusion applied with even greater force to the state's efforts in other areas of special education. Educational facilities for children suffering from a severe physical disability were provided mainly by schools organised by the authorities in various hospitals and the department gave little consideration to extending such services in the 1960s. Ó Cuilleanáin commented in *Oideas* that the department was beginning to investigate the problem of providing a suitable education for such children by 1968.[239] But it is evident that the provision of improved educational opportunities for children with physical disabilities received little or no attention from the state for most of the decade. The department in the late 1960s gave greater attention to the development of special education for children with impaired hearing, although the progress made by the state in providing the necessary facilities was still very limited. O'Malley established a committee in May 1967 'to review the provision made for the education of deaf

3 Young artist Paddy Casserley enjoys doing some transcripts from the blackboard with his right foot, c. 1955. Courtesy of the National Library of Ireland.

and partially deaf children and to make recommendations'.[240] The final report of the committee, which was chaired by Ó Cuilleanáin, was completed only in February 1972.[241] The report contained a series of recommendations to the government, covering in a comprehensive fashion the problems of providing adequate educational services to children with impaired hearing. The committee emphasised the importance of early identification and assessment of children with impaired hearing. They advised that facilities should be provided to enable a high proportion of such children to be educated in ordinary national schools.[242] The committee also recommended the development and expansion of existing special educational facilities in Dublin and Cork, rather than the establishment of new residential schools at other centres, to provide for children whose hearing was severely impaired.[243] The committee provided a detailed blueprint for the expansion and reorganisation of educational services for children with impaired hearing. The report also underlined the limited progress made by the department in developing proper facilities for several forms of special education in the 1960s. Ó Cuilleanáin himself acknowledged in 1968 that while some progress had been made in improving educational facilities for deaf pupils, 'much more, however, remains to be done'.[244] This assessment by the department's senior expert on special provision for children with disabilities was a fair commentary on the state's efforts in the whole area of special education in the 1960s. The department under Colley and his successors established a firm commitment by the state to the expansion of special education and began to implement new initiatives to provide specialised facilities for children with various forms of disability. But the department was only beginning to address the task of delivering adequate educational services to disabled pupils. The problem of designing and implementing adequate programmes of special education remained a formidable challenge for the state in the 1970s.

Traveller education

If the department at least made a promising beginning in the development of special education, official efforts to provide for the education of Travellers showed little innovation and were seriously inadequate. The report of the Commission on Itinerancy, which was completed in 1963, emphasised the urgency of providing education for children of the nomadic community.[245] The department under successive ministers took the cautious position that education for Travellers could be provided only through ad hoc measures, which took full account of local circumstances.[246] Some piecemeal measures were taken within this framework to provide education for Travellers at primary level. A special school in Ballyfermot, Dublin, was established for Traveller children in the late 1960s.[247] The department was, however, reluctant to make special provision for Travellers on an ongoing basis.

The limitations of the department's approach to Traveller education were vividly illustrated in a report produced by a committee of officials in 1970, on 'the provision of facilities for the education of itinerants'.[248] The report was a mixture of well-intentioned piecemeal measures for Traveller education and conventional social thinking reflecting the low status of Travellers in Irish society. The committee asserted that the educational system should meet the 'special needs' of Traveller children but also adopted the objective of achieving 'the general integration of itinerants with the community'.[249] The official commitment to the 'integration' of Travellers within the settled community informed the department's limited and conventional approach to the development of educational facilities for Traveller families. The committee recommended that the children of Travellers should generally attend 'ordinary classes in ordinary schools', with the intention that 'they would proceed through school in a normal way'.[250] The department did not favour the establishment of more special schools for the children of Travellers living in housing or semi-permanent sites; instead the committee aimed to encourage the gradual integration of Traveller children into mainstream national schools.[251] The committee was willing to designate certain national schools to accommodate the children of nomadic travellers who followed a regular itinerary every year; the report held out the prospect that such national schools would receive additional support from the department, but emphasised that the number of these schools 'would have to be strictly limited'.[252] As for the education of Traveller families who travelled a wide circuit each year, the department decided that little could be done.

Moreover the committee concluded that 'there is no machinery at departmental level for initiating local schemes' and therefore the initiative in developing facilities for the education of Traveller children 'must come from local persons and bodies', such as school managers, teachers and voluntary associations.[253] This carefully worded disclaimer effectively rendered redundant the more constructive recommendations of the report and left the implementation even of the department's modest proposals to school managers or other voluntary groups. Having identified Traveller children as a category that required special provision at least in some circumstances, the department then backed away from meaningful initiatives to include them within the educational system. The state made very little progress by the early 1970s in providing education for Traveller children, not least due to official ambivalence over the need to undertake special educational initiatives for the nomadic community at all and to official reluctance to support in any way the distinctive culture of the Traveller community.

Implementing the *White Paper*: the Irish language

Colley's term of office brought no significant policy change in the state's approach to the revival of the Irish language, which was very much the concern of the government as a whole and not simply the Department of Education by 1965. The Minister pledged on 16 June 1965 to implement the government's decisions on the promotion of the Irish language in the schools, which had been outlined by the *White Paper on the Restoration of the Irish Language*.[254] Colley, who was fluent in Irish, shared with senior officials of the department a strong commitment to the revival of the language.[255] He emphasised to the Cork Branch of Tuairim on 19 November that the special position given to Irish as a subject in the schools was based on patriotic rather than utilitarian considerations: 'In fact its right to a place in an Irish school is the intrinsic one that it is not French, German, Italian or Spanish, but Irish.'[256] Colley believed that the schools should make an important contribution to the restoration of Irish and that the adoption of more effective teaching methods would allow them to play their part in achieving the national objective of language revival. The Minister was particularly concerned to improve the methods for teaching oral Irish and to promote Irish as a spoken language, in accordance with the government's policy.

The *White Paper* endorsed the recommendation made by the Commission on the Restoration of the Irish Language for a linguistic analysis of Irish as a spoken language, with the objective of devising a graded course of instruction in the language.[257] The linguistic research, which was conducted by Fr. Colmán Ó hUallacháin of the Franciscan order in collaboration with the department, was completed during Colley's term. The findings were published in June 1966, in the form of a report entitled *Buntús Gaeilge*.[258] Colley established committees, composed of departmental officials and teachers, to prepare graded courses for primary and post-primary schools on the basis of this research into spoken Irish. The effects of the new initiative were felt first at primary level. The department initiated experimental Irish language courses based on the new research in twelve national schools in 1965–66.[259] The courses were intended to apply the new methods of language teaching on a trial basis and to assist in the production of the graded courses in oral Irish. The Minister extended the pilot project for the following school year, introducing experimental courses based on *Buntús Gaeilge* in 150 primary schools in 1966–67: a separate experimental course designed for infants' classes was also introduced in fifty schools.[260] Colley sought to modify the state's approach to the language revival in the schools, by promoting Irish as a spoken language and developing new Irish language courses. The department under

Colley's direction initiated a process of experimentation in the teaching of oral Irish, which led before the end of the decade to the introduction in all primary schools of new Irish language courses based on *Buntús Gaeilge*.[261] But the Minister's commitment to the introduction of new methods of language teaching was coupled with firm support for the traditional national objective of restoring the Irish language. Colley initiated changes in the state's approach to the teaching of Irish as a means of giving renewed strength to the established policy of language revival. The Minister's approach reflected both his personal commitment to the revival of Irish and the overall policy of the government, as expressed in the *White Paper*. Colley undertook a limited and incremental reform of the traditional policy for the revival of Irish in the schools, which contrasted with Hillery's more sceptical approach to the state's attempt to revive the language through the educational system.

Lemass and educational expansion

The effective reforming approach pursued by the department under Colley, especially in dealing with the challenges of educational expansion at primary and post-primary level, owed much to the critical analysis of *Investment*. But Colley could hardly have initiated controversial educational reforms without the full support of the Taoiseach. Lemass's vigorous support for long-term educational planning and the importance that he attached to the expansion of the Irish educational system shaped the political context for the initiatives undertaken by Colley. The Taoiseach elaborated on the government's commitment to educational expansion in the course of a general policy statement, which he delivered to the Dáil on 7 July 1966. Lemass argued that the state had to compensate for its limited resources by 'the fullest and most economical use of the resources which are available'.[262] This would involve the concentration of available resources on the development of educational and technical training arrangements to utilise 'our main assets, the intelligence and adaptability of our people'.[263] The Taoiseach also noted that the commentary on *Investment* by the NIEC emphasised the need for a substantial increase in the financial allocation devoted to educational development.[264] This meant either the acceptance of further taxation to fund such development or giving priority to educational expansion in the allocation of public funds over other desirable objectives. As he considered that further tax increases would unduly restrict economic expansion, Lemass pledged that the government would give education 'the priority it deserves' in the future allocation of public funds.[265] He reiterated his consistent belief that the future economic development of the country would depend on enhancing the level of education and training secured by the Irish workforce. Lemass commented that: 'To an ever-increasing degree the policy of the Government will be directed to this end and we will have to endure the political criticisms which it may evoke from the unthinking as other desirable developments are necessarily slowed down to enable this essential educational programme to be fulfilled.'[266] The Taoiseach's statement firmly established that the government would give precedence to education in the allocation of public expenditure. Lemass's commitment to give priority to education in the allocation of scarce national resources reflected the importance attached to educational expansion by policy-makers in 1966; this marked a fundamental change from the state's traditional policy approach. It was to be Colley's successor, Donogh O'Malley, who benefited most from the Taoiseach's decision to give the highest priority to educational expansion.

Colley served as Minister for Education for barely fifteen months, from 21 April 1965 until 13 July 1966, but his relatively brief term left an enduring legacy in Irish education. The critical analysis of the Irish educational system provided by *Investment* shaped Colley's reforming approach. The amalgamation of small national schools brought about a radical reorganisation of primary education, which was based on the conclusions of the report. The Minister also developed more fully the state's policy for the expansion of post-primary education. Colley identified the achievement of equality of educational opportunity and the raising of the statutory school leaving age by 1970 as definite and urgent objectives. He sought to break down the traditional barriers between the divided systems of second-level education to facilitate the achievement of these key objectives. The Minister's attempt to establish a comprehensive post-primary system, on the basis of a pooling of resources between secondary and vocational schools, was one of the most ambitious initiatives undertaken by the state in education since 1922. The department had little success in achieving voluntary collaboration between the two systems, but the introduction of a common Intermediate Certificate examination was an important achievement. Colley adopted long-term planning of educational needs as an indispensable element of the government's policy for the development of second-level education. But the department's insistence on effective planning did not yet extend to higher education, where long-term policy decisions were deferred pending the completion of the report of the Commission on Higher Education. Colley also sought to promote the expansion of special education with mixed results. The Minister maintained the state's established policy on the Irish language, seeking to reinvigorate the language revival in the schools through the revision of teaching methods. Colley's reforming approach proved most successful when it was supported by the analysis of *Investment*; in policy areas where the influence of the pilot study was not apparent, such as special education or the universities, the state's approach was less clearly defined and less effective.

The pilot study paved the way for policy changes which ministers and officials had not previously contemplated. The department under Colley's direction acted decisively to launch radical reforms in primary and post-primary education, which were inspired largely by the analysis of *Investment*. Colley firmly established the central role of the state in the development and implementation of educational policy. The Taoiseach played a crucial part in sustaining the Minister's reforming approach. Lemass not merely endorsed significant policy changes but advised Colley on how to promote controversial initiatives. The Taoiseach also affirmed unequivocally that educational expansion would be given the highest priority in the allocation of available resources. The policy initiatives taken by Colley, with the active support of Lemass, greatly accelerated the process of educational reform and made the expansion of the educational system a key policy priority for the Irish state.

Notes

1 Interview with Dr. Patrick Hillery, 25 February 2002.
2 O'Connor, *A Troubled Sky*, p. 94.
3 Ibid.
4 Ó Buachalla, '*Investment in Education*', pp. 10–20.
5 NA D/T 96/6/355, S.12891E, Interview by Seán Lemass with *Open*, 29 January 1965.
6 *Dáil Debates*, vol. 216, col. 954, 16 June 1965.
7 NESC, *Educational Expenditure in Ireland*, no. 12 (Dublin, 1975), p. 38; see Apprendix 1, Tables 2 and 4, pp. 328–9.
8 *Dáil Debates*, vol. 216, col. 964, 16 June 1965.
9 Ibid.
10 Ibid., col. 978.
11 Ibid., col. 969.
12 Ibid.
13 Ibid., col. 970.
14 Ibid.
15 Ibid., col. 977.
16 O'Connor, *A Troubled Sky*, p. 95.
17 *Investment in Education, Part 1*, p. 387.
18 Ibid., pp. 252–4.
19 O'Sullivan, *Cultural Politics and Irish Education*, p. 140.
20 Interview with Professor Martin O'Donoghue, 10 January 2005.
21 *Investment in Education, Part 1*, p. 201.
22 Ibid., p. 391.

23 Ibid., p. 141.
24 Ibid., pp. 160–1.
25 NIEC, *Comments on Investment in Education* (Dublin, 1966), p. 12.
26 *Investment in Education, Part 1*, p. 12.
27 Ibid., p. 172
28 Ibid., p. 157; Appendix 2, Figure 2, p. 331.
29 *Investment in Education, Part 1*, p. 389.
30 Ibid., p. 392.
31 Ibid., pp. 228–9.
32 Ibid., p. 252.
33 Ibid., pp. 247–9.
34 Ibid., p. 242.
35 Ibid., pp. 262–3.
36 Ibid., p. 233.
37 Ibid., p. 264.
38 Ibid., p. 392.
39 Ibid.
40 O'Connor, *A Troubled Sky*, p. 120.
41 Ibid., p. 110.
42 *Investment in Education, Part 1*, p. 12.
43 Ibid., p. 353, *Second Programme, Part I*, p. 13.
44 NA D/T 97/6/437, S.17913, Lemass to G. Colley, Minister for Education, 27 November 1965.
45 Colley to Lemass, 30 November 1965.
46 NA D/T 97/6/437, *Press Release, Investment in Education: Irish-OECD Survey of Needs and Costs of Irish Education*, 23 December 1965, pp. 1–10.
47 *Dáil Debates*, vol. 216, col. 977–8, 16 June 1965.
48 Ibid., O'Connor, *A Troubled Sky*, p. 95.
49 *Dáil Debates*, vol. 217, col. 1960–8, 21 July 1965.
50 Ibid.
51 Ibid.
52 Ibid., col. 1968–9.
53 Ibid., col. 1969.
54 Ibid., col. 1970.
55 Ibid.
56 NA D/T 96/6/355, S.12891E, *Irish Press*, 13 September 1965.
57 Ibid.
58 Ibid.
59 Colley to Lemass, 24 September 1965.
60 Colley to Lemass, *Memorandum*, 24 September 1965, p. 1.
61 Ibid.
62 Ibid.
63 Lemass to Colley, 25 September 1965.
64 Ibid.
65 Colley to Lemass, 27 September 1965.

66 Ibid.

67 INTO, Annual Report, CEC 1965–66 (Dublin, 1966), pp. 25–7.

68 NA D/T 96/6/355, S.12891E, Colley to Lemass, 27 September 1965.

69 Ibid.

70 DDA AB8/B/XV/b/05, *McQuaid Papers*, Minutes, General Meeting of the Hierarchy, 12 October 1965, p. 3.

71 Ibid.

72 Ibid.

73 Fergus to Colley, 17 October 1965.

74 DDA AB8/B/XV/b/05, *McQuaid Papers, Report by Dr. D. Herlihy, Bishop of Ferns, Meeting of the Episcopal Commission on Primary Education with Mr. Colley, Minister for Education*, 10 January 1966, pp. 1–2.

75 Ibid.

76 Ibid.

77 Minutes, Standing Committee of the Hierarchy, 11 January 1966, p. 2.

78 Ibid.

79 Ibid.

80 Minutes, General Meeting of the Hierarchy, 21–22 June 1966, p. 7.

81 Ibid.

82 INTO, Annual Report, CEC 1965–66, pp. 20–1.

83 Ibid., p. 21.

84 Ibid., p. 24.

85 *Dáil Debates*, vol. 220, col. 1790, 17 February 1966.

86 INTO, Annual Report, CEC 1965–66, pp. 21–2.

87 Ibid.

88 Ibid.

89 Ibid.

90 *Official Programme of the 98ʰ Annual Congress of the INTO*, 12–15 April 1966, pp. 34–5.

91 Ibid.

92 INTO, Annual Report, CEC 1965–66, pp. 21–5.

93 NA D/T 96/6/355, S.12891E, *Speech by George Colley TD, Minister for Education, Rural Week, Ballinrobe*, 11 November 1965.

94 Ibid.

95 *Dáil Debates*, vol. 218, col. 433, 21 October 1965.

96 Ibid., col. 434.

97 Ibid., col. 436.

98 *Dáil Debates*, vol. 220, col. 1514, 15 February 1966.

99 NA D/T 96/6/355, S.12891E, *Irish Press*, 'Mr. Colley's Lecture', 7 February 1966.

100 Ibid.

101 *Irish Press*, 'School Closures Unconstitutional, says Dr. Browne', 7 February 1966.

102 Ibid.

103 Ibid.

104 Ibid.
105 Ibid.
106 Interview with Tony Ó Dálaigh, 3 May 2002.
107 *Irish Press*, 'No Further Comment - Dr. Browne', 8 February 1966.
108 NA D/T 96/6/355, S.12891E, *Irish Press*, 'Minister Replies to Bishop's Criticisms', 7 February 1966.
109 Ibid.
110 *Irish Press*, 'Mr. Colley on Galway Meeting', 8 February 1966.
111 Ibid.
112 Ibid.
113 *Irish Press*, 'Minister Replies to Bishop's Criticisms', 7 February 1966, 'Mr. Colley on Galway Meeting', 8 February 1966.
114 O'Connor, *A Troubled Sky*, p. 127.
115 NA D/T 96/6/355, S.12891E, *Irish Press*, 'No Further Comment – Dr. Browne', 8 February 1966.
116 *Irish Independent*, 'Clash at Galway', 7 February 1966.
117 Ibid.
118 UCDA, *Fianna Fáil Papers*, P.176/448, Minutes of the Parliamentary Party, 9 February 1966.
119 *Dáil Debates*, vol. 220, col. 1504, 15 February 1966.
120 Ibid., col. 1546–7.
121 Ibid., col. 1513.
122 Ibid., col. 1505–6.
123 Ibid., col. 1547.
124 *Dáil Debates*, vol. 220, col. 1711–21, 16 February 1966.
125 Ibid., col. 1729–31.
126 *Dáil Debates*, vol. 220, col. 1548–50, 15 February 1966.
127 Ibid.
128 Ibid.
129 *Dáil Debates*, vol. 220, col. 1749, 16 February 1966.
130 *Dáil Debates*, vol. 220, col. 1807, 17 February 1966.
131 Ibid., col. 1780–1.
132 Ibid., col. 1795–6.
133 Ibid., col. 1783–4.
134 Ibid., col. 1795.
135 NA DFA 2003/17/383, Talk by Tomás Ó Floinn, *Recent Developments in Education in Ireland*, June 1972.
136 Ibid., Coolahan, 'National schools 1960–1985', in Mulcahy and O'Sullivan, *Irish Educational Policy*, p. 42.
137 *Clonmel Nationalist and Munster Advertiser*, 'Intermediate Certificate for Vocational Pupils, Minister's Clonmel Announcement', 9 October 1965.
138 Ibid.
139 Ibid.
140 Ibid.

141 Ibid.
142 Ibid.
143 Ibid.
144 Minutes, Standing Committee, ASTI, 29 October 1965, p. 3.
145 Ibid.
146 O'Connor, *A Troubled Sky*, p. 95.
147 Ibid., p. 104.
148 NA D/T 96/6/356, S.12891F, *Address by George Colley TD, Minister for Education, on Changes in Irish Education to the Cork Branch of Tuairim*, 19 November 1965.
149 Ibid.
150 *Irish Press*, 'Discussion Needed on Education', 20 November 1965.
151 Ibid.
152 Ó Buachalla, *Education Policy*, pp. 277–83.
153 *Investment in Education, Part 1*, p. 392.
154 Ibid.
155 Letter by George Colley, Minister for Education, *To the Authorities of Secondary and Vocational Schools*, 4 January 1966, *Official Programme, 44ᵗʰ Annual Convention*, ASTI (Dublin, 1966), pp. 26–9.
156 Ibid.
157 Ibid.
158 Ibid.
159 Ibid.
160 NA D/T 17405 C/63, *Statement by Dr. P.J. Hillery T.D., Minister for Education, in relation to Post-Primary Education*, 20 May 1963, p. 7.
161 Colley, *To the Authorities of Secondary and Vocational Schools*, 4 January 1966, *Official Programme, 44ᵗʰ Annual Convention*, ASTI, pp. 26–9.
162 Ibid.
163 Ibid.
164 Ibid.
165 *Dáil Debates*, vol. 220, col. 1753–4, 16 February 1966.
166 Colley, *To the Authorities of Secondary and Vocational Schools*, 4 January 1966, *Official Programme, 44ᵗʰ Annual Convention*, ASTI, pp. 26–9.
167 Ibid.
168 Ibid.
169 Randles, *Post-Primary Education*, p. 96.
170 *Dáil Debates*, vol. 220, col. 1755, 16 February 1966.
171 O'Connor, *A Troubled Sky*, p. 129.
172 IVEA, *Congress Report 1966* (Dublin, 1966), pp. 28–36.
173 Ibid., pp. 31–2.
174 *Sunday Press*, 'Our Future in Education: the Role of Vocational Schools', 16 January 1966.
175 Ibid.
176 Randles, *Post-Primary Education*, p. 200.
177 Minutes, Standing Committee, CCSS, 18 February 1966.

178 Irish Christian Brothers' Archives, St. Mary's Province, Br. P.J. Walsh and Br. F.B. Donovan to Colley, 20 February 1966.

179 Randles, *Post-Primary Education*, p. 199.

180 DDA AB8/B/XV/b/05, *McQuaid Papers*, Minutes, Standing Committee of the Hierarchy, 11 January 1966, p. 1.

181 Ibid.

182 *Journal of the 31st General Synod of the Church of Ireland, 1962* (Dublin, 1962), pp. 119–20.

183 *Report of the Advisory Committee on Secondary Education in the Republic of Ireland, Journal of the 32nd General Synod of the Church of Ireland*, 2nd session, *1965* (Dublin, 1965), pp. 140–3.

184 Ibid., p. 143.

185 *Journal of General Synod, 1965*, lxxxiii.

186 *Journal of the 32nd General Synod of the Church of Ireland*, 3rd session, *1966* (Dublin, 1966), pp. 86–7.

187 *Report of the SEC, 1966, Journal of General Synod, 1966*, pp. 133–5.

188 Ibid., p. 135.

189 Ibid.

190 Irish Christian Brothers' Archives, St. Mary's Province, Br. Walsh and Br. Donovan to Colley, 20 February 1966.

191 Minutes, Central Executive Committee, CCSS, 6 October 1966.

192 Randles, *Post-Primary Education*, pp. 200–1.

193 Ibid.

194 *Official Programme, 45th Annual Convention*, ASTI (Dublin, 1967), p. 24.

195 Ibid.

196 Ibid., pp. 65–7.

197 *Dáil Debates*, vol. 220, col. 1755, 16 February 1966.

198 Randles, *Post-Primary Education*, pp. 200–1.

199 Minutes, Standing Committee, ASTI, 21 May 1966, p. 1.

200 O'Connor, *A Troubled Sky*, p. 129.

201 Ibid., p. 130.

202 Minutes, Standing Committee, ASTI, 15 May 1965, p. 1.

203 Minutes, Standing Committee, ASTI, 5 June 1965, p. 2.

204 Minutes, Standing Committee, ASTI, 2 October 1965, pp. 2–3.

205 Ibid.

206 Minutes, Standing Committee, ASTI, 7 May 1966, p. 4.

207 Minutes, Standing Committee, ASTI, 24 June 1966, p. 1.

208 Circular M27/66, Department of Education, June 1966.

209 Ibid., p. 1.

210 Circular M54/66, Department of Education, December 1966.

211 Circular M27/66, *Section B, Intermediate Certificate Examination*, Department of Education, June 1966, p. 1.

212 *Dáil Debates*, vol. 220, col. 1501–2, 15 February 1966.

213 DDA AB8/B/XV/b/05, *McQuaid Papers*, Minutes, Standing Committee of the Hierarchy, 11 January 1966, p. 1.

214	Ibid., *Observations on regulations for Comprehensive Schools*, January 1966.

215	Minutes, Standing Committee of the Hierarchy, 11 January 1966, p. 1.

216	Ibid., *Regulations for Comprehensive Schools*.

217	Minutes, General meeting of the Hierarchy, 21–22 June 1966, p. 7.

218	S. Ó Mathúna to H. Murphy, 24 April 1967.

219	NA D/T 98/6/144, S.12891F, *List of the Schools Providing Free Post-Primary Education for day pupils from September 1967*.

220	*Committee of Public Accounts, Appropriation Accounts 1966–67* (Dublin, 1968), pp. 117–18.

221	L. O'Flaherty, *Management and Control in Irish Education: The Post-Primary Experience* (Dublin, 1992), p. 40.

222	O'Connor, *A Troubled Sky*, p. 135.

223	*Dáil Debates*, vol. 218, col. 431–2, 21 October 1965.

224	NA 97/5/1, G.C.11/39, Cabinet Minutes, 3 December 1965, p. 2.

225	NA 97/5/1, G.C.11/14, Cabinet Minutes, 13 July 1965, p. 3.

226	NA 97/5/1, G.C.11/23, Cabinet Minutes, 7 September 1965, p. 2.

227	Ibid.

228	Interview with James Dukes, 28 April 2003.

229	*Second Programme, Part II*, p. 206.

230	*Dáil Debates*, vol. 216, col. 960, 16 June 1965.

231	*Report of the Commission on Mental Handicap* (Dublin, 1965).

232	*Dáil Debates*, vol. 216, col. 976–7, 16 June 1965.

233	*Report, Commission on Mental Handicap*, xv–xvi, T. A. Ó Cuilleanáin, 'Special education in Ireland', Oideas, no. 1 (Autumn 1968), pp. 5–17.

234	Ó Cuilleanáin, 'Special education in Ireland', pp. 5–17.

235	Ibid.

236	*Dáil Debates*, vol. 232, col. 462, 6 February 1968.

237	Ó Cuilleanáin, 'Special education in Ireland', p. 10.

238	Ibid., p. 13.

239	Ibid., p. 14.

240	NA D/T 2003/16/556, S.18579, Ref.113013, *Memorandum for the Government, Report of Committee on the Education of Children who are handicapped by impaired hearing*, 19 June 1972, p. 1.

241	Ibid., Hyland and Milne, *Irish Educational Documents 2*, pp. 473–6.

242	*Education of Children who are Handicapped by Impaired Hearing, Report of a Committee appointed by the Minister for Education* (Dublin, 1972), pp. 146–7.

243	Ibid., p. 148.

244	Ó Cuilleanáin, 'Special education in Ireland', p. 10.

245	*Report of the Commission on Itinerancy* (Dublin, 1963), p. 67.

246	A. Bhreathnach, *Becoming Conspicuous: Irish Travellers, Society and the State 1922–70* (Dublin, 2006), p. 122.

247	Ibid.; *Oideas, Committee Report: Educational Facilities for the Children of Itinerants*, no. 5 (Autumn 1970), p. 46.

248	*Oideas, Committee Report: Educational Facilities for the Children of Itinerants*, p. 44.

249 Ibid., pp. 44–5.
250 Ibid., p. 45.
251 Ibid., pp. 45–6.
252 Ibid., p. 47.
253 Ibid., p. 50.
254 *Dáil Debates*, vol. 216, col. 975, 16 June 1965.
255 Interview with Tony Ó Dálaigh, 3 May 2002, O'Connor, *A Troubled Sky*, p. 132.
256 NA D/T 96/6/356, S.12891F, Address by Colley, *Changes in Irish Education*, 19 November 1965, Ó Buachalla, *Education Policy*, p. 283.
257 *White Paper on the Restoration of the Irish Language*, p. 102, *Final Report, Commission on the Restoration of the Irish Language*, p. 417.
258 *Progress Report for the period ended 31 March 1966, for White Paper on the Restoration of the Irish Language* (Dublin, 1966), p. 24.
259 Ibid.
260 Ibid.
261 Hyland and Milne, *Irish Educational Documents* 2, pp. 534–5.
262 *Dáil Debates*, vol. 223, col. 2194, 7 July 1966.
263 Ibid.
264 NIEC, *Comments on Investment in Education*, p. 21.
265 *Dáil Debates*, vol. 223, col. 2194–5, 7 July 1966.
266 Ibid., col. 2195.

5

The politics of transformation: 1966–68

'A man deserves to be remembered for the positive things he did, and his single sweeping reform of second level education, more than any other of his actions, has made Donogh O'Malley a folk-hero.'[1] This assessment of Donogh O'Malley's career by one of the officials who worked most closely with him, Seán O'Connor, accurately illustrated the popular perception of O'Malley's impact as Minister for Education. O'Malley is best remembered for the introduction of the scheme for free post-primary education in September 1967. The initiative launched by O'Malley was widely regarded by scholars and contemporaries as the key development in the transformation of the Irish educational system; this view was shared by officials such as O'Connor and by some educationalists, especially Séamas Ó Buachalla. Ó Buachalla's verdict on O'Malley's career reflected this interpretation: 'His early death in 1968 cut short a political career which in a short period had transformed the system.'[2] The introduction of free post-primary education at O'Malley's instigation was a landmark of profound importance in the history of Irish education. But for all its undoubted importance, the initiative should not obscure the significant implications of other reforms implemented by the state in this period, not least other measures initiated by O'Malley himself. Similarly O'Malley's career was not a bolt of lightning illuminating the surrounding darkness, but a dramatic development of an ongoing process of transformation.

Following George Colley's appointment as Minister for Industry and Commerce in July 1966, Lemass maintained his consistent practice of appointing dynamic, ambitious members of Fianna Fáil's younger generation to head the Department of Education. Donogh O'Malley was appointed as Minister for Education on 13 July 1966. He owed his advancement to Lemass, who had appointed O'Malley as Parliamentary Secretary to the Minister for Finance in October 1961 and elevated him to the Cabinet as Minister for Health in April 1965. O'Malley displayed an interest in education, especially the development of higher education, as a backbench TD.[3] He also took a leading role, as Parliamentary Secretary to Jim Ryan, in promoting the use of prefabricated buildings to reduce the backlog in the national school building programme.[4] O'Malley was regarded by parliamentary colleagues and officials as a forceful, impetuous and unconventional figure.[5] O'Connor summarised the general reaction of the department's officials after O'Malley's appointment: 'From O'Malley, we expected fast and furious action.'[6] The new Minister did not disappoint the expectations of his officials.

O'Malley lost no time in outlining his priorities to the Taoiseach, in a letter addressed to Lemass on 29 July 1966, within a month of his appointment. The new Minister told Lemass that as he was going away on holiday he wished to inform the Taoiseach of his proposals for education and 'to refer in some detail to the major new educational services I propose to introduce, and to the existing services I wish extended'.[7] O'Malley emphasised firstly the importance of the new comprehensive schools. While the first three schools were ready for occupation by September 1966, the building programme was incomplete, as sufficient funding was not available: the provision of various facilities had been deferred. The Minister described this approach as 'an unacceptable procedure', which was undesirable, costly and inefficient.[8] He aimed to arrange for the rapid completion of the three new schools at Carraroe, Cootehill and Shannon and to proceed with the construction of a fourth comprehensive school at Glenties, Co. Donegal; he envisaged too the establishment of new comprehensive schools in other areas. O'Malley also warned of the need to develop vocational and technical education, as an essential means of sustaining the economic progress of the state.

O'Malley argued for the introduction of a variety of new services, including a national transport scheme for second-level pupils subsidised by the state, a school meals service at post-primary level and a scheme of grants for audio-visual teaching aids. He particularly emphasised the urgent need for a national scheme of school transport at primary and post-primary level. The Minister considered that a school transport service subsidised by the state at post-primary level should be introduced as soon as possible. He regarded such a national scheme as an essential reform in the context of the government's commitment to raise the school leaving age to fifteen by 1970 and its policy of providing three years of post-primary education for all children. O'Malley freely admitted that he had presented an extensive programme of new initiatives to Lemass in his first month as Minister for Education, but had no hesitation in demanding urgent action by the government to implement his plans: 'This is an imposing list of new and extended services but, in my short period as Minister for Education, it has become abundantly clear that we shall have to introduce them quickly if we want to make any progress in education.'[9]

The new Minister's letter indicated the wide-ranging – and expensive – character of his plans. He made no secret of his belief that it would be costly to develop education properly, but emphasised that adequate state support for education was vital to sustain economic expansion. He warned the Taoiseach that immediate and decisive action was required to overcome severe educational problems. 'If we do not now proceed as I suggest, a serious position, already apparent, will become more aggravated.'[10] The new Minister implicitly challenged the Taoiseach to support further substantial investment in education. The key priorities outlined by O'Malley on 29 July, especially the development of the comprehensive schools and the initiation of a public transport service at post-primary level, displayed considerable continuity with the policies of his immediate predecessors. O'Malley's letter to Lemass did not, however, reveal the full extent of his ambitions. O'Malley did not even mention the abolition of post-primary school fees as a possible objective, although he was undoubtedly contemplating the prospect of introducing free second-level education from the outset of his term. But the wide variety of the new or expanded services demanded by O'Malley underlined the new Minister's impatience with spending constraints and his determination to achieve rapid and far-reaching changes in the educational system. O'Malley's letter to the Taoiseach provided an early indication of his reforming zeal and his intention to implement a wide range of new educational initiatives as a matter of urgency.

Reforming primary education

Although primary education did not receive great attention in O'Malley's letter, the new Minister maintained and extended the reforms undertaken by his immediate predecessors, especially the amalgamation of the small national schools championed by Colley. The policy of amalgamation was firmly defended by O'Malley, who told the Dáil on 6 February 1968 that larger schools not only ensured a more rational use of teaching personnel but also delivered better education for primary school pupils.[11] The amalgamation of small schools in rural areas facilitated the department's efforts to reduce the pupil-teacher ratio in large urban schools. O'Malley announced in February 1968 that his department's approach was designed to achieve a maximum class size of thirty-five pupils in all national schools.[12] The department sought to improve the pupil-teacher ratio by making more effective use of the available teaching personnel through amalgamation and by increasing the supply of trained teachers. The target of a maximum of thirty-five pupils in each class proved elusive, but the department's approach delivered a gradual improvement in the pupil-teacher ratio.[13] The department amended the regulations on the appointment of teachers in July 1966 and February 1968, allowing national schools to appoint additional teachers on the basis of smaller enrolment figures.[14] The improvements were incremental rather than dramatic, but it was significant that the department's solution to the familiar challenge of high pupil-teacher ratios in urban schools was inextricably linked to the new policy of amalgamation and the resulting redistribution of the teaching force.

The amalgamation of small national schools was combined with a greater commitment by the state to the improvement of conditions in existing schools. The Minister's approach was heavily influenced by the INTO, which launched a campaign in 1967 to remedy the appalling conditions in many national schools. The INTO general secretary, Senator Seán Brosnahan, made a public statement in the Senate on 9 February 1967, drawing attention to the unsatisfactory level of maintenance in many national schools.[15] Brosnahan proceeded to inform the department, the Clerical Managers' Association and the Office of Public Works on 27 February 1967 that the union considered the conditions in many schools to be 'sub-standard and in some cases uncivilised'.[16] Brosnahan warned that the union would investigate any serious complaint about sub-standard conditions in national schools and would withdraw its members from such schools if any complaints were substantiated.[17] The INTO's case was not disputed by the Minister. O'Malley freely admitted in the Senate on 9 February that 'there are thousands of schools which can only be classified, I am sorry to admit, as hovels'.[18] He convened a meeting of all the relevant organisations to consider the conditions in national schools on 7 July: the conference was chaired by Seán MacGearailt, recently appointed as Deputy Secretary of the department, and attended by representatives of the INTO, the managers and the Office of Public Works.[19] Following this meeting MacGearailt issued a circular to the managers in September 1967, which outlined new guidelines for the maintenance of national schools. The Deputy Secretary instructed the school managers to seek three tenders for essential maintenance work and to initiate the process immediately, wherever the provision of heating and sanitary facilities was an urgent necessity. He confirmed that a state grant amounting to at least two-thirds of the cost of renovation work would be provided, while a higher grant was available if necessary.[20] The department's revised guidelines were designed to ensure that the managers fulfilled their responsibilities to undertake essential maintenance work in the schools.

The department's initiative certainly facilitated the improvement of conditions in the schools, but the INTO also played a key role in expediting the process as a result of a protest organised by the union early in 1968. The

INTO withdrew its members from five schools in Ardfert, Co. Kerry, between 16 January and 5 February 1968, until maintenance work to remedy defective facilities in the schools was completed.[21] The success of the INTO action, which generated considerable publicity, placed effective pressure on managers to expedite maintenance work in schools throughout the country.[22] The INTO exerted a considerable influence on the department's approach to the improved maintenance of national schools. O'Malley's intervention to expedite the necessary renovation of national schools was undertaken in the context of the INTO campaign and especially the union's threat of industrial action. The undoubted influence exerted by the INTO was due not only to the effective action initiated by the union's leadership, but also to the Minister's concern to maintain constructive relations with the organisation, which supported key elements of the government's policy, including amalgamation. The preservation of amicable relations with the INTO was important especially because the state was taking a much more proactive and interventionist approach in primary education in the late 1960s than at any time previously.

The department under O'Malley broke new ground in educational policy at primary level, promoting a range of reforming initiatives. The senior officials showed a new confidence in their ability to reform and reorganise primary education. The department took effective action to ensure the regular progression of pupils through the national school. *Investment* had illustrated the delayed progression of pupils at primary level: the report indicated that in 1963 30% of all national school pupils in the fifth class were delayed by one year, while 13.5% were delayed by two or more years. *Investment* also underlined that the percentage of 'delayed' pupils rose steadily with progression through the classes.[23] The department acted to break this traditional pattern in 1967. Ó Raifeartaigh issued a circular to the school authorities in March 1967 which established definite principles for the regular promotion of pupils in national schools. The circular stipulated that 'The normal procedure should be that a pupil is promoted to a higher standard at the end of each school year.'[24] The Secretary warned that pupils should be held back only on an exceptional basis – such cases should be 'minimal'.[25] Moreover pupils should not be held back for more than one year throughout their time in the national school. The circular gave a clear message that regular progression through the national school should be the norm. The department moved to ensure regular promotion of pupils without any consultation with the managers or school staff, who had previously determined the rate of progression. The initiative exerted a significant influence on the age of completion for primary education. The official circular, combined with the introduction of free education in most post-primary schools from September 1967, helped to establish twelve as the normal age for completing the national school course. There were 37,173 primary school pupils aged thirteen years or over in 1964, while only 6,091 pupils from this age group were in primary education in 1980.[26] The department's intervention was successful in promoting the transfer of national school pupils to second-level education at an earlier age.

The reforming approach of the department under O'Malley also brought significant changes in the state's policy towards examinations at primary level. The Minister's decision to abolish the Primary Certificate was perhaps the most obvious policy change in primary education. The INTO had consistently sought the removal of the Primary Certificate since it became compulsory in 1943, but their efforts had been frustrated by the opposition of most managerial associations, who supported the concept of an examination at primary level.[27] The officers of the INTO made a renewed appeal for the abolition of the Primary Certificate directly to O'Malley on 20 January 1967.[28] The union's representatives made their case to the Minister and Seán MacGearailt for the replacement of the examination with a system of record cards. Significantly O'Malley did not defend the Primary Certificate, but told the INTO representatives to outline their alternative. He commented that he could not act unilaterally to abolish the examination, but undertook to call a conference of all the interested parties to consider the case for abolition.[29] While the Minister avoided precipitate action to abolish the Certificate, he made no secret of his opposition to it. O'Malley told the Senate on 9 February 1967 that he wished to express 'utter disgust at this form of examination'.[30] O'Malley's public comments made clear that the Primary Certificate's days were numbered, although a viable alternative had yet to be devised.

The conference convened by O'Malley, which brought together representatives of the INTO, the Catholic and Protestant managers and the department itself, was held on 30 June 1967.[31] MacGearailt, who presided over the conference on the Minister's behalf, set out to secure an acceptable alternative to the examination. The Deputy Secretary's opening statement to the conference clarified the department's approach. He told the representatives that 'fundamental changes were taking place in Irish education' and these changes had to be taken into account at the primary stage.[32] MacGearailt noted that the government's policy of providing three years of second-level education for all children and the introduction of free post-primary education from September 1967 meant that formal education would no longer end at primary level: these policy changes called into question the need for a Primary Certificate. Moreover he argued that the limited written examination had tended to dominate educational practice in the national schools, narrowing the work of the senior classes. While MacGearailt emphasised that he sought only to initiate the discussion, his statement underlined that the officials were content to drop the Primary Certificate. The INTO delegation presented their proposed alternative, arguing for the replacement of the examination by a system of record cards for each pupil, which would be made available to post-primary schools. The union's representatives asserted that the examination was damaging in its effect on the work of the primary school and detrimental to the welfare of pupils who failed the examination. They also considered that the Certificate served no useful purpose, as post-primary education was being made available to all. The INTO delegation argued that the record card would provide an objective assessment of each pupil's aptitudes and abilities.[33] The managerial authorities were by no means fully reconciled to the abolition of the examination. Monsignor Martin Brenan of the Catholic Managers' Association warned that 'everything would not be rosy if the Primary Certificate were abolished here'.[34] Most managerial representatives agreed that the Primary Certificate was flawed but favoured some form of objective test at primary level. The Catholic managers sought a revised test conducted by an external authority, which was entirely unacceptable to the INTO.[35] MacGearailt instead proposed that an assessment of pupil attainment for the record card should be carried out by the teachers, subject to evaluation by the department's inspectors. This formula secured general support from the conference. The managerial representatives accepted the introduction of a system of record cards and internal tests, on the basis suggested by MacGearailt.[36] The Deputy Secretary, who had deftly guided the deliberations of the conference, was able to present an agreed solution for the abolition of the Primary Certificate to the Minister.

O'Malley submitted the revised arrangements for the assessment of primary school pupils to the government on 26 July 1967. The Minister's proposal, based on the conclusions of the conference, provided for the replacement of the Primary Certificate by a system of record cards for all pupils in the fifth and sixth classes.[37] The record card was intended to include the results of an intelligence test, to be undertaken by all pupils, as well as information concerning the achievements of pupils in each subject.[38] The attainment of the pupils would be assessed on the basis of tests carried out by the teachers, subject to evaluation by the inspectors: school reports would also be circulated to the parents of each pupil. The Minister's initiative was not controversial within the government. The Cabinet approved O'Malley's proposal for the abolition of the Primary Certificate on 12 September.[39] The replacement of the state examination by a system of record cards and internal school tests was a significant policy change. While the INTO's persistent lobbying for the abolition of the compulsory examination proved influential, it was O'Malley who took the

decision, which had been avoided by his predecessors, to replace the examination with an alternative form of assessment. The senior officials, who
no longer wished to defend the Primary Certificate, rapidly implemented
the policy change. MacGearailt played a crucial part in persuading the
managerial authorities to accept a viable alternative. The abolition of
the Primary Certificate was influenced by the expansion of second-level
education and by the planned introduction of the initiative for free post-
primary education.[40] The department recognised that the purpose of the
state examination was increasingly undermined, as it ceased to be a final
examination for most pupils. MacGearailt saw the abolition of the Primary
Certificate as a logical consequence of fundamental changes in post-
primary education. The policy of educational expansion encouraged a
radical reappraisal by the senior officials of the assessment of primary
school pupils.

The Minister and officials of his department did not have a comprehensive or fully worked out programme of reform for primary education, but
the various reforming initiatives undertaken under O'Malley and his two
predecessors transformed the state's policy approach at primary level.
Initial proposals for the reform of the national school curriculum were also
developed by officials in this period, although the revision of the national
programme would not come to fruition until the early 1970s. Coolahan
points out that while no overall plan for reform existed, the measures taken
by the state after about 1960 amounted to a far-reaching shift in policy
on primary education.[41] The significant changes in the state's policy
towards primary education, initiated by the department especially under
Colley and O'Malley, were heavily influenced by the government's commitment to deliver some post-primary education for all. The need to
encourage an orderly and regular transfer of pupils to second-level education shaped the context for the reforms in primary education. The reforming initiatives at primary level also underlined a key feature of O'Malley's
overall approach, which involved extensive ministerial intervention to
direct the transformation of the educational system.

Rationalisation and resistance

The Development Branch clarified and extended the policy of rationalisation at post-primary level following O'Malley's appointment. O'Malley
himself identified the development of new comprehensive schools as an
important priority in his letter to Lemass on 29 July 1966.[42] But despite
the new Minister's initial views, the department initiated the building of
only a limited number of comprehensive schools. The first three new
schools were fully completed by 1968. The department placed the contract

for the fourth comprehensive school in Glenties, Co. Donegal, during O'Malley's term and the new school was opened in 1968.[43] O'Malley also facilitated the creation of the first Protestant comprehensive school in East Donegal, which was based on the amalgamation of two Protestant schools in Raphoe and Lifford. The Minister agreed to finance the building of the new school, which was established at Raphoe in 1971.[44] The department sanctioned a distinctive management structure for the Protestant comprehensive schools, which allowed the church authorities to have three nominees on a board of five members.[45] The Protestant church authorities secured more favourable terms from the state for the management of the new schools than the Catholic bishops. The Minister was willing to agree favourable terms with the Protestant educational authorities mainly because their desire to provide comprehensive education was a welcome development for the department. O'Malley sanctioned the same managerial arrangements for the Jesuit order, which transformed an existing secondary school in Limerick into a comprehensive school by 1971. The Deed of Trust for Crescent Comprehensive school allowed the Provincial of the order to nominate three of the five members of the board of management.[46] O'Malley encouraged the initiative by the Jesuits, hoping that their participation would lend prestige to comprehensive education and help to make the new schools acceptable to parents.[47] But despite the willingness of the Protestant church authorities and the Jesuits to participate in comprehensive education, the state still confronted considerable difficulties in establishing comprehensive schools, which were underlined when O'Malley sought to extend comprehensive education in Dublin.

O'Malley's concern to establish comprehensive schools in the capital for the first time caused considerable tension between the Department of Education and Dr. McQuaid. McQuaid clashed with MacGearailt over the proposal, which was raised by the Deputy Secretary with the Archbishop in July 1967. McQuaid's secretary, Fr. Liam Martin, warned MacGearailt on 26 July that the Archbishop had already made ample provision for post-primary education in Ballymun, in consultation with religious orders and the City of Dublin VEC.[48] MacGearailt told McQuaid bluntly on 1 August that the Minister was determined to establish comprehensive schools to serve the new Ballymun development and did not expect the Archbishop to assess the educational needs of the area: 'He would have felt that it would be recognised that he had functions in the matter.'[49] McQuaid took grave exception to this pointed reminder that the Minister was responsible for educational policy, complaining directly to O'Malley that MacGearailt's comments were 'gravely erroneous' and seeking a meeting with the Minister to clarify his position.[50] O'Malley, however, maintained that comprehensive schools were required in Ballymun, sending McQuaid a memorandum on post-primary education in Dublin, which made a strong case for comprehensive education in the Ballymun area.[51] The dispute was resolved following a meeting between O'Malley and McQuaid on 5 October 1967, when the Archbishop claimed that MacGearailt had misrepresented his position. McQuaid was willing to accept comprehensive schools in Ballymun, provided that local religious orders played an important role in providing comprehensive education.[52] This pragmatic position was not fundamentally opposed to the Minister's approach and O'Malley was able to proceed with the project. The Minister announced on 20 December 1967 that two comprehensive schools would be established in Ballymun. He envisaged two single-sex schools each accommodating about 750 pupils, one for boys and the other for girls. The Minister's decision to proceed with single-sex schools was dictated mainly by the politics of Irish education. The Catholic bishops had previously objected to co-education in comprehensive schools as a general principle and any attempt to introduce co-education in Ballymun would certainly have inflamed the dispute between the Archbishop and the Minister. The two new comprehensive schools in Ballymun were established by 1970. But the creation of a network of comprehensive schools for the entire country was not a practical proposition due to financial and political constraints. The foundation of comprehensive schools not only was a substantial financial commitment but also required tortuous negotiations with the Catholic bishops, who continued to regard state post-primary schools with considerable suspicion and were firmly opposed to co-education.[53] MacGearailt told the Public Accounts Committee on 6 March 1969 that the department had initiated the establishment of only four new comprehensive schools after the implementation of the initial pilot project by 1968.[54] O'Malley soon accepted that the ambitious restructuring of the post-primary sector which he sought could not be achieved through the comprehensive schools. The department sought instead to secure the delivery of comprehensive education through a far-reaching rationalisation of post-primary schools.

Colley had aimed to promote extensive collaboration between the secondary schools and the vocational sector, with the intention of creating an integrated post-primary system. The new Development Branch played the central part in the implementation of the policy of integration at local level. The Development Branch undertook between 1966 and 1967 surveys of the educational facilities in every county, which were intended to provide the necessary statistical data to implement the state's new approach. The surveys gave detailed information on the number of pupils who required post-primary education in each area and on the extent of the local facilities available for secondary or vocational education.[55] The

Development Branch issued county reports on the basis of the surveys, making wide-ranging proposals for the reorganisation of post-primary education in each county. The planning work undertaken by the Branch was designed to ensure that facilities for comprehensive education were provided in every local area and that educational resources were used as economically as possible.[56] The officials acknowledged that comprehensive schools would be few in number, concluding that comprehensive education could only be achieved through a process of collaboration between existing schools.[57] The Development Branch outlined common general principles in each county report for the development of post-primary centres. These principles laid down that each post-primary centre should offer both academic and vocational subjects, so that all pupils would have the opportunity of choosing the subjects best suited to their aptitudes: most counties would have three or four post-primary centres.[58] The officials set out minimum requirements for such centres, which would serve either the junior or senior cycle. A junior centre would consist of about 150 pupils and would provide education to the Intermediate Certificate level: for the senior cycle, pupils would be transported to a major post-primary centre, providing accommodation for up to 400 pupils. The officials envisaged that areas which had a total school population of less than 150 pupils would be best served by providing transport for local pupils to post-primary centres. In the long term small schools that were not viable on this basis would be closed, although they might be retained in the short term.[59] The officials essentially sought to achieve the expansion and reorganisation of post-primary education on the basis of minimum school units for the junior and senior cycles. The officials emphasised that they were merely present-ing the results of the surveys and suggesting possible solutions for educa-tional problems, leaving the decisions to the school authorities.[60] But the Development Branch was in effect proposing a far-reaching rationalisation of the post-primary sector, which had the potential to transform the tradi-tional pattern of second-level education.

The county reports were considered at a series of local meetings through-out the country, which were initiated by the department in December 1966.[61] The secondary school authorities and representatives of the VECs were invited to the meetings, which were chaired by O'Connor or his col-league Seán Ó Mathúna, Principal Officer in the Development Branch. O'Malley also agreed to allow the ASTI and VTA to nominate representa-tives to the meetings.[62] The meetings were intended to secure agreement between the school authorities on the plans for the local co-ordination of educational resources, in accordance with the policy of rationalisation pursued by Colley and O'Malley. But it soon became obvious that collabo-ration would not be easily achieved. O'Connor, who was responsible for the organisation of the meetings as head of the Development Branch, described the first meeting he convened as a complete failure: 'Neither of the two sectors of the post-primary system wanted anything from the other sector and could not spare any part of its services for the other side.'[63] The Minister soon decided to publicise the process of consultation. He ensured that the meetings were open to the general public and the Development Branch gave notice of them in the local newspapers. This approach at least ensured that parents were able to participate in the consultative process. But the meetings largely failed to produce any positive results. O'Connor acknowledged that the Development Branch achieved minimal progress in promoting educational planning at a local level: 'though discussion was more open, the meetings achieved very little.'[64]

The local meetings proved unproductive largely because the department's rationalisation proposals were received with widespread suspicion, especially on the part of the Catholic managerial bodies and the secondary teachers. Fr. John Hughes, a prominent Catholic headmaster and manager, told McQuaid in January 1967 that it was 'not humanly possible' for the schools to implement both the reorganisation of post-primary education and the introduction of the scheme for free education: the Minister should be asked to choose which initiative he wished to implement in the short term.[65] The leadership of the CCSS was also seriously alarmed by the activity of the Development Branch, considering that its approach to collaboration was both unrealistic and dangerous. Sr. Jordana Roche, President of the CCSS, warned the Conference's Executive Committee on 6 October 1966 that the activism of the officials threatened to undermine the independence of voluntary secondary schools: 'What kind of system of education have we? Is it no longer private?'[66] The scepticism of the most powerful Catholic managerial bodies was fully matched by the hostility of the secondary teachers. The Central Executive Committee (CEC) of the ASTI insisted on 4 January 1967 that 'no existing secondary teacher be obliged to teach in other than a secondary school'.[67] The ASTI criticised the proposal for post-primary centres on the basis that the creation of two distinct types of school was undesirable and harmful to the junior cycle school. The union found common ground with the managerial authorities in their shared reservations about the policy of rationalisation.[68] An ASTI delegation discussed the policy with the Joint Managerial Body (JMB) on 30 May 1967 and the school managers undertook to protect the interests of the lay secondary teachers.[69] The ASTI and the managerial authorities developed a joint approach to the process of rationalisation. The managerial bodies assisted the association in establishing contact with county committees of secondary school heads in each area, while the ASTI asked all its representatives at the planning meetings to co-operate fully with local managerial committees.[70] The co-ordination between the managerial representatives and the ASTI was based on their common suspicion of the department's agenda and their shared opposition to a radical reshaping of secondary education.

The suspicious response of the secondary school associations was influenced by the rapid transformation of the department's approach to educational policy. The confident and proactive style adopted by the Development Branch in promoting the reorganisation of post-primary education contrasted sharply with the low profile and tentative practice of the department for the previous generation. The department's willingness to promote new policy ideas in a public setting was unexpected and often unwelcome to the secondary school authorities and teachers. Charles McCarthy considered that the relatively sudden transformation in the department's approach also inspired scepticism: 'if a tiger changing its spots is never very credible, neither is a central bureaucracy coming down from heaven and asking advice'.[71] The entrenched divisions between the different systems of second-level education and the considerable suspicion of the department's approach on the part of most secondary school associations presented formidable obstacles to the creation of an integrated post-primary system.

4 Class in Christian Brothers School, Synge St., 1941. Courtesy of the National Library of Ireland.

The rationalisation of post-primary education sought by the Minister and senior officials made only limited progress between 1966 and 1968. But the proactive reforming agenda adopted by the Development Branch was in itself a significant advance, which underlined the extent of the change from the department's previous tentative and conservative practice in post-primary education. The new Branch's proactive approach underlined its considerable potential as a force for reform in second-level education. The reluctance of established educational interests to collaborate with the department's plans curtailed the prospects for a far-reaching restructuring of post-primary education. But O'Malley himself did not give the process of rationalisation the same emphasis as his predecessor George Colley. O'Malley's key priority in the second-level sector was not rationalisation but the introduction of free post-primary education.

'A dark stain on the national conscience'

The new Minister raised the possibility of introducing a scheme of free education at post-primary level with Seán O'Connor shortly after his appointment in July 1966. The Assistant Secretary advised O'Malley that it would be best to wait until 1970 to begin the introduction of such a scheme in accordance with plans for raising the school leaving age, which were under consideration by the department.[72] The introduction of free post-primary education was being considered by the department well before O'Malley's appointment as Minister for Education. The confidential report of the internal departmental committee headed by Duggan had recommended in December 1962 a period of free and compulsory post-primary education for all children aged between twelve and fifteen.[73] Moreover *Investment in Education* had illuminated the severe social disparities in educational participation at post-primary level, identifying a 'very marked association' between social group and participation in full-time education, which grew more evident as pupils progressed to higher levels.[74] The conclusions of the survey team underlined the extent of the inequalities in the educational system and reinforced the case for a far-reaching reform of second-level education. The government's policy of raising the compulsory school leaving age to fifteen by 1970 also provided a compelling rationale for free post-primary education at least for junior cycle pupils. The senior officials of the department intended to combine the raising of the school leaving age in 1970 with the introduction of free education for all pupils in compulsory attendance at post-primary schools.[75] This approach was intended to give time for the development of greater collaboration between secondary and vocational schools, which was essential to facilitate a comprehensive curriculum. Certain officials, including O'Connor, believed that the delay until 1970 was also necessary to enable vocational education to fulfil its potential following the recent removal of the restrictions that had prevented vocational schools from pursuing the Intermediate and Leaving Certificate courses. As the vocational schools were preparing pupils for the Intermediate Certificate only from September 1966, the officials considered that the vocational sector would require some years to adapt successfully to the new arrangements.[76] O'Malley inherited an established policy approach, which implicitly involved the introduction of free post-primary education in some form by 1970. O'Malley's initiative to introduce a scheme of free education did not mean a sudden and complete break with the past, but in many respects marked the culmination of a gradual transformation of the state's policy since 1959.

The new Minister was, however, entirely responsible for the scope and timing of the initiative. O'Malley rejected the time frame favoured by the officials. Despite the advice given by the senior officials to wait until the raising of the school leaving age before taking any action, the Minister soon made clear his intention to introduce a scheme of free post-primary education as soon as possible. He requested the Development Branch to prepare a scheme, which was drafted in its original form by O'Connor and two other officials, Seán Ó Mathúna and William Hyland, the senior statistician of the Branch.[77] The officials produced two possible options for free education, Scheme A and Scheme B. Scheme A provided for free education up to the Intermediate Certificate level for all pupils in vocational and comprehensive schools, as well as all day pupils in secondary schools which charged an annual fee of no more than £20.[78] This option envisaged that financial assistance from the state at Leaving Certificate level should be means-tested and confined to pupils whose families enjoyed incomes under £12 a week.[79] Scheme B was a more wide-ranging proposal, which offered fee relief up to the Leaving Certificate level without any means test. The second option provided for free education up to the Leaving Certificate for all pupils in secondary schools charging fees of no more than £20 in 1965–66, as well as the abolition of vocational and comprehensive school fees.[80] O'Malley rejected the inclusion of a means test for access to free post-primary education and decided to proceed on the basis of Scheme B, which offered the prospect of free tuition for most pupils up to the end of second-level education.[81] As it was very much an outline of the basic elements required by a potential scheme, rather than a detailed proposal, many of the ideas contained in Scheme B were later amended, but the Minister adopted the key features of the outline. O'Malley's exclusion of any means test for free post-primary education at an early stage underlined his crucial role in determining the scope and cost of the proposed scheme.

The Minister was well aware that he faced a formidable challenge in securing the government's agreement for such a radical and costly reform. He first sought to win Lemass' support for the initiative, proposing the introduction of free post-primary education at a meeting with the Taoiseach on 7 September 1966.[82] He addressed a letter to Lemass, marked 'Personal – By Hand', immediately in advance of the meeting, enclosing a memorandum 'in connection with an approach to free education'.[83] O'Malley told Lemass that he hoped, in a forthcoming speech, 'to make a general reference – without going into details – to some of the matters referred to in this Memorandum, should you so approve'.[84] The Minister warned Lemass that Fine Gael was about to launch its plan for education: 'They are evidently panicking at the fact that in their publication *The Just Society*, they have no proposals whatsoever on education.'[85] He emphasised the importance of pre-empting the largest opposition party with a policy announcement by the government. The memorandum presented by O'Malley made a strong case for the introduction of free post-primary education. He relied heavily on the analysis of *Investment* to support his argument, drawing attention to the social disparities in educational participation revealed by the pilot study. The memorandum noted the report's conclusion that 17,459 pupils, 31% of national school leavers in 1962–63, dropped out of full-time education on leaving the national schools.[86] The study also underlined that a relatively high proportion of pupils who entered post-primary schools left full-time education early without securing any post-primary certificate. The early drop-out rate was particularly high in vocational schools, as about 7,000 pupils left annually without undertaking the Day Group Certificate. This drop-out rate was regarded by the survey team as 'strikingly high' for a two-year course with an entry cohort of 16,000.[87] The rate of early school leaving in secondary schools was also considerable, as approximately 6,500 pupils, out of a total cohort of 25,000, dropped out of secondary education without undertaking the Intermediate Certificate examination. The report identified the substantial drop-out rate at junior cycle level as a key area in which improvement in participation could be achieved.[88] The analysis of *Investment* provided a firm foundation for the Minister's case, underlining that over half of the cohort aged between thirteen and sixteen in the early 1960s dropped out of full-time education without receiving any post-primary qualification.

The Minister argued that the high drop-out rate at post-primary level and the social disparities in participation were explained largely by the inability of parents to pay school fees and other educational costs. O'Malley made the case to Lemass that the presence of tuition fees was often 'the decisive influence' in the decision of many parents to withdraw their children from full-time education at the age of 14 or 15.[89] He emphasised the need to overcome the financial barriers to participation on social and economic grounds. He drew attention to the apparent social inequalities within the existing educational system: 'It must be acknowledged that the picture presented above discloses a state of serious social injustice.'[90] O'Malley did not neglect the economic implications of the substantial drop-out rate, commenting that the situation also entailed 'a serious drawback to the country's economic progress'.[91] The Minister deliberately linked the achievement of equality of educational opportunity with the economic imperative to secure an adequate supply of well-qualified school leavers, who could provide the necessary expertise and skills to sustain economic progress. O'Malley's case for free post-primary education was clearly influenced by the analysis of *Investment*, although the report did not recommend the introduction of free second-level education.

While O'Malley categorically rejected a means test for secondary school pupils, he was much less definite about the details of his own proposals. The Minister's memorandum outlined the two options formulated by the officials, Scheme A and Scheme B.[92] The options submitted by O'Malley to Lemass on 7 September did not amount to a definitive proposal for free post-primary education. The schemes were marked 'Preliminary' by the department and contained only an outline of the necessary elements which would be required to deliver free education: indeed Scheme B, which was the option favoured by O'Malley, consisted only of a single-page summary of the department's ideas.[93] Moreover any costings or assessments of student numbers given by the preliminary schemes were approximate and not necessarily reliable. O'Connor warned the Minister that the officials 'would simply have to guess the number of additional students that might be attracted by free education'.[94] O'Malley certainly made a persuasive case to the Taoiseach for the early abolition of post-primary school fees, but as the department's planning for the initiative was still at an early stage, he did not present a definite scheme for free second-level education to Lemass. The Minister's proposal left many details of the proposed scheme unclear and indicated no definite timescale for its introduction. Lemass' immediate response to O'Malley's approach was not recorded, perhaps because any formal response was overtaken by events. But the Minister's determination to secure the implementation of his initiative had the most profound repercussions for Irish education.

O'Malley chose with deliberation the timing and circumstances for the most sensational policy announcement of his term and arguably of the decade. He made his first major speech since his appointment as Minister for Education at a weekend seminar of the National Union of Journalists (NUJ), in Dún Laoghaire on Saturday, 10 September 1966.[95] The timing of his speech and the fact that it was made to an audience of journalists guaranteed extensive media coverage of any significant policy statement by O'Malley, especially in the print media in both the Sunday and Monday editions. O'Malley was clearly concerned to communicate his message effectively to the media: he told his audience that he was pleased to be making his maiden speech as Minister before a body composed mainly of journalists. He drew attention to Lemass' public statement in July 1966 that education was to receive priority in the allocation of scarce financial resources, seeking to place his own announcement within the context of the government's policy.[96] O'Malley identified the inability of lower-income families to keep their children in education, due to financial and social barriers to participation, as the fundamental flaw of the educational system. He emphasised that the inequalities in educational participation had a severe impact on the economic and cultural development of the state: 'I think it is one of the great tragedies of our history since independence that we have not found the means to check this terrible loss to the national potential for economic and cultural advancement.'[97] He pointed out that approximately 17,000 primary school pupils left school without receiving any post-primary education and were permanently relegated to an inferior economic and social status: 'This is a dark stain on the national conscience. For it means that some one-third of our people have been condemned – the great majority through no fault of their own – to be part-educated unskilled labour, always the weaker who go to the wall of unemployment or emigration.'[98] The new Minister passionately condemned the inequalities entrenched in the post-primary educational system. His solution was sweeping and dramatic: 'I am glad to be able to announce that I am drawing up a scheme under which, in future, no boy or girl in this State will be deprived of full educational opportunity – from primary to university level – by reason of the fact that the parents cannot afford to pay for it.'[99]

This sweeping commitment to full educational opportunity for all was a dramatic advance in the state's approach to education, which on its own would have commanded favourable headlines. O'Malley, however, proceeded to make a definite commitment to the introduction of free post-primary education from the beginning of the next school year. The Minister announced that he would introduce a scheme, beginning from September 1967, which would make the opportunity for free post-primary education available to all families up to the end of the Intermediate Certificate course.[100] He aimed to abolish tuition fees in most post-primary schools, arguing that even modest school fees were beyond the means of many parents. The proposed scheme would include all the vocational and comprehensive schools, while it would be available 'in the general run of secondary schools'.[101] The high-fee secondary schools were not expected to adopt the scheme and parents would still be free to send their children to high-fee schools.

O'Malley proceeded to outline other key elements of his plan to guarantee 'full educational opportunity' for all children.[102] He promised to ensure that no pupil would be prevented by lack of means from reaching the end of the Leaving Certificate course. The Minister also announced that the state would provide financial aid towards the cost of school books to students who experienced hardship in attempting to meet such costs.[103] He indicated too that consideration would be given to the introduction of financial assistance for pupils who could receive post-primary education only by attending a boarding school. O'Malley was marginally more circumspect in his comments on higher education, because the Commission on Higher Education had not completed its report. He disclaimed any intention to cut across the recommendations of the Commission but announced that the state would act to assist able pupils who were unable to proceed to higher education due to their financial circumstances.[104] The Minister's proposals were outlined only in general terms, as the department had not yet completed the formulation of the necessary schemes. O'Malley told the NUJ that he hoped to give the Dáil the full details of the proposals sometime before Christmas. But while O'Malley presented his proposals in a general fashion, his commitment to the achievement of a radical advance in educational participation at post-primary level was definite and unequivocal. O'Malley's policy announcement clearly set out a wide-ranging programme of reform for post-primary education, which gave the state a central role in the transformation of the educational system. The statement implicitly rejected any piecemeal effort to reduce social inequalities in educational participation and proposed a comprehensive reform seeking to deal with all the various elements that contributed to the high drop-out rate from post-primary education. The Minister made a firm commitment that the state would intervene decisively to overcome traditional barriers to educational participation, from the primary schools to the universities.

O'Malley sought to reinforce the case for a far-reaching reform of second-level education, by emphasising the importance of free education in providing a supply of well-qualified school leavers for the developing economy. He argued that the need to secure an increased supply of 'better-educated young people' to sustain economic progress made the introduction of free education at post-primary level even more urgent.[105] The consensus among leading politicians and officials that investment in education contributed significantly to economic development certainly formed part of the context for O'Malley's initiative. The Minister aimed to place his initiative firmly within this political consensus and to portray free education as an economic imperative, as well as a social advance. But this skilful portrayal of his policy by O'Malley did not mean that the early introduction of free post-primary education was in any sense part of a national consensus in September 1966. O'Malley himself told the NUJ seminar that it would take some time to implement 'such a revolutionary change in our approach to the provision of education for our people'.[106] O'Malley's definite commitment to the introduction of free post-primary education from September 1967 certainly marked a significant change in the state's policy for educational expansion. O'Malley made the rapid achievement of free second-level education a central objective of the department, which had previously been preoccupied with the gradual development and reform of post-primary education to facilitate the raising of the school leaving age. The announcement did not mark a fundamental reappraisal of the state's policy objectives. The raising of the school leaving age and ensuring three years of post-primary education for all were already key objectives of the government, while Lemass had sought to encourage the reform and expansion of the educational sector long before O'Malley's appointment. But the means employed by the state to achieve these objectives faced radical change as a result of O'Malley's initiative. The department under his immediate predecessors sought to facilitate educational expansion in a measured way through detailed planning of educational needs and the establishment of an integrated post-primary system. O'Malley's policy announcement held out the prospect of a much more rapid expansion of post-primary education, underpinned by the early availability of free education in the secondary and vocational schools. His dramatic announcement set out publicly a fixed timescale for the introduction of free education. The Minister's initiative made free post-primary education a likely prospect in the short term, rather than a possible option for the future. It was in this sense that O'Malley's announcement marked a dramatic new departure in the state's policy.

O'Malley arranged the timing of his policy announcement to secure the maximum effect, not least in terms of favourable publicity by the media.[107] The impact of the announcement certainly did not disappoint him: his speech was widely portrayed by the media as a sensational advance. The initiative was the subject of leading articles in the *Sunday Press* and *Sunday Independent* on 11 September.[108] Likewise the announcement received coverage in leading stories in all three major daily newspapers on 12 September.[109] The *Irish Press* welcomed the Minister's approach with great enthusiasm in an editorial on 12 September. The editorial argued that O'Malley's announcement was 'a vote of confidence by the Government in the people who instructed them to govern and more particularly in the unproven children of those people'.[110] The *Irish Press* emphasised that investment in education was an investment in the potential of the Irish people, while educational expansion was an inescapable necessity to fulfil the national demand for skilled manpower. The editorial concluded that O'Malley's initiative would help to lift poorer children out of 'the serfdom of ignorance'.[111] The ringing endorsement of the initiative by the *Irish Press* was hardly surprising. But the *Irish Times* also firmly supported O'Malley's initiative. The newspaper's editorial of the same date noted that scepticism might well be regarded as a legitimate reaction to O'Malley's announcement, due to the startling content of his statement and the lack of detailed information about the proposals.[112] But the *Irish Times* considered that the initiative should be welcomed and concerns about its potential cost should be balanced by an appreciation of the value of education: 'The scheme will cost us dear, but a sense of proportion will remind us that if we can pay £15 a head subsidy for a heifer or a calf, we can afford to think in generous terms for the education of a child.'[113] The Minister's initiative received a more cautious response from the *Irish Independent*, although its editorial noted that O'Malley had effectively caught the attention of the country. The editorial expressed some scepticism about his purpose in announcing a future policy without providing details concerning his plans. But the *Irish Independent* also recognised that O'Malley had initiated a new departure in Irish education, acknowledging the important implications of his statement and the favourable public reaction generated by the announcement.[114] O'Malley's well-calculated manoeuvre produced an avalanche of generally favourable publicity for his initiative in the national press.

O'Malley also achieved the short-term political objective which he had outlined to Lemass on 7 September – namely to seize the political initiative on education and to outflank Fine Gael, which was preparing to launch its policy on educational reform. Fine Gael's reaction to the announcement was tentative and uncertain. Mark Clinton, Fine Gael TD for Dublin South-West, unwisely attacked O'Malley's statement as an opportunistic manoeuvre, which the government would never implement: it was 'a long-term shot delivered for political reasons'.[115] The leader of Fine Gael, Liam Cosgrave, was more cautious, declining to make any comment on the initiative until he had studied the plans more closely and discussed it with his parliamentary colleagues.[116] The Labour Party made a more definite response, giving a qualified endorsement of the Minister's approach. Brendan Corish, the Party leader, commented that he would be 'very pleased' if the Minister succeeded in implementing his initiative, as it was consistent with the Labour Party's policy.[117] Corish, however, also expressed scepticism about O'Malley's ability to secure the necessary funding for the initiative. The doubts expressed by representatives of the two main opposition parties about the initiative itself or the government's willingness to provide resources for it certainly appeared reasonable in September 1966. But the scepticism of the opposition merely increased the pressure on the government to deliver additional resources to implement O'Malley's initiative, by underlining the political cost to Fianna Fáil if the scheme did not materialise. Moreover O'Malley's policy announcement was designed to appeal strongly to a substantial section of the population, who were likely to benefit from the implementation of his plans. The Education Correspondent of the *Irish Times* on 12 September noted the favourable impact made by the Minister's statement on public opinion and provided a perceptive analysis of O'Malley's tactics: 'With this public opinion behind him, Mr. O'Malley evidently is confident that he has set a ball rolling which will be difficult to halt, whatever opposition it encounters.'[118]

The Minister succeeded in securing a generally favourable response to his initiative from the national media and effectively outmanoeuvred the opposition parties. It is equally evident that O'Malley acted deliberately to pre-empt critical consideration by the government of his proposals. O'Malley's initiative was publicly announced without any consultation with the Department of Finance or the government as a whole: indeed Jack Lynch, the Minister for Finance, was attending a conference in Athens and knew nothing at all about O'Malley's intentions.[119] T.K. Whitaker responded furiously to the announcement, complaining directly to Lemass on 12 September about O'Malley's disregard for official procedures: 'It is astonishing that a major change in educational policy should be announced by the Minister for Education at a weekend seminar of the National Union of Journalists.'[120] Whitaker pointed out that as the new policy had not been examined by the Department of Finance or the government, it 'should have received no advance publicity, particularly of the specific and definite type involved in Mr. O'Malley's statement'.[121] The Secretary commented scathingly that O'Malley should have had all the more reason for caution since he had recently left the Department of Health 'gravely insolvent'.[122] The Minister had also acted without the approval of the Taoiseach, although O'Malley subsequently claimed to have secured Lemass' support for his initiative at the meeting on 7 September.[123] This contention is highly implausible. The Minister had presented only preliminary options, not a specific and definitive proposal for approval, to the Taoiseach on 7 September. Moreover O'Malley's announcement that the state would introduce a wide-ranging scheme of free education within a single year was a definite commitment with a specific time frame, which had certainly not been presented to the Taoiseach in the Minister's original outline. Lemass was willing to consider the introduction of some form of free education at post-primary level and may well have allowed O'Malley to float the possibility of a scheme publicly. But the Taoiseach certainly did not give O'Malley a blank cheque to introduce free post-primary education within a single year.

Lemass issued a rebuke to O'Malley on 12 September, bluntly warning the Minister that his announcement did not constitute a policy commitment by the government to any scheme advanced by O'Malley. The Minister's plans would have to be considered by the government in accordance with normal procedures and would be subjected to 'meticulous examination' by the Department of Finance.[124] Lemass pointedly observed that 'if other Ministers, in respect of their own work, were to seek to commit the Government, by making speeches about their intentions in advance of Government approval of their plans, everything would become chaotic'.[125] Lemass' warning did not deter O'Malley, who replied on 14 September, forcefully defending his initiative and assuring the Taoiseach that he intended to submit detailed proposals to the government. The Minister argued that it would have been 'disastrous' if Fine Gael had been allowed to take the initiative on education.[126] O'Malley also commented on the 'unprecedented' favourable response by the public to his initiative, making the plausible claim that there was widespread support for the proposals. The Minister even suggested that he was simply following Lemass' own practice in proposing new policies which caught the imagination of the public and mobilised popular demand for new initiatives. He claimed that the policy announcement was made on the basis of his discussion with Lemass on 7 September and sought the Taoiseach's support in getting the proposals approved by the government: 'If I was under a misapprehension in believing that I had your support for my announcement, I must apologise. I would hope, however, that what I have said will persuade you that I was right in making it and that you will give me your full support in getting my plans approved by the Government.'[127]

O'Malley's steadfast defence of his policy approach underlined the Minister's determination to secure the government's approval for the initiative. Lemass was, however, also receiving alarmed representations from the Minister for Finance about the cost of the proposals. Lynch raised O'Malley's announcement with Lemass on 21 September, expressing his 'grave concern' about the financial implications of the proposed scheme.[128] The Taoiseach addressed another warning letter to O'Malley on the following day, conveying Lynch's serious reservations about the initiative. Lemass told O'Malley to develop his ideas in detail without delay and submit his proposals for consideration by the government, 'before any further public statement is made about them'.[129] Lemass was not opposed to the proposal for free post-primary education, but was concerned at the potential cost of the initiative and aimed to ensure that any new scheme was phased in by the state on a gradual basis, to avoid an excessive burden on the Exchequer in a single year.[130] The Taoiseach was also wary of the Minister's penchant for short-circuiting normal government procedures and aimed to ensure that O'Malley adhered closely to the usual Cabinet procedures in future.

O'Malley submitted the first detailed proposals for free education prepared by his department to the government on 14 October 1966.[131] The Minister proposed an ambitious scheme for free post-primary education. The first key element of the memorandum proposed 'to make free tuition in post-primary schools available to all'.[132] The plan envisaged the payment of a special state grant of £30 for each day pupil to secondary schools that agreed to make free education available to all pupils. The state would provide free education for all full-time students in vocational schools, while the fees in comprehensive schools would also be abolished. The Minister proposed free post-primary education for most day pupils up to the end of the Leaving Certificate course. The proposals included a scheme of financial assistance to poor children for the purchase of school books. O'Malley also sought the introduction of a scheme of state grants to enable pupils from low-income families to proceed to higher education.[133] The department estimated that the cost of the proposals would amount to over £3 million annually. The Minister sought approval for the introduction of the new schemes by the beginning of the next school year.[134] O'Malley's proposals were breathtakingly ambitious, justifying the worst fears of the Department of Finance. The irrepressible Minister requested the government to approve the proposals as a matter of urgency before 21 October 1966. He attached an urgency certificate to the memorandum which stipulated that 'the Minister requires decision before the television debate on Education scheduled for Friday 21 Deireadh Fomhair'.[135] But the Department of Finance was firmly opposed to various aspects of the proposals and Lynch was expected to oppose the memorandum at the Cabinet meeting.[136] There was no prospect of achieving a favourable decision from the government in such a restricted time frame.

Lemass intervened to guarantee a more measured consideration of O'Malley's plans by the government. The Taoiseach told officials of his department to hold the memorandum without circulating it to the Cabinet. He then wrote to O'Malley on 17 October, telling him that it would be unreasonable to expect the government to consider his proposals without following the full Cabinet procedure, including a detailed assessment of the scheme by the Department of Finance: it was also 'very improbable' that other ministers would readily agree to the proposals, which involved additional expenditure of £3 million on education in 1967–68.[137] Lemass advised O'Malley that 'You should therefore consider what it may be possible to achieve in the next few years in the post-primary education sphere at a lower cost.'[138] Lemass' intervention ensured that the Cabinet's decision on the initiative was postponed until November. The Taoiseach acted to block O'Malley's attempt to secure approval of a far-reaching and controversial reform, within a week of its submission to the government. But Lemass' intervention ultimately proved beneficial to O'Malley. The postponement of the government's deliberations gave the Department of Education time to formulate a more acceptable and comprehensive plan for free post-primary education.

The officials of the department used their time well. The revised plan maintained the principal features of O'Malley's previous proposals, but scaled back the more ambitious elements of the initiative, producing more conservative costings. The proposal for the free tuition scheme on this occasion set the more modest target of 'making free tuition available in certain post-primary schools'.[139] The revised plan did, however, firmly maintain the principle that there should be no means test for free education. The officials proposed a special state grant in lieu of fees to secondary schools in certain fee ranges, on condition that they would cease to charge school fees. The scheme involved the payment of a supplemental grant, which would vary between a minimum of £15 and a maximum of £25 to accommodate different fee ranges, for each day pupil attending secondary schools that adopted free education. The state would act to abolish fees in vocational schools, secondary tops and comprehensive schools, as outlined in the original plan.[140] The introduction of a differential in the rate of the grant to secondary schools was a significant modification of O'Malley's initial proposal. The department considered that the proposed scheme would deliver free education for approximately 75% of the day pupils in secondary schools.[141] The plan also envisaged a state grant to cover a portion of the boarding school fee, up to a maximum limit of £25, for all pupils who were unable to attend day schools due to the location of their homes. The revised proposals made special provision for Protestant secondary education. O'Malley proposed a separate scheme for Protestant secondary schools, with the intention of delivering the same level of state support that would be available to Catholic students.[142] Despite the special provision for Protestant secondary schools, the estimated cost of the free tuition scheme came to about £1,442,000 annually, showing a reduction of over £1 million from the original proposal.[143] While this estimate later proved entirely inadequate, the department had succeeded in crafting a free tuition scheme which appeared more limited and reasonable than O'Malley's initial proposal.

The Minister's plan emphasised that free tuition was not enough to secure greater participation in post-primary education by low-income social groups. O'Malley favoured the introduction of financial assistance towards the cost of books for low-income families, as defined by the Health Acts.[144] He proposed that the state should provide free books to low-income pupils: the scheme for free books was to be limited to 25% of all pupils receiving free education, but the Minister would be able to allocate a higher proportion of grants to schools with a high percentage of low-income pupils. The department also proposed the introduction of a maintenance allowance of £40 per annum for 'very poor pupils' who continued in full-time education after the compulsory school leaving age: this allowance would benefit the children of families receiving social welfare or other means-tested assistance from the state.[145] The plan also made special provision for low-income pupils who could secure post-primary education only by attending boarding schools: it was suggested that the state should pay the full boarding school fee up to a maximum of £100 for such pupils.[146] These elements of the initiative underlined O'Malley's concern to increase educational participation from low-income social categories and to expand overall participation beyond the compulsory school leaving age.

The revised proposals submitted by O'Malley reaffirmed the need for a scheme of higher education grants. The proposed scheme provided for assistance to students who attained a high standard in the Leaving Certificate but lacked the financial support to proceed to higher education. The department guaranteed full assistance for a family with one child, earning less than £1,200 per annum, while the income threshold would be adjusted upwards with reference to the number of children in the family.[147] The Minister aimed to discontinue the existing schemes of post-primary and university scholarships and divert the funding made available to meet the cost of the new scheme.

The final key element in the revised proposals and the most significant addition to the original plan was a nation-wide scheme for school transport, to be subsidised by the state. O'Malley recognised that the plan for free post-primary education was incomplete unless it provided for general access to school transport. The introduction of free education would not take effect fully without a national transport scheme, as greater participation at post-primary level in rural areas required the alleviation of the heavy transport costs faced by parents.[148] The departmental submission emphasised that the rationalisation of post-primary education could not be implemented in the absence of a viable transport service: the policy of refusing to sanction small post-primary schools would be 'impossible to maintain' unless transport was provided to larger centres.[149] The submission also made the case that a national transport scheme was essential to achieve equality of educational opportunity: 'The underlying factor behind the proposal to establish a State supported transport scheme is to remove inequalities based on geographical location.'[150] The free transport scheme was designed to overcome the severe regional disparities in educational participation, which had been identified by *Investment*.[151] The scheme provided that the state would pay the full cost of transport for pupils living more than three miles from a post-primary school, on the basis that a free transport service would be initiated in any area with a minimum of seven eligible children.[152] The prevalence of the geographical inequalities identified by *Investment* established a compelling rationale for state aid for school transport. Moreover the government's policy of rationalisation demanded a transport scheme subsidised by the state. It was virtually impossible for the government to oppose a nation-wide public transport scheme, although the idea of free transport for all was not so easily accepted.

The revised proposals were circulated to the government on 11 November 1966, the day after Lemass' retirement as Taoiseach. The latest proposals formed a comprehensive and viable blueprint for the introduction of free post-primary education. The core principles of O'Malley's initial submission in October were maintained and even extended, but the revised plan made a much more detailed and plausible case for free education. The officials significantly modified the proposed free tuition scheme to reduce the estimated costs, especially in the first year of its operation. The estimated cost of the overall proposals remained high, amounting to £3,002,000 on an annual basis.[153] But the revised plan provided for the gradual implementation of the free tuition and free transport schemes, so that the total cost in the first year came to just over £1,000,000.[154] The department crafted a more workable and cautious plan for free second-level education, which enjoyed a greater prospect of acceptance by the government than the original submission. Lemass' intervention, which compelled O'Malley to defer the initial proposals, worked in his favour by ensuring the development of a more viable and politically acceptable plan for free education. The initiative presented by O'Malley to the Cabinet in November 1966 was, however, still remarkably ambitious: he was proposing a radical reform of the existing system of second-level education. The initiative involved not a single scheme for free tuition, but several interdependent elements, which were designed to provide free post-primary education and expand significantly the level of participation by low-income social groups in second-level and higher education. The radical implications of the proposals were not lost on the Department of Finance, which firmly opposed key elements of the initiative.

Following Jack Lynch's election as Taoiseach on 10 November 1966, the new Minister for Finance, Charles Haughey, submitted a memorandum to the government on 17 November, which raised a series of objections to O'Malley's proposals.[155] The submission, which reflected the concerns of the senior officials of the Department of Finance, correctly pointed out that the net direct cost of about £3,000,000 annually was by no means a complete estimate of the expenditure required by the plan. The increased student numbers generated by the initiative would lead to further expenditure to provide additional accommodation and teachers.[156] The Department of Finance's submission initially urged the government to defer the proposals indefinitely, advising against the acceptance of an initiative involving such extensive financial commitments: 'The Minister for Finance must ask the Government to view very critically proposals which will add so substantially to public expenditure.'[157] But Haughey recognised that the Cabinet was going to approve some initiative based on O'Malley's plan. The Minister for Finance therefore proposed a series of amendments if the initiative was to be approved in some form.

The Department of Finance's submission gave a critical commentary on the initiative as a whole and was particularly dismissive of the free tuition scheme: 'To describe this scheme as "free" is misleading. The scheme really means that many parents at present paying moderate school fees voluntarily will have to pay an equal or greater amount compulsorily in the form of additional taxation.'[158] The Department of Finance argued that free education should be restricted to the junior cycle level and introduced even at this level only on a phased basis: the separate scheme for Protestant schools should be deferred indefinitely.[159] The department considered that while the transport scheme was acceptable in principle, school transport should not be entirely free for all: a state transport scheme should be undertaken only on the basis of a local contribution of at least half of the cost in each case.[160] The submission acknowledged the need to provide free books for low-income pupils, but objected to the proposed maintenance allowance to 'very poor' children. The Department of Finance was also firmly opposed to the scheme for financial assistance to university students.[161] Finally the submission requested that if the government approved the proposals, its approval should be given only subject to the modifications demanded by the Department of Finance: O'Malley should be allowed to implement the plan only on a phased basis with the prior agreement of the Minister for Finance to each element of the initiative.[162] The Department of Finance presented a series of specific objections to O'Malley's proposals, which would have nullified or at least greatly restricted the effect of the initiative. While Haughey acknowledged that the government might wish to approve the proposals, his department's submission was designed to obstruct or delay the implementation of key elements of the initiative. O'Malley's proposals would have been mutilated beyond recognition if the government had accepted all of the Department of Finance's amendments.

As O'Malley had no intention of accepting such a drastic revision of his proposals, Lynch was obliged to adjudicate the conflict between O'Malley and the Department of Finance in his first month as Taoiseach. Officials of the Department of Education considered that O'Malley, who had enjoyed a friendly working relationship with Lemass, was less sure of himself in dealing with the new Taoiseach.[163] O'Malley had sidelined Lynch in making his policy announcement on free education and Lynch had complained to Lemass about the cost of the initiative. But the new Taoiseach, who had previously served as Minister for Education, did not depart from Lemass' approach of giving priority to education in the allocation of national resources. While Lynch shared Lemass' caution about the scope and timing of O'Malley's proposals, he showed no inclination to obstruct the introduction of free post-primary education. The political circumstances favoured O'Malley's initiative. The Minister's policy announcement had created a public and media expectation that free education would be introduced. A withdrawal from O'Malley's dramatic statement was fraught with political danger for the government. It was even more difficult for a newly elected Taoiseach, who faced early by-elections in December 1966, to withdraw from the definite statement of intent made by O'Malley. Moreover the launch of Fine Gael's policy document on education in November 1966 underlined the political case for an ambitious initiative by the government. The Fine Gael document, which was composed mainly by Senator Garret FitzGerald, proposed a complex scheme which would allow most secondary schools to offer free education at least to a minimum proportion of their pupils.[164] Fine Gael proposed that the state should offer a substantial increase in the capitation grants per student in secondary schools that agreed to offer free education: all pupils would receive free education in schools where the increased capitation grant exceeded the income previously derived from fees. High-fee schools, where the increased grant would not fully cover the income received from fees, would offer a proportion of free places under this plan, amounting to at least one-third of all places in a day school.[165] The plan was perhaps too complex and technical to win popular support and was in any event overshadowed by O'Malley's initiative. The launch of Fine Gael's policy made the swift approval of O'Malley's proposals even more likely. O'Connor considered that 'the issue of the Fine Gael policy document silenced any opposition to the proposals within the Government'.[166] Fine Gael's initiative certainly reinforced the political imperative for the government to finalise a wide-ranging plan of its own for free second-level education. Fianna Fáil could not allow the largest opposition party to seize the initiative on education policy, especially on the eve of two by-elections. The launch of Fine Gael's policy strengthened O'Malley's hand, in his efforts to secure the government's approval for his initiative.

The Cabinet considered the proposals on 29 November 1966, devoting a full meeting to the discussion on the Minister's initiative.[167] The Cabinet approved the proposed free tuition scheme up to the Leaving Certificate: the level of the special grant paid by the state per pupil in secondary schools would be fixed by agreement between the ministers for Education and Finance. O'Malley succeeded in preventing a fundamental revision of the scheme, securing the government's agreement that the differential in the special grant for each day pupil would vary from £15 to £25.[168] The Cabinet agreed that special consideration should be given to pupils who could only secure post-primary education through attendance at boarding schools as they lived in remote areas outside the range of a school transport scheme. The principle of a remoteness grant for such pupils, who lived mainly on islands off the coast, was approved and a maintenance grant of £50 per pupil was introduced in 1967, with an exceptional allocation of £95 for poor pupils attending boarding schools.[169] The government fully endorsed the nation-wide free transport scheme, which was to be introduced on a gradual basis from 1 April 1967. The proposed scheme for the supply of free books to pupils from low-income families was also approved, although the terms of the scheme were to be settled between O'Malley and Haughey.[170] Most of the specific amendments sought by the Department of Finance in their counter-memo were ignored or rejected by the Cabinet. Lynch's government accepted most core elements of the plan for free post-primary education, although the Cabinet also sought to ensure that the initiative would be introduced on a phased basis to spread the costs over a number of years.

O'Malley did not, however, secure unqualified support for his radical initiative. Certain elements of the Minister's plan were deferred or sidelined by the government, at the instigation of the Department of Finance. The Cabinet deferred the proposal for a maintenance allowance to subsidise 'very poor' pupils, which was designed to encourage the children of low-income families to remain in full-time education.[171] It was agreed that the terms of the allowance were to be settled through further consultation between O'Malley and Haughey; but in fact the proposal was never implemented.[172] The Cabinet also decided not to proceed in the short term with the proposal for state aid to third-level students: it was agreed that the government's decision should make no reference to Part C of the proposals, which related to higher education.[173] This decision marked a delay rather than a permanent setback for O'Malley's plans. He secured Haughey's agreement to a scheme of higher education grants early in 1968 following protracted negotiations between their departments. The scheme, which was submitted to the government on 20 February 1968, was means-tested and based on a relatively high standard of attainment. The minimum standard for the award of assistance was four Honours in university matriculation subjects at the Leaving Certificate, with a requirement for 70% in one of these subjects.[174] The proposal required all local authorities to provide for the grants annually an equivalent amount to their existing allocation for university scholarships: the additional funding required to meet the cost of the scheme would be provided directly by the state.[175] Despite the opposition of the Department of Local Government, the Cabinet authorised O'Malley on 27 February 1968 to draft a Bill introducing higher education grants. The Local Authorities (Higher Education Grants) Bill was approved by the Cabinet on 2 April 1968, less than a month after O'Malley's sudden death.[176] His successor, Brian Lenihan, piloted the Bill through the Dáil and the legislation came into effect for the beginning of the next college year in 1968–69. The new legislation initially benefited only first year students and was ultimately intended to assist only about 14% of the total cohort receiving higher education. But the initiative was a significant advance on the haphazard collection of local authority scholarship schemes which it replaced. The new scheme offered grants to about 800 students annually, compared to the previous allocation of only 275 university scholarships.[177] The scheme marked the first serious attempt by the state to reduce the traditional barriers restricting access to higher education for low-income students. The legislation delivered a restructuring and extension of the limited provision for state assistance at university level, although the extent of the improvement was restricted by financial constraints.

Despite its limitations the plan for free post-primary education was undeniably a landmark reform in Irish education. Certainly the proposals approved by the Cabinet were less obviously ambitious than the initial plan submitted by O'Malley in October. But various financial conditions built into the revised plan as a result of pressure from the Department of Finance, especially the variation in the grant to secondary schools, proved temporary due to representations by influential educational authorities for increased state funding of secondary education. While the cautious safeguards secured by the Department of Finance proved transitory, the government's decision to approve proposals for free second-level education marked an irrevocable policy commitment. The government adopted for the first time a definite and far-reaching plan to increase educational participation by low-income social groups. The initiative was a decisive intervention by the state to transform educational participation at the post-primary level. O'Malley's dramatic announcement on 10 September 1966 and the Cabinet's decision to honour his unauthorised initiative marked a firm policy commitment by the state to the democratisation of the post-primary educational system.

The Minister lost no time in publicising the proposals agreed by the government, outlining the main elements of the initiative to the Dáil on 30 November 1966, the day after the Cabinet's decision.[178] He anticipated that the scheme would make free second-level education available to about 75% of day pupils in Catholic schools. O'Malley did not attempt to mini-mise the cost or scale of his proposals, telling the Dáil that he was not placing 'any Utopian scheme' before the House.[179] He openly acknowl-edged that his initiative would require additional expenditure to provide increased accommodation and more teachers at post-primary level. The Minister assured the Dáil that the scheme of free post-primary education would be delivered in a responsible way. Indeed O'Malley commented that the educational advances envisaged by his proposals would have to be financed through additional taxation, which would fall on the wealthy: 'Every worthwhile development in the social and economic advancement of any nation calls for some sacrifice on the part of those best able to bear it – that is what we will be asking our people to accept in the implementa-tion of these proposals.'[180]

Conflict and consensus: church–state negotiation

The successful implementation of O'Malley's initiative required the collabo-ration of the influential private stakeholders in the secondary school system. The initial reaction of the private school authorities to O'Malley's policy announcement tended to be mildly positive, but cautious and non-committal. Fr. John Hughes S.J., chairman of the Catholic managerial com-mittee, welcomed the principle of free education, but declined to make any further comment until he had examined the detail of the scheme. O'Malley's initiative was also welcomed in general terms by Dr. R.W. Reynolds, secre-tary of the Irish Schoolmasters' Association (ISA), the representative body for Protestant headmasters.[181] The representatives of the Catholic and Protestant managerial authorities were understandably cautious in their initial response to the announcement, awaiting the full details of the Minister's scheme. The Protestant educational authorities, however, soon took a markedly more positive approach to the initiative than the Catholic managers and religious orders, in part because the representatives of the Protestant authorities secured much greater influence over the final version of the proposals than their Catholic counterparts.

The SEC, which represented the interests of the Protestant churches in post-primary education, took a proactive approach following O'Malley's initial announcement, making representations to the department to secure special arrangements for the Protestant secondary schools.[182] O'Malley readily accepted the SEC case that an alternative scheme of assistance was required for Protestant children. The department calculated that only 7.5% of Protestant pupils would benefit from the proposed free tuition scheme, which was primarily designed to provide for day pupils. This discrepancy was explained in part by the higher cost of education in Protestant schools, as the Protestant community lacked the service of the religious orders, which heavily subsidised Catholic secondary education. Moreover 40% of all Protestant pupils could receive denominational education only by attending boarding schools, due to the lack of suitable Protestant day schools.[183] O'Malley's submission to the government on 11 November 1966 therefore accepted the case for special provision for Protestant secondary education: 'The Protestant schools are a special problem and it is submitted, require special assistance.'[184] The SEC was deeply involved in the formulation of the separate scheme of assistance for Protestant schools, as the Minister sought their advice on the details of the scheme and SEC members held a series of discussions with officials. The scheme involved the payment by the state of a block grant of £70,000 for day pupils to the Protestant educational authorities, for distribution by the SEC to the Protestant schools. The Minister made only limited provision initially for Protestant boarding pupils, allocating a block grant of £10,000 to the Protestant educational authorities.[185] The SEC soon lobbied successfully for an increased allocation for Protestant boarding schools. O'Malley secured the agreement of the Cabinet on 4 August 1967 to pay the tuition element of the boarding fee for all Protestant boarding pupils from 1967–68. The revised scheme involved the payment of a block grant of £60,000 to the SEC for boarding school pupils in 1967–68.[186] The SEC's lobbying was successful in securing a highly favourable scheme of assistance, which did much to meet the special requirements of the Protestant schools. O'Malley and the senior officials took great care to accommodate the concerns of the Protestant educational authorities. The special arrangements authorised by the Minister did not deliver free education for most Protestant pupils, but provided an invaluable subsidy to the Protestant secondary schools and allowed considerable flexibility to the Protestant authorities in the implementation of the scheme. It was not surprising that the SEC paid a warm tribute to O'Malley after his death in 1968, declaring that he 'had laboured unceasingly and with vision to implement an enlightened policy'.[187]

The Minister received few tributes from the Catholic managerial authorities then or later. O'Malley calculated correctly that the support of the Catholic Hierarchy for his proposals would be crucial in securing the collaboration of the Catholic managers and religious orders. He began preliminary discussions with the bishops on the initiative even before the government approved it. O'Malley, accompanied by three senior officials, met leading representatives of the Hierarchy, including Conway and McQuaid, in Maynooth on 3 October 1966.[188] The Minister outlined the proposals for free education in general terms, acknowledging that the details had not yet been worked out. The officials clarified that the scheme for free tuition was based on the principle that free post-primary schools should be available to all: free education would not simply be given to the poorer pupils in each school and the special grants would be paid only to schools giving free education to all their pupils. Cardinal Conway objected strongly to the proposal to vary the rate of the state's grant from £15 to £25 per pupil depending on the level of the school fees: he argued that a standard rate for all secondary schools was essential to avoid injustice to low-fee schools.[189] The Hierarchy's representatives also sought clarification on the provision to be made for secondary boarding schools. The Minister indicated that assistance to Catholic boarding pupils would be undertaken in some way, but did not clarify the scope or level of this assistance. Ó Raifeartaigh promised that special provision would be made by the state for the Catholic Diocesan Colleges, which prepared candidates for the priesthood, but the bishops expressed concern about the position of low-fee boarding schools provided by the religious orders.[190] The discussion at Maynooth was inconclusive. The bishops expressed no objection to the initiative for free education, but raised serious reservations about the arrangements for implementing the Minister's plans in the voluntary secondary schools. O'Malley's meeting with the Catholic bishops on 3 October was only the beginning of a tortuous process of negotiation between the state and the Hierarchy.

Ó Raifeartaigh and MacGearailt conducted the negotiations initially. The two officials arranged to meet James Fergus and Henry Murphy, Bishop of Limerick, in Ballaghaderreen on 10 December 1966 to discuss the initiative. They assured the bishops that O'Malley intended to offer a grant of £25 for all students in the Diocesan Colleges, on the basis that such pupils formed an exceptional category due to their religious vocation.[191] The two bishops expressed disquiet at the exclusion of boarding schools in general from the initiative, urging that low-fee boarding schools should be enabled to participate in the scheme. But they reserved their strongest objection for the variation in the state grant to secondary schools. Fergus outlined the bishops' objections to the differential in no uncertain terms, issuing a letter to Ó Raifeartaigh on 14 December: 'We have serious misgivings about the application of the sliding scale in respect to any school. We feel that it is not a good or fair method.'[192] Fergus described the differentiated grant as a 'discriminatory' measure, which would condemn low-fee schools to 'a perpetual position of inferiority'.[193] The Secretary replied on 17 December, informing the Bishop that O'Malley also wished to secure a fixed grant of £25 for all day pupils within the scheme: 'His ultimate intention is to have an adequate flat rate for all day pupils and he hopes to achieve this sooner rather than later.'[194]

O'Malley also received vehement complaints from the TBA concerning the differential in the state grant. The Provincials of the six male teaching orders submitted a memorandum to O'Malley and Lynch on 6 December 1966, which made the case that the variation in the grant discriminated against low-fee schools. The Provincials refused to accept the scheme as it stood and declined to participate in it unless the same grant was offered to all secondary schools.[195] Brother T.G. Moynihan, one of the two Provincials of the Irish Christian Brothers, appealed directly to the Taoiseach to help the religious orders in securing a fixed grant. Moynihan told Lynch on 6 December that the male teaching orders sought a standard grant of £30 per pupil for all schools within the scheme.[196] O'Malley swiftly arranged a meeting with the Provincials on 9 December and bluntly challenged them to participate in the scheme. This set the scene for a highly charged and acrimonious encounter, which failed to produce any agreement at all between the Minister and the teaching orders.[197] The disagreement was temporary, however, as O'Malley had considerable sympathy with the concerns of the TBA and was determined to secure their collaboration in implementing the initiative.

The Minister soon acted decisively to eliminate the differential in the grant to day pupils. He sought the agreement of the government on 26 January 1967 for the removal of the differential on a phased basis. O'Malley informed the Cabinet that the Hierarchy, the clerical managers and the teaching orders were all implacably opposed to any variation in the state grant.[198] He agreed with them that the payment of a minimum grant of only £15 per pupil to low-fee schools effectively penalised those schools for providing low-cost education. O'Malley proposed instead the payment of a fixed grant of £25 for each day pupil to all schools within the scheme by September 1969. The revised scheme provided for a sliding scale of £15 to £25 only in 1967–68: the minimum grant would then be increased to £20 in 1968–69 and a flat rate of £25 per pupil would be paid to all secondary schools within the scheme by September 1969.[199] The Cabinet rapidly approved O'Malley's revised scheme on 31 January, not least because he had secured Haughey's agreement to the proposal.[200] While the demand for a fixed grant of £30 was not conceded, O'Malley had secured a significant improvement in the terms of the free tuition scheme, which satisfied a key concern of the Hierarchy and the TBA. The Minister employed the objections of the bishops and the religious orders to good effect in winning the government's approval for an important extension of the scheme, which brought the terms more closely in line with his original intentions.

But the amendment did not go far enough to secure the support of the Catholic bishops or managerial authorities for the initiative. The Hierarchy still maintained reservations about the exclusion of low-fee boarding schools from the scheme. O'Malley's offer to pay the tuition fees of all boarding pupils in the Diocesan Colleges on an exceptional basis did not find favour with the bishops. The Standing Committee of the Hierarchy on 10 January 1967 recommended that the bishops should reject the offer of preferential treatment for the Diocesan Colleges.[201] Fergus told Ó Raifeartaigh on 17 January that acceptance of the offer would lay the bishops open 'to the accusation of having made a bargain favourable to themselves without concern for the interests of the other low fee boarding schools'.[202] The Standing Committee advised the Minister instead to extend the tuition grant to boarders in all low-fee schools. The Secretary responded on 30 January by urging the bishops to reconsider their position on O'Malley's offer. Ó Raifeartaigh emphasised that the Minister's initiative was never intended to deliver free education in boarding schools as a whole.[203] He warned Fergus that there was no immediate prospect of the introduction of grants to cover even the tuition fee for boarding school pupils generally. The Secretary outlined the recent concessions made by the Minister, emphasising the benefits of eliminating the differential in the state grant for day pupils.[204] Fergus welcomed the elimination of the differential, but gave no indication that the bishops would reconsider their position concerning the Minister's offer.[205] Moreover the Catholic managerial authorities raised more fundamental objections to O'Malley's approach early in 1967.

The Catholic managerial committee, which included representatives of the CHA, TBA and the CCSS, objected strongly to key elements of the scheme. They regarded even a temporary differential as unjust and considered that the maximum rate of £25 per pupil was inadequate.[206] The Catholic managerial representatives considered that O'Malley had wrongly excluded schools catering for 25% of the secondary school population from the scheme. When the Minister met the representatives of the managerial bodies for the first time on 16 December 1966, they argued that he should facilitate the entry of all secondary schools into the scheme.[207] The phased introduction of a fixed rate of £25 per pupil by 1969–70 therefore did not pacify the Catholic managerial associations. The Catholic managers instead began to explore an alternative to the Minister's scheme. The clerical and religious Superiors of the archdiocese of Dublin authorised Fr. Hughes and Mother Jordana to draft an alternative to O'Malley's scheme in January 1967.[208] Hughes suggested an alternative proposal to O'Malley on 27 January 1967, seeking 'an unofficial meeting' with the Minister to discuss the situation further.[209] The Jesuit headmaster told O'Malley that the clerical and religious authorities were supportive of free education, but disagreed fundamentally with the mechanism proposed by the Minister to achieve it – the special grant to schools opting for the scheme. He stated bluntly that even a temporary differential in the grant was unacceptable: 'there is not the slightest hope that a differential of £15 to £25 would be acceptable to anyone'.[210] Hughes proposed that as an interim solution the government should increase the capitation grant to all secondary schools on the condition that the schools would lower their fees by a similar amount: this approach would make free places available wherever the reduction eliminated fees completely. Moreover he indicated that the Catholic managers were seeking an Act of the Oireachtas to clarify the future relations between the state and the secondary schools.[211]

The proposed alternative presented by Hughes, on behalf of the Catholic managerial authorities, was a serious challenge to the basic principle which underpinned the Minister's scheme for free education. The free tuition scheme was designed to ensure that a large majority of secondary schools offered free education to all their pupils, not to provide free places on a piecemeal basis. O'Malley quickly dismissed the proposed alternative. He outlined the government's approach to the managerial authorities in a definitive fashion on 31 January 1967.[212] O'Malley delivered an uncompromising message in separate meetings with the Provincials of the TBA and the representatives of the other managerial bodies. When Hughes proposed the alternative approach favoured by the Catholic managers, O'Malley firmly rejected the idea, on the basis that it would reduce considerably the number of pupils within the free education scheme. The Minister urged the managerial representatives to accept his scheme, pointing out that he had secured the removal of the differential in the state grant for day pupils by 1969. He also confirmed that the state would pay the tuition fee for boarding school pupils, who lived in remote areas outside the effective range of a school transport service, in schools charging fees of no more than £120 annually. The managerial representatives welcomed the removal of the differential but told the Minister that they could not endorse the scheme without consulting their members. O'Malley told them that the initiative was now being presented to the managerial bodies as a definitive offer, brushing aside any attempts to amend the scheme further.[213] The Minister was sufficiently emphatic to convince the Catholic managerial representatives that he had presented them with 'his final offer – and equivalently, with an ultimatum'.[214] Hughes reported to McQuaid on 2 February 1967 that O'Malley wanted the secondary schools to enter the scheme entirely on his terms. Hughes expressed vividly the disquiet and resentment of the Catholic managerial authorities at O'Malley's approach: 'On the whole, I was, and still am, depressed and bewildered. We are dealing with a very clever man, who can, of course, be charming, but whose political career comes first – the rest, nowhere.'[215] The meetings on 31 January ended in deadlock, as the Catholic managerial authorities declined to endorse the Minister's scheme and O'Malley flatly refused to contemplate their alternative.

O'Malley sought to overcome the objections of the Catholic managerial authorities through direct negotiations with the Hierarchy. Ó Raifeartaigh, who enjoyed close and friendly connections with McQuaid, undertook private discussions with the Archbishop of Dublin on the scheme. McQuaid was seriously dissatisfied with the financial arrangements proposed by O'Malley for the voluntary secondary schools. He considered that the proposed state grant to the secondary schools was completely inadequate and could cause the disappearance of schools run by the religious orders. The Archbishop told Hughes on 3 February 1967 that O'Malley's initiative marked a crisis for the secondary schools: 'It is on the result of this crisis that we shall be required to live for very many years to come.'[216] But McQuaid also advised the Catholic Major Superiors in his archdiocese to accept the scheme in principle, insisting that the church could not oppose an initiative which promised to deliver free post-primary education for all.[217] He informed Ó Raifeartaigh that he had discussed the initiative with the Catholic managerial representatives on 26 January 1967: 'I succeeded well, I thought. But am I right?'[218] This remarkably opaque comment suggested that McQuaid was seeking to persuade the Catholic educators to accept the scheme, but the Archbishop's approach was more complex and ambiguous. McQuaid maintained close contact with Hughes and allowed him to proceed with the formulation of an alternative to O'Malley's scheme, although the Archbishop did not officially sanction the initiative.[219] Moreover McQuaid informed O'Malley on 2 February 1967 that all the Catholic managerial bodies and religious orders in his archdiocese were 'profoundly disturbed' by the Minister's approach. The Archbishop endorsed their view that the scheme did not provide a satisfactory basis for the introduction of free education.[220] When O'Malley demanded to know the grounds for their dissatisfaction, McQuaid responded that he could not add anything to the comments already made by the Catholic school managers.[221] This did not necessarily imply the rejection of the Minister's initiative, but underlined that McQuaid was determined to extract more concessions from the state for the Catholic secondary schools. O'Malley later told Cardinal Conway that he understood McQuaid's letter to indicate the rejection of the plan for free education by the Catholic educational authorities.[222] But the Archbishop was adopting a hardline approach to promote a revision of the scheme, not to block the introduction of free post-primary education.

The Minister, however, was seriously alarmed by the tone of McQuaid's communication. O'Malley was also infuriated at the criticisms of the scheme made by leading Catholic managerial representatives and educators.[223] He made an impassioned defence of his policy in the Senate on 9 February 1967, in the course of a debate on *Investment*. O'Malley commented on the large volume of supportive messages that he had received from parents and then launched into a scathing denunciation of his critics. He claimed that vested interests were attempting to sabotage the initiative so as to maintain socially exclusive secondary schools.[224] O'Malley assured the Senate that critics of his policy would not prevail: 'I know I am up against opposition and serious organised opposition but they are not going to defeat me on this. I shall tell you further that I shall expose them and I shall expose their tactics on every available occasion whoever they are.'[225] O'Malley's denunciation of his critics was a thinly veiled attack on the secondary school authorities and religious orders who were sceptical about his scheme. O'Connor, who disapproved of the Minister's vehemence, commented that the onslaught was 'uncalled for, was foolishly undiplomatic and was never forgiven'.[226] Certainly O'Malley's fierce attack on critics of the scheme dismayed and alienated secondary school managers and teachers.[227] But the Minister's onslaught did not at all impede the successful conclusion of the negotiations with the Hierarchy. Ó Raifeartaigh resumed private negotiations with McQuaid and the Archbishop assured O'Malley on 11 February that the clerical and religious authorities had not rejected his scheme, but were merely seeking to revise the terms to secure the future of the secondary schools.[228] Moreover within a week of his speech in the Senate, the Minister reached agreement with Cardinal Conway on most key aspects of the initiative for free education.

O'Malley and Ó Raifeartaigh arranged to meet the Cardinal privately in Dundalk on 15 February 1967 to discuss the initiative. Conway took a positive line on the free tuition scheme, rejecting the assertion by Hughes on 27 January that even a temporary differential in the state grant to the secondary schools would be unacceptable.[229] He expressed satisfaction with the phased elimination of the differential and assured O'Malley that the schools whose fees came within range of the scheme would participate in it. The Minister defended his remarks in the Senate, complaining that the managerial authorities had ignored the important concession made by the government in abolishing the differential. Conway told O'Malley that the male teaching orders would now be willing to opt for the scheme, following the removal of the differential. The Cardinal effectively disassociated the Hierarchy from the position on the scheme taken by the Catholic managerial representatives: 'He added that the managerial bodies on whose behalf Fr. Hughes was writing had no authority from the church to seek an Act which would regulate the relations between their schools and the State.'[230] Conway assured the Minister that Hughes's approach did not represent the position of the Catholic Church. The Cardinal was confident that the Hierarchy would formally approve the plan at its next meeting.[231] Conway's broadly positive approach towards the initiative illustrated a significant divergence between the Catholic managerial representatives and the Hierarchy. This did not mean that the Cardinal was entirely satisfied with the terms of the scheme. He reiterated that the bishops could not accept the Minister's offer of special grants for the Diocesan Colleges, arguing instead for a state subsidy for all pupils in low-fee boarding schools. O'Malley replied that the government could not currently afford to subsidise boarding pupils in general, but that tuition grants for all boarding pupils could be provided in the future.[232] He hinted at the prospect of a future state grant, which would cover the tuition element of the boarding school fee. Conway in turn assured O'Malley that the Diocesan Colleges would certainly participate in the scheme so far as their day pupils were concerned. The Cardinal's conciliatory approach underlined that continuing episcopal reservations about the position of the low-fee boarding schools would not prevent the acceptance of the scheme by the Hierarchy.

The influence of the Catholic bishops proved decisive in securing the general acceptance of O'Malley's scheme by the managerial authorities. The differences between the Hierarchy and the leading Catholic managerial representatives became evident in February 1967. The Catholic managerial committee submitted a memorandum to the bishops on 12 February 1967, outlining their reservations about the scheme.[233] The managerial representatives endorsed the principle of free education but condemned the Minister's scheme as unacceptable. The committee saw 'a basic objection' to a scheme which made the secondary schools completely dependent on the state for their income: economic dependence without any legal guarantees was an unacceptable prospect for the school managers.[234] They feared that the autonomy of the secondary schools would be decisively undermined; 'under the O'Malley Plan, without legal guarantees, the situation of the schools could be intolerable'.[235] The committee concluded that while the managers could not reject free education, they dared not accept the Minister's scheme without the inclusion of stringent legal conditions. They proposed that the Hierarchy and the religious orders should seek the Minister's agreement to a fixed grant of £25 per pupil immediately as an interim solution: the bishops should then negotiate legal guarantees for the voluntary secondary schools, which would be enshrined in a new statute. The bishops lost no time in rejecting the committee's approach. A delegation from the Hierarchy, including Fergus, Murphy and Dr. John Ahern, Bishop of Cloyne, met Fr. Hughes and Mother Jordana on 16 February to clarify the church's response to the Minister's initiative.[236] The Hierarchy's representatives ruled out any official intervention by the bishops on behalf of the managers. The three bishops instead instructed the managerial representatives to recommend immediate acceptance of the scheme to the relevant secondary schools in their associations:

> The Episcopal Commission for post-primary education met the Joint Committee of the Catholic Managerial Bodies, at the latter's request, in Dublin, on 16th February 1967 and strongly advised that, in the interests of religion and to forestall the misrepresentation of which the Church in Ireland was bound to be made the victim, it was imperative (a) that they should recommend the acceptance of the scheme, whatever its defects, to the schools for which it was envisaged and (b) that this should be done and made known to have been done, with the least possible delay.[237]

The Hierarchy acted to protect the prestige of the Catholic Church and prevent accusations that the church was obstructing the introduction of free education, by directing the Catholic managerial representatives to endorse the initiative. The bishops told the managers that efforts could be made to resolve the defects in the scheme at a later stage. They directed Hughes to issue a letter to the Minister on behalf of the committee indicating that the managerial representatives were recommending the acceptance of the scheme. The bishops avoided any official intervention in the negotiations, instead directing the joint managerial committee to issue the recommendation in favour of the initiative.[238] But the reality was that the Hierarchy had issued a direct instruction to the managerial representatives, which left no room for ambiguity.

Hughes informed O'Malley on 24 February 1967 that the Catholic managerial committee had decided to recommend acceptance of the free education scheme to all the schools in their associations which came within the scheme announced by the Minister. The committee still maintained that there were serious defects in the scheme and Hughes told the Minister that the managerial representatives would seek further negotiations with him to overcome these flaws.[239] Hughes also informed the Catholic educational authorities and Provincials of the religious orders throughout the state of the committee's recommendation to accept the free tuition scheme.[240] The Hierarchy's intervention broke the deadlock in the negotiations between the state and the managerial bodies, securing the endorsement of the most influential Catholic managerial authorities for the Minister's initiative. The private negotiations conducted by O'Malley and his officials with the Hierarchy successfully sidelined the objections of the Catholic managerial representatives, who were obliged to accept the initiative essentially on the Minister's terms. The concern of the bishops that the church should not even appear to oppose free post-primary education contributed significantly to the outcome, as McQuaid acknowledged to Fergus on 21 February 1967: 'From the outset I have urged that as Catholic educators we must not even seem to oppose a scheme that would make available post-primary education for all children.'[241] The Hierarchy's representatives openly expressed their concern to protect the prestige of the church on 16 February, when they instructed the Catholic managerial representatives to accept the scheme.[242] There is little doubt that O'Malley's explosive outburst in the Senate hastened the Hierarchy's intervention in favour of the initiative. While the Minister did not criticise the bishops, his statement opened up the prospect of a divisive public debate on free education, which might well have damaged the prestige of the church. The Hierarchy was determined to avoid a public confrontation between the Minister and the Catholic school authorities over free education. The bishops acted to forestall such an appalling prospect by instructing the Catholic managerial representatives to accept the free tuition scheme.

The Catholic and Protestant school managers generally accepted the Minister's initiative by the autumn of 1967. Ó Raifeartaigh issued Circular M15/67, which outlined the detailed terms of the free tuition scheme and the grants for the supply of free books, in February 1967. The department set a deadline of 16 May 1967 for the acceptance of the initiative by secondary schools.[243] The influence of individual bishops, especially McQuaid, proved important in securing the acceptance of the scheme by most Catholic secondary schools. McQuaid advised the Major Superiors of his archdiocese to accept the scheme wherever it was financially feasible for schools to do so: he urged them to accept the scheme 'under protest' as it was launched without consultation with the managers and the Minister had failed to show sufficient consideration for the financial position of schools provided by the religious orders.[244] Despite his dissatisfaction with O'Malley's tactics, McQuaid played a crucial part in ensuring that the secondary school authorities in Dublin accepted the Minister's initiative. McQuaid's collaboration proved an invaluable asset to O'Malley, who was concerned that the success of the initiative would be compromised if a substantial number of higher-fee secondary schools in Dublin failed to join the scheme. Officials of O'Malley's department believed that McQuaid's influence proved decisive in bringing many higher-fee convent schools in Dublin within the free education scheme.[245] O'Malley was not satisfied with the original estimate by the department that 75% of day pupils would be included and sought to bring the maximum number of secondary schools within the scope of his initiative. The Minister emphasised that his initiative was intended to guarantee the right of access to post-primary education for all children, at a public meeting in Clontarf on 16 February.[246] O'Malley's success in attaining his objectives exceeded the original estimates of his officials. The vast majority of secondary schools entered the free tuition scheme by September 1967. A total of 485 out of 551 secondary schools catering for day pupils opted to enter the scheme for 1967–68: only 26 Catholic day schools did not participate in the initiative.[247] The department informed the Public Accounts Committee that 92% of all day pupils in secondary schools were covered by the scheme in 1967–68.[248] The general acceptance of the initiative by the educational authorities far exceeded the expectations of the Department of Education.

O'Malley also succeeded in expanding the scope of the scheme well beyond the original intentions of the government. Following persistent representations by the Hierarchy, the Minister secured the extension of the scheme to cover the tuition element of the fee for boarding pupils in low-fee schools. The bishops had consistently made the case to O'Malley that such secondary schools made great sacrifices to provide low-cost education for the children of poor families.[249] O'Malley brought the Hierarchy's concerns to Haughey's attention in June 1967, securing his agreement to the extension of the scheme. The revised scheme provided for the payment from 1969–70 of a state grant of £25 for each boarding pupil in low-fee schools charging an annual fee of no more than £120.[250] The latest modification of the scheme also involved the payment by the state of the tuition fee for boarding pupils in the Diocesan Colleges from 1967–68. The extension of the free tuition scheme meant that pupils in the low-fee boarding schools would be subsidised at least in part by the state. The revision of the scheme met to some extent the concerns of the bishops about the future viability of low-fee schools provided by the religious orders. The initiative as it was implemented was even more comprehensive and far-reaching than the plan originally approved by the government.

The impact of the initiative on second-level education was not fully anticipated even by O'Malley himself. O'Malley and the officials of his department greatly underestimated the likely rate of increase in educational participation at post-primary level as a result of the scheme. The department estimated that an additional 7,000 students might well seek admission to post-primary schools in September 1967, although its

officials recognised that accurate prediction of the additional enrolment
was problematic.[251] O'Malley himself expressed scepticism about the possibility of a massive influx of pupils into post-primary education. He told
the Senate on 9 February 1967 that the state still confronted a formidable
challenge in persuading low-income families of the value of education
beyond the compulsory phase, even with the introduction of free post-
primary education.[252] The Minister and his officials did not anticipate the
dramatic advance in educational participation, which was a direct consequence of the new initiative. The total pupil enrolment in secondary schools
surged from 103,588 in September 1966 to 118,807 in September 1967,
marking an extraordinary increase of over 15,000 in a single year.[253] The
vocational system experienced a less dramatic but still considerable
increase of about 5,000 in the number of day pupils undertaking full-time
continuation courses in the same period.[254] This advance was deceptive in
some respects due to the high drop-out rate in vocational courses: the
actual number of day pupils undertaking continuation courses by February 1968 showed an increase of about 4,000 from the previous year.[255]
The post-primary schools were already enjoying a considerable expansion
in pupil enrolment in the early 1960s, but the gradual flow of pupils into
second-level education became an avalanche with the advent of free education. The increased rate of expansion was particularly evident in the
secondary schools. The secondary system enjoyed an additional influx of
approximately 5,000 pupils annually immediately before the introduction
of the new scheme.[256] The initiative roughly trebled the annual intake of
pupils to the secondary schools. The accelerated rate of expansion was
sustained for the remainder of the decade. The secondary school population expanded by no less than 39% between September 1966 and September 1969. The total pupil enrolment in post-primary education increased
by 34% between 1966–67 and 1969–70.[257] The initiative for free post-
primary education succeeded, beyond the expectations even of O'Malley
himself, in achieving a rapid and dramatic expansion of educational participation at post-primary level.

Several scholars have suggested that the initiative changed the balance
of advantage between secondary and vocational schools and had the effect
of sidelining vocational education once again.[258] The concerns of the senior
officials who had advised O'Malley to defer his initiative until 1970, on the
basis that vocational schools would not benefit fully from free education,
certainly proved well founded. The timing of the reform worked against
the vocational schools, not least because they were generally unable to
offer courses for the Leaving Certificate until 1969–70.[259] The Minister's
initiative reinforced the existing pattern of post-primary education, in
which the large majority of pupils attended secondary rather than voca-

tional schools. But the initiative did not undermine the position of vocational education. The inferior status of technical education was a legacy of the state's policy from 1930 until the late 1950s. The department under successive ministers had overturned the traditional policy, but the profoundly negative influence of the traditional consensus could not be eliminated overnight. It required more than simply the removal of traditional restrictions on the vocational sector to change the obvious preferences of many parents, which favoured secondary education. The greater rate of expansion in the secondary system was dictated at least as much by the established pattern of second-level education as by the timing of the Minister's initiative. Moreover O'Connor later acknowledged that a delay in the introduction of free second-level education until 1970 might well have ensured that it never happened at all, in the very different political and economic climate of the following decade.[260] O'Malley's initiative offered a practical means of expanding access to post-primary education, which took account of the realities of the Irish educational system in the 1960s.

The unexpected and dramatic impact of the initiative made most of the department's original estimates redundant. O'Malley acknowledged in the Dáil on 6 February 1968 that the cost of the free tuition scheme and the grant for free books would exceed the original estimates by over £150,000.[261] The initial success of the free transport scheme also surpassed the expectations of the department. The Minister entrusted the organisation of the nation-wide transport scheme to Córas Iompair Éireann (CIÉ), appointing the Chief Executive Officers of the relevant VECs as the transport liaison officers between the educational authorities and the company.[262] The free transport service was organised on the basis of catchment areas for about 350 post-primary centres throughout the country; students living at least three miles from the nearest post-primary school providing free education were eligible for free transport.[263] The department envisaged that the free transport service would be phased in by CIE over two to three years from April 1967. But the scheme was successfully introduced for most eligible pupils between April 1967 and February 1968. CIE took over the administration of 120 existing school transport services organised by the school authorities, parents' associations and Roinn na Gaeltachta.[264] O'Malley informed the Dáil on 6 February 1968 that free transport had been provided to 52,500 of the 55,000 children who were eligible for the service.[265] The rapid implementation of the scheme was a significant logistical achievement, which placed a considerable strain on CIE's resources. The cost of the scheme in the first year of its operation amounted to £840,000, which was almost three times the original estimate of £300,000.[266] The substantial cost of the transport service underlined its importance in making free second-level education widely accessible. The swift implementation of the free transport scheme made an indispensable contribution to the dramatic expansion of post-primary education.

The initiative for free post-primary education brought the largest increase in the Exchequer's spending on second-level education since the foundation of the state. The net expenditure for secondary education increased spectacularly by over £3,500,000 in a single year. While the Minister's initiative brought unprecedented state support for secondary education, the vocational system was by no means neglected. The government provided additional funding of almost £1,000,000 for vocational education in 1967–68.[267] The massive increase in state expenditure was explained primarily by the three new schemes for free tuition, free transport and free books. The department also expanded the existing scheme of building grants to secondary schools in 1967, to finance the extensive programme of school building, which was essential following the introduction of free education.[268] The revised scheme offered a free grant by the state amounting to 70% of the cost of a building programme, while the remaining 30% was advanced to the school authorities as a loan, repayable over fifteen years.[269] The more generous allocation of capital funding to school building was an inevitable consequence of free second-level education. The initiative for free education involved an unprecedented increase in the level of state funding for the post-primary system. Lemass' assessment that O'Malley's initiative would add £3,000,000 to the Estimates in a single year proved entirely justified. If anything the Taoiseach's prediction was on the conservative side.

The eventual outcome was certainly a tribute to O'Malley's political skill: few other ministers would have shown the daring and the tenacity required to persuade the government to introduce such a far-reaching scheme of free second-level education in the first place. Moreover the Minister dealt skilfully with the complex process of negotiation, which was needed to ensure the implementation of the initiative. He made sufficient concessions to secure the collaboration of the Catholic Hierarchy and effectively outmanoeuvred the most influential clerical and religious managerial bodies. Ó Raifeartaigh played an important part in smoothing the way for the introduction of O'Malley's initiative by acting as an intermediary with various members of the Catholic Hierarchy. The success of the initiative also had something to do with the reality that neither the department nor the government as a whole had a clear understanding in 1966 of the eventual scale of the plan. O'Malley's task would have been much more difficult had his ministerial colleagues realised in advance the full cost of the initiative, which vastly exceeded the Minister's estimates. But the dramatic increase in state expenditure on education also reflected the settled policy of the government. It was Lemass, more than any other political figure, who created the conditions necessary for the introduction of free post-primary education. O'Malley's initiative made rapid progress at least in part because education had already been identified as the most urgent national priority in the allocation of scarce resources by Lemass himself. Educational expansion had become a central priority for the state and this policy approach provided the essential context for the introduction of free second-level education.

O'Malley and 'free education'

There is no doubt that O'Malley's initiative for free post-primary education made a greater impression on contemporaries than any other educational reform introduced then or since. But O'Malley's term saw the development of a series of reforms in primary and post-primary education, which were designed to facilitate the expansion of the educational system and fulfil the social and economic objectives of the government. The Minister himself made a key contribution to a wide variety of reforming measures, from the improvement of sub-standard conditions in national schools to the introduction of free post-primary education. But the influence exerted by leading officials of the department, especially MacGearailt, O'Connor and the members of the Development Branch, should not be underestimated. It was MacGearailt who skilfully secured wide agreement from the educational interest groups for a workable alternative to the Primary Certificate. The Development Branch began a radical programme of rationalisation at post-primary level; although their efforts were not crowned with success in the short term, the proactive approach taken by the officials laid the groundwork for further educational reforms under O'Malley's successors. The dramatic public initiatives taken by the Minister should not obscure the pervasive influence exerted by the officials on the transformation of the educational system.

It is evident, however, that O'Malley himself dictated the sweeping and ambitious nature of the initiative for free second-level education. O'Malley's endorsement of the principle of free education was not a fundamental policy change by 1966, as the government's policy of raising the school leaving age demanded the introduction of some form of free education at post-primary level. But he exerted a decisive influence on the content and timing of the initiative, so that the reform proved much more radical and far-reaching than the government had originally intended. The introduction of the schemes for free tuition and free transport brought an immediate and dramatic expansion in the overall level of participation in post-primary education. Yet the transformation of the educational system did not begin or end with free post-primary education, it was an evolving process, which began in the late 1950s under O'Malley's predecessors and continued after his death in 1968. While Lemass did not authorise the Minister's sensational announcement, O'Malley's initiative was undertaken in the context of the policy of educational expansion pursued by the Taoiseach since 1959. O'Malley ensured that free second-level education became a reality and not merely a pious aspiration; but his daring initiative was possible because Lemass had firmly established education as a key national priority throughout his term as Taoiseach.

Notes

1 O'Connor, *A Troubled Sky*, p. 192.
2 Ó Buachalla, *Education Policy*, pp. 284–5.
3 Horgan, *Seán Lemass*, p. 297.
4 NA D/T 96/6/355, S.12891E, O'Malley to Lemass, 8 January 1965.
5 O'Connor, *A Troubled Sky*, p. 139, Interview with Tony Ó Dálaigh, 3 May 2002.
6 O'Connor, *A Troubled Sky*, p. 139.
7 NA D/T 97/6/437, S.17913, O'Malley to Lemass, 29 July 1966, p. 1.
8 Ibid.
9 Ibid., p. 2.
10 Ibid., p. 4.
11 *Dáil Debates*, vol. 232, col. 460, 6 February 1968.
12 Ibid.
13 Coolahan, 'National schools 1960–1985', in Mulcahy and O'Sullivan, *Irish Educational Policy*, pp. 34–6.
14 Circular 12/66, Department of Education, July 1966, *Dáil Debates*, vol. 232, col. 460, 6 February 1968.
15 *Seanad Debates*, vol. 62, col. 1062–3, 9 February 1967.
16 INTO, Annual Report, CEC 1966–67, S. Brosnahan to Department of Education; Clerical Managers' Association; Office of Public Works (Dublin, 1967), p. 19.
17 Ibid., p. 20.
18 *Seanad Debates*, vol. 62, col. 1083, 9 February 1967.
19 O'Connell, *History of the INTO*, p. 448.
20 Circular 22/67, Department of Education, September 1967.
21 O'Connell, *History of the INTO*, pp. 448–9.
22 Coolahan, 'National schools 1960–1985', in Mulcahy and O'Sullivan, *Irish Educational Policy*, p. 42.
23 *Investment in Education, Part 1*, p. 241.
24 Circular 10/67, Department of Education, March 1967.
25 Ibid.
26 Coolahan, 'National schools 1960–1985', in Mulcahy and O'Sullivan, *Irish Educational Policy*, pp. 33–43.

27 O'Connell, *History of the INTO*, pp. 422–5.

28 INTO, Annual Report, CEC 1966–67, pp. 24–5.

29 Ibid.

30 *Seanad Debates*, vol. 62, col. 1078, 9 February 1967.

31 NA D/T 98/6/143, S.12935B, *Memorandum for the information of the Government, Primary Certificate Examination, Appendix B*, 26 July 1967.

32 Ibid., p. 2.

33 Ibid., pp. 3–5.

34 Ibid., p. 8.

35 Ibid., pp. 10–14.

36 Ibid., p. 15.

37 *Memorandum, Primary Certificate Examination*, 26 July 1967, p. 1.

38 Ibid., *Appendix A*.

39 NA 99/5/1, G.C.12/60, Cabinet Minutes, 12 September 1967, p. 3.

40 Coolahan, 'National schools 1960–1985', in Mulcahy and O'Sullivan, *Irish Educational Policy*, p. 63.

41 Ibid., pp. 62–3; Chapter 7, pp. 251–8.

42 NA D/T 97/6/437, S.17913, O'Malley to Lemass, 29 July 1966, pp. 1–4.

43 *Committee of Public Accounts, Appropriation Accounts 1967–68*, p. 122.

44 *Journal of the 33rd General Synod of the Church of Ireland, 1968* (Dublin, 1968), p. 99.

45 O'Flaherty, *Irish Education*, p. 36.

46 Ibid., p. 167.

47 Bonel-Elliott, 'La Politique de l'enseignement', p. 318.

48 DDA AB8/B/XVIII/18, *McQuaid Papers*, Fr. L. Martin to S. MacGearailt, 26 July 1967.

49 MacGearailt to McQuaid, 1 August 1967.

50 McQuaid to O'Malley, 19 August 1967.

51 O'Malley to McQuaid, 20 September 1967, Memorandum, *Post-Primary Education in Dublin County Borough*, 1967.

52 McQuaid to O'Malley, 5 October 1967.

53 Chapter 3, pp. 92–4.

54 *Committee of Public Accounts, Appropriation Accounts 1967–68*, p. 122.

55 *Dáil Debates*, vol. 220, col. 1753–4, 16 February 1966.

56 NA D/FIN 2001/3/1073, D2/14/65, Ó Raifeartaigh to Murray, *Draft of Second Progress Report on the Second Programme for Economic Expansion*, Department of Education, 9 February 1966, pp. 1–4.

57 Ibid.

58 Department of Education, *County Report for Co. Cavan, Projected Organisation for Post-Primary Education: General Principles*, 1966, p. 1.

59 Ibid.

60 O'Connor, *A Troubled Sky*, p. 159.

61 *Dáil Debates*, vol. 226, col. 104, 6 December 1966.

62 *Official Programme, 45th Annual Convention*, ASTI, Report of Deputation to Minister for Education, 3 February 1967, pp. 65–7.

63 O'Connor, *A Troubled Sky*, p. 159.

64 Ibid.
65 DDA AB8/B/XVIII/18, *McQuaid Papers*, Note by Fr. L. Martin of meeting with Fr. J. Hughes, 9 January 1967.
66 Minutes, Central Executive Committee, CCSS, 6 October 1966.
67 Minutes, CEC, ASTI, 4 January 1967, p. 2.
68 D. Barry, 'The involvement and impact of a professional interest group' in D.G. Mulcahy and D. O'Sullivan (eds), *Irish Educational Policy: Process and substance* (Dublin, 1989), pp. 140–3; Chapter 4, pp. 146–7.
69 Minutes, Standing Committee, ASTI, 4 July 1967, p. 1.
70 *Official Programme for 47ᵗʰ Annual Convention*, ASTI, CEC Report 1968–69 (Dublin, 1969), p. 77.
71 C. McCarthy, *The Decade of Upheaval: Irish Trade Unions in the Nineteen Sixties* (Dublin, 1973), p. 206.
72 O'Connor, *A Troubled Sky*, p. 141.
73 Departmental Committee, *Tuarascáil Shealadach*, 8 December 1962, p. 9; see Chapter 3, pp. 84–5.
74 *Investment in Education, Part 1*, p. 150.
75 O'Connor, *A Troubled Sky*, p. 141.
76 Ibid.
77 Ibid.
78 NA D/T 96/6/356, S.12891F, *Memorandum to An Taoiseach on the necessity for improvement in full-time attendance at school at secondary level, Scheme A*, Department of Education, 7 September 1966, p. 2.
79 Ibid., p. 4.
80 NA D/T 96/6/356, S.12891F, *Memorandum to An Taoiseach, Scheme B*, 7 September 1966, p. 1.
81 O'Connor, *A Troubled Sky*, p. 142.
82 NA D/T 96/6/356, S.12891F, O'Malley to Lemass, 7 September 1966, Horgan, *Seán Lemass*, p. 298.
83 NA D/T 96/6/356, S.12891F, O'Malley to Lemass, 7 September 1966.
84 Ibid.
85 Ibid.
86 *Investment in Education, Part 1*, pp. 139–41, NA D/T 96/6/356, S.12891F, *Memorandum to An Taoiseach*, 7 September 1966, pp. 1–3.
87 *Investment in Education, Part 1*, pp. 135–6.
88 Ibid., p. 176.
89 NA D/T 96/6/356, S.12891F, *Memorandum to An Taoiseach*, 7 September 1966, pp. 1–2.
90 Ibid., p. 2.
91 Ibid., p. 2.
92 Ibid., pp. 1–3.
93 Ibid., *Scheme B*.
94 O'Connor, *A Troubled Sky*, p. 141.
95 Press Statement, *Speech by Donogh O'Malley, Minister for Education, to the National Union of Journalists at the Royal Marine Hotel, Dún Laoghaire, on Saturday*, 10 September 1966 (Ref. Aine Hyland).

96 Ibid.
97 *Irish Times*, 'State Plans Free Education for All Children', 12 September 1966.
98 Ibid., *Sunday Press*, 'Free education: Highlights of O'Malley's plan', 11 September 1966.
99 *Irish Times*, 'State Plans Free Education for All Children', 12 September 1966.
100 Ibid.
101 *Sunday Independent*, 'Schools to be Free', 11 September 1966.
102 *Irish Times*, 'State Plans Free Education for All Children', 12 September 1966.
103 Ibid.
104 Ibid.
105 Press Statement, *Speech by Donogh O'Malley, Minister for Education*, 10 September 1966.
106 *Irish Times*, 'State Plans Free Education for All Children', 12 September 1966.
107 Horgan, *Seán Lemass*, p. 298.
108 *Sunday Press*, 'Free Education: Highlights of O'Malley's Plan', 11 September 1966, *Sunday Independent*, 'Schools to be Free', 11 September 1966.
109 *Irish Times*, 'Sketch Plan for Free Schooling: Surprise at Breadth of Scheme', 12 September 1966, *Irish Press*, 'Teachers Hail New Education Proposals', 12 September 1966, *Irish Independent*, 'Doubts on Plan for Free Education: Guarded Reaction to Schooling Scheme', 12 September 1966.
110 *Irish Press*, 'Investment in People', 12 September 1966.
111 Ibid.
112 *Irish Times*, 'On the Double', 12 September 1966.
113 Ibid.
114 *Irish Independent*, 'Opening Shot', 12 September 1966.
115 *Irish Times*, 'Sketch Plan for Free Schooling: Surprise at Breadth of Scheme', 12 September 1966.
116 *Irish Independent*, 'Doubts on Plan for Free Education: Guarded Reaction to Schooling Scheme', 12 September 1966.
117 Ibid.
118 *Irish Times*, 'Sketch Plan for Free Schooling: Surprise at Breadth of Scheme', 12 September 1966.
119 O'Connor, *A Troubled Sky*, p. 146, Interview with Tony Ó Dálaigh, 3 May 2002.
120 NA D/T 96/6/356, S.12891F, Whitaker to Lemass, 12 September 1966.
121 Ibid.
122 Ibid.
123 *Irish Times*, 'Education Review: the Day O'Malley Jumped the Gun', 9 November 1971.
124 NA D/T 96/6/356, S.12891F, Lemass to O'Malley, 12 September 1966.
125 Ibid.
126 O'Malley to Lemass, 14 September 1966.

127 Ibid.
128 Lemass to O'Malley, 22 September 1966.
129 Ibid.
130 Ibid.
131 NA D/T 97/6/638, S.12891F, F.111668, *Memorandum to the Government, Provision of Free Post-Primary Education, Office of the Minister for Education*, 14 October 1966.
132 Ibid., p. 1.
133 Ibid., pp. 1–3.
134 Ibid., pp. 3–8.
135 *Form A, Submission to the Government*, 14 October 1966.
136 *Form B, Submission to the Government*, 14 October 1966.
137 Lemass to O'Malley, 17 October 1966.
138 Ibid.
139 NA D/T 97/6/638, S.12891F, F.111668, *Memorandum to the Government, Provision of Free Post-Primary Education, Office of the Minister for Education*, 11 November 1966, p. 1.
140 Ibid.
141 Ibid., p. 8.
142 Ibid., p. 12.
143 Ibid., p. 32.
144 Ibid., p. 16.
145 Ibid., p. 20.
146 Ibid., p. 21.
147 Ibid., pp. 22–7.
148 Ibid., p. 28.
149 Ibid., p. 28.
150 Ibid., p. 29.
151 *Investment in Education, Part 1*, p. 157.
152 NA D/T 97/6/638, S.12891F, F.111668, *Memorandum, Provision of Free Post-Primary Education*, 11 November 1966, p. 31.
153 Ibid., p. 32.
154 Ibid., p. 32.
155 NA D/T 97/6/638, S.12891F, *Memorandum to the Government, Provision of Free Post-Primary Education, Office of the Minister for Finance*, 17 November 1966.
156 Ibid., p. 1.
157 Ibid., p. 2.
158 Ibid., p. 2.
159 Ibid., pp. 3–4.
160 Ibid., p. 6.
161 Ibid., p. 5.
162 Ibid., p. 6.
163 O'Connor, *A Troubled Sky*, p. 162, Interview with Tony Ó Dálaigh, 3 May 2002.

164 Fine Gael, *Policy for a Just Society 3, Education* (Dublin, 1966), pp. 32–3.
165 Ibid., pp. 33–4.
166 O'Connor, *A Troubled Sky*, p. 146.
167 NA 99/5/1, G.C.12/2, Cabinet Minutes, 29 November 1966, pp. 1–2.
168 Ibid., p. 2, NA D/T 98/6/144, S.12891F, F.111668, *Memorandum to the Government, Office of the Minister for Education*, 26 January 1967, p. 1.
169 *Committee of Public Accounts, Appropriation Accounts 1967–68*, p. 116.
170 NA 99/5/1, G.C.12/2, Cabinet Minutes, 29 November 1966, p. 2.
171 Ibid.
172 Ibid., Horgan, *Seán Lemass*, p. 298.
173 NA D/T 97/6/638, S.12891F, Decision slip, *Cruinniú Rialtais, Item 3, Post-Primary Education*, 29 November 1966.
174 NA D/T 99/1/332, S.16890, *Memorandum to the Government, Scheme of Grants for Higher Education, Office of the Minister for Education*, 20 February 1968, pp. 1–3.
175 Ibid.
176 NA 99/5/1, G.C.12/91, Cabinet Minutes, 27 February 1968, p. 2; NA 99/5/2, G.C.12/99, Cabinet Minutes, 2 April 1968, p. 2.
177 NA D/T 99/1/332, S.16890, *Memorandum, Scheme of Grants for Higher Education*, 20 February 1968, p. 3.
178 *Dáil Debates*, vol. 225, col. 1872–94, 30 November 1966.
179 Ibid., col. 1893–4.
180 Ibid.
181 *Irish Press*, 'Teachers Hail New Education Proposals', 12 September 1966.
182 *Report of the SEC, 1967, Journal of the 33rd General Synod of the Church of Ireland*, 1st session, *1967* (Dublin, 1967), pp. 112–13.
183 NA D/T 97/6/638, S.12891F, F.111668, *Memorandum, Provision of Free Post-Primary Education*, 11 November 1966, pp. 10–11.
184 Ibid., pp. 11–12.
185 *Report of the SEC, 1967, Journal of the 33rd General Synod*, pp. 112–13.
186 NA D/T 98/5/951, S.16890, F.113233, *Memorandum to the Government, Office of the Minister for Education*, 27 June 1967, pp. 12–13, NA 99/5/1, G.C.12/55, Cabinet Minutes, 4 August 1967, pp. 1–2.
187 *Report of the SEC, 1968, Journal of the 33rd General Synod*, 2nd session, p. 131.
188 DDA AB8/B/XV/b/05, *McQuaid Papers*, Minutes of the Hierarchy, Meeting of the Minister for Education with the Hierarchy at Maynooth on 3 October 1966, p. 1.
189 Ibid., p. 2.
190 Ibid., p. 2.
191 NA D/T 98/6/144, S.12891F, Ó Raifeartaigh to Fergus, 17 December 1966.
192 Fergus to Ó Raifeartaigh, 14 December 1966.
193 Ibid.
194 Ó Raifeartaigh to Fergus, 17 December 1966.

195 Irish Christian Brothers' Archives, St. Helen's Province, A4 R2.11, *Memorandum presented to An Taoiseach and An tAire Oideachais on Points arising from the Proposed Scheme for Free Post-Primary Education as presented to Dáil Eireann on 30ᵗʰ November 1966*, 6 December 1966.

196 A4 R2.10, Br. T.G. Moynihan to Lynch, 6 December 1966, A4 R2.09, Br. Moynihan to O'Malley, 6 December 1966.

197 A4 R2.07, *Note of meeting with the Minister*, 9 December 1966, Doyle, *Leading the Way*, p. 131.

198 NA D/T 98/6/144, S.12891F, *Memorandum to the Government, Provision of a grant in lieu of school fees to Secondary Schools opting for the Minister's scheme, Office of the Minister for Education*, 26 January 1967, pp. 1–3.

199 Ibid.

200 NA 99/5/1, G.C.12/15, Cabinet Minutes, 31 January 1967, pp. 2–3.

201 DDA AB8/B/XV/b/05, *McQuaid Papers*, Minutes, Standing Committee of the Hierarchy, 10 January 1967, p. 2.

202 Fergus to Ó Raifeartaigh, 17 January 1967.

203 NA D/T 98/6/144, S.12891F, Ó Raifeartaigh to Fergus, 30 January 1967.

204 Ibid.

205 Fergus to Ó Raifeartaigh, 2 February 1967.

206 DDA AB8/B/XV/b/05, *McQuaid Papers, Memorandum from the Catholic Managerial Committee to the Episcopal Commission for Post-Primary Education*, 12 February 1967, p. 1.

207 NA D/T 98/6/144, S.12891F, *The Minister's Scheme for Free Education, Office of the Minister for Education*, February 1967, p. 5, CCSS, *Meeting of Managerial Associations with An tAire on 16/12/1966*, p. 1.

208 DDA AB8/B/XV/b/05, *McQuaid Papers*, Note by Martin of meeting with Hughes, 9 January 1967.

209 NA D/T 98/6/144, S.12891F, Hughes to O'Malley, 27 January 1967.

210 Ibid.

211 Ibid.

212 DDA AB8/B/XV/b/05, *McQuaid Papers, Summary of points made by the Minister to the Joint Managerial Committee*, 31 January 1967.

213 Ibid.

214 DDA AB8/B/XV/b/05, *McQuaid Papers, Memorandum by the Catholic Managerial Committee to the Hierarchy*, 12 February 1967.

215 Hughes to McQuaid, 2 February 1967.

216 McQuaid to Hughes, 3 February 1967.

217 McQuaid to Fergus, 21 February 1967.

218 NA D/T 98/6/144, S.12891F, McQuaid to Ó Raifeartaigh, 27 January 1967.

219 DDA AB8/B/XV/b/05, *McQuaid Papers*, Note by Martin, Meetings of Fr. Hughes and Mother Jordana with the Major Superiors, 26 January 1967.

220 Ibid., McQuaid to O'Malley, 2 February 1967.

221 O'Malley to McQuaid, 7 February 1967, McQuaid to O'Malley, 8 February 1967.

222 NA D/T 98/6/144, S.12891F, Note of discussion between the Minister, Mr. Donogh O'Malley, and His Eminence Cardinal Conway at Dundalk on 15th February 1967, p. 2.

223 Randles, *Post-Primary Education*, pp. 255–60, 'ASTI Presidential Address by Seán Bromell', *Secondary Teacher*, vol. 2, no. 4, April 1967, pp. 6–11.

224 *Seanad Debates*, vol. 62, col. 1074–111, 9 February 1967.

225 Ibid., col. 1090.

226 O'Connor, *A Troubled Sky*, p. 155.

227 Randles, *Post-Primary Education*, p. 261, T. O'Dea, Editorial, *Secondary Teacher*, vol. 2, no. 5, May 1967, p. 5.

228 DDA AB8/B/XV/b/05, *McQuaid Papers*, McQuaid to O'Malley, 11 February 1967.

229 NA D/T 98/6/144, S.12891F, Ó Raifeartaigh, Note of discussion between O'Malley and Cardinal Conway, 15 February 1967, pp. 1–3.

230 Ibid., p. 1.

231 Ibid., pp. 1–2.

232 Ibid., p. 3.

233 DDA AB8/B/XV/b/05, *McQuaid Papers*, *Memorandum from the Catholic Managerial Committee to the Episcopal Commission for Post-Primary Education*, 12 February 1967.

234 Ibid., pp. 1–2.

235 Ibid., p. 2.

236 Hughes to McQuaid, 17 February 1967.

237 DDA AB8/B/XV/b/05, *McQuaid Papers*, *The O'Malley Scheme, Note for the information of the Bishops*, February 1967.

238 Hughes to the Clerical Major Superiors, 17 February 1967, Doyle, *Leading the Way*, p. 133.

239 DDA AB8/B/XV/b/05, *McQuaid Papers*, Hughes to O'Malley, 24 February 1967.

240 Hughes to the Clerical Major Superiors, 17 February 1967.

241 McQuaid to Fergus, 21 February 1967.

242 Fergus to McQuaid, 20 February 1967.

243 Circular M15/67, Department of Education, February 1967, Circular M32/67, Department of Education, May 1967.

244 DDA AB8/B/XV/b/05, *McQuaid Papers*, McQuaid to Fergus, 21 February 1967.

245 O'Connor, *A Troubled Sky*, pp. 152–5.

246 *Irish Times*, 'O'Malley – Don't Expect Miracles: Handling of Free Education', 17 February 1967.

247 Randles, *Post-Primary Education*, p. 276, Doyle, *Leading the Way*, p. 134.

248 *Committee of Public Accounts, Appropriation Accounts 1967–68*, p. 118.

249 DDA AB8/B/XV/b/05, *McQuaid Papers*, Minutes, General Meeting of the Hierarchy, 20–1 June 1967, p. 5, O'Malley to Fergus, 16 June 1967.

250 NA D/T 98/6/95, S.16890, F.113233, *Memorandum to the Government, Office of the Minister for Education*, 27 June 1967, pp. 10–12.

251 O'Connor, *A Troubled Sky*, p. 141, Doyle, *Leading the Way*, p. 134.

252 *Seanad Debates*, vol. 62, col. 1108, 9 February 1967.

253 *Tuarascáil, Tablaí Staitistic, An Roinn Oideachais 1966–67* (Dublin, 1968), p. 36, *Tuarascáil, Tablaí Staitistic, An Roinn Oideachais 1967–68* (Dublin, 1969), p. 3.

254 *Tuarascáil, An Roinn Oideachais 1966–67*, p. 65, *Tuarascáil, An Roinn Oideachais 1967–68*, p. 73.

255 *Tuarascáil, An Roinn Oideachais 1967–68*, p. 4.

256 *Tuarascáil, Tablaí Staitistic, An Roinn Oideachais 1965–66* (Dublin, 1967), p. 3, *Tuarascáil, An Roinn Oideachais 1966–67*, p. 36.

257 NA DFA 2003/17/383, Ó Floinn, *Recent Developments in Education*, June 1972; *Tuarascáil, Tablaí Staitistic, An Roinn Oideachais 1968/69–1971/72* (Dublin, 1974), p. 26.

258 Horgan, *Seán Lemass*, pp. 300–1, T. Garvin, *Preventing the Future: Why was Ireland so Poor for so Long* (Dublin, 2004), p. 158.

259 Horgan, *Seán Lemass*, pp. 300–1.

260 O'Connor, *A Troubled Sky*, p. 141.

261 *Dáil Debates*, vol. 232, col. 464, 6 February 1968.

262 Circular M1/67, Department of Education, February 1967, pp. 1–2.

263 Department of Education, *Memorandum, Organisation of Post-Primary Transport Scheme*, February 1967, pp. 1–2.

264 Circular M2/67, Department of Education, June 1967, p. 5.

265 *Dáil Debates*, vol. 232, col. 468, 6 February 1968.

266 Ibid.

267 Appendix 1, Table 2, p. 328; *Committee of Public Accounts, Appropriation Accounts 1966–67*, p. 156, *Committee of Public Accounts, Appropriation Accounts 1967–68*, p. 266.

268 *Dáil Debates*, vol. 232, col. 463–5, 6 February 1968.

269 *Committee of Public Accounts, Appropriation Accounts 1967–68*, p. 121.

6

A quiet revolution – higher education: 1966–68

Donogh O'Malley's term of office and indeed the whole process of educational expansion in the 1960s have been inextricably linked with free post-primary education, but it was by no means the sole policy advance promoted by the Minister. The most striking aspect of O'Malley's term was not any single educational advance but the wide range of initiatives undertaken by the state in almost every aspect of the educational system. The expansion of higher technical education was an equally enduring and influential legacy of O'Malley's term as Minister for Education, although it was largely overshadowed by the introduction of free education. O'Malley also made a determined attempt to reshape the structure of university education. He sidelined the long-awaited report of the Commission on Higher Education and vigorously promoted a merger between Trinity College and University College Dublin. While the Minister's dramatic initiative for university merger did not transform the landscape of university education as he had hoped, O'Malley played a crucial part in achieving a quieter but much more radical transformation in higher technical education.

Founding the RTCs

O'Malley identified the foundation of the Regional Technical Colleges (RTCs) as a key priority in his letter to Lemass on 29 July 1966.[1] The establishment of the RTCs had been a policy objective of the government since Hillery's policy announcement in May 1963 and O'Malley played a leading role in making the proposal a reality. He appointed a special consortium of architects, engineers and quantity surveyors to supervise the construction of the colleges shortly after taking up office. O'Malley requested the consortium, Building Design Associates, to design the proposed colleges in Waterford, Galway, Sligo and Dundalk, while they were also requested to act as consultants to the architects appointed by the local VECs at the other centres. The appointment of the consortium was intended to reduce the costs to the state and the time required to build the colleges. O'Malley told Lynch on 24 February 1967 that the work of the consortium would reduce the estimated building time for the RTCs by 20%, while the adoption of a common building system for the whole project would bring a saving of about 10% in the building costs.[2] O'Malley also appointed a Steering Committee on Technical Education to formulate a definite plan for the development of the colleges, dealing with the educational require- ments, courses and organisation of the new institutions. The Minister established the Steering Committee on 20 September 1966, to advise him on technical education generally but primarily to provide the building consortium with a detailed educational brief for the establishment of the RTCs.[3] The Committee, which was chaired by Noel Mulcahy, senior man- agement specialist at the Irish Management Institute, was composed of members drawn from the business community, the trade union movement and universities, as well as officials from various departments.[4] O'Malley selected a broad-based committee, which included members who would bring a business or managerial perspective to the development of technical education.

The Steering Committee was given the considerable responsibility of producing an educational brief for the regional colleges, which would take into account all relevant considerations. They were informed that the Minister had decided to build eight RTCs and were asked to advise on the need for a ninth college in Letterkenny, Co. Donegal. This substantial undertaking had to be completed in the short term, as the consortium was awaiting an educational brief for the colleges.[5] The Minister's decision to appoint the consortium almost simultaneously with the establishment of the Steering Committee placed considerable pressure on the Committee to produce its report as quickly as possible.[6] The Steering Committee submit- ted a Preliminary Brief to the department in January 1967, which outlined the accommodation requirements of the colleges by making projections for the target population of students in each region. The Committee's final report, which was completed in April 1967, dealt more fully with the role of the RTCs and the expansion of the limited facilities for higher technical education.[7]

The final report emphasised that the availability of increased technical knowledge and skill at all levels was a necessary condition for further eco- nomic growth and the promotion of enterprise among the Irish people. The Committee asserted that the Irish state had generally failed to give its people a genuine opportunity to become technically skilled, due at least in part to the established academic bias in the educational system: 'Ireland has largely failed to provide this resource.'[8] They considered that the RTCs would help to fulfil the national need for a greater supply of skilled technical personnel, which was an essential requirement if the national economy was to adapt successfully to free trade with Britain and the likely accession of the state to the EEC. The report envisaged that the new colleges would be concerned with filling gaps in the supply of industrial manpower, particularly in the technician area: but the main long-term function of the new institutions would be to provide education for trade and industry over a wide range of occupations, especially in engineering and science but also in business, languages and other subjects.[9] The Committee emphasised that planning for the colleges should take account of the economic and social needs of developing regions, where investment in education was a necessary element of industrial development.[10] Their conclusions reflected the prevailing consensus that investment in technical education was an indispensable prerequisite for economic progress and underlined that O'Malley was not alone in regarding the establishment of the Regional Technical Colleges as an urgent necessity.

The Committee envisaged a wide variety of courses for different age cohorts within the colleges. The RTCs were intended to provide senior cycle post-primary courses leading to the Leaving Certificate, with a bias towards science and technical subjects.[11] Significantly, the original purpose of the new colleges had altered considerably since May 1963, when Hillery proposed that the Technical Schools Leaving Certificate would be provided for students in the 'Regional Technological Colleges'.[12] Hillery's proposal had been quietly dropped; neither the Committee nor Hillery's successors favoured the idea of a separate public examination for technical subjects. The Committee envisaged that the new colleges would provide apprenticeship training and courses for technician qualifications at various levels. The colleges would also offer third-level courses leading to higher technician or professional qualifications, as well as adult education courses.[13] The wide range of technical courses envisaged by the Committee reflected their concern that the new institutions should not only meet the short-term demand for more technicians but also expand the limited provision for higher technical education.

The Steering Committee's recommendations gave a powerful impetus to the rapid development of the RTCs. They advised the Minister to proceed with all eight of the colleges, whose location had already been fixed, as soon as possible.[14] The department was encouraged to investigate the possibility of phasing the construction programme at each college to ensure a reasonable rate of capital expenditure. The Committee did not favour a delay in providing any of the colleges, but recommended that if part of the project was to be deferred, then the colleges in Cork, Limerick, Waterford and Galway should have priority and should proceed without delay.[15] The Committee also recommended that a Local Technical College, providing mainly for Leaving Certificate courses and apprentice training, should be established at Letterkenny. They considered that it was not necessary to provide the full range of courses appropriate to a regional college in Donegal initially, but that the site for the institution should be large enough to accommodate its expansion to full RTC status at a later stage.[16] The Steering Committee emphasised that the colleges must be allowed to adapt to social, economic and technological changes: 'we do not foresee any final fixed pattern of courses in the Colleges'.[17] They also warned that the progress of the RTCs should not be restricted by 'any artificial limitation of either the scope or the level of their educational achievements'.[18] The Committee declined to set any limit to the future development of the new institutions.

O'Malley generally accepted the recommendations of the Steering Committee. He fully endorsed the recommendation in favour of proceeding immediately with the construction of the eight colleges, whose location had already been fixed, in a submission to the government on 15 June 1967.[19] The Minister proposed to phase the building work over an extended period to enable the capital cost to be spread over five to six years.[20] The adoption of a phased process of construction for the RTCs closely followed the advice of the Committee. Moreover O'Malley shared the Committee's conviction that the development of technical education and technician training was an economic imperative. He told the government that 'The availability and demand for technical education are of the essence in relation to our future industrial progress.'[21] One of the few differences between O'Malley and the Steering Committee concerned the establishment of a ninth college in Letterkenny. O'Malley had already decided to propose a regional college for Donegal well before the Committee completed its deliberations. He informed Lemass on 8 November 1966 that he intended to seek the government's approval for an additional college in Letterkenny.[22] The establishment of an additional RTC in Donegal was, however, the only significant issue concerning the new colleges where the Minister paid little attention to the views of the Steering Committee.

The report was influential in shaping the state's approach not only to the foundation of the RTCs but also to the wider development of higher technical education. The Committee asserted that the need for skilled technical education was sufficiently great that the state should act to stimulate demand for the new institutions if necessary, by giving appropriate recognition to the awards conferred by the new colleges.[23] They recommended the establishment of a national Council for Educational Awards, which would set the standards for admission to and qualification from courses in technical education. The proposed Council was intended to approve examination syllabuses and courses in the regional colleges and technical schools, awarding certificates and diplomas to those successful in the approved examinations.[24] This recommendation proved influential, although it was not implemented immediately, as the department wished to consult the newly formed Higher Education Authority (HEA) on the proposal. The Authority soon endorsed the Steering Committee's case for formal recognition of technical courses and qualifications. The HEA's first report to the government in March 1969 recommended the establishment of a national Council, which would award qualifications for the successful completion of courses undertaken at third-level institutions other than the universities.[25] The government agreed on 9 March 1971 that the department should proceed to draft legislation for the creation of the National Council for Educational Awards (NCEA).[26] The NCEA was established on an ad hoc basis in April 1972, as the relevant legislation faced a lengthy delay before its enactment.[27] The foundation of the NCEA provided an institutional framework for the recognition of technical courses and qualifications at a national level for the first time.

The Committee also proposed a radical restructuring of the educational system on a regional basis. They recommended the establishment of Regional Education Councils, which would absorb the local VECs and take responsibility for all strands of education in each region. The proposed regional councils would include representatives of the Minister, the ecclesiastical authorities, trade unions, employers, local councillors and all the educational interests.[28] This proposal, which would have involved the creation of a unified educational system with common regional structures, proved too radical even for O'Malley. Most officials of the department did not support a regional reorganisation of the educational system and the proposal was ignored. But the report of the Steering Committee exerted considerable influence on the rapid expansion of higher technical education. The Committee had provided a wide-ranging educational brief for the foundation of the colleges within a remarkably short period of time.[29] The efficiency of the Committee ensured that the construction of the RTCs proceeded with minimal delay, while its report provided an essential basis for the planning of the educational facilities to be provided by the new colleges. The recommendations of the Steering Committee paved the way for the expansion and development of the traditionally neglected area of technical education.

O'Malley initially proposed that the state should finance the building and operation of the new colleges even before the Committee completed its report, but failed to secure the approval of the Cabinet for his plans. He first raised the need for the state to finance the RTCs in October 1966, but his initial proposal was withdrawn due to the opposition of the Department of Finance.[30] O'Malley submitted a more detailed proposal to the government on 2 December 1966: he argued that both the capital cost of building the colleges and the current costs of administration should be financed entirely by the state.[31] He also made the case to his colleagues for the establishment of a ninth college in Co. Donegal. The Minister for Finance, Charles Haughey, agreed in principle that the cost of building the RTCs should be covered by the state, but rejected any suggestion that the operational costs of the new colleges should also be met from the Exchequer. Haughey firmly rejected the provision of an additional college for Donegal, on the basis that the state faced a 'critical financial position' and could not afford a ninth RTC when it was already proposed to establish such a college in Sligo.[32] O'Malley submitted another memorandum on 6 January 1967 which reiterated the case for a college in Donegal, but the Department of Finance remained implacably opposed to the establishment of an additional college. O'Malley therefore withdrew his proposals from the Cabinet agenda on 10 January.[33] He made little progress with his proposals for higher technical education before the Steering Committee completed its report.

The Minister for Education's next submission to the government on 15 June 1967 drew heavily on the analysis of the Steering Committee. O'Malley's proposal echoed the report in arguing that it was necessary not simply to satisfy the existing demand for technical education, but to stimulate 'a swing towards technical education and technician training in all its aspects'.[34] The detailed study carried out by the Committee indicated that the number of students and variety of courses in the colleges would far exceed those originally visualised by the department: it was estimated that the RTCs would serve over 11,000 students outside Dublin by 1975. The revised estimate of student numbers demanded more extensive accommodation than the department had anticipated, significantly increasing the estimated building costs.[35] But O'Malley asserted that as a result of the analysis undertaken by the Committee, the floor areas of the colleges were being kept to the minimum level necessary for the projected student numbers: moreover the work of the consortium was reducing the unit building costs. He argued therefore that, in view of the extensive scope of the colleges, they represented good value for money.[36] O'Malley sought the approval of the government to proceed with the establishment of nine RTCs, including an additional college in Donegal. He again proposed that the state should finance the capital cost of building all the colleges, as well as their annual operational costs.[37]

This ambitious proposal met with firm opposition from the Minister for Finance. Haughey argued that the operational costs of the colleges should be met by the relevant VECs: he was also alarmed at the escalation in the building costs for the colleges and warned that they should not be planned 'on an over-ambitious scale'.[38] He argued that only four RTCs should be established initially, at Cork, Limerick, Galway and Waterford. O'Malley immediately rejected the proposal that the government should proceed with only four colleges immediately. He argued that the state had to make a firm commitment to the development of technical education and any retreat from the establishment of all the colleges in the short term would 'cast considerable doubt on the Government's confidence in the entire project'.[39] The Cabinet did not make a definite decision between the opposing positions taken by the two ministers at its meeting on 4 July 1967, instead seeking more detailed information from O'Malley on the capital costs of the colleges.[40]

The officials wasted no time in compiling the supplementary information: O'Malley submitted a further proposal to the government on 7 July.[41] On this occasion the department outlined not only a detailed breakdown of capital costs for each college but also a definite time scale for phasing the programme of building work for the RTCs. It was proposed that building works on the six smaller colleges would start in the spring of 1968, while the work on the colleges in Cork, Limerick and Galway would not begin until 1969. The department envisaged that the RTCs would become operational on a phased basis from September 1969, anticipating that the building process would be completed by September 1972.[42] O'Malley and the senior officials tenaciously lobbied the government to secure an early decision on the foundation of the RTCs and to maximise the level of direct state support for the new colleges. Leading officials of the Department of Education, including MacGearailt and O'Connor, strongly promoted the RTCs in discussions with the Department of Finance.[43] The persistent efforts of the Minister and key officials were rewarded on 11 July 1967, when the Cabinet agreed that the state should finance the building costs of the eight colleges, whose location had already been announced. The Cabinet approved the proposal for the capital financing of eight RTCs by the Exchequer, subject to further consultation between O'Malley and Haughey on the date for the start of building works at the three larger colleges in Cork, Limerick and Galway.[44] Despite this proviso to the Cabinet decision, O'Malley secured a definite commitment by the government to proceed with eight new colleges in the short term. The Cabinet approved the approach favoured by O'Malley and the Steering Committee, authorising the building of all these colleges on a phased basis, over the recommendation of the Department of Finance to proceed with only four RTCs initially.

The Minister was, however, not entirely successful in his lobbying within the government. The Cabinet on 11 July postponed any decision on the funding of the operational costs for the RTCs and on the proposal for a ninth college in Donegal.[45] O'Malley's determination to secure an additional RTC in Letterkenny soon became another bone of contention with the Minister for Finance. When O'Malley again sought the government's approval for a new college in Donegal on 8 September, Haughey strongly opposed the establishment of an additional college. He argued that the RTCs were meant to serve regional rather than local needs and that providing such facilities for a single county would create an unwelcome precedent, which would encourage demands for the establishment of further colleges in other local areas.[46] Moreover Haughey commented that 'a convincing case has not been made for this College', especially as Donegal lacked the industrial base which was essential to the success of such colleges.[47] O'Malley, however, made a plausible case for the establishment of an additional college in Letterkenny. He considered that Donegal should be treated as a regional college area in its own right, on the basis of the size of the county and of the geographical reality that at most only part of Donegal could be directly served by an outside centre for technical education.[48] O'Malley argued too that the establishment of a centre of technical education would provide the necessary trained personnel for local economic progress and would help to stimulate industrial development in the county.[49] The report of the Steering Committee had emphasised the positive impact of an RTC on the economic and social development of its catchment area.[50] O'Malley's proposal made explicit a key consideration which influenced the government's support for the new colleges – namely the conviction that the RTCs would directly promote economic development in the regions.

The Minister for Education had some powerful allies in his efforts to secure a college for Donegal, including Neil Blaney, Minister for Agriculture, and Dr. Anthony MacFeely, Bishop of Raphoe. Blaney had unsuccessfully lobbied Hillery in February 1965 for the establishment of a regional college in Donegal: as a TD representing a Donegal constituency, Blaney was a reliable supporter of O'Malley's proposal within the Cabinet.[51] MacFeely provided another influential voice in favour of the idea. He appealed directly to Lemass on 23 August 1966, urging the Taoiseach to ensure that Donegal did not become 'the Cinderella of the country' due to its geographical isolation and the lack of adequate facilities for technical education.[52] Lemass retired from office before the issue was resolved, but MacFeely lost no time in renewing his representations to the new Taoiseach, appealing to Lynch on 15 December to consider favourably the establishment of a third-level college in Letterkenny.[53] O'Malley made sure to inform the Cabinet of the Bishop's representations, enclosing a copy of MacFeely's appeal to Lemass with the Department of Education's proposal on 8 September.[54] The Minister's lobbying, which was reinforced by powerful supporters inside and outside the government, carried the day despite the objections of the Department of Finance. The Cabinet agreed on 17 October 1967 that a Regional Technical College should be established in Co. Donegal.[55] There is no doubt that O'Malley's persistent advocacy for an additional college made a crucial difference to the outcome. He took the decision to propose an RTC in Donegal despite the Steering Committee's recommendation against it and he submitted at least four separate proposals for a ninth RTC to the government before a favourable decision was secured.

O'Malley did not, however, secure the government's approval for the payment of the operational costs of the RTCs by the Exchequer during his term of office. The Cabinet again deferred the issue on 17 October 1967.[56] The question of financing the operational costs of the new colleges was constantly deferred over the next year and was not considered by the government again during O'Malley's term. It was not until July 1968 that O'Malley's successor, Brian Lenihan, submitted a revised proposal to the government, which reiterated that the current costs of the RTCs should be met directly by the state. The Department of Finance remained opposed to this approach and the proposal was deferred once again.[57] Although the arrangements for funding the RTCs remained ill-defined until the new colleges were actually in operation, the state soon took responsibility for financing the operational costs of the colleges through the VECs. The Department of Education made grants to the VECs from 1970–71 to meet the running costs of the colleges, on the basis of estimates submitted by the committees.[58] While all the arrangements for financing the RTCs were not finalised during his term, O'Malley and the senior officials of his department secured the government's approval for the key policy decisions, which ensured the establishment of new technical colleges in most regions of the country.

The policy decisions initiated by O'Malley in 1967, mainly but not entirely on the basis of the recommendations of the Steering Committee, exerted a profound influence on the future development of technical education in the Republic. The decision by the state to finance the establishment of a network of RTCs opened the way for a rapid expansion of higher technical education and the creation of a new sector in higher education during the following decade. The first five colleges, in Athlone, Carlow, Dundalk, Sligo and Waterford opened their doors to students for the first time in September 1969, while a sixth RTC was founded in Letterkenny in 1971.[59] The remaining colleges were established on a phased basis by 1975, with the exception of the proposed RTC in Limerick where the government did not proceed with a regional college in the short term, deciding instead to establish a National Institute of Higher Education.[60]

The foundation of the RTCs transformed the educational opportunities available to vocational pupils, who had previously been denied any real avenue to higher education especially in rural areas. The proactive approach taken by O'Malley and officials of his department made an invaluable contribution to the development of higher technical education. O'Malley acted decisively to implement key recommendations of the Steering Committee, although his approach was not simply dictated by the Committee. Following the Minister's death, Seán Cooney, President of the VTA, paid a warm tribute to O'Malley, giving his key role in planning the development of the RTCs the same weight as the introduction of free post-primary education: 'Free post-primary education, the free transport scheme and his plans for the development of regional colleges will remain everlasting monuments to him.'[61] The VTA at least fully recognised the high priority given by O'Malley to the foundation of the RTCs and his considerable influence on the expansion of higher technical education. The importance attached to the rapid establishment of the RTCs by O'Malley himself, the Steering Committee and the government as a whole reflected the transformation in the state's policy towards technical education within the space of a single decade. The government promoted the expansion of technical education, which had been neglected and even restricted by the state and the Catholic Hierarchy until the late 1950s, as an indispensable element in the economic development of the nation.

Merger

The Minister also sought to achieve a radical reshaping of university education. The department under O'Malley formulated a definite overall policy for the development of university education for the first time. The state's newly developed policy approach owed more to O'Malley's zealous promotion of a merger between Trinity College and UCD than to the report of the Commission on Higher Education. The report of the Commission, which had been awaited with increasing impatience by the government, was completed in February 1967.[62] The Cabinet agreed to publish the summary of the report on 7 March 1967.[63] But the lengthy delay in the deliberations of the Commission greatly reduced the impact of its recommendations. James Dukes, who later became the first secretary of the HEA, even commented that 'they had no impact that I can recall'.[64] While Dukes overstated the case, there is no doubt that by 1967 the Minister and senior officials were no longer willing to wait for the Commission's report before formulating plans for the future development of higher education. Although O'Malley avoided any policy statement on university education until he received the report, he first submitted proposals for the merger of

Trinity College and UCD to the Cabinet on 15 December 1966. The Minister's memorandum, which was entitled *The Problem of Trinity College Dublin*, emphasised that Trinity College was seeking extensive capital investment by the state in the short term, at a time when the college still contained a substantial proportion of non-Irish students, who were drawn especially from Britain.[65] O'Malley argued that 'the State should not have to shoulder the enormous expense of duplication that will be involved' in financing the expansion of two rival universities in Dublin, especially as the additional funding for one of those colleges represented a commitment to the education of non-Irish students.[66] The Minister's proposals envisaged the establishment of a single University of Dublin with Trinity College and University College as its two constituent colleges 'and with each complementary to the other'.[67] The government deferred any decision on O'Malley's plan until it received the report of the Commission, which decided against a formal association between Trinity College and UCD and recommended instead close collaboration and joint development in some areas between the two colleges.[68] The Minister was convinced, however, that it was essential 'to rationalise the university position in Dublin' through the establishment of a formal relationship between the two colleges.[69] O'Malley had already privately ruled out a key recommendation of the Commission even before he received its report.

The Commission produced an immensely detailed and comprehensive report, which dealt with all areas of higher education and contained thirty-seven principal recommendations. The report favoured the absorption of the increasing demand for third-level education by new institutions and a more limited expansion of university education, which would protect high academic standards. The Commission asserted that it was the responsibility of the universities to match student numbers with available resources of staff, accommodation and equipment: 'It is essential that the present inadequate staff/student ratio be amended and overcrowding eliminated before further expansion is undertaken.'[70] They recommended that no additional university should be established. Instead the report proposed the creation of a new type of institution, the New College, to meet part of the expanding demand for higher education. The new institutions, which were to be established initially in Dublin and Limerick, would award a pass degree for three-year courses and diplomas for shorter courses.[71] The recommendation for New Colleges proved to be one of the most controversial proposals made by the Commission: it was criticised by educationalists and officials of the Department of Education for setting a ceiling to the aspirations of students within the proposed institutions.[72] The Commission also considered that technical training and research should be undertaken outside the universities under the auspices of a Technological Authority:

they suggested that the training of technicians should be a primary function of the vocational education system. They recommended, however,
that new research developments should usually be accommodated in the
universities or existing research institutes.[73] The Commission was concerned to protect the interests of the universities and feared that excessive
student numbers would damage the quality of university education. The
report was emphatic in its conclusion that the universities had to safeguard academic standards at a time of increasing demand for higher education: 'If the universities should falter, they must inevitably be swamped
by the flood of undergraduates; and the consequent lowering of standards
will be transmitted throughout the entire educational system, with grave
consequences in every department of the nation's activities.'[74]

The Commission proposed various institutional modifications in the
university system but did not favour far-reaching changes in the existing
pattern of higher education. They acknowledged that the system of academic appointments in the NUI was unsatisfactory and recommended that
permanent academic appointments in all universities should be made by
the governing authority on the basis of nominations by expert committees.[75] The Commission opposed any formal amalgamation between Trinity
College and UCD and recommended that the constitution of Trinity College
should be reaffirmed by an Act of the Oireachtas. The report proposed that
the NUI should be dissolved so that its three constituent colleges, UCD, UCC
and UCG, could be reconstituted as separate universities: it was envisaged
that the Catholic ecclesiastical authorities would decide the future of
St. Patrick's College, Maynooth, a recognised college of the NUI.[76] This
recommendation certainly proposed an important alteration of the formal
relationship between the three colleges, but it did not involve a dramatic
change in the workings of university education at a practical level. The
Commission itself acknowledged that the NUI worked 'rather as a loose
aggregation of colleges than as an integrated system'.[77] They recommended its abolition on the basis that its organisation was inadequate and
that the colleges had in practice assumed university functions with regard
to courses and examinations. The Commission's recommendation in
favour of three independent universities was an attempt to formalise an
existing pattern of university development rather than an initiative to
reshape fundamentally the structures of higher education.

The Commission endorsed the principle of institutional autonomy for
the universities, although they acknowledged that such autonomy should
be subject to some limitations, as the institutions depended heavily on state
funding. The report therefore proposed the establishment by statute of a
permanent Commission for Higher Education, consisting of nine part-time
members appointed by the government and drawn from outside the

institutions of higher education. Significantly it was envisaged that the new Commission would report directly to the Taoiseach, not the Minister for Education.[78] The permanent Commission would be responsible for the distribution of state funding to the institutions and would undertake a continual review of the development of higher education. The report also proposed the establishment by the Oireachtas of a Council of Irish Universities, which would have the power to set minimum requirements for entry and degree standards; the Council would also oversee the transfer of students and the exchange of information between institutions.[79] The proposed Council, to be composed of members from each college, was intended to provide for formalised co-operation between the institutions of higher education without affecting their autonomy.

The Commission's report received a sceptical response from the Minister for Education. O'Malley thanked the Commission for their work and commented that they had 'served the nation truly and well', at the same press conference where he explicitly rejected their recommendation for the retention of Trinity College and UCD as independent institutions.[80] The Minister acted swiftly following the submission of the report, seeking the approval of the Cabinet for a formal merger between the two colleges on 9 March 1967, shortly after the summary of the report was presented to the government.[81] O'Malley argued that the state had to address the anomalous position of Trinity College, which stood apart 'from the main stream of the nation'.[82] He commented that 'the Commission has to all intents and purposes shied away from the problem'.[83] The Cabinet agreed on 31 March that O'Malley should approach the university authorities with a proposal for the creation of a single University of Dublin, which would incorporate the two existing colleges on a complementary basis.[84] The Minister quickly publicised the government's decision, making his policy announcement on higher education at a press conference on 18 April 1967. O'Malley announced his initiative well before the main body of the report was published: it was not until 1 August 1967 that the first volume of the report was presented to the Cabinet prior to publication.[85] Moreover he informed the authorities of the two colleges about the content of his statement only on the morning of the press conference.[86] O'Malley launched the initiative for the merger of Trinity College and UCD publicly in advance of any consultation with the university authorities, clearly intending that negotiations on the proposal would be undertaken after the announcement in an atmosphere of public approval for the idea.

The Minister told an audience of educational and political journalists that the government aimed in the public interest to establish a formal relationship between the two colleges, despite the contrary views of the Commission.[87] O'Malley proposed the creation of a single university authority, established on a statutory basis, with a subsidiary authority for each constituent college: the powers and composition of each governing body had yet to be decided. O'Malley commented that the government had taken the basic policy decision in favour of a merger and expressed confidence that a viable solution would be found provided that the necessary goodwill was forthcoming.[88] The *Irish Times* accurately commented that the Minister had assumed 'a cheerful, confident, shoot-first-and-ask-questions-afterwards mood'.[89] While he presented the terms of the initiative only in a general fashion, O'Malley made a detailed case for the proposed merger. He emphasised that the pattern of university education in Dublin was profoundly unsatisfactory, presenting a compelling rationale for change on economic, political and educational grounds. The Minister gave the greatest attention to the economic case for a formal co-ordination of activity between the two institutions. He warned that the state could not be expected to subsidise 'avoidable duplication' of university services due to the competing claims of the two colleges.[90] The prospect of a substantial increase in student numbers and the considerable commitment of the state to the university building programmes meant that the government had to insist upon 'a joining of forces with a view to obviating all unnecessary duplication'.[91] He suggested the merger of certain faculties within the new university, arguing that the veterinary faculties of the two colleges could sensibly be merged into a single institution: it would make economic sense too for all science students to be taught under a single roof. While these suggestions were examples of the opportunities offered by a merger rather than final proposals, the Minister's intent to end unnecessary duplication of services and resources was unmistakable. O'Malley emphasised that 'the whole thing cries out for some kind of complementary allocation'.[92] Economic and financial considerations certainly loomed large in the Minister's proposal for the university merger.

O'Malley, however, was concerned to point out that the initiative was not driven solely by economic necessity. He argued that in this instance 'what makes economic sense makes educational sense too'.[93] He believed that the new University of Dublin would be able to provide education of a higher quality than the colleges under existing conditions: the collaboration produced by merger would help to alleviate high staff/student ratios and to raise academic standards.[94] O'Malley also combined appeals to history and national tradition with his analysis of economic realities, arguing that the existing situation was not only financially intolerable but culturally and politically undesirable. He asserted that the government aimed to end 'a most insidious form of partition on our doorstep', the traditional division between Trinity College, once the bastion of the Protestant ruling class, and UCD, which had originally been founded to provide university education for Catholics.[95] The Commission had declined to make any substantive comment on the regulation maintained by the Catholic Hierarchy, which banned the attendance of Catholic students at Trinity College.[96] O'Malley had not sought the agreement of the Hierarchy for the removal of the ban, but aimed to make the regulation redundant through the merger. The Minister was lyrical in his evocation of the cultural and political benefits of merger for the nation in general and Trinity College in particular: 'Trinity is not going to pass away. It will be merely taking the final step across the threshold of that mansion to which it properly belongs, the Irish nation.'[97] O'Malley did not openly challenge the bishops' position, but clearly intended that the merger would circumvent the ban. He asserted that the new University of Dublin would not be 'neutral' but would be multi-denominational, giving full respect and recognition to all denominations of students.[98] He firmly opposed any form of religious segregation within the new university, hoping to create a multi-denominational university institution in Dublin. O'Malley expressed confidence that his initiative would evoke the necessary goodwill among the university authorities and staff to achieve the merger, declaring that 'we are at the opening of a new era in higher education'.[99]

O'Malley's statement on 18 April 1967 was the most dramatic and significant attempt by any Irish government to transform the structures of higher education since the foundation of the state. While the state's policy towards higher education in general was not yet fully clarified, the Minister's announcement had the potential to reshape the pattern of university education in Dublin. The policy statement identified the merger of Trinity College and UCD as the government's most urgent priority in the development of higher education. The Minister's statement received an almost universally positive response across the political spectrum. Fine Gael issued a statement welcoming the proposed merger, although they criticised O'Malley's failure to outline fully his proposed university structure. Likewise Brendan Corish welcomed the Minister's proposal on behalf of the Labour Party, expressing the hope that it would lead to a process of closer integration between the two colleges.[100] The initiative also drew praise from the Church of Ireland Archbishop of Dublin, George Otto Simms and from the Catholic Bishop of Cork, Cornelius Lucey, although the Catholic Hierarchy as a whole made no comment on the proposed merger.[101] The announcement was a public relations triumph for O'Malley. But the implementation of the policy itself was fraught with difficulties and the Minister's strategy of announcing a policy decision in advance of serious negotiations with the relevant stakeholders proved much less effective on this occasion than it had in securing the introduction of free second-level education. O'Malley's confident rhetoric did not reflect the reality of the situation. The Minister had easily brushed aside the views of the Commission on Higher Education, but he faced far greater obstacles in securing the agreement of the two universities to a mutually acceptable form of merger.

The very different reactions of the provost of Trinity College and the authorities of UCD to O'Malley's statement underlined the deep divergence between the two colleges. The provost, Dr. A.J. McConnell, issued a personal statement welcoming O'Malley's initiative. McConnell expressed confidence that Trinity College would 'look at the Minister's plans with the utmost sympathy' and he looked forward to the development of a single university on the basis of the Minister's proposals.[102] The governing body of UCD, which met on 18 April, also immediately announced their support for the initiative in principle, endorsing O'Malley's criticism of wasteful duplication within the university sector. But the governing body disagreed with the Minister's approach to merger, arguing instead that the benefits sought by O'Malley would best be achieved by 'a complete unification of the two institutions'.[103] The UCD authorities urged that the new university should combine all the material and intellectual resources of the two colleges under a single unitary authority.[104] This statement immediately set the scene for confrontation between the Minister and the authorities of UCD, as O'Malley told the press conference on 18 April that a complete fusion of the two institutions would be 'an appallingly bad decision', which would threaten the distinctive identity of the colleges.[105] The emergence of a crucial disagreement on the nature of the merger between the authorities of the two colleges immediately after the Minister's statement did not augur well for the success of his initiative.

The fundamental differences between the official position of UCD and the approach favoured by most staff within Trinity College were fully exposed by a symposium on the university merger in *Studies*. J.P. MacHale, secretary and bursar of UCD, argued strongly for a full unification of the two institutions.[106] MacHale considered that a unitary structure would create a fully integrated university and would minimise avoidable duplication of scarce resources: such an institution would be able to maintain its autonomy, while the Senate of a two-college institution would be dominated by nominees of the government and external bodies. He claimed that the governing body of UCD was willing to sacrifice the traditional identity of the college to create a new university: 'That a university institution should agree to liquidate itself as a separate entity in order that a new and better university structure should rise, phoenix-like, from the ashes, is a very unusual occurrence.'[107] It was evident, however, that UCD, which was the larger institution, was likely to become the dominant force in a unified university. MacHale represented the views of the UCD authorities, who were clearly unwilling to accept merger on an equal basis with a smaller college in a federal structure. MacHale's generous interpretation of the motives of the UCD authorities was not shared in Trinity College. Basil Chubb, Professor of Political Science in TCD, commented that a unitary university would be entirely unacceptable to the staff and graduates of Trinity College.[108] He supported the proposal for a single university with two colleges, on the basis that such a structure would allow the preservation of Trinity's existing academic community and provide the necessary co-operative arrangements to exploit the academic potential of the two colleges in Dublin.[109] While Chubb made his contribution to *Studies* as a personal opinion, his comments accurately reflected the position of the academic staff within Trinity College. Chubb's opposition to a unitary structure was fully endorsed by all the other contributors to *Studies* from Trinity College; the point was reiterated with particular force by Professor T.W. Moody, who had served as a member of the Commission on Higher Education. Moody considered that the proposals for a unitary university would mean 'the extinction of TCD' and warned that only a two-college structure stood any chance of acceptance by the college's staff: 'There being no death-wish in TCD, it will resist a unitary university to the utmost.'[110] The authorities and staff of TCD certainly had no intention of accepting a merger based on unification, which was regarded as a thinly veiled attempt to absorb Trinity into the larger institution. The authorities of Trinity College were concerned to maintain the college's independence and were wary of a merger in which TCD became the junior partner in a combination with a larger institution shaped by a different ethos.[111] The *Studies* symposium underlined that severe and probably irreconcilable differences existed between the UCD authorities and the staff of Trinity College on the nature of any merger from the outset of the debate.

The position of the governing body did not command universal support in UCD. An article in *Studies* by Denis Donoghue, Professor of Modern English and American Literature in UCD, made the case for a single university with two colleges and asserted that the governing body's decision did not accurately represent the views of the academic staff.[112] Certainly many members of the Academic Staff Association in UCD expressed opposition to the idea of a unitary university at a meeting on 12 May 1967.[113] The Minister sought to mobilise support for his proposals within UCD on 12 July, when he addressed the academic staff of the college. O'Malley reiterated his proposal for a single university with two constituent colleges, outlining certain details of the proposed structure.[114] He emphasised that the university would own most of the property of the two colleges and that the university governing body would exercise authority over the entire institution. He envisaged that the central authority would appoint staff and determine the distribution of faculties; the university would also control the admission of students. Both colleges would have equal representation on the university authority, which would also include a minority of government nominees.[115] O'Malley's address underlined that he favoured a strong central authority for a university institution based on a two-college structure. But various proposals outlined by O'Malley on 12 July were deeply unwelcome to the authorities in both colleges. The governing body of UCD was firmly opposed to the idea of equal representation for the two colleges in a merged university: MacHale criticised such a provision as unworkable and unfair to UCD.[116] O'Malley's proposal for a strong university authority, which would control the admission of students, was unwelcome to a strong element in TCD, who sought at most a loose alignment between the two colleges. T.W. Moody strongly argued that control of admissions must remain with each college authority if merger went ahead.[117] The Minister's address did not allay the fear of the authorities and staff in Trinity College that they faced the prospect of losing their independence. O'Malley's clarification of his original announcement did little to advance the prospects for merger.

The sharp division between the UCD authorities and the academic officers and staff of TCD militated against the success of the Minister's plans, despite the positive public response given by representatives of both institutions to the principle of merger. The two colleges initiated negotiations concerning a possible merger, but failed to reach a mutually acceptable settlement. Professor James Meenan, who was a member of UCD's negotiating team, commented in 1968 that the discussions between the colleges were conducted with good will on both sides, but conceded that the negotiations appeared increasingly to be 'an attempt to square a circle'.[118] The disagreement over the unitary solution favoured by the authorities of UCD marked a fundamental division between influential forces in each college, which could not be readily overcome. This basic divergence of opinion meant that no agreement on a joint approach to a merger was possible and it gave strength to those in both institutions who were already sceptical of the benefits of merger. The impasse ensured that merger was not a practical proposition unless the Minister was willing to impose a solution on the universities, which would certainly have united influential elements in both colleges against his initiative. Moreover even if the government was willing to take such a hazardous approach, O'Malley had not initially formulated a definitive proposal for the establishment of the new university and the department lacked detailed information about the staffing requirements and accommodation needs of various faculties in the event of merger.[119] The early death of Donogh O'Malley in March 1968 deprived the initiative of its most eloquent and persistent advocate. But

O'Connor, who supported the proposals for merger, commented that even during O'Malley's term, 'many of us feared that the battle could not be won'.[120] The outlook for the policy of university reorganisation was certainly problematic even before O'Malley's death. The mercurial Minister's confidence that he could overcome the traditional division between the two institutions proved misplaced, not least because the authorities of each college endorsed fundamentally incompatible forms of merger virtually from the outset of the debate. The initiative for the university merger, which was launched with great fanfare, proved to be much less significant than the policy decisions initiated by O'Malley on the expansion of higher technical education, which attracted much less public and media attention.

The dramatic but ultimately fruitless initiative for university merger also contrasted sharply with the low-profile but influential deliberations of a committee of senior officials on the future of higher education. O'Malley established a committee within the department in 1967 to examine the recommendations of the Commission on Higher Education. The committee, which was headed by Ó Raifeartaigh, included MacGearailt, the Deputy Secretary, as well as the Assistant Secretaries and the Chief Inspectors.[121] The committee did not focus primarily on the initiative for merger, as the government had already decided to propose a single University of Dublin by the time the officials began their deliberations.[122] While O'Malley himself shaped the state's policy on the proposed merger, the task of producing a detailed response to the recommendations of the Commission on most other issues was delegated to the officials. The committee endorsed the reconstitution of UCC and UCG as independent universities, although they advised that any action to confer full university status on the colleges in Cork and Galway should be delayed until the negotiations on the merger had been completed.[123] But the officials expressed strong opposition to other key recommendations made by the Commission. They categorically rejected the proposal for New Colleges. The committee considered that the concept of a non-university institution with the power to award pass degrees was unacceptable and likely to undermine the status of all Irish degrees. Moreover they commented that 'the idea is psychologically unsound', as such colleges with a lower entry standard and inferior degrees would merely promote an inferiority complex among their students and staff.[124] The committee therefore also rejected the recommendation that primary teacher training colleges should be attached to the New Colleges: the officials agreed that the period of training for national teachers should be extended to three years but stipulated that the training colleges should be linked to the universities. They dismissed without hesitation the Commission's suggestion that vocational and comprehensive schoolteachers should receive degrees from the New Colleges, while the training of secondary school teachers would remain concentrated in the universities. The officials regarded the Commission's approach to teacher training as divisive and contrary to the established policy of the government.[125] They also rejected the recommendation for a Technological Authority, which would supervise technical training and research.[126] The departmental committee strongly disputed a central conclusion of the report, namely the contention that it was the responsibility of the universities to match student numbers with the available resources. The officials stated bluntly that the ultimate responsibility for the regulation of student numbers rested with the state: 'The issue is fundamentally a national one.'[127] They commented that 'it would be a grave abuse of the universities' autonomy' if they attempted to restrict the level of student access to their institutions without prior consultation with the state.[128] The committee considered that the only proper solution to the challenge of increased student numbers was to be found in regular consultation between the universities and the state. O'Connor, who was a member of the internal committee, believed that 'the Commission was determined to protect the universities at all costs and to make them even more elite than they already were'.[129] The officials were critical of the underlying philosophy of the report, which gave the highest priority to preserving academic standards at university level in an era of rapid expansion.

The committee's comments on the report were not entirely critical. The officials supported various recommendations made by the Commission, including the establishment of a Council of Irish Universities.[130] They also endorsed the creation of a permanent Commission for Higher Education but specified that the new Commission should report to the Minister for Education rather than the Taoiseach.[131] The committee of officials exerted considerable influence in blocking or modifying key proposals made by the Commission. Successive ministers generally accepted the conclusions of the committee and several important recommendations made by the Commission were rejected or amended. The controversial proposal for New Colleges came to nothing. Likewise the related recommendations on teacher training were not implemented. The Higher Education Authority (HEA) was established on a non-statutory basis in August 1968 to oversee the development of higher education.[132] The HEA reported to the Minister for Education and included members drawn from institutions of higher education, in accordance with the recommendation of the departmental committee. The Commission's proposal that the members should be 'persons outside the institutions of higher education' was rejected.[133] The reconstitution of UCC and UCG as independent universities was endorsed by successive ministers, but deferred indefinitely following the failure of the initiative for the university merger.[134] The influence of the Commission on the development of higher education was relatively limited, not least as a result of the critical commentary on their proposals delivered by the internal departmental committee.

The committee's influence, however, was not restricted to a negative critique of specific recommendations in the report. The officials disagreed with the Commission's view that no additional universities should be established. They considered that a new university would help to meet the expanding demand for higher education, if the authorities of the new institution took an innovative approach and offered courses in disciplines, which had traditionally been avoided by the older universities, including higher technological training.[135] The committee proposed the establishment of a new university college in Limerick, which would be linked initially to UCC. They envisaged that the new institution would include an Institute of Technology and an Institute of Education, as well as university arts and science faculties.[136] The proposed institution was very different from the limited concept of the New College, which was to be deliberately restricted in its role and functions. The committee's proposal was not fully implemented, as the HEA later recommended the creation of a national institute of higher education instead of a new university in Limerick.[137] But a key element of the committee's proposal, namely the establishment of a new type of third-level institution offering qualifications in higher technological education, became the cornerstone of the HEA's recommendation.[138] While the proposal for a university did not come to fruition in the short term, the report by the officials was a major constructive contribution to the government's deliberations and helped to influence the eventual decision in favour of a new national institute of higher education in Limerick. The private recommendations of the internal committee were much more influential in shaping the state's policy on higher education for the next decade than the painstaking deliberations of the Commission on Higher Education.

O'Malley: change and continuity

Donogh O'Malley's highly successful and memorable term as Minister for Education ended abruptly with his sudden death on 10 March 1968. O'Malley's dynamic and ambitious approach to the achievement of policy objectives, combined with his skilful use of the media, identified him more firmly with the reform and expansion of the educational system than any other public figure. But O'Malley's political style should not conceal the considerable continuity between his policy approach and the reforming initiatives pursued by his immediate predecessors. O'Malley sought in many areas to implement or extend initiatives first promoted by Hillery or Colley. Perhaps the best example was the development of higher technical education, which was first proposed by Hillery in May 1963. The development of the RTCs was one of the most far-reaching and lasting educational advances delivered by the state in the entire period of economic expansion. This advance was due largely to O'Malley's initiative in establishing the Steering Committee on Technical Education and to the influence which he exerted on the government's policy in the late 1960s. The government's decision to promote the upgrading of technical education, as a significant element in economic development, marked a fundamental break with the tentative and restrictive approach of the previous generation, which had gravely limited the potential of the vocational sector. The development of higher technical education on a national basis for the first time was easily the most radical reform undertaken by the state in the era of educational expansion. O'Malley also gave a higher priority to the restructuring of university education than any of his predecessors, essentially sidelining the report of the Commission on Higher Education and seeking to develop an alternative policy. While the Minister's initiative for the merger of Trinity College and UCD ultimately failed, the deliberations of the departmental committee established by O'Malley proved influential in shaping the state's policy for the development of higher education. The Minister's dynamic reforming approach greatly extended the process of far-reaching change within the educational sector. O'Malley's term essentially completed the transformation of the state's educational policy, which had been initiated by Lemass and Hillery in 1959. Perhaps O'Malley's most significant legacy was not any single initiative, but his successful development of the state's policy of educational expansion to its fullest extent.

Notes

1 NA D/T 97/6/437, S.17913, O'Malley to Lemass, 29 July 1966, pp. 1–2.
2 NA D/T 98/6/831, S.18047A, O'Malley to Lynch, 24 February 1967, 20 June 1967.
3 Steering Committee on Technical Education, *Report to the Minister for Education on Regional Technical Colleges, 1967* (Dublin, 1969), p. 5.
4 Ibid., p. 2.
5 Ibid., p. 5.
6 O'Connor, *A Troubled Sky*, p. 140.
7 Steering Committee on Technical Education, *Report*, pp. 32–3.
8 Ibid., p. 7.
9 Ibid., p. 11.
10 Ibid., p. 8.
11 Ibid., p. 12.

12 NA DFA 2003/17/383, Ó Floinn, *Recent Developments in Education*, June 1972, p. 13; Chapter 3, p. 88.

13 Steering Committee on Technical Education, *Report*, p. 12.

14 Ibid., p. 39.

15 Ibid., pp. 36–9.

16 Ibid., pp. 38–9.

17 Ibid., p. 11.

18 Ibid.

19 NA D/T 98/6/831, S.18047A, G.O. F.39/1/31, *Memorandum to the Government, Regional Technical Colleges, Office of the Minister for Education*, 15 June 1967.

20 Ibid., p. 4.

21 Ibid., p. 6.

22 NA D/T 97/5/510, S.18047A, O'Malley to Lemass, 8 November 1966.

23 Steering Committee on Technical Education, *Report*, p. 8.

24 Ibid.

25 NA D/T 99/1/311, S.16735B, *Memorandum A, Initial Recommendation by the HEA on the question of establishing a Body which would award national qualifications at technician and technological levels*, 20 March 1969, p. 2.

26 NA D/T 1/2002/6/1, G.C.13/104, Cabinet Minutes, 9 March 1971, pp. 1–2.

27 NA D/T 2003/16/448, S.18592A, C.O. 1253, *Memorandum for the Government, Establishment of a temporary ad hoc National Council for Educational Awards*, 11 February 1972, NCEA, *First Annual Report 1972–73* (Dublin, 1973), p. 7.

28 Steering Committee on Technical Education, *Report*, p. 40.

29 O'Connor, *A Troubled Sky*, pp. 176–7.

30 NA D/T 97/6/510, S.18047A, G.O. F.39/1/31, *Memorandum to the Government, RTCs, Office of the Minister for Education*, 28 October 1966.

31 *Memorandum, RTCs*, 2 December 1966, pp. 1–9.

32 Ibid., p. 5.

33 NA D/T 97/6/510, S.18047A, G.O. F.39/1/31, *Memorandum to the Government, RTCs*, 6 January 1967, pp. 1–2, Ó Nualláin to Ó Dálaigh, 10 January 1967.

34 NA D/T 98/6/831, S.18047A, G.O. F.39/1/31, *Memorandum to the Government, RTCs, Office of the Minister for Education*, 15 June 1967, p. 5.

35 Ibid., p. 3.

36 Ibid., p. 4.

37 Ibid., p. 8.

38 Ibid., p. 4.

39 Ibid., p. 6.

40 NA D/T 98/6/831, S.18047A, Ó Nualláin to Ó Dálaigh, 4 July 1967.

41 NA D/T 98/6/831, S.18047A, *Memorandum to the Government, RTCs, Office of the Minister for Education*, 7 July 1967, pp. 1–4.

42 Ibid.

43 Interview with Tony Ó Dálaigh, 3 May 2002.

44 NA 99/5/1, G.C.12/46, Cabinet Minutes, 11 July 1967, pp. 4–5.

45 NA D/T 98/6/831, S.18047A, Ó Nualláin to Ó Dálaigh, 11 July 1967.

46 NA D/T 98/6/831, S.18047A, *Memorandum to the Government*, RTCs, 8 September 1967, pp. 3–4.

47 Ibid., p. 4.

48 Ibid., p. 4.

49 Ibid., p. 2.

50 Steering Committee on Technical Education, *Report*, p. 8.

51 NA D/T 97/6/510, S.18047A, N. Blaney to Hillery, 5 February 1965.

52 A. MacFeely to Lemass, 23 August 1966.

53 MacFeely to Lynch, 15 December 1966.

54 NA D/T 98/6/831, S.18047A, *Memorandum to the Government*, RTCs, 8 September 1967, p. 1.

55 NA 99/5/1, G.C.12/65, Cabinet Minutes, 17 October 1967, p. 3.

56 NA D/T 98/6/831, S.18047A, Ó Nualláin to Ó Dálaigh, 17 October 1967.

57 NA D/T 99/1/481, S.18047B, *Memorandum to the Government, Financing of annual operational costs of RTCs, Office of the Minister for Education*, 26 July 1968, p. 2.

58 *Committee of Public Accounts, Appropriation Accounts 1969–70* (Dublin, 1974), pp. 53–4.

59 NA DFA 2003/17/383, Ó Floinn, *Recent Developments in Education*, June 1972, p. 14.

60 NA D/T 99/1/311, S.16735B, Decision slip, *Cruinniú Rialtais*, 6 December 1968.

61 VTA, *General Secretary's Report 1967–68, Annual Congress 1968* (Dublin, 1968), p. 1.

62 *Report, Commission on Higher Education, Summary*, p. 14, UCDA, *Cearbhall Ó Dálaigh Papers*, P51/39 (12–15), M. Carty to C. Ó Dálaigh, 2 December 1966.

63 NA 99/5/1, G.C.12/22, Cabinet Minutes, 7 March 1967, pp. 2–3.

64 Interview with James Dukes, 28 April 2003.

65 NA D/T 98/6/195, S.13962C, C.O.686/4, *Memorandum for the Government, The Problem of Trinity College Dublin, Office of the Minister for Education*, 15 December 1966, pp. 1–3.

66 Ibid., p. 2.

67 *The Problem of Trinity College Dublin*, p. 23.

68 NA D/T 98/6/195, S.13962C, Ó Nualláin to Ó Dálaigh, 20 December 1966, *Report, Commission on Higher Education, Summary*, pp. 47–51.

69 *Irish Times*, 'TCD and UCD to be United, O'Malley Announces Wedding Plans', 19 April 1967.

70 *Report, Commission on Higher Education, Summary*, p. 95.

71 Ibid.

72 O'Connor, *A Troubled Sky*, p. 167.

73 *Report, Commission on Higher Education, Summary*, pp. 95–6.

74 Ibid., p. 98.
75 Ibid., p. 64.
76 Ibid., pp. 48–9.
77 Ibid., p. 47.
78 Ibid., p. 54.
79 Ibid., p. 53.
80 *Irish Times*, 'TCD and UCD to be United, O'Malley Announces Wedding Plans', 19 April 1967.
81 NA D/T 98/6/195, S.13962C, C.O.686/4, *Memorandum, The Problem of Trinity College Dublin*, 9 March 1967, p. 1.
82 Ibid.
83 Ibid.
84 NA 99/5/1, G.C.12/22, Cabinet Minutes, 31 March 1967, pp. 3–4.
85 NA D/T 98/6/747, S.17744, Ó Nualláin to Ó Dálaigh, 1 August 1967.
86 *Irish Times*, 'TCD and UCD to be United, O'Malley Announces Wedding Plans', 19 April 1967.
87 *Irish Press*, 'UCD and TCD to Merge: Opening of New Era in our Higher Education', 19 April 1967.
88 *Irish Independent*, 'UCD and TCD to Merge: Minister Outlines University Plan', 19 April 1967.
89 *Irish Times*, 'TCD and UCD to be United, O'Malley Announces Wedding Plans', 19 April 1967.
90 D. O'Malley, 'University education in Dublin: Statement of Minister for Education – 18 April 1967', *Studies*, vol. 56, no. 2 (Summer 1967), p. 113.
91 Ibid., p. 116.
92 Ibid., p. 120.
93 Ibid., p. 120.
94 *Irish Times*, 'TCD and UCD to be United, O'Malley Announces Wedding Plans', 19 April 1967.
95 Ibid.
96 *Report, Commission on Higher Education, Summary*, p. 51.
97 O'Malley, 'University education in Dublin', p. 118.
98 Ibid., p. 121, Hyland and Milne, *Irish Educational Documents* 2, pp. 418–20.
99 *Irish Times*, 'TCD and UCD to be United, O'Malley Announces Wedding Plans', 19 April 1967.
100 *Irish Times*, 'O'Malley Describes New University', 19 April 1967.
101 *Irish Press*, 'UCD Calls for New Foundation', 19 April 1967.
102 *Irish Times*, 'Statements by Provost and UCD Governors', 19 April 1967.
103 Ibid.
104 Ibid.
105 *Irish Times*, 'O'Malley Describes New University', 19 April 1967.
106 J.P. MacHale, 'The university merger', *Studies*, vol. 56, no. 2 (Summer 1967), pp. 122–9.
107 Ibid., pp. 122–3.

108 B. Chubb, 'The university merger', *Studies*, vol. 56, no. 2 (Summer 1967), pp. 130–7.

109 Ibid.

110 T.W. Moody, 'Comment', *Studies*, vol. 56, no. 2 (Summer 1967), p. 174.

111 O'Connor, *A Troubled Sky*, p. 181.

112 D. Donoghue, 'Comment', *Studies*, vol. 56, no. 2 (Summer 1967), pp. 160–4.

113 Ibid.

114 O'Connor, *A Troubled Sky*, p. 180.

115 Ibid.

116 MacHale, 'The university merger', p. 128.

117 Moody, 'Comment', pp. 173–5.

118 J. Meenan, 'The University in Dublin', *Studies*, vol. 57, no. 3 (Autumn 1968), p. 317.

119 O'Connor, *A Troubled Sky*, p. 203.

120 Ibid., p. 204.

121 NA D/T 99/1/438, S.17744, *Departmental Committee's Observations on the Recommendations of the Commission on Higher Education*, 1967.

122 Ibid., p. 1.

123 Ibid., p. 35.

124 Ibid., p. 11.

125 Ibid., p. 30.

126 Ibid.

127 Ibid., p. 10.

128 Ibid.

129 O'Connor, *A Troubled Sky*, p. 173.

130 NA D/T 99/1/438, S.17744, *Departmental Committee's Observations on Recommendations of the Commission*, 1967, p. 2.

131 Ibid., p. 30.

132 DDA AB8/B/XVIII/18, *Higher Education: Statement issued by the Minister for Education on behalf of the Government*, 16 August 1968, pp. 1–4.

133 *Report, Commission on Higher Education*, p. 54.

134 Hyland and Milne, *Irish Educational Documents 2*, pp. 422–5.

135 NA D/T 99/1/438, S.17744, *Departmental Committee's Observations on Recommendations of the Commission*, 1967, p. 11.

136 Ibid., p. 34.

137 NA D/T 99/1/311, S.16735B, *Memorandum B, Recommendation of the Higher Education Authority on the Provision of Third-Level Educational Facilities at Limerick*, 20 March 1969, pp. 6–7.

138 Ibid., p. 8.

7

The limits of reform: 1968–72

The approach pursued by the department under O'Malley's successors, Brian Lenihan and Pádraig Faulkner, was greatly influenced by policy decisions taken between 1959 and 1968. The state had developed a coherent overall policy for educational expansion by March 1968, when Lenihan succeeded O'Malley as Minister for Education. Important reforms in primary and post-primary education were announced or implemented between 1968 and 1972, which were largely based on plans already initiated or formulated by the officials. The state was also obliged to confront new challenges associated with the swift transformation of the educational system. Key problems that ministerial intervention had failed previously to resolve, notably the reorganisation of the rapidly expanding second-level sector, provoked conflict between the state and established educational interests. The HEA exerted a significant influence on the state's approach to the development of higher education, modifying the policies originally outlined by O'Malley. The department was preoccupied with implementing and managing the rapid expansion of the educational system.

A new national curriculum

The most far-reaching change at primary level since the 1930s was the development of a new curriculum for national schools. There had been no fundamental changes in the national school programme since 1934, when the *Revised Programme of primary instruction* was introduced.[1] The established curriculum was greatly influenced by cultural nationalism in the 1920s, which demanded precedence for the Irish language in primary education. The revival of the national language through the schools was a key objective of the programme of primary instruction.[2] The existing curriculum also reflected the importance placed on formal, written examinations at all levels by officials and educationalists in the first generation of the independent Irish state; the programme was influenced by the requirement to prepare students for the compulsory Primary Certificate from 1943. The policy priorities of the new state in the 1920s shaped the character of the national school curriculum for over a generation. The traditional programme was highly restrictive and inflexible, giving little freedom to teachers and taking no account of differences in size and location between national schools.[3] The curriculum also offered a narrow range of subjects, made no attempt to link the different subject elements and placed little emphasis on the learning experience of the child.[4] Successive governments maintained the traditional national school programme with only minor changes until the 1960s.

The first indications of more radical change emerged in the early 1960s, when Hillery amended the department's regulations to dilute the traditional policy of teaching through the medium of Irish in junior classes.[5] The abolition of the Primary Certificate in 1968 formed part of a broader reappraisal within the department concerning the primary school curriculum. Seán O'Connor reflected the new thinking at official level in his contribution to the Jesuit periodical *Studies* in 1968: 'We have buried without regret the Primary Certificate examination. Let us now bury, again without regret, the present National School Curriculum.'[6] While O'Connor was certainly more outspoken than any of his colleagues, other officials did not greatly dissent from his sentiments. Initial proposals to revise the primary school curriculum emerged within the department by 1967. The Development Branch began preparations in 1966 for the publication of a White Paper on education and a steering committee, composed mainly of primary school inspectors, was established in December 1966 to advise the Minister on the primary education aspects of a White Paper.[7] O'Malley did not proceed with the publication of a White Paper, giving priority to other issues which he considered more urgent.[8] But the abortive project gave an important impetus to curriculum reform in primary education. The steering committee concluded that a new curriculum was required for primary schools. They recommended a fundamental revision of the national school programme, which they considered rigid, inflexible and insensitive to the diversity offered by any group of children.[9] The committee, which was influenced by the ideas of Jean Piaget and by the Plowden Report published in England in 1966, made the case for a flexible and child-centred curriculum.[10] The senior officials soon accepted the principle of a new curriculum. The first definite indication that the department was committed to far-reaching reform came in December 1967, when a working group, composed of primary school inspectors, was established to develop detailed plans for a new curriculum.[11] O'Malley himself did not give a high priority to the reform of the national school programme, although the revision of the curriculum began during his term of office. The initiative was taken instead by senior officials and primary school inspectors. While the new programme would not take effect in most national schools until 1971, the department was committed to the introduction of curriculum reform at primary level by December 1967.

The senior officials approved the draft proposals for a new curriculum, produced by the committee of inspectors, in the autumn of 1968. The department issued a working document outlining the proposals for a revised curriculum to the INTO on 26 September 1968.[12] The working document envisaged a child-centred programme, which set out to provide for the full development of each individual child.[13] Tomás Ó Floinn, the Assistant Secretary with responsibility for primary education, believed that the existing programme was inflexible and outdated, treating a child as 'the passive recipient of knowledge'.[14] He indicated that the new child-centred approach was based on the belief that 'the learning process should be active and not passive': the new programme was intended to promote learning at the child's own pace and to encourage the child to engage more actively in the learning process.[15] The working document also emphasised the necessity for a flexible curriculum, which took account of the diverse mental and physical capacity of different pupils. The proposals for change were designed to promote a more flexible and integrated learning process, which envisaged a greater focus on the child as an individual and closer interaction between subjects.[16] The proposed curriculum involved the introduction of new teaching methods, including group teaching, individual teaching and project methods. The department also proposed to expand the range of subjects offered at primary level through the introduction of social and environmental studies, physical education and arts and crafts.[17] The official proposals for a new curriculum involved a radical reform of the existing national school programme.

The department moved rapidly to involve educational interest groups in the process of curriculum reform. Seán MacGearailt, who succeeded Ó Raifeartaigh as Secretary of the department in August 1968, convened a meeting of all the primary managerial bodies, as well as the INTO, to discuss the working document on 11 October.[18] MacGearailt himself and Gearóid Ó Súilleabháin, Deputy Chief Inspector for primary schools, outlined the thinking behind the proposed curriculum in terms which illustrated the recent transformation in the department's approach to primary education: 'They stated that they wished a new spirit to permeate the working of the national school, with more flexibility in the Curriculum and Timetable.'[19] The officials indicated that the new curriculum aimed to place children at the centre of the educational process, relegating programmes and timetables to second place. The department's approach to the revision of the curriculum met with general approval on the part of the managers and the INTO representatives. The union's delegates, Senator Brosnahan and A.J. Faulkner, were strongly supportive of the new initiative in principle, although they raised some practical reservations. They correctly warned that improved school accommodation and adequate equipment were essential prerequisites for the implementation of the new curriculum. But in general the INTO representatives indicated that teachers were likely to welcome a child-centred curriculum. The officials promised to consider the INTO's concerns and asked all the organisations concerned to submit their observations on the working document.[20] The department took care on this occasion to inform the relevant educational interests fully of the proposed changes and to initiate a process of consultation on the reform of the curriculum.

The working document was reviewed by the department in conjunction with the managerial bodies and the INTO. Lenihan addressed the INTO congress in April 1969 to encourage widespread acceptance of the draft programme.[21] The department's proposals received a broadly positive response from most educational interests. The Teachers' Study Group, which had previously called for a reform of the curriculum, welcomed the new proposals in January 1969.[22] Their response drew attention to certain deficiencies in the department's approach, notably the lack of co-ordination between the reform of the primary curriculum and the revision of post-primary courses, but enthusiastically endorsed the introduction of the new curriculum.[23] The INTO also warmly welcomed the proposals in January 1970, arguing that the new programme fulfilled many of the ideals first raised by the organisation in its own document, *A Plan for Education*, as far back as 1947.[24] The primary teachers' union gave a strong endorsement to the principles underlying the new curriculum 'on philosophical, psychological and educational grounds'.[25] The CEC warned, however, that some suggestions made in the working document, especially for the teaching of Irish, were too ambitious and would require adaptation to local school conditions. They also emphasised that adequate accommodation and suitable teaching materials would be essential to achieve the satisfactory implementation of the new curriculum.[26]

Senior officials of the department swiftly reassured the union that the curriculum would be implemented gradually and at least initially on the basis of voluntary co-operation by teachers. Ó Súilleabháin informed INTO members that there would be 'no coercion'; existing national teachers who were unable or unwilling to undertake the new curriculum would not be compelled to do so.[27] The officials readily acknowledged that the new curriculum could not be implemented in the short term in many schools. Tomás Ó Floinn publicly admitted in 1969 that the implementation of the new curriculum in the remaining one or two-teacher schools was 'simply an impossibility'.[28] Ó Floinn recognised that in very small schools, where a teacher had to cope with several classes and a wide range of age groups, the only viable option was the teaching of a minimum programme with minimal flexibility: 'In other words the very opposite of the position envisaged in the new curriculum.'[29] The introduction of the new programme in a majority of national schools could be achieved only through the creation of larger school units. The need for extensive amalgamation and an improvement in the pupil-teacher ratio to allow the introduction of the new curriculum shaped the gradual approach taken by the department to the implementation of the initiative. The department's decision to introduce the new curriculum in a measured way was also dictated by other challenges than the physical constraints imposed by the prevalence of small schools. The introduction of new teaching methods and new subjects demanded more teachers and an extensive supply of modern teaching aids.[30] Additional facilities were also required for the introduction of new activities in subject areas such as physical education and environmental studies. Moreover the implementation of the new curriculum involved retraining the vast majority of serving national teachers, who had been trained in a very different tradition and were accustomed only to teaching the existing programme.[31] The department had little choice but to initiate the new curriculum in a gradual fashion.

The introduction of the new programme began with the organisation of an extensive pilot project in primary schools. The department initially selected about 300 pilot schools in 1968 to implement different elements of the proposed curriculum on an experimental basis.[32] This project was soon extended and approximately 600 national schools throughout the country were operating as pilot schools for the new programme by 1971.[33] The department also initiated a comprehensive retraining programme for serving national teachers. Special in-service training courses for principal teachers began in the summer of 1969 and continued for several years, involving over 4,000 principal teachers.[34] The department organised an extensive in-service training programme, which benefited most primary teachers between 1969 and 1972. The officials promoted organised visits by teachers to the pilot schools, which acted as demonstration centres for various aspects of the new curriculum, as an important part of the process of in-service training.[35] MacGearailt moved to facilitate the retraining programme in 1971, directing that a leave of absence of one half-day could be granted to teachers to visit a pilot school, subject to the consent of the manager and local inspector.[36] The officials also provided a comprehensive outline of the new programme by producing handbooks on the curriculum changes for all national teachers.[37] The department prepared two volumes of a *Teachers' Handbook* by 1971. The handbooks, which were issued to all national teachers, contained details of the new curriculum and suggested methods for implementing it.[38] The new curriculum became the official programme for all national schools in September 1971.

The senior officials and national school inspectors managed the planning and introduction of the new curriculum with considerable skill. They conducted successful pilot projects and finalised a new official programme within a relatively short period of time and in the face of considerable difficulties.[39] Moreover the department succeeded in securing widespread support for the new curriculum from the educational interest groups, especially the INTO, and prepared the way effectively for its introduction. The official introduction of the new curriculum in 1971 did not mean, however, that it was fully adopted overnight by most national schools. The programme was implemented on an uneven basis due to the considerable educational and structural difficulties that prevented the immediate adoption of the curriculum by all national schools. Pádraig Faulkner, who succeeded Lenihan as Minister for Education on 2 July 1969, publicly acknowledged that the new curriculum could only be implemented gradually. He informed the Dáil on 3 November 1971 that 'it is hoped to have it in operation in the schools generally in about five or six years'.[40] The full implementation of the programme was delayed by the continued existence of a substantial number of very small schools in 1971, despite the rapid progress of the policy of amalgamation. The persistence of high pupil-teacher ratios in many schools, which militated strongly against the employment of innovative methods such as individual and group teaching, also obstructed the full introduction of the new curriculum.[41] Moreover the programme of in-service training courses initiated by the department in 1969 was not maintained throughout the following decade due to increasing financial constraints, which brought a reduction in the funding for teacher training courses by 1975. The new curriculum was not fully implemented in many areas, due to the persistence of educational and structural problems, as well as the inadequate resources available for the introduction of the programme.[42] The full implementation of the new curriculum depended on a continuing flow of increased resources for primary education, which was not guaranteed in the more uncertain economic climate of the 1970s.

Despite the gradual and often imperfect implementation of the initiative, the development and introduction of the new curriculum marked a far-reaching change in the state's policy towards primary education. John Coolahan points out that the new programme itself involved a radical shift in the ideology underlying the curriculum and in the methodological approach to primary education adopted by the state.[43] Ó Floinn drew attention to the fundamental character of the curriculum reform in a speech in 1972, when he emphasised that the new curriculum was designed to deliver child-centred learning rather than the subject-centred instruction provided by the traditional programme.[44] Certainly the child-centred approach underlying the new programme, combined with the wide range of subjects and the greater flexibility given to teachers, contrasted sharply with the rigidity and narrow subject concentration of the traditional programme. The Assistant Secretary also made the more dubious claim that the new curriculum was in essence 'a comprehensive type of primary education', which was essential as a preparation for comprehensive post-primary education.[45] Ó Floinn was attempting to portray the developments of the past decade as the product of coherent overall planning by the department. He therefore gave an impression that there was a high level of deliberate co-ordination between the reforms at primary and post-primary level, which was in fact usually notable by its absence. There had been no real effort by the department to align the new primary curriculum with the earlier reform of the post-primary curriculum at junior cycle level.[46] The officials made no attempt to involve the post-primary school associations in the formulation of the new programme for national schools and there was little evidence even of much liaison between different branches of the department itself.[47] There was no indication that the officials who initiated the reform of the primary school curriculum in the late 1960s were particularly concerned to prepare pupils for comprehensive post-primary education. This lack of cohesion reflected the reality that the reforms in this period were not inspired by any definitive master plan, but were frequently incremental and unco-ordinated, driven by the policy priorities of individual ministers and various groups of officials.

The development of the new curriculum was not, however, an isolated event. It took place in the context of fundamental policy changes in the state's approach to primary education. The necessity to deliver other key changes to facilitate the new programme reinforced the state's commitment to a far-reaching reform of primary education. The evolution of the new programme was inextricably linked with the department's effective implementation of initiatives such as amalgamation of small schools and improvements in the pupil-teacher ratio. Official concern to create the physical conditions to facilitate the new curriculum reinforced the department's commitment to the amalgamation of small schools. The increasing success of the policy of amalgamation paved the way for the introduction of a more flexible and innovative school programme. The new programme itself marked a significant break with the past. The state abandoned its previous attempt to achieve key policy objectives, such as the revival of the Irish language, by imposing a rigid uniformity on the national schools through an inflexible, subject-centred school programme. Instead the department took the lead in developing a new curriculum, which promoted a flexible and integrated learning process and sought to place the ideal of child-centred education at the core of the primary school experience. While the objectives of the department were not fully achieved, the introduction of the new primary school curriculum was a key element in the transformation of the state's policy towards primary education. The initiative underlined that the department was willing and able to carry through far-reaching educational reforms which marked a fundamental break with traditional policies and methods.

Towards community schools

The department under O'Malley's successors also began to devise a new approach to the rationalisation of post-primary education, following the very limited progress achieved by the Development Branch in its efforts to promote an integrated post-primary system. The Development Branch's attempt to provide a comprehensive curriculum through the pooling of resources between secondary and vocational schools proved largely unsuccessful. The process of general rationalisation envisaged by Colley's letter in January 1966 simply never materialised. The initiative for free post-primary education had an unanticipated effect on the process of rationalisation, as it ensured that many small secondary schools increased their enrolments.[48] This made secondary schools even less likely to regard amalgamation or institutionalised collaboration with any favour. The department's efforts to promote collaboration had also been effectively obstructed by the secondary managerial authorities and the ASTI. While thirty-five schools were closed or amalgamated as a result of the policy of rationalisation between 1966 and 1969, twenty-six of these schools were drawn from the vocational system.[49] The impact of the state's policy on the much larger secondary system was minimal. The department therefore proposed new forms of institutional collaboration in the late 1960s.

The officials of the Development Branch fully recognised that the rationalisation of post-primary education on the basis of a voluntary pooling of resources between secondary and vocational schools was unattainable at least in the short term. An internal working document prepared by the officials in 1967, *Notes on the Organisation of Secondary Education in a sample rural area*, commented that the difficulty of securing collaboration to provide a single wide-ranging curriculum between two different systems should not be underestimated: 'Experience indicates that only in rare cases is it fully achieved.'[50] The Development Branch considered that its current rationalisation plans might not be achieved for up to fifteen years: moreover even the department's own proposals were not sufficient to deliver a broad post-primary curriculum. The officials therefore proposed that a long-term plan for reorganisation should be combined with a short-term approach involving experiments in selected areas, which would introduce the principles of the long-term plan on a pilot basis.[51] The officials presented several options to allow the establishment of new pilot centres, which would provide instruction in subjects requiring specialised facilities, including Science and practical subjects. The proposed alternatives included the conversion of existing vocational schools into post-primary centres for special subjects, the building of new centres that could later form part of a new school and the establishment of pilot centres to be shared by more than one school.[52] While the unpublished document attracted no public attention, the analysis outlined by the *Notes* proved influential. The creative thinking of the officials provided the basis for a more successful restructuring of second-level education in the following years.

The Development Branch's bleak assessment of the shortcomings of the rationalisation process laid the groundwork for various initiatives promoted by the department in the late 1960s. The official analysis provided a compelling rationale for the adoption of a revised approach to post-primary rationalisation. The Development Branch's suggestion for the establishment of educational centres shared by more than one school found expression in the idea of common enrolment. The department proposed common enrolment in 1967 to facilitate the joint provision of comprehensive education by two or more small post-primary schools. The proposal envisaged that all the children in the schools concerned would be included on a common roll and treated as if the schools formed a single educational unit.[53] Common enrolment was intended to allow two or more schools to form a single educational centre, while maintaining independent managerial arrangements within a co-operative system: the principals shared responsibility for the running of the schools, while a committee of the relevant managerial interests decided educational policy.[54] Common enrolment was initially implemented only in Boyle, Co. Roscommon, in September 1968. The co-operative arrangements involved three local schools, including a vocational school and two secondary schools.[55] Although there was no formal arrangement for joint ownership or management of the schools, the experiment in Boyle was successful due to effective collaboration between the individual principals and managers.[56] But common enrolment was not widely accepted on a national basis due to the opposition of the ASTI and the Catholic managerial bodies. The Standing Committee of the ASTI did not initially object to the co-operative arrangements at Boyle, although it identified 'possible disadvantages for members if common enrolment became general'.[57] But the association, which was concerned to protect the status of secondary teachers within a private educational sector, firmly opposed common enrolment at rationalisation meetings.[58] Moreover the Executive Committee of the CCSS flatly rejected common enrolment on 21 March 1968, advising all its members 'to have nothing to do with "common entry" or "community school" proposals' from the department.[59] The Council of Managers of Catholic Secondary Schools (CMCSS), which was established in June 1968 as a co-ordinating organisation for the Catholic managerial bodies, was also suspicious of the concept. A confidential report by the CMCSS recognised that common enrolment worked smoothly in Boyle but commented that 'there is serious reason to anticipate trouble, were it applied generally'.[60] The Catholic managerial bodies feared that the spread of common enrolment would lead to the absorption of secondary schools into the vocational system or even their extinction.[61] Despite its success at Boyle, common enrolment did not provide a viable basis for an integrated system of post-primary education.

The failure of common enrolment and the limited progress towards collaboration at the rationalisation meetings made the establishment of a new type of school an increasingly attractive option. The department began to consider more formal arrangements for the integration of secondary and vocational education, which came to fruition in 1970 with the proposal for community schools. William Hyland had first proposed the idea of a community school in 1964 in the course of the *Investment* study. He suggested the establishment of a single 'comprehensive or community school' providing both practical and academic education, which could replace a number of existing vocational or secondary schools.[62] The reference to community schools was not clarified or even included in the final report, following an objection from Hyland's colleague Pádraig Ó Nualláin, senior inspector with the department, who commented 'Surely the plain people of Ireland are sufficiently confused as it is, without introducing more undefined terms?'[63] The establishment of comprehensive schools meant that the senior officials in 1964 had little interest in the idea of a 'community school', which was designed to serve essentially the same function. But the Development Branch, with Hyland as its chief statistician, returned to the concept of the community school in the late 1960s as a solution to its difficulties with the rationalisation of post-primary education. The proposal in the *Notes* for the establishment of new centres to be shared by more than one school, which would serve as pilot centres for the provision of special subjects, was never implemented in its original form.[64] But the analysis by the officials pointed the way towards the development of a new educational model, which would deliver comprehensive education.

The Development Branch certainly favoured the idea of the community school by 1968 when the head of the Branch, Seán O'Connor, raised the concept publicly in an article, which was published in the autumn edition of *Studies*.[65] O'Connor outlined the significant policy initiatives taken by reforming ministers between 1963 and 1968. He identified the 'two fundamental purposes' of the reforms undertaken by the state as the achievement of equality of educational opportunity for all and the restructuring of the educational system to provide for the needs and aptitudes of the individual pupil.[66] O'Connor's commentary on the objectives of successive ministers at least since 1963 was essentially accurate although he could also have added that the government regarded the expansion of the educational system as an essential element in economic development. But the Assistant Secretary did not confine himself to a summary of the government's initiatives or objectives. He also offered a highly controversial vision of the future, emphasising that he alone took responsibility for his comments, which were not made on behalf of the Minister or the department.[67]

O'Connor argued that the traditional distribution of schools in the Irish educational system, which had developed 'as a hodge podge of very small units', was no longer sustainable.[68] He warned that within a few years the Irish educational sector would not be able to meet the demands of a changing society, which would depend increasingly on the technical skills of its people. Moreover the state could not afford to waste its modest resources on expanding a network of small and inadequate post-primary schools: the viability of school units had to be judged by economic as well as educational criteria. O'Connor urged that post-primary schools should be amalgamated to create viable educational units: 'Single community schools are the rational requirement in most centres outside the large urban areas.'[69] He commented that the Development Branch had made 'no significant gains in our drive for community schools'.[70] O'Connor's comment was the first explicit statement by a senior official that the establishment of another new type of school was envisaged by the Department of Education. He did not outline the concept of the community school in detail, but indicated that it could involve the joint management of new or existing schools by the secondary and vocational authorities, as well as the closer identification of schools with their local communities.[71]

O'Connor pointed out that co-education was required to achieve viable educational centres in many areas and identified the opposition of the Catholic church authorities to co-education as a major obstacle to the reorganisation of post-primary education. He accused the bishops and religious orders of taking an entirely unreasonable approach, which was detrimental to the education of individual pupils: 'It seems clear that education is being adversely affected by institutional considerations not related to education.'[72] The Assistant Secretary considered co-education to be an essential feature of future community schools in many areas. While this analysis was certainly controversial enough, it was O'Connor's assessment of relations between church and state in education that proved explosive. He correctly noted that clerical and religious vocations were declining and emphasised the need to give greater responsibility to lay secondary teachers.[73] O'Connor advocated the development of a partnership between the state, lay teachers and the Catholic Church, in place of the traditional dominance of post-primary education by Catholic clerical and religious authorities. 'No one wants to push the religious out of education; that would be disastrous, in my opinion. But I want them in it as partners, not always as masters.'[74] He argued for a constructive dialogue between the state and the churches to achieve the necessary changes in the educational system.

O'Connor's article in *Studies* was an unprecedented public intervention by a senior official of the Department of Education. The outgoing Secretary, Ó Raifeartaigh, was strongly opposed to O'Connor's action and advised Lenihan to block the publication of the article. Tony Ó Dálaigh recalled that Ó Raifeartaigh was 'appalled' that a civil servant was writing such a controversial piece.[75] The Minister initially withdrew his permission for the piece due to Ó Raifeartaigh's intervention but later allowed the Assistant Secretary to proceed with the article, following strong representations from O'Connor himself and Fr. Peter Troddyn, the editor of *Studies*.[76] Ó Raifeartaigh then sought McQuaid's intervention to suppress the article.[77] McQuaid requested the Provincial of the Irish Jesuits, Fr. Cecil McGarry, to prevent the publication of the article on the basis that it would cause 'great damage, here and abroad by its presentation of what is supposed to be the position and influence of Religious in Irish Education'.[78] But the Provincial refused to suppress O'Connor's article, expressing confidence that the discussion in *Studies* would do more good than harm in the long term.[79] The efforts made by Ó Raifeartaigh and McQuaid to suppress O'Connor's contribution foreshadowed the intense controversy provoked by its publication. The content of O'Connor's article was sensational and indeed explosive in the context of the educational system in the late 1960s, which was still heavily influenced by the Hierarchy and the religious orders. O'Connor's open criticism of the Catholic church authorities and his call for the dilution of the power traditionally held by the bishops and religious orders in the educational sector drew an avalanche of outraged responses from the secondary school authorities and teachers. Fr. Troddyn led the way with a critical editorial, disagreeing especially with the amalgamation of small post-primary schools.[80] The editor's commentary was relatively mild, however, compared to the vitriolic tone and content of several other contributions published in *Studies* in response to the article.

The Executive of the TBA denounced not only O'Connor's contribution but also the approach to rationalisation taken by the department. The TBA criticised the department's plans for the reorganisation of second-level education on the basis of larger school units as 'unjust and educationally unsound'.[81] Moreover they asserted that O'Connor's approach to school management amounted to 'nationalisation by stealth', in which the state left undisturbed the property of the religious orders but took over the management of the schools which they had established.[82] The TBA warned bluntly that they intended to preserve their position in the face of encroachment by the department. 'We know our rights. We intend to stand by them.'[83] O'Connor's article was also fiercely criticised by a representative of the secondary teachers and a leading member of the academic establishment in UCD. Denis Buckley of the ASTI disputed the accuracy of O'Connor's comments about the limited role of lay secondary teachers and claimed that the article involved 'a sinister denigrating' of the role of Catholic religious orders in education.[84] He believed that politicians and civil servants were seeking to dominate the educational system and exclude the religious communities, as the state had done in France during the Third Republic. Denis Donoghue, a senior academic in UCD, made a vitriolic attack on the Department of Education. He argued that O'Connor did not understand the aims of education while the department as a whole was incompetent and autocratic: 'It is not pleasant to see so much power entrusted to mediocre men.'[85] Many of the contributors to *Studies* saw O'Connor's vision as a nightmare scenario, which did not merely represent his personal viewpoint but the secret programme of the department. The explosion of outrage provoked by O'Connor's article was not simply a negative reaction to the content of his contribution. The force of the hostile response reflected the considerable resentment among most established educational interests at the department's vigorous advocacy for educational reform since the early 1960s. The debate in *Studies* underlined that influential elements in the educational system, including the male teaching orders and the ASTI, were profoundly suspicious of the department and hostile to its plans for the reform of post-primary education.

The reaction to O'Connor's intervention was by no means entirely unfavourable. The secretary of the Church of Ireland Board of Education, Kenneth Milne, welcomed the article for initiating a valuable debate on the future of education. Milne pointed out that Protestant schools had accepted the principle of co-education, while the SEC fully agreed with the department on the need for rationalisation and was actively seeking the amalgamation of many Protestant schools.[86] Milne's contribution underlined the contrast between the broadly favourable approach of the Protestant educational authorities towards rationalisation and the more suspicious attitude of the Catholic managerial bodies. O'Connor's vision of the future was also warmly welcomed by Charles McCarthy, who congratulated O'Connor for breaking through the veil of anonymity which usually concealed the views of senior officials. McCarthy firmly supported the creation of 'a new sense of partnership' between the state and the church authorities in education.[87] The VTA was broadly supportive of the state's policy and O'Connor enjoyed constructive relations with the association's leadership, as he was known to be sympathetic to vocational education.[88]

While O'Connor's vision of the future was expressed as a personal viewpoint, there was little doubt that it reflected the position of the department on several key issues. Other senior officials did not support O'Connor's open criticism of the power of the church authorities. But his contribution reflected the department's dissatisfaction with the limited success of its efforts to restructure post-primary education and illustrated the frustration of the officials with the Catholic Church's opposition to co-education. The storm of controversy ignited by O'Connor's contribution focused especially on his comments about church–state relations and the role of religious orders in school management, but his general reference to the need for community schools provided the most significant indicator of the state's future policy. O'Connor's article underlined that the department was considering a new form of integration in post-primary education based on the concept of the community school.

The department's concern to achieve new forms of institutional collaboration at post-primary level was influenced by its plans for the revision of the Leaving Certificate. The revision of the senior cycle courses was initiated in January 1967, when a departmental committee was established to conduct a reappraisal of the structure of the Leaving Certificate course and examination.[89] The committee, which was chaired by O'Connor, included representatives of the second-level managerial bodies and teaching associations, as well as the universities. The rationale for changes in the senior cycle programme was compelling. The Leaving Certificate programme was dominated by academic subjects and largely neglected technical or vocational studies; the senior officials hoped to transform the scope and content of the secondary school programme through reform of the Leaving Certificate.[90] The department also aimed to modernise the examination structure and to introduce new forms of assessment, including orals in language subjects and practical tests. The committee's report, which was issued to the various educational bodies in October 1967, generally fulfilled the department's aspirations. The committee proposed a radical reform of the

Leaving Certificate. They envisaged an extension of the traditional curriculum to incorporate a range of practical and technical subjects in the Leaving Certificate for the first time. The report concluded that the two-year Leaving Certificate course should be retained, with the establishment of an additional course of one year leading to an Advanced Certificate.[91] The committee also recommended the introduction of subject grouping, which would require pupils to concentrate their efforts on a particular field of related subjects. The committee envisaged the introduction of five broad subject groupings, based on languages, science, commerce, social studies and technical subjects: students would be required to take three subjects from one of the groupings.[92] Grouping involved a considerable degree of specialisation at Leaving Certificate level. It was also proposed to introduce grading of results for all public examinations in place of the traditional classification of Honours, Pass or Fail. The committee recommended too the introduction of oral tests in all modern languages and practical tests in science and technical subjects.[93] The proposals amounted to a wide-ranging restructuring of the Leaving Certificate, which reflected the department's concern to expand the scope of the senior cycle programme and to encourage a degree of specialisation at this level.

But the implementation of such a complex and far-reaching package of reforms, which required the support or at least the acquiescence of managers and secondary teachers, was always likely to be difficult and the outlook was not improved by O'Malley's decision to present the educational associations with a fait accompli. O'Malley immediately offended most of the groups whose support the department needed by publicly accepting the key recommendations of the report before the educational associations were given an opportunity to consider their response to it.[94] Following O'Malley's death, Brian Lenihan vigorously pursued the committee's recommendations for reform and secured the government's approval for the proposals in April 1968.[95] The Minister proposed to introduce subject grouping on a voluntary basis in 1969 and to initiate the additional course for the Advanced Certificate from 1971.[96] Grouping would become compulsory at Leaving Certificate level in 1972. The proposals involved the most radical revision of the Leaving Certificate since its introduction in 1924.

But a key element of the proposed changes met with almost unanimous opposition. The introduction of subject grouping was rejected in 1968 by all the secondary school managerial bodies and representatives of the NUI.[97] The ASTI soon added its voice to the opposition: the union's CEC resolved on 18 January 1969 to oppose 'the inflexible grouping of subjects at Leaving Cert. as educationally questionable and socially undesirable'.[98] Grouping received vocal support only from the VTA, which endorsed it as the only means to provide a broad, integrated curriculum to all students on a national basis.[99] Lenihan retreated from the proposal for grouping in the face of intense opposition from the secondary school authorities. The proposal for compulsory grouping was withdrawn in June 1969: post-primary schools could still undertake subject grouping on a voluntary basis.[100] The widespread suspicion about the department's intentions on the part of the secondary school associations led not only to the with-drawal of grouping but also to a significant scaling back of the reform of the Leaving Certificate. The proposed Advanced Certificate was never implemented. Moreover the Secretary informed school managers in May 1969 that the department did not intend to require the organisation of oral or practical tests for the new Leaving Certificate subjects in the short term.[101] The department quietly dropped the most ambitious proposals for the reform of senior cycle courses.

This did not mean, however, that the reform of the Leaving Certificate itself was abandoned. Lenihan and the senior officials proceeded with the revision of the examination and the introduction of new subjects, giving priority to more easily achievable objectives than the imposition of group-ing. Lenihan announced on 31 October 1968 that the traditional classifi-cation of results would be replaced with a new system of grading for all public examinations.[102] The grading of results for the Leaving and Inter-mediate Certificate was introduced in 1969: it was one of the few areas where the committee on the Leaving Certificate exerted a lasting influence on the public examinations system. More significantly, the department succeeded in implementing a wide-ranging reform of the senior cycle curriculum. The examination programme was extended from 1969 to include a wide range of technical and practical subjects.[103] MacGearailt outlined to the schools in June 1969 the broad programme of subjects that could be taken by pupils for the new Leaving Certificate.[104] The new courses added to the curriculum included commercial subjects such as accounting and economics, while new technical subjects were also introduced, includ-ing mechanics and technical drawing.[105] The syllabuses for all Leaving Certificate subjects were revised by the summer of 1969.[106] The academic programme for the revised Leaving Certificate came into effect in 1969–70 and the first common examination for both secondary and vocational pupils was held in 1971.[107] While the revision of the senior cycle pro-gramme was less radical than the department had initially planned, it was nonetheless a far-reaching and ambitious educational reform. The revi-sion of the Leaving Certificate greatly expanded the subject options poten-tially available for pupils, although it did not force secondary schools to provide practical subjects. The curriculum reform enabled vocational schools to provide senior cycle courses and prepare their pupils for the

Leaving Certificate for the first time. While this did not guarantee parity of esteem for the vocational sector, it was certainly an important educational advance.

The wide-ranging revision of the Leaving Certificate programme reinforced the department's commitment to the rationalisation of post-primary education. Close collaboration between secondary and vocational schools appeared a logical imperative to ensure that the wide array of subjects available at Leaving Certificate level were provided to all pupils. The Development Branch devised a new proposal for the integration of the two systems of post-primary education, which was based on the concept of the community school. The department's revised approach envisaged the joint management and operation of post-primary schools by the secondary and vocational authorities. The existing legislation did not allow VECs to co-operate with other educational authorities in establishing or operating second-level schools. Faulkner therefore secured the agreement of the government on 4 November 1969 for the preparation of legislation which would enable VECs to collaborate with other authorities in the establishment and management of post-primary schools.[108] The Minister also intended to provide for the reconstitution of the VEC in the city of Limerick, which had been dissolved by O'Malley in 1967.[109] But the main concern of the senior officials was to enable VECs to participate in joint arrangements with other educational interests for the operation of post-primary schools. The department's proposal emphasised the need for 'jointly operated post-primary schools to be established in areas where separate secondary and vocational schools would not be viable'.[110] The department clearly intended that the powers of the VECs should be extended to facilitate the creation of a new type of school.

The draft legislation, which was submitted by Faulkner to the government in April 1970, provided for 'co-operation by vocational education committees with certain other schools regarding continuation and technical education'.[111] This clause enabled the VECs to establish and maintain schools in collaboration with other educational authorities, subject to the consent of the Minister for Education. The draft Bill also permitted the Minister to reconstitute the membership of a VEC within a specified time frame following its dissolution: this opened the way for Faulkner to reconstitute the committee for the city of Limerick.[112] The Cabinet approved the Bill on 26 May 1970 and it became law by July.[113] The Vocational Education (Amendment) Act, 1970, received little public attention but was an essential element of the department's strategy for the integration of post-primary education. The legislation gave the VECs the necessary powers to engage in joint management and ownership of post-primary schools with the secondary school authorities.[114] It removed formal obstacles to institutional collaboration and gave legal support to the government's policy of breaking down the traditional barriers between secondary and vocational education. Most significantly, the new Act provided the legislative basis for the creation of community schools.

The department developed definite proposals for community schools by the autumn of 1970, when Faulkner began negotiations with the Catholic Hierarchy on the establishment of a new type of post-primary school. The Minister sent a detailed proposal entitled 'Community School' to the Hierarchy on 26 October 1970.[115] While the proposal took the form of a working document and was unsigned, it fully outlined the department's revised approach to the integration of post-primary education. This approach involved the creation of a new institutional arrangement involving joint management of schools by the secondary school authorities and the VECs. The proposed community schools would be governed by a board of management composed of representatives of the secondary school managers and the local VEC, with an independent chairman, either the bishop of the diocese or another agreed nominee.[116] The document emphasised that the creation of community schools flowed directly from the government's policy for the reform and expansion of post-primary education. The key elements of this policy included 'the creation of a unified post-primary system of education' and the achievement of free post-primary education for all children irrespective of ability and without academic selection.[117] The policy also demanded the establishment of facilities for comprehensive education in all areas of the country and the elimination of duplication in providing facilities or teachers.[118] The officials of the Development Branch hoped that the proposed community schools would provide a viable framework for the full establishment of comprehensive education on a national basis. The officials aimed to provide comprehensive education through a new type of school, which would have formal arrangements for joint management acceptable to the secondary and vocational school authorities. The proposal was designed to resolve the central problem confronting the Development Branch since its foundation, namely the development of an integrated system of post-primary education within a fragmented second-level sector, in which influential private interests jealously guarded their autonomy.

The proposal envisaged that community schools would be formed as a result of the amalgamation of secondary and vocational schools or through the establishment of single schools in city areas instead of separate secondary and vocational schools.[119] The department considered that the optimum size for post-primary school units was about 800 pupils and aimed to establish schools which would accommodate 400 to 800 students. The document proposed that the state would provide the full capital

costs for the establishment of the new schools, although there would be a
nominal local contribution. The state would also finance the current costs
of the schools, by covering the costs incurred by the board of management,
within a budget agreed between the board and the department.[120] The new
schools would provide a broad range of post-primary courses leading to
the national state examinations. The officials also envisaged that the community school would provide adult education for the local area. The document emphasised that education was a life-long process, looking forward
to a substantial development of adult education in the 1970s: 'On another
level there is growing acceptance throughout the world that education is
a life-long process and that second chance education must be provided at
all levels.'[121] The proposal also commented that 'there is in all countries a
growing community consciousness', leading to a demand for school facilities to be made available to voluntary organisations and the local community.[122] The community school was intended to meet this demand by
providing facilities for voluntary organisations. The officials hoped that the
community school would develop a distinctive identity as a centre of community activity. The aspects of the department's plan concerning adult
education and community-based activities were influenced by developments in education internationally. The *Irish Times* recognised that the
officials were drawing inspiration from the practice of comprehensive
schools in Britain and the USA.[123] Certainly it was intended that the community schools would share significant features of the comprehensive
model in Ireland and abroad, but the proposal was also clearly shaped by
the demands of the Irish educational sector. The department was proposing a new type of school, one which would provide comprehensive education but would safeguard the position of established educational interests
through its distinctive management structure.

The Minister issued the proposal only to the Catholic Hierarchy initially,
although it was subsequently circulated to the secondary managerial
authorities and the IVEA.[124] Faulkner's caution did not prevent the rapid
leak of the document to a national newspaper. The department's proposal
received extensive coverage in the *Irish Times* on 12 November 1970: John
Horgan and Michael Heney accurately identified the proposal for community schools as 'the logical culmination' of the policy for the restructuring
of post-primary education launched by Hillery in 1963.[125] The journalists
fully appreciated the significance of the initiative, describing the document
as 'the most important single policy statement by the Department' since
the decision to establish comprehensive schools.[126] The Minister insisted
in the Dáil on 18 November that the proposal was merely a working document, which had been sent to the Hierarchy as a prelude to a process
of general consultation.[127] But it was evident that the department had

produced a new policy initiative with the potential to reshape the second-level sector. A senior representative of the Catholic managerial authorities recognised the profound implications of the proposal in his anonymous comment to the *Irish Times*: 'He said that while the Department might claim it was merely a working document, it did not read like that.'[128] The department was seeking an advanced form of integration between the secondary and vocational systems in various areas. The premature publication of the document revealed that the establishment of community schools had become an integral part of the state's policy to secure a cohesive system of post-primary education.

The Minister sought to gain the support of the Catholic bishops for the proposal before consulting with other educational interests. Faulkner was following a tried and tested strategy, which had worked for several of his predecessors, but on this occasion the premature publication of the document on community schools upset his plans. Various interests that were not consulted at all initially, notably the IVEA and vocational teachers, were alarmed at the content of the proposal itself and affronted by Faulkner's tactics in promoting it.[129] The Hierarchy itself reacted cautiously to the initiative, seeking a discussion with the Minister to clarify the implications of the working paper. Faulkner, accompanied by MacGearailt, O'Connor and Patrick Moloney, met the Hierarchy's representatives and members of the CMCSS on 10 December to discuss the proposal.[130] The Minister made the case for community schools on educational and financial grounds. A broad curriculum and a wide choice of subjects could not be delivered in many small secondary schools, which confined their pupils to academic subjects and sometimes to the Pass Leaving Certificate course. Moreover the Minister was faced with the problem of 'providing the best educational facilities at the most economical rate'.[131] Faulkner told the bishops and managers that a fiscally responsible solution had to be found to the acute educational needs of many small rural towns. The department had identified twenty-five rural centres throughout the country where post-primary educational needs had to be met as a matter of urgency.[132] The officials considered that the introduction of community schools would meet essential educational needs in an economical way.

The bishops and the Catholic managerial representatives sought clarification on a series of issues, including the likely size of the community schools, the prospect of amalgamation for existing schools and the management structure.[133] Faulkner and the senior officials defended the proposal for a minimum school unit containing at least 400 pupils, arguing that such a school unit was necessary to provide a minimum level of educational facilities and a reasonable number of highly qualified specialist teachers.[134] The Minister clarified that amalgamation would occur mainly where all schools in an area required replacement, when they would be replaced by a single community school. He pledged that amalgamation would take place on a voluntary basis, but warned that if a school refused to amalgamate the department would have to review the payment of building grants to that school. The department was no longer willing to finance the rebuilding or extension of three small schools in a rural town when a single community school offered a viable solution.[135] Faulkner also commented bluntly that while it would be theoretically possible for a school to opt out of a community school arrangement subsequently, 'in practice it would be almost impossible'.[136] The Minister was conciliatory, however, in dealing with the question of management. He assured the Hierarchy that the denominational character of the new schools would be guaranteed. He aimed to secure agreement with the bishops and other educational interests on a satisfactory management structure. The department was not seeking any representation on the board of management for community schools, although they were represented on the board of management for comprehensive schools. Instead the officials envisaged that if three traditional schools formed a community school the board of management would be composed of two members drawn from each of the existing schools. The official delegation also gave an assurance that the local VEC would have no control over the management of the school or particularly the appointment of teachers.[137] Faulkner and the senior officials were particularly concerned to secure the support of the Catholic Hierarchy and the CMCSS for the plan, to the extent that they were willing to risk offending the vocational education authorities.

The Minister also sought to play down the significance of the proposal. He indicated that the document was prepared in the context of the urgent educational needs in Ardee and other small rural centres, remarking that 'as of now he was interested only in the smaller areas'.[138] MacGearailt too commented that the department was currently planning only for the provision of community schools in small centres where the situation was 'critical'.[139] This line of argument was disingenuous, as the department was proposing the community school as a model for the reorganisation of post-primary education throughout the country. The importance of community schools to the state's approach was underlined when Faulkner declined to give any assurance that the document was drawn up to deal with specific cases only.[140] The CMCSS representatives asked the Minister to clarify publicly that the proposal for community schools did not involve an overall policy affecting the entire country. Faulkner flatly refused to do so, on the flimsy basis that further comment from him would only be misconstrued, following 'so much uninformed comment already' as a result of the article in the *Irish Times*.[141] In fact the journalists had correctly construed the proposal as a far-reaching policy initiative with profound implications for the future of Irish education. Faulkner and the senior officials regarded community schools as a key element of the state's policy for the expansion of the educational system on a national basis. They sought to minimise the importance of the initiative only because it had been published prematurely, before the Minister could reach an agreement with the Catholic Hierarchy.

The Hierarchy and the Catholic managers agreed to consider the proposal and continue negotiations with the Minister: a statement issued by the CMCSS after the meeting on 10 December referred to their 'exploratory discussion' with the Minister and his officials on community schools.[142] The representatives of the VECs and the vocational teachers were, however, deeply discontented with Faulkner's approach, not least because of the complete absence of consultation with them initially. The Minister sought the views of the IVEA on the document only in January 1971, over two months after its publication in the *Irish Times*.[143] The Standing Council of the IVEA, which met Faulkner on 19 February 1971, assured the Minister that they favoured his policy in principle, but raised severe reservations about key elements of the proposal. They expressed 'qualified agreement' with the general outline of the state's policy for post-primary education, but firmly opposed the proposed system of administration for the community schools.[144] The IVEA representatives told Faulkner that the creation of independent boards of management to control the schools, which would be financed directly by the department, was unacceptable to the VECs.[145] They warned the Minister against the imposition of a system of administration which would be unaccountable to the public and dominated by departmental officials in close collaboration with the Catholic bishops: 'It would be a tragedy if the important decisions concerning post-primary education in future were to be taken behind closed doors by people with whom the public will feel no close identification and over whom they will have no control.'[146] The IVEA representatives feared that the proposal would mean the absorption of the vocational schools into the new system and the complete elimination of the VECs.

The concerns of the vocational education authorities were fully shared by the VTA. The association's Executive acknowledged that effective educational development in certain areas might well require the establishment of community schools, but strongly criticised the proposed management structure for the new schools.[147] Charles McCarthy communicated the union's view to Faulkner in December 1970, objecting to the allocation of full managerial authority to the board of the school, especially as the department had suggested that the local Catholic bishop might act as chairman of the board.[148] The VTA was entirely opposed to such an arrangement, which would effectively turn vocational teachers into employees of the local bishop. McCarthy urged instead that the local community itself should manage a new community school. The VTA and the vocational education authorities were broadly supportive of the concept of the community school, but were seriously alarmed by the system of administration for the new schools envisaged by the department.

The Minister, however, essentially ignored the concerns expressed by the IVEA and the vocational teachers. The Catholic bishops and the CMCSS agreed in March 1971 that any community school resulting from the amalgamation of existing schools should be a Catholic school, with the trustees for each school appointed by the local bishop.[149] Moreover they considered that at least two-thirds of the board of management in any new community school should be nominated by the trustees, leaving one-third to be appointed by the local VEC. The bishops resolved that they would attempt 'to have the 4/2 ratio apply in all cases', regardless of the number of Catholic secondary schools involved in the establishment of the community school.[150] Faulkner sought to accommodate fully the concerns of the bishops. He issued a press statement on 13 May 1971, which clarified the management structure for the community schools. The Minister proposed that the board of management for each school would consist of six members, including four nominees of the secondary school authorities and two representatives of the local VEC.[151] He envisaged that two of the representatives nominated by the secondary school authorities would be parents of children in the school. Faulkner also stipulated that the school site and building would be vested in three trustees nominated by the local Catholic bishop: one of these trustees would be appointed from a list of nominees supplied by the local VEC.[152] The proposed management structure clearly favoured the Catholic Church and marginalised the VECs in the restructuring of post-primary education. The Minister's approach was designed to secure the support of the Catholic Hierarchy by giving majority representation to secondary managerial interests within the governing structures of community schools.[153] But in his overriding concern to win the support of the Catholic bishops for community schools, Faulkner ignited a firestorm of controversy.

The IVEA unanimously rejected the Minister's proposals at its annual congress between 31 May and 3 June 1971.[154] The representative body for the VECs did not oppose the idea of the community school, which was praised by most members at the congress. But a series of delegates from VECs around the country denounced the Minister's approach as undemocratic, dictatorial, sectarian and disastrous for the vocational system.[155] The IVEA emphatically rejected the Minister's current proposals for the establishment of community schools, 'with particular reference to the management structure'.[156] The VTA also opposed Faulkner's plan at a special congress on 4 June 1971, urging the government to produce a White Paper before proceeding with such fundamental changes in the post-primary sector. They argued that the new schools should reflect the best of both educational traditions and provide for equal representation in their administrative structures for secondary school and vocational interests.[157] The opposition to the Minister's latest initiative was by no means restricted to the representatives of vocational education. Faulkner's proposals were also criticised by representatives of the Church of Ireland and by the General Assembly of the Presbyterian Church.[158] The Church of Ireland Board of Education warned the Minister in June 1971 that they were 'gravely disturbed' by various aspects of his proposals.[159] Several prominent opposition TDs, including Garret FitzGerald of Fine Gael and Barry Desmond of the Labour Party, attacked the proposed management arrangements as sectarian.[160] The numerous critics of the Minister's approach expressed a well-founded suspicion that Faulkner's proposals would create a single denominational system of public education in the state, which would be dominated by the Catholic bishops.[161]

The Minister soon modified his initial proposals in the face of severe pressure from various educational interests and opposition political parties. Faulkner announced on 30 July 1971 that the first community schools would be established in Tallaght and Blanchardstown: he also indicated that two of the secondary school representatives on the boards of management would be elected by the parents of pupils attending the new schools, after each school had been in operation for three years.[162] While these concessions applied initially only to the two schools in Co. Dublin, Faulkner's statement signalled the beginning of a more general reassessment. The Minister revised his proposals again in February 1972, announcing that the boards of management would consist of two representatives nominated by the VECs and two by the secondary school authorities, as well as two elected representatives of the parents.[163] The parents would elect their own representatives in all community schools with the temporary exception of the schools in Blanchardstown and Tallaght, on the basis that there were initially too few parents to select representatives in these schools. Faulkner also announced that the Minister rather than the Catholic bishop would appoint the school trustees.[164] But the controversy over the management and ownership of the community schools was not fully resolved and it continued well beyond Faulkner's term as Minister for Education. The disagreements between the various educational interests over the control of the new schools persisted throughout the 1970s and were not fully overcome until the Deed of Trust for the community schools was generally agreed in 1979: even then several VECs approved the Deed only in 1981.[165] The Deed provided for boards of management which included three nominees of the religious authorities, three VEC nominees, two elected representatives of the parents and two teachers selected by the permanent teaching staff of each school: the principal of the school was also a non-voting member of the board.[166] The final Deed of Trust represented a compromise, which emerged from prolonged and frequently acrimonious negotiations between the department, the different managerial authorities and the teaching unions.

It was significant, however, that many critics of the Minister's proposals nevertheless expressed their support for the restructuring of post-primary education and the principle of establishing community schools. The IVEA generally supported the educational reforms sought by the department, although they feared the political and administrative implications of the changes for the vocational system.[167] Likewise the VTA had consistently favoured the rationalisation of post-primary education since January 1966 and was willing to support the establishment of community schools in certain areas, if the management structure protected the interests of its members.[168] The VECs and the vocational teachers were by no means opposed to the state's policy, although they were deeply dissatisfied with the administrative arrangements adopted by the department to implement it. The Protestant educational authorities were also broadly supportive of the department's latest attempt to restructure second-level education. The SEC advised the Protestant churches that the concept of a community school had 'much to recommend it', although the scheme originally proposed by the Minister was clearly unsatisfactory.[169] Moreover the SEC considered in March 1972 that the revised proposals announced by Faulkner met many of their concerns and recommended that Protestant school authorities should seriously consider collaboration with the department in developing new community schools.[170] Although the methods proposed by the Minister to implement the policy aroused intense controversy, the state's initiative for community schools later secured widespread support from most educational interest groups.

The department proceeded rapidly with the establishment of community schools despite the unresolved issues concerning the management structure. The first community schools were established at Blanchardstown and Tallaght in 1972.[171] The department acted decisively to build community schools in areas where new educational facilities were required. Indeed twelve community schools were established before the formal Deed of Trust was published.[172] Despite the prolonged controversy over school management, the department succeeded in devising a viable new approach for formal collaboration between the secondary and vocational authorities, which was more widely acceptable than its previous initiatives. The publication of the document on the community school in November 1970 was certainly premature, but it accurately represented the department's latest and most determined attempt to secure the integration of second-level education.[173] The initiative also proved the most influential and effective measure taken by the officials to achieve the restructuring of post-primary education and the implementation of a comprehensive curriculum. The establishment of community schools would remain an essential part of the state's policy for the expansion and reorganisation of post-primary education throughout the following decade.

Teachers in turmoil

The creation of a unified teaching profession emerged as a key element of the state's policy for the restructuring of the educational system by the late 1960s. The department considered that the introduction of a common basic scale of salary for all teachers was vital to facilitate the integration of second-level education and the elimination of traditional barriers between primary and post-primary teaching.[174] The officials envisaged that secondary and vocational teachers would be taking classes in each other's schools, while national schoolteachers with appropriate qualifications would be employed in post-primary schools.[175] Circular M44/66, which was issued by the Secretary in October 1966, ensured that trained national teachers and vocational teachers who held the necessary qualifications for secondary teaching would be able to transfer to the secondary teaching service.[176] The circular was designed to encourage inter-group mobility between the three categories of teachers and to facilitate a more efficient distribution of the teaching force throughout the educational system.

The department was concerned not only to facilitate a more rational use of scarce resources but also to deal with a series of competing salary claims by different groups of teachers. All three teaching unions were pursuing pay claims through separate arbitration schemes by 1967, with each group seeking to improve its own salary position relative to the other groups of teachers.[177] The officials were determined to get away from the traditional practice of leapfrogging by different teaching unions, favouring a common arbitration scheme for all teachers. The department envisaged the introduction of a common basic scale, with additional remuneration for qualifications and the exercise of extra responsibilities.[178] This proposal had far-reaching implications for the teaching profession as a whole; it raised particularly sensitive issues for lay secondary teachers, who received a basic salary from the secondary schools and in most cases were also entitled to an incremental salary from the state. O'Malley endorsed the principle of a common salary scale and secured the agreement of the government on 19 September 1967 for the establishment of an ad hoc tribunal to recommend the appropriate salary level for the scale.[179] The Tribunal on Teachers' Salaries was asked to recommend a common basic scale of salary for all primary and second-level teachers and to report on the appropriate allowances to be added to the common scale.[180] The Tribunal was designed to establish the basic conditions for the establishment of a unified teaching profession. All three teaching unions agreed to co-operate with the Tribunal, although the ASTI successfully sought a commitment from O'Malley that they would be able to fall back on their separate conciliation and arbitration scheme if they were dissatisfied with the findings.[181] This stipulation by the ASTI proved an ominous portent of future conflict between the department and secondary teachers.

O'Malley formally established the ad hoc Tribunal on 15 December 1967, with Professor Louden Ryan of Trinity College Dublin as its chair. The Tribunal concluded its deliberations within five months, presenting its report to Lenihan on 23 April 1968.[182] The Tribunal recommended that a common basic scale of salary and a common system of allowances for all teachers should come into effect on 1 September 1968. The new arrangements would apply to all new teachers from that date.[183] The proposed common scale was fixed at approximately the same level as the existing scale for vocational teachers.[184] The report set out transitional arrangements for existing teachers. All vocational teachers were to be assimilated to the common scale at a level two increments above the point they had reached on their existing scale. Secondary teachers receiving incremental salary were to be given the option of joining the new scale on the same basis as vocational teachers or remaining on the existing salary scale.[185] Significantly the Tribunal recommended that the special salary agreement between the ASTI and the secondary school managers in 1964, which involved an increase of 12.5% in basic salary for lay secondary teachers, should be set aside, due to its 'divisive effects within the teaching profession'.[186] The report concluded that ad hoc payments by schools could jeopardise the emergence of a single teaching profession and recommended that the department should take responsibility for the payment of the full salary of secondary teachers. The new arrangements provided for the payment of allowances for university qualifications and a range of new allowances related to specific duties. Allowances would be paid to principals and vice-principals in secondary schools for the first time, while posts of special responsibility would be created in all schools.[187] The Tribunal also proposed a single scheme of conciliation and arbitration, which would replace the separate schemes for each group of teachers.[188] The Tribunal fulfilled admirably the objectives set by the Department of Education, outlining a comprehensive blueprint for the creation of a unified teaching profession. But the report provoked a storm of controversy within the teaching profession, due to the very different impact of its recommendations for each group of teachers.

The Tribunal's report was broadly satisfactory for the primary teachers, as it conceded the traditional demand by the INTO for a common salary scale and delivered a moderate salary increase for primary teachers. While the INTO considered that the level of basic salary offered by the Tribunal was still too low, the union urged the Minister in July 1968 to implement the report.[189] But the report offered much less favourable terms to both categories of post-primary teachers. The VTA favoured the principle of a common scale, but was deeply disappointed at the level of the salary proposed by the Tribunal. Moreover many vocational teachers were appalled by the proposal for degree allowances in the vocational sector, which created a differential between university graduates and teachers of practical subjects in vocational schools.[190] The VTA initially rejected the findings of the Tribunal, seeking further salary negotiations with the Minister.[191] But it was the secondary teachers who reacted most vehemently to the recommendations. The ASTI was deeply dissatisfied with the level of the salary scale proposed by the Tribunal, which involved an actual pay reduction for many secondary teachers.[192] Certainly the offer of posts of responsibility did nothing to reconcile the ASTI to the proposals of the Tribunal.[193] This offer depended on the willingness of clerical and religious managers to allocate posts of responsibility to their lay staff. The Catholic managers, however, were reluctant to delegate such authority to the lay teachers in the short term and had no desire to facilitate official plans for a restructuring of the teaching profession.[194] The CMCSS refused to accept the proposal that the department would pay all school salaries, in the absence of legal guarantees for the financial position of the managers.[195] The ASTI categorically rejected the findings of the Tribunal on 1 June 1968 and threatened 'immediate action' by the union if the Minister accepted the report.[196] The Tribunal's recommendations for sweeping change in the salary structure of the teaching profession had set the scene for a trial of strength between the government and the secondary teachers.

There was no doubt that the government would endorse the report and Lenihan duly accepted the Tribunal's recommendations in September 1968.[197] The Minister sought to avert industrial action by making moderate improvements in the common scale envisaged by the report. Lenihan issued salary proposals on 18 October, which involved increases in the figures proposed by the Tribunal amounting to £125 at the top of the scale for married men and £100 at the maximum point for women and single men: the allowances for honours' degrees were also increased by £50.[198] The INTO quickly accepted the salary offer, having secured the introduction of a common scale and the Minister's commitment to a common scheme of arbitration.[199] The VTA accepted the Minister's proposals by postal ballot in late October on the basis that no better terms could be secured at present.[200] But Lenihan's proposals failed completely to pacify the secondary teachers. The Standing Committee of the ASTI on 26 October unanimously recommended rejection of Lenihan's offer. A ballot of ASTI members resulted in an emphatic dismissal of the salary proposals, with a vote of 92% against the Minister's offer.[201] The ASTI moved rapidly towards large-scale industrial action. The union demanded the right to proceed with its salary claim through the traditional scheme of conciliation and arbitration for secondary teachers. The Minister could not concede this demand without making nonsense of the government's policy and enraging the other teaching unions, who would be affected by the outcome of separate negotiations. The CEC of the association resolved on 18 January 1969 to hold a ballot providing for 'a withdrawal of services' by secondary teachers.[202] Further negotiations in January proved fruitless and the union's membership voted heavily in favour of a strike.[203] The ASTI began its first full-scale strike since the foundation of the state on 1 February 1969.

The association secured the full support of the secondary managerial authorities for their action. The CHA gave an assurance of their 'fullest support' for the ASTI's salary claim as early as October 1968.[204] Moreover the managers decided to suspend all school activities for the duration of the strike. The managerial bodies issued a press statement on 31 January 1969, which announced the closure of the schools until further notice and emphasised their determination to retain 'the loyalty and co-operation of their staffs'.[205] The catalyst for the ASTI action and the closure of the schools was a salary dispute, but the secondary teachers and their allies were clearly making a sustained protest against the state's policy towards secondary education. The union's Action Committee issued a wide-ranging denunciation of the Department of Education in January 1969, which was by no means restricted to the unsatisfactory salary offer. They accused the department of attempting to implement a reduction in the salary of secondary teachers and to downgrade the status of secondary teaching as a profession. The Action Committee also denounced the department for attempting to attain absolute power over secondary education: 'The Department of Education is seeking to gain absolute control of secondary schools, thereby interfering with the private nature of our employment.'[206] The ASTI argued that the state had no legal right to interfere in an agreement between secondary teachers and school authorities, which involved the payment of part of the teachers' salaries. Moreover they emphasised the danger of giving 'absolute control in the framing of educational policy to Departmental administrators'.[207] While pronouncements issued in the course of a strike are rarely notable for their restraint, the statement underlined the hostility of the secondary teachers' association to the state's overall policy for second-level education.

The ASTI was deeply discontented with the government's policy for the restructuring of post-primary education, especially the department's efforts to break down traditional barriers between different groups of teachers. The association found common ground with the secondary school managerial bodies, especially the Catholic managers, in their shared reservations about the state's agenda in education. The department's attempts to rationalise post-primary education had provoked a suspicious reaction on the part of many secondary managerial authorities, who regarded the actions of the officials as arrogant and bureaucratic.[208] Sr. Eileen Randles recalled the resentment of the Catholic secondary school authorities at the department's assertive approach, arguing that opposition to change was often provoked by 'the intemperate zeal of the Department of Education officials'.[209] O'Connor's article in *Studies* intensified the widespread distrust of the department's intentions among the Catholic managerial authorities.[210] The co-operation of the managerial bodies with the ASTI strike was based not simply on their support for a salary claim, but on their opposition to key elements of the policy of rationalisation promoted by the department. Charles McCarthy commented accurately: 'This was more than a strike of teachers; it was a revolt of the schools.'[211] The secondary teachers and managerial authorities had joined in a common protest against the policies of the state.

The ASTI strike continued for three weeks and did not conclude until the Catholic bishops intervened to mediate the dispute. The Hierarchy's Commission for Post-Primary Education opened separate discussions with the Minister and the ASTI on 12 and 13 February.[212] Following the intervention of the bishops, Lenihan issued new salary proposals to the ASTI on 14 February. The Minister offered increases in various degree allowances and a marginal increase in incremental salary for secondary teachers.[213] The revised offer also involved the award of special functions allowances, ranging from £100 to £300, to a majority of secondary teachers. The new allowances were to be made to all teachers placed on or above the tenth point of the common scale without any requirement for the performance of specific duties.[214] This was effectively a separate salary increase for secondary teachers, which undermined the principle of the common basic scale. The CEC recommended acceptance of the new offer and the ASTI membership approved the agreement in a ballot, concluding their strike on 24 February.[215] The settlement, which was formally signed in March 1969, ended the secondary teachers' strike but it also made further industrial unrest in the educational sector inevitable. The agreement was a significant setback for the department's declared aim of a unified teaching profession. Lenihan managed to end the strike, but only at the price of undermining the recommendations of the Tribunal and making a unilateral pay settlement with secondary teachers. The agreement was never likely to be a permanent settlement, not least because of the hostile reaction of the other teaching unions.

The representatives of primary and vocational teachers were outraged by the Minister's unilateral agreement with the ASTI. Charles McCarthy recalled that 'the VTA were on the warpath'.[216] The vocational teachers were deeply dissatisfied not only with the concessions to the ASTI but also due to the limited progress of their own negotiations with the department for the creation of posts of responsibility in vocational schools. The VTA therefore conducted a two-day strike on 26 and 27 May, which was coupled with threats of further action.[217] The INTO, which protested vehemently to the government over the undermining of the principle of the common scale, also began a campaign of action, beginning with a strike by primary teachers in Dublin on 28 May.[218] All three teaching unions had taken strike action within the same year and the Minister was still in dispute with two of them. The government's approach to the revision of teacher salaries was in complete disarray and a unified teaching profession appeared a more distant prospect than ever. The Minister decided to summon Professor Ryan back in an attempt to pacify the INTO and the VTA. Ryan was asked to assess the agreement with the ASTI and to recommend means of resolving the dispute.[219] Ryan's second report, which was issued on 13 June 1969, not surprisingly concluded that the Minister's agreement with the ASTI had breached the principle of the common basic scale.[220] The department accepted Ryan's analysis and aimed to replace the special allowances for secondary teachers with posts of responsibility in accordance with the original recommendations of the Tribunal.[221] Faulkner, who inherited the dispute in July 1969, was determined to depart from the agreement with the ASTI on the basis that it undermined the common scale.[222] This approach was at least consistent with the objective of a unified teaching profession but it involved the department in protracted negotiations with all three teaching unions from July 1969 until February 1971, against a background of continuing industrial unrest and regular threats of further action.

The department under Faulkner cautiously manoeuvred to implement the common basic scale by phasing out the special allowances for secondary teachers. The Minister outlined new salary proposals on 16 September 1969, which involved a gradual dismantling of the agreement with the ASTI.[223] Faulkner reiterated that a common basic scale and a common system of allowances would be introduced. Serving secondary teachers would be obliged to choose between a general salary increase available on the new common scale or the continued payment of the special allowances.[224] The ASTI condemned Faulkner's approach, arguing that the Minister was breaking the agreement concluded by his predecessor. Michael Sheedy, the ASTI President, accused Faulkner of operating 'a wage freeze' against the secondary teachers and protested against the Minister's attempt to depart from the agreement with the ASTI.[225] The ASTI's reaction underlined that the union would not abandon their special agreement without a prolonged struggle. The Minister also moved to establish a common scheme of conciliation and arbitration for the teaching profession, which was agreed by the INTO and VTA in 1970.[226] The ASTI, however, rejected the proposed scheme and refused to participate in joint negotiations with the other teaching unions on their pay claim.[227]

The deadlock in the salary dispute persisted throughout 1970, as the Minister's proposals for the new salary structure failed to satisfy either the secondary or vocational teachers. Faulkner moved to phase out the special salary arrangements for secondary teachers. The department instructed school managers in May 1970 that all new entrants to secondary teaching after 31 May should be placed on the common basic scale and should not be eligible to receive the benefits of the separate salary agreement negotiated in 1969.[228] The ASTI immediately directed its members not to correct the Certificate examinations in 1970, although the ban on examination work was later applied only to the Leaving Certificate.[229] The Minister also came into dispute with the VTA, which was dissatisfied with the department's refusal to grant allowances for most qualifications other than university degrees. The vocational teachers undertook a campaign of industrial action, which culminated in a nation-wide strike from 11 to 17 February 1970.[230] MacGearailt sought to improve the department's fraught relations with the VTA by giving Seán O'Connor responsibility for conciliation and arbitration, as well as the Development Branch, in February 1970.[231] This measure had some effect, as the department managed to avoid further industrial action by the VTA. But the Minister's dispute with the ASTI soon intensified, as the government completed the dismantling of the special agreement with the secondary teachers.[232] Faulkner issued further salary proposals on 3 July 1970, reiterating that the special functions allowances for secondary teachers would not be paid to any new entrants to the profession. He proposed to phase out the special allowances and to compensate secondary teachers through pay increases on the new common scale, as well as the creation of posts of responsibility.[233] Faulkner's latest offer proved broadly acceptable to the VTA and the INTO, but was firmly rejected by the Standing Committee of the ASTI.[234] The secondary teachers' association again prepared for strike action. An ASTI member, Michael Mac-Mahon of Limerick, warned the Taoiseach on 2 November 1970 that 'another disastrous strike' was likely if Lynch did not compel Faulkner to uphold the original agreement.[235] The Taoiseach refused to intervene in the dispute, not least because such an intervention would have undermined the authority of the Minister.[236] The stage seemed set for another confrontation between the state and the secondary teachers.

The real prospect of another ASTI strike was averted only by the intervention of the Irish Congress of Trade Unions (ICTU). The CEC resolved that their strike would begin on 16 February, if a ballot of the union's membership favoured strike action.[237] Although the ballot produced a narrow majority in favour of a strike, Maurice Cosgrave, President of ICTU, made a last-minute appeal to the association on 15 February to defer their action; he invited all three teaching unions to engage in joint discussions under the auspices of ICTU.[238] The Standing Committee agreed to defer the strike and to participate in joint negotiations with the other teaching unions. The intensive negotiations mediated by the officers of ICTU succeeded in finding common ground between the three teaching associations, securing their agreement for a joint salary claim to the Department of Education. The agreed claim envisaged short-term compensation to secondary teachers in return for the acceptance by the ASTI of the common salary scale.[239] MacGearailt and other senior officials met representatives of the teaching unions on 22 February and broadly accepted their joint proposals, after consulting with Faulkner and Lynch. A lump sum of £60 was to be paid to all secondary teachers receiving the special allowances on 1 August 1970, while secondary teachers who reached the tenth point of the common scale during 1970–71 would receive a one-off payment of £116. A new allowance would also be paid to all post-primary teachers over the age of fifty who did not hold a university degree.[240] The ASTI was deeply divided over the proposed settlement and the CEC put the salary offer to its members without any recommendation. The union's membership accepted the offer by a relatively narrow margin of 56.6% to 43.4%.[241] While the final salary proposals did not fully satisfy the ASTI or the VTA, the settlement in February 1971 resolved the dispute triggered by the department's attempts to implement a common salary structure for all teachers.

All three teaching unions finally accepted the introduction of a common salary scale and system of allowances, although the new salary structure was introduced on a phased basis for secondary teachers. But the department achieved its key objective of a revised salary structure with a common basic scale only at the price of a bitter and protracted conflict with the ASTI and to a lesser extent with the other teaching unions. It was significant that the prolonged salary dispute was finally resolved not by the state but by the intervention of the Irish Congress of Trade Unions. The state could no longer afford to treat lightly the grievances of the increasingly self-confident and militant teaching unions. The department's efforts did much to achieve a more unified teaching profession based on the common scale. The officials, however, also came close to unifying post-primary teachers only against the department itself in the course of the dispute. The department's tactics were frequently ill-judged and damaging to its objective of a unified teaching profession.[242] McCarthy commented that 'some of the approaches of the Department seemed to bring mayhem more than peace'.[243] Yet the department's controversial attempt to promote a unified teaching profession was a key part of the state's policy of rationalisation. The department was not simply seeking to save money, as some of its critics assumed, but to achieve an ambitious restructuring of post-primary education with scarce financial resources.

Raising the school leaving age

The policy of rationalisation was designed to ensure that comprehensive education was widely available when the school leaving age was raised to fifteen years. The extension of the statutory school leaving age to fifteen years by 1970 was a key policy objective accepted by the government since the early 1960s. The *Third Programme, Economic and Social Development*, which was published in March 1969, treated the raising of the school leaving age in 1970 as a certainty: the programme noted its likely effect on the number of pupils in post-primary education. 'The raising of the school leaving age to 15 years in 1970 will cause some further increase, though a large proportion of the 14 to 15 age group is already receiving whole-time education.'[244] The commentary on education in the *Third Programme* underlined the impact of the free tuition and free transport schemes in promoting an increased demand for second-level education. The initiative for free post-primary education had already substantially increased the proportion of pupils remaining in full-time education on a voluntary basis, before any move was made to raise the school leaving age; so the original rationale for raising the school leaving age was overtaken by events and the reform no longer had the same importance which was initially attached to it.[245] But the effect of the new schemes also meant that an extension of the school leaving age was a more attainable objective, which could be implemented more easily due to the impact of O'Malley's initiative. The senior officials of the Department of Education, who had pursued the extension of the school leaving age as a key objective throughout the previous decade, aimed to secure the government's approval for the reform in January 1970.

Faulkner submitted a proposal to the government on 13 January 1970, seeking the approval of the Cabinet for the extension of the school leaving age to fifteen from 1 July 1970.[246] The introduction of legislation was unnecessary, as the Minister for Education was empowered to make a statutory order extending the period of compulsory attendance at school under Section 24 of the School Attendance Act, 1926.[247] Faulkner therefore proposed to raise the school leaving age by making an order, which deemed children to have reached the age of fifteen at the end of the quarter during which they attained that age.[248] The department supported its case with a comparative analysis of other European states, correctly identifying 'a world wide trend towards compulsory full-time attendance at school up to 16 years at least'.[249] Compulsory education extended to at least fifteen (and sometimes sixteen) years in most western European countries, including Britain, France, the Netherlands, Luxembourg, Austria, Sweden and Finland. Indeed in West Germany educational instruction was compulsory up to the age of eighteen, including nine years of full-time education and a further period of part-time instruction.[250] The officials, however, placed more emphasis on the effects of the initiative for free second-level education than on their analysis of European trends. They estimated that extending the age of compulsory attendance at school would mean an increase in pupil enrolments of only 6,750 over and above the projected expansion based on existing trends.[251] The impact of the schemes introduced by O'Malley had already triggered a dramatic expansion of second-level education. The department admitted that the building programme for post-primary schools was 'already overloaded', as a result of the need for additional accommodation since 1967.[252] But the officials considered that the relatively small proportion of additional places required could be provided without great difficulty. They also envisaged that the number of additional teachers required by post-primary schools as a result of the extension of the school leaving age would not be very great. The only real disadvantage anticipated by the department was a marginal increase in the shortage of teachers in specialist categories, including mathematics, science and some practical subjects.[253] The officials made a plausible case that the availability of free second-level education had paved the way for the raising of the school leaving age without much additional cost to the state.

The department's argument had considerable force. The extension of the statutory period of compulsory education was certainly a much more modest reform in 1970 than it would have been in 1967. But the cost of the proposed advance was by no means negligible. The department estimated that the cost of the reform in terms of current expenditure was £785,900. The estimated capital cost for the proposal, which would create a demand for additional building programmes, equipment and school buses, came to over £2.3 million within a period of three to four years. The officials suggested that the capital costs could be significantly reduced by allowing for some increase in class sizes and employing lower-cost building methods.[254] The department's efforts to play down the scope and financial implications of the proposal were not fully justified. The extension of the school leaving age was an important educational reform, which required further extensive capital investment in post-primary education if the idea was to be transformed into reality. Moreover the officials also raised the possibility of special assistance for 'needy parents', which had been unsuccessfully proposed by O'Malley in November 1966 as part of his plans for free second-level education.[255] They considered that the extension of the school leaving age would increase pressure for maintenance allowances to low-income families, which would compensate them for loss of earnings and enable them to keep their children at school.[256] Although no definite provision for such allowances was included in the proposal, the Department of Education was sympathetic to the idea, pointing out that special assistance to low-income families might be required as a direct result of the raising of the school leaving age. This was a revealing admission by the officials, which underlined that they were seeking to achieve a significant educational advance, not simply a minor sequel to the initiative for free post-primary education.

The cost of the proposal certainly alarmed the Department of Finance, which vehemently opposed the initiative. Senior officials of the Department of Finance gave a highly critical response, expressing deep dissatisfaction with the escalating costs of the initiative for free education. They pointed out that the cost of the schemes for free tuition, free transport and higher education grants had far exceeded original estimates and would continue to increase steadily for some years. The Department of Finance even questioned whether the schemes were sustainable in financial terms: 'It is very doubtful whether these schemes can continue in their present form or whether they will have to be modified substantially.'[257] They commented too that the financial outlook was so negative in the short term that severe cutbacks would be required: the rapid increase in expenditure on education had contributed greatly to 'this serious budgetary imbalance'.[258] Having sounded this ominous warning note, the Department of

Finance firmly dismissed the proposal to extend the school leaving age. They considered that in a situation where financial stringency was imperative and educational costs were still rising rapidly, the adoption by the state of a further substantial commitment in the area of education was 'completely out of the question'. The proposal should be 'deferred for the present'.[259] This deceptively mild conclusion did nothing to conceal Finance's opposition to any extension of the school leaving age in the foreseeable future. The officials of the Department of Finance were seriously alarmed at the escalating cost of the state's policy in education, especially in the costly aftermath of free post-primary education. They were increasingly dissatisfied with the government's policy of giving precedence to education in the allocation of resources and demanded instead the application of financial stringency to education with greater rigour. It was a significant intervention by the Department of Finance, which was critical not merely of the proposal to extend the school leaving age but implicitly of the government's entire approach to the management of educational expansion. The proposal submitted by Faulkner received considerable support from other ministers. George Colley, now Minister for Industry and Commerce and Joseph Brennan, Minister for Labour, both endorsed the extension of the school leaving age.[260] The main obstacle to the extension of compulsory education was undoubtedly the opposition of the Department of Finance.

The government's decision on the proposal was a neat political compromise. The Cabinet decided on 20 January 1970 to authorise the Minister for Education to take the necessary measures for the extension of the statutory school leaving age to fifteen years from 1 July 1972.[261] The proposal to raise the school leaving age was accepted, but the implementation of the decision was postponed for two years. It was a compromise solution, which paved the way for the important educational reform sought by the Department of Education, but delayed its implementation until 1972 in deference to the objections of Finance. There was no fundamental change in the government's policy for educational expansion. The Cabinet endorsed an expensive reforming initiative which was designed to sustain the expansion of the educational system and achieve full educational participation by children of all social categories at post-primary level. But the Department of Finance's intervention had some effect, although its officials were strongly opposing the implementation of a policy objective repeatedly endorsed by the government itself. The Department of Finance had challenged not only the proposal itself but also the state's established approach of providing the necessary resources to sustain the transformation of the educational system. The delay in the extension of the school leaving age underlined that the government's educational policy was losing some of the focus and urgency which had characterised the state's approach towards educational expansion in the later part of the 1960s.

The scope for far-reaching new initiatives in education was significantly curtailed by 1970. The Department of Finance sought to reassert greater financial constraints on future educational initiatives, having lost the opportunity to control the substantial costs of free post-primary education. The increasingly critical approach taken by the Department of Finance towards new educational reforms by the early 1970s occurred in the context of an extraordinary advance in educational spending during the previous decade. The rapid transformation of the educational system was sustained by a striking increase in the level of state investment in education.[262] Current spending by the Exchequer on education trebled in less than a decade: education's share of all public current expenditure increased from 9.37% in 1961–62 to 12.33% in 1969–70.[263] Capital spending by the national government on education enjoyed an even more dramatic expansion, growing from 4.22% of overall public capital expenditure in 1961–62 to 9.02% by 1969–70.[264] Likewise the state's expenditure on education increased dramatically as a proportion of GNP from 3.05% to 5.53% in the same period.[265] The substantial cost of the educational advances implemented or initiated in the 1960s reinforced the Department of Finance's opposition to new financial commitments in education and limited the scope for further reforming initiatives.

Moreover the rapid and wide-ranging changes introduced by the state since 1959 provoked a suspicious and increasingly hostile reaction from many educational interest groups, especially the ASTI and the secondary school managerial authorities. The traditional stakeholders in the educational system, including the religious orders, were seriously alarmed at the unprecedented range and extent of state intervention in second-level education. The proactive reforming approach pursued by successive ministers and officials greatly reduced the influence of the private interests, which had previously dominated the educational system, especially at post-primary level. The pace and scope of the changes surprised even their most dedicated advocates and left many traditional stakeholders in the educational system with little time to adapt to new realities. Charles McCarthy was surely correct in commenting that for many managers and teachers the changes appeared 'to put in question not only the environs of a job but a whole ethos, a way of life'.[266] Even the representatives of vocational education, who generally supported the government's initiatives to transform the status of technical education, were distrustful of the department's approach by 1970. The VTA and the vocational education authorities were concerned that the state was making too many concessions to traditional stakeholders, especially the Catholic Church, to win their support for the restructuring of post-primary education. The reservations of many private interest groups concerning educational reforms were effectively brushed aside by a succession of dynamic ministers and reforming officials throughout the 1960s. The state was able to achieve many of its objectives by winning the acquiescence of a small number of powerful interest groups, notably the Catholic Hierarchy and the INTO, for its reforming initiatives. But by 1970 industrial action by all the teaching unions and the open collaboration of clerical and religious managers with the strike by the secondary teachers underlined that private educational interest groups would no longer accept the state's policies without serious and prolonged protest. The Minister's policy approach could no longer be carried through with minimal concern for the reservations of most private educational interests.

Pádraig Faulkner, who served as Minister for Education from July 1969 until February 1973, therefore took a much more cautious approach than his immediate predecessors. Faulkner avoided major policy statements to the media or in public speeches outside the Dáil, in stark contrast to the assiduous public promotion of controversial policies undertaken by Colley and O'Malley. He focused primarily on the implementation of reforms initiated by his predecessors, launching few new policy initiatives of any significance. While the proposal for community schools was certainly a development of profound importance for second-level education, officials of the department had devised the idea of the community school well before 1970 and indeed O'Connor publicly suggested it in September 1968. The department under Faulkner took a more measured and cautious approach to the implementation of educational reforms. Faulkner's caution did not mark a reversion to the conservatism of the 1950s. The state's policy for the expansion and reshaping of the educational system was firmly established by 1970 and Faulkner sought to achieve essentially the same objectives as his immediate predecessors. The reforms pursued by the state since 1959 had initiated a lasting transformation of the educational system. Faulkner and the senior officials were confronted with the task of implementing an extraordinary range of reforming policies, especially at post-primary level, which had been adopted by previous ministers. The exceptional creativity of the policy development undertaken by reforming politicians and officials in the 1960s created a new and formidable challenge for the Department of Education in the 1970s. The department under Faulkner was obliged to manage the successful implementation of the initiatives formulated or introduced by the state in the previous decade.

The impact of the HEA

The development of higher education presented a complex challenge for the government not least as a result of O'Malley's initiative for university merger. Lenihan inherited the established policy of university reorganisation at a time when the prospects for a successful merger were already receding. He clarified the state's policy for the restructuring of the university sector in a public statement on 6 July 1968.[267] The Minister announced that the government would act to dissolve the NUI and to reconstitute UCC and UCG as separate universities. A permanent authority would be established to oversee the financial and organisational issues involved in the state's relationship with the institutions of higher education, while a Conference of Irish Universities would deal mainly with the academic problems common to all the university institutions.[268]

Lenihan devoted the bulk of his statement, however, to a detailed summary of the department's proposals for a reconstituted University of Dublin, which would combine the two existing university institutions in the city. He announced that the university would be a corporate body forming 'one indivisible whole', which would allow each college to retain its identity.[269] The key elements of Lenihan's announcement on the governing structures of the new institution were consistent with the terms of O'Malley's original initiative, but the latest ministerial announcement also recommended a redistribution of faculties between the two colleges. The faculties of medicine and veterinary science would be based entirely in Trinity College. The law faculty was also to be located in TCD under Lenihan's plan, while engineering, social science and commerce would be based in UCD. Each college would retain its existing range of disciplines in the arts and sciences.[270] Lenihan asserted that the plan provided for 'a fruitful intermingling' of the best qualities of the two institutions.[271] The Minister's statement underlined that the merger remained a key element of the government's policy for university education. But Lenihan would have very limited success in implementing the government's agenda.

The establishment of the Higher Education Authority as a permanent executive body to advise the Minister and allocate state funding to the institutions of higher education was the only element of the programme outlined by Lenihan that was fully implemented in the short term.[272] The Minister announced the establishment of the HEA on 16 August 1968.[273] The government delegated wide-ranging functions to the new Authority, which was established on an ad hoc basis initially. The HEA was required to maintain 'a continual review of the country's needs in higher education' and to advise the Minister on issues related to higher education.[274] The new Authority was also intended to explore ways of eliminating 'unnecessary duplication' at university level and to promote the development of higher education generally. In addition, the Authority would examine budgets prepared by the institutions of higher education and make recommendations concerning the allocation of state funding for each institution.[275] It was obvious that the HEA would have important executive functions when it was established on a statutory basis.

The composition of the new Authority provided some reassurance to the universities that the HEA was not intended to infringe upon their autonomy. The Authority consisted initially of fourteen members, who were drawn from the universities and other institutions of higher education as well as semi-state bodies and private business. Ó Raifeartaigh was appointed as the first chair of the HEA, retiring as Secretary of the department to take up the new full-time position, while James Dukes became the secretary to the Authority.[276] Lenihan affirmed that the HEA was an autonomous body in his speech to the first meeting of the Authority on 12 September 1968, assuring its members that the new body was not 'an executive arm' of the government or the Department of Education.[277] The Minister invited the HEA to advise the government on the forthcoming legislation for the restructuring of higher education, which would provide for the autonomous status of the Authority itself. The HEA was certainly not simply an extension of the Department of Education. James Dukes recalled that 'Many of them were university figures; it wasn't about state control. What we wanted was to develop the universities.'[278] The new Authority was designed to provide an overall framework for the development of higher education, assessing educational needs and overseeing the state's contribution to the expansion of the sector. The HEA operated, however, in the context of the state's educational policies. Ó Raifeartaigh commented in a letter to Mac-Gearailt on 7 March 1970 that the achievement of rationalisation and coordination in higher education was the 'raison d'être' of the HEA.[279] The Authority was intended to co-ordinate future state assistance for higher education and to minimise avoidable duplication of resources. While the HEA did not set out to interfere with the autonomy of the universities on an operational basis, the new body was designed to introduce effective planning and greater accountability in the distribution of state funding to institutions of higher education.

The legislation to establish the HEA on a statutory basis was formulated by the Department of Education in close consultation with the Authority itself, which was successful in maintaining the wide-ranging role assigned to it by the Minister in 1968. The Department of Education's initial proposals, which were agreed with the HEA by March 1970, proved generally acceptable to the government.[280] The Cabinet decided, however, to add a clause requiring the HEA to take account of the national aims of restoring the Irish language and developing the national culture.[281] The draft legislation gave the HEA the general functions of advancing the development of higher education, assisting in the co-ordination of state investment in the sector and promoting an appreciation of the value of higher education.[282] The legislation confirmed that the Authority would act as an advisory body to the Minister, incorporating the advisory functions outlined by Lenihan in August 1968. The draft Bill outlined the considerable executive powers of the Authority with regard to institutions of higher education. The Authority was given the responsibility of evaluating the financial requirements of each institution and assessing any request for state funding by an institution of higher education. The HEA was also given the power to allocate state funding to all the institutions within its remit and to recommend the overall level of state expenditure for higher education.[283] The Higher Education Authority Bill, 1970, secured parliamentary approval in July 1971, allowing the Minister to give statutory recognition to the Authority from May 1972.[284] The legislation established firmly the extensive powers delegated by the government to the HEA over the universities and other established institutions of higher education. Significantly the RTCs and the Colleges of Technology were not designated under the Act as institutions that came under the remit of the HEA. Although the Authority had a general advisory role for the entire third-level sector, it lacked any executive function over an important and rapidly expanding segment of higher education.[285] The result of the government's policy in the late 1960s was the emergence in the following decade of a binary system of governance for third-level education. While the government delegated important executive functions to the HEA in dealing with the majority of the institutions of higher education, the state retained a high degree of control over the development of the RTCs and the technological colleges in Dublin.[286] The department was unwilling to surrender its ability to exert influence directly over the development of higher technical education. The establishment of the HEA was the most significant innovation in the governance of higher education since the foundation of the Irish state, but it was an incomplete reform as higher technical education remained directly under the authority of the Department of Education.

The new Authority was immediately asked to advise the Minister on the restructuring of university education.[287] But the state's policy for university reorganisation already faced formidable and probably insurmountable obstacles by the time the HEA was established. The proposals for merger announced by Lenihan on 6 July 1968 proved utterly unacceptable to the authorities and staff of UCD. Professor James Meenan's contribution to *Studies* in September 1968 noted that the Minister's proposals were being decisively rejected by various faculties: 'It could be said with great truth that University College has never been so united about any issue through-out its existence as it is about this.'[288] The events of the following year proved Meenan's analysis essentially correct. The Academic Staff Associa-tion of UCD approved two resolutions on 4 November 1968, which endorsed the retention of two separate universities in Dublin.[289] The gov-erning body of UCD also firmly rejected Lenihan's proposals and adopted the development of four separate universities in Ireland as its favoured solution.[290] Professor J.J. Hogan, the President of UCD, submitted a lengthy document, entitled *The Case for University College Dublin*, to the Taoiseach, the Minister and the HEA on 1 April 1969.[291] The case presented by the college authorities amounted to a damning indictment of the Minister's plans. The document asserted that the proposals involved 'the partial destruction and total discouragement' of UCD as a university institution.[292] The authorities of UCD protested vehemently against the proposals for the transfer of medicine and law to Trinity College. They made a strong case for the reconstitution of UCD as an independent university, which would co-operate closely with Trinity College.[293] The Senate of the NUI supported the position of the UCD authorities. When the Taoiseach agreed to receive a deputation from the Senate to discuss general university business on 6 February 1969, the deputation took the opportunity to urge Lynch and Lenihan not to dissolve the NUI in the short term.[294] The representatives of all three university colleges within the NUI argued that the National University should not be dissolved until all of its colleges were satisfied with the future status proposed for them. The firm opposition of UCD and the Senate of the NUI to the Minister's proposals underlined that the prospects for merger were bleak by the spring of 1969.

It is unlikely that merger could have been implemented even with the enthusiastic support of Trinity College; in any event this was certainly not forthcoming. While the government had not overcome the reservations of many staff in TCD about the potential loss of their college's identity in a merger, there was also increasingly little incentive for the college's author-ities to embrace the initiative. A merger did not offer any great advantage to Trinity College by 1969, as it was already attracting a high proportion of Catholic students despite the ecclesiastical ban. Ó Raifeartaigh pointed out to Lynch on 5 February 1969 that the majority of new students enter-ing TCD in 1968–69 were Catholics and accurately predicted that the institution would have a large majority of Catholic students within a decade.[295] The ban had increasingly little impact on Trinity College even before the Hierarchy changed its policy in 1970. The authorities of the two universities found common ground in their scepticism about the govern-ment's policy. The authorities of Trinity College and the National University of Ireland agreed to propose an alternative solution to the HEA in April 1970. The NUI/TCD agreement envisaged two independent universities in Dublin, which would collaborate closely together and co-ordinate their academic activity in certain areas.[296] The successful negotiations between the NUI and TCD appeared to offer the prospect of effective collaboration between the two universities without a merger.

The removal of the ban itself dealt a further blow to the prospects for the university reorganisation. The Hierarchy agreed at its general meeting on 22–24 June 1970 to repeal their regulation restricting the entry of Catholics to Trinity College.[297] The bishops announced in a public statement on 25 June that they were acting to remove the ban in response to constructive developments in the relations between the two universities.[298] The decision by the Hierarchy rendered redundant a key political argument for merger, which had been promoted by successive ministers as a solution to traditional political and religious divisions. While the government maintained its public commitment to university merger until 1972, senior officials of the department privately recognised that the initiative could not be implemented.[299] The HEA sounded the final death knell for merger in their report on university reorganisation, which was presented to the Minister on 9 December 1971. The Authority accepted that there should be two separate universities in Dublin, in accordance with the proposals made by the university authorities.[300] The HEA considered that the proposed merger was no longer a compelling necessity, as the circumstances had changed dramatically since the policy was adopted. They drew attention particularly to the removal of the ecclesiastical ban, the reduction in the proportion of non-Irish students in Trinity College and the agreement between the university authorities for closer co-ordination of their activity. The HEA recommended the establishment of a Conjoint Board linking the two universities to guarantee an effective joint approach by the institutions to common challenges in the Dublin region.[301] The HEA's recommendation for a change in the government's policy enhanced its reputation with the universities, which generally opposed the initiative.[302] But the HEA report simply recognised the reality that merger was not a viable project by the early 1970s, due to the scepticism of the university authorities and the considerable changes in higher education. The government quietly abandoned not only the merger, but also the more general business of university reorganisation, making no attempt to dissolve the NUI when it became clear that the merger would never be implemented. The ambitious plans for the restructuring of university education initiated by O'Malley therefore had little practical effect on the development of higher education.

While the overall restructuring of higher education did not materialise, the HEA played a crucial part in determining the role and functions of a new institution of higher education in Limerick. The Limerick University

Project Committee had undertaken a sustained public campaign for a university in the city since 1959. O'Malley and Lenihan both expressed support for Limerick's claim to a third-level institution, but no proposal was brought to the government concerning the demand for a new university until November 1968.[303] Lenihan initially recommended the establishment of a university institution in Limerick to the government on 12 November 1968. The Cabinet was supportive of his proposal but delayed any final decision pending consultation by the Taoiseach with the Minister for Finance and by Lenihan with the HEA.[304] Lenihan informed the HEA at its meeting in November 1968 that the government had taken 'a decision in principle' to establish a new third-level institution in Limerick.[305] But Lenihan's announcement to the Authority was vague concerning the nature of the new institution. He told the HEA only that degree courses in the arts and sciences would be provided within the new college, in addition to an Institute of Technology.[306] The Minister indicated that he would seek the advice of the Authority on 'the form and content of the new institution within the general university complex'.[307] Lenihan's statement was highly ambiguous and potentially contradictory. He stated that the government had already decided to allocate capital funding for a new university in Limerick, but then promised to seek the HEA's advice on the nature of the new institution.[308] Lenihan correctly feared that the HEA would oppose a new university in Limerick. He informed the Cabinet on 19 November that he would consult the Authority concerning a new university to 'avoid any danger of a clash with the Higher Education Authority'.[309] The Minister was seeking to avoid any conflict with the established universities represented on the HEA over his proposal, but also to satisfy the vocal demands of the Project Committee for a new university. Lenihan's ambivalent approach gave the HEA considerable scope to influence the government's policy.

Following consultation by the Minister with the HEA, the government stopped well short of making a commitment to a new university in Limerick. The Cabinet decided on 6 December 1968 to provide the necessary capital funding for the establishment of a new third-level institution in Limerick, which would provide qualifications in the arts and sciences as well as technological courses.[310] The HEA was asked to advise how such an institution might be fitted into the existing or future provision for higher education.[311] The representatives of the Project Committee expressed 'bitter disappointment' at the Minister's failure to announce a university for Limerick and were not at all pacified by the government's decision to refer the issue to the HEA.[312] Lenihan, however, pledged in an interview with the *Limerick Leader* on 12 December that Limerick was about to secure 'a better Institution than any University'.[313] He also informed a deputation from the Project Committee on 2 January 1969 that he had sought the recommendations of the HEA concerning the nature of the new institution and the full details of the proposed courses.[314] The Minister had in effect delegated to the HEA the task of determining the character and functions of the new institution.

The HEA made influential policy recommendations, which proved profoundly significant not only for the Limerick region but for the upgrading of technical education in Ireland. The Authority, which submitted its report on 20 March 1969, agreed with the Commission on Higher Education that there was 'no national need' for another university.[315] But the HEA also identified the development of higher technological education as an urgent national requirement, noting that technological education in Ireland 'has not yet found its proper level'.[316] They emphasised the necessity to upgrade and expand technological education if it was to contribute to national economic requirements: 'If, in accordance with its function, it is to keep in step with the growth of the nation's economy, its content must be further upgraded and the scope of its operation extended.'[317] It was envisaged that a new institution in Limerick would lead the way in meeting the national need for higher technological education. The Authority did not go as far as the committee of officials who had recommended a new university in Limerick in 1967, but accepted the case for a new third-level institution offering qualifications in higher technological education. The report argued that such education did not simply consist of practical training but encompassed the teaching of humanities subjects as an ancillary to technological studies. The HEA recommended the establishment of a new type of third-level institution, which would combine the prestige of degree courses with extensive provision for non-degree technological qualifications.[318] The new institution would mainly concentrate on technological studies, but would also include a significant element based on arts humanities courses. The Authority's recommendations were influenced by the report in 1966 of the Robbins Committee in Britain, which facilitated the development and expansion of the polytechnics as an important sector in higher education.[319] The influence of the Robbins Committee helped to explain the creative and innovative approach recommended by the HEA, in contrast to the much more conservative ideas of the Commission on Higher Education.

The HEA outlined a series of principles, which were intended to govern the establishment of the new College of Higher Education in Limerick. The new college was intended both to meet the specific needs of the region and to serve as a national institution, which would meet the requirements of the country as a whole and attract students from a wide area.[320] The new institution would offer degree, diploma and certificate courses, although the diploma and certificate courses would form the major part of its work initially. The HEA stipulated that the entry standards for degree courses should be the same as those required in the universities; the Authority sought to ensure that degrees awarded by the new institution would enjoy a comparable status to degrees offered by the existing universities. The report also recommended that the new college should have an independent governing body.[321] While the new institution would not be a university in the traditional sense, it was certainly designed to incorporate important features of university education, not least degree courses in the arts and sciences. The HEA outlined detailed measures to ensure the effective implementation of its recommendations. They advised the Minister to establish a Planning Board, which would engage in detailed planning for the foundation of the new institution. The board was also intended to draw up a draft constitution for the college. The HEA also recommended the early appointment of a Director and senior staff for the college by the Minister.[322] The Authority clearly did not intend their first report to gather dust on a ministerial shelf.

The HEA's report not only outlined a viable blueprint for a new type of educational institution but also firmly endorsed the expansion of technical education within the third-level sector. The report acknowledged the underdevelopment of technical education, which had been illustrated by *Investment* and the OECD study on the training of technicians in Ireland.[323] The Authority urged the government to promote more third-level courses in technical education and to support the development of technological studies at a more advanced level.[324] The HEA made a sustained and convincing case for the further upgrading and development of higher technical education.

Lenihan quickly accepted the HEA recommendations. The Minister altered only the proposed title of the institution, which became the National Institute of Higher Education rather than a 'College of Higher Education' as proposed by the HEA. He calculated correctly that the revised title would be more acceptable to the advocates for a university in Limerick.[325] Lenihan and MacGearailt outlined the HEA recommendations to the Limerick University Project Committee on 11 April 1969, promising that the new institute of higher education would be established in September 1971.[326] The Committee strongly disagreed with the HEA's decision to rule out the option of a new university, but did not reject the proposed National Institute. Lenihan assured the Committee's representatives that the new institution would not be prevented by its constitution from expanding to meet future educational and cultural demands. While MacGearailt firmly rejected a suggestion from the Committee that the new institution should be known as Limerick University, the Minister indicated that the matter might be discussed again in due course.[327] Lenihan held out the vague but tantalising prospect that the Institute might well achieve university status in the near future. He also sought with some success to foster the impression that Limerick was receiving a third-level institution, which would be a university in all but name.[328] The Project Committee vowed in May 1969 to continue their efforts to secure a university, but acknowledged that the new third-level institution was 'a worthwhile acquisition' for the Limerick region.[329] The Committee reluctantly accepted the government's proposals. Indeed by October 1970 its representatives were complaining about the slow progress made by the state in establishing the Institute, rather than the HEA's rejection of Limerick's claim for a university.[330]

Although the department did not adhere to the timescale promised by Lenihan, the new National Institute of Higher Education (NIHE) opened its doors to students in 1972.[331] The foundation of the NIHE in Limerick marked a valuable contribution by the state to the expansion of higher technical education. The establishment of the new institute, which offered both non-degree qualifications and degree courses, was an important innovation in higher education. The HEA played a crucial role in the creation of a new type of third-level institution, which combined a strong technological orientation with the provision of more traditional arts courses. The foundation of the new Institute was a key feature in the gradual upgrading of higher technical education, which had become a central element of the state's educational policy by 1972.

Managing educational expansion

The Minister and senior officials were increasingly preoccupied with managing the problems of educational expansion as the new decade dawned. Several key policy developments came to fruition by 1971, notably the introduction of the new curriculum for national schools. Similarly the department under Lenihan successfully extended the Leaving Certificate programme to incorporate technical subjects for the first time; the introduction of a broad-based curriculum at Leaving Certificate level was a significant educational reform. The senior officials of the department also developed and launched the initiative for community schools, which had a lasting impact on the post-primary system in the following decade. The department made considerable progress towards the creation of a unified teaching profession, although its tactics also provoked an unprecedented series of strikes by the teaching unions. But the scope for ambitious new initiatives was increasingly curtailed and even the timely implementation of established policies, such as the extension of the school leaving age, became more difficult by the end of the decade. The transformation of the educational system was achieved on the basis of substantial and escalating costs, which dismayed the Department of Finance and intensified its resistance to new initiatives in education. The success of the state's educational policy in the 1960s created its own problems, notably the greatly increased demands for funding of educational services and the widespread discontent among private educational interests at the government's methods of achieving educational reform. Lenihan's attempts to manage these intractable problems had very mixed success and could not prevent a full-scale conflict between the state and established educational interests at secondary level. The state's reforming policy was confronted with significant political and fiscal limits by the end of the decade. These difficulties led Faulkner to take a more measured approach than his immediate predecessors, seeking primarily to consolidate the progress already achieved and to implement the government's established policies. The reversion by the Minister to a more cautious approach after 1969 was also apparent in higher education, where the plan for university merger was quietly dropped and the HEA secured an influential role in shaping the future of third-level education. But there is no doubt that the outlook for Faulkner and the senior officials of his department in 1972 was very different from the vista of stagnation and limited development which had confronted Lemass and Hillery in 1959.

Notes

1 Coolahan, *Irish Education*, p. 42.
2 Coolahan, 'National schools 1960–1985', in Mulcahy and O'Sullivan, *Irish Educational Policy*, p. 47.
3 Coolahan, *Irish Education*, p. 43.
4 Coolahan, 'National Schools 1960–1985', in Mulcahy and O'Sullivan, *Irish Educational Policy*, pp. 47–9.
5 Chapter 2, pp. 42–46.
6 S. O'Connor, 'Post-primary education now and in the future', *Studies*, vol. 57, no. 3 (Autumn 1968), p. 241.
7 Coolahan, 'National schools 1960–1985', in Mulcahy and O'Sullivan, *Irish Educational Policy*, p. 48.
8 O'Connor, *A Troubled Sky*, p. 192.
9 S. De Buitléar, 'Curaclam Nua le hAghaidh na Bunscoile', *Oideas*, no. 3 (Autumn 1969), pp. 4–12.
10 Coolahan, 'National schools 1960–1985', in Mulcahy and O'Sullivan, *Irish Educational Policy*, p. 49, *Children and their Primary Schools: A Report of the Central Advisory Council for Education (England)*, vol. 1 (London, 1966), pp. 189–202.

11 Coolahan, 'National schools 1960–1985', in Mulcahy and O'Sullivan, *Irish Educational Policy*, pp. 49–50.

12 INTO, *Annual Report*, CEC 1968–69 (Dublin, 1969), p. 35.

13 De Buitléar, 'Curaclam Nua le hAghaidh na Bunscoile', pp. 4–12.

14 NA DFA 2003/17/383, Ó Floinn, *Recent Developments in Education*, June 1972, p. 17.

15 Ibid.

16 De Buitléar, 'Curaclam Nua le hAghaidh na Bunscoile', pp. 4–12.

17 Ibid., Department of Education, *Ár ndaltaí uile – All Our Children* (Dublin, 1969), pp. 9–11.

18 INTO, *Annual Report*, CEC 1968–69, p. 35.

19 Ibid., p. 36.

20 Ibid.

21 Coolahan, 'National schools 1960–1985', in Mulcahy and O'Sullivan, *Irish Educational Policy*, p. 49.

22 Teachers' Study Group, K. McDonagh (ed), *Reports on the Draft Curriculum for Primary Schools* (Dublin, 1969), p. 9.

23 Ibid., pp. 46–7.

24 INTO, *Annual Report*, CEC 1969–70 (Dublin, 1970), pp. 13–16.

25 Ibid., p. 24.

26 Ibid., pp. 24–5.

27 Ibid., p. 25.

28 Speech by Tomás Ó Floinn, 1969, INTO, Annual Report, CEC 1969–70, p. 26.

29 Ibid.

30 NA DFA 2003/17/383, Ó Floinn, *Recent Developments in Education*, June 1972, p. 17.

31 INTO, *Annual Report*, CEC 1969–70, pp. 24–6.

32 De Buitléar, 'Curaclam Nua le hAghaidh na Bunscoile', pp. 4–12, Coolahan, 'National Schools 1960–1985', in Mulcahy and O'Sullivan, *Irish Educational Policy*, p. 49.

33 INTO, *Annual Report*, CEC 1971–72 (Dublin, 1972), p. 42.

34 Coolahan, 'National schools 1960–1985', in Mulcahy and O'Sullivan, *Irish Educational Policy*, p. 50.

35 De Buitléar, 'Curaclam Nua le hAghaidh na Bunscoile', pp. 4–12.

36 INTO, *Annual Report*, CEC 1971–72, p. 42.

37 INTO, *Annual Report*, CEC 1969–70, p. 25.

38 INTO, *Annual Report*, CEC 1971–72, p. 41.

39 Coolahan, 'National schools 1960–1985', in Mulcahy and O'Sullivan, *Irish Educational Policy*, p. 53.

40 *Dáil Debates*, vol. 256, col. 943, 3 November 1971.

41 Coolahan, 'National schools 1960–1985', in Mulcahy and O'Sullivan, *Irish Educational Policy*, p. 51.

42 Ibid., pp. 52–3.

43 Ibid., p. 50.

44 NA DFA 2003/17/383, Ó Floinn, *Recent Developments in Education*, June 1972, p. 17.

45 Ibid., p. 18.

46 Teachers' Study Group, McDonagh, *Reports on the Draft Curriculum*, pp. 45–7.

47 Coolahan, 'National schools 1960–1985', in Mulcahy and O'Sullivan, *Irish Educational Policy*, p. 50.

48 Barry, 'Impact of a professional interest group', in Mulcahy and O'Sullivan, *Irish Educational Policy*, p. 144.

49 Ibid., Randles, *Post-Primary Education*, p. 300.

50 Department of Education, *Notes on the Organisation of Secondary Education in a Sample Rural Area*, internal document, 1967, p. 2.

51 Ibid., pp. 3–4.

52 Ibid., pp. 13–14.

53 Barry, 'Impact of a professional interest group', in Mulcahy and O'Sullivan, *Irish Educational Policy*, p. 141.

54 *Roscommon Herald*, 'Federal System of Schools in Boyle: Vocational Committee Adopts Rules for Common Enrolment', 21 February 1969.

55 Ibid.

56 Ibid., Fr. P. Troddyn, Editorial, *Studies*, vol. 59, no. 4 (Winter 1970), pp. 349–50.

57 Minutes, Standing Committee, ASTI, 2 March 1968, p. 2.

58 ASTI, *Official Programme for the 47th Annual Convention*, p. 77.

59 Minutes, Central Executive Committee, CCSS, 21 March 1968.

60 CMCSS, *Report of CMCSS on Amalgamation and/or Co-operation between Secondary and Vocational Schools*, 1968, pp. 1–3.

61 CMCSS, *Comments on Report by CMCSS*, 1968, pp. 1–2.

62 Department of Education, *Draft of Investment in Education report*, 1964.

63 Ibid.

64 Department of Education, *Notes on Secondary Education*, 1967, p. 14.

65 O'Connor, 'Post-primary education', pp. 233–49.

66 Ibid.

67 Ibid., p. 240.

68 Ibid., pp. 246–7.

69 Ibid., p. 247.

70 Ibid.

71 Ibid., p. 240.

72 Ibid., p. 247.

73 Ibid., pp. 248–9.

74 Ibid., p. 249.

75 Interview with Tony Ó Dálaigh, 3 May 2002.

76 Irish Jesuit Archives, CM/LEES/357 (23), Troddyn to O'Connor, 8 August 1968.

77 CM/LEES/357 (28–29), Note by Troddyn, *Distribution of Mr. Seán O'Connor's article 'Post-Primary Education: Now and in the Future'*, 14 August 1968.

78 Irish Jesuit Archives, Admin/3/86(1), McQuaid to Fr. C. McGarry, 13 August 1968.
79 Admin/3/86(1), McGarry to McQuaid, 17 August 1968.
80 Fr. P. Troddyn, Editorial, *Studies*, vol. 57, no. 3 (Autumn 1968), pp. 226–32.
81 Executive of the TBA, 'Teaching Brothers', *Studies*, vol. 57, no. 3 (Autumn 1968), p. 277.
82 Ibid., pp. 282–3.
83 Ibid., p. 281.
84 D. Buckley, 'Secondary teacher (2)', *Studies*, vol. 57, no. 3 (Autumn 1968), p. 296.
85 D. Donoghue, 'University professor', *Studies*, vol. 57, no. 3 (Autumn 1968), pp. 286–7.
86 K. Milne, 'A Church of Ireland view', *Studies*, vol. 57, no. 3 (Autumn 1968), pp. 261–9.
87 McCarthy, 'Vocational teachers', *Studies*, vol. 57, no. 3 (Autumn 1968), p. 273.
88 *Sunday Press*, 'The role of Vocational Schools', 16 January 1966, J. Logan, 'The making of a modern union: The Vocational Teachers' Association 1954–1973', in J. Logan (ed.), *Teachers' Union: The TUI and its Forerunners 1899–1994* (Dublin, 1999), p. 178.
89 O'Connor, *A Troubled Sky*, p. 189.
90 O'Connor, 'Post-primary education', p. 235.
91 Department of Education, *Structure of the Leaving Certificate Course and Examination, Summary of the Conclusions reached on the various items of the agenda by the committee set up to examine the matter*, 1967, pp. 2–5.
92 Ibid.
93 Ibid., pp. 7–8.
94 O'Connor, *A Troubled Sky*, p. 190.
95 NA 99/5/2, G.C.12/103, Cabinet Minutes, 23 April 1968, p. 3.
96 *Dáil Debates*, vol. 236, col. 1787, 31 October 1968.
97 Executive of the TBA, 'Teaching Brothers', pp. 274–83.
98 Minutes, CEC, ASTI, 18 January 1969, p. 4.
99 VTA, *General Secretary's Report 1968–69, Annual Congress 1969* (Dublin, 1969), p. 25, *General Secretary's Report 1969–70, Annual Congress 1970* (Dublin, 1970), p. 21.
100 Circular M43/69, Department of Education, June 1969.
101 Circular M39/69, Department of Education, May 1969.
102 *Dáil Debates*, vol. 236, col. 1787, 31 October 1968.
103 NA DFA 2003/17/383, Ó Floinn, *Recent Developments in Education*, June 1972, p. 13.
104 Circular M43/69, Department of Education, June 1969.
105 VTA, *General Secretary's Report 1969–70, Appendix V: Memorandum on New Leaving Certificate, Annual Congress 1970*, p. 32.
106 Circular M39/69, Department of Education, May 1969.

107 NA DFA 2003/17/383, Ó Floinn, *Recent Developments in Education*, June 1972, p. 13.

108 NA D/T 2000/6/324, S.17238, F.3/20/12, *Memorandum to the Government, Amendment of the Vocational Education Acts 1930–62*, 28 October 1969, p. 3; Ó Nualláin to Ó Dálaigh, 4 November 1969.

109 NA D/T 2000/6/324, S.17238, F.3/20/12, *Memorandum, Amendment of the Vocational Education Acts 1930–62*, 28 October 1969, p. 3.

110 Ibid., pp. 1–6.

111 NA D/T 2001/6/248, S.17238, F.3/20/12, *Memorandum for the Government, Vocational Education (Amendment) Bill 1970, Office of the Minister for Education*, 20 April 1970, p. 1.

112 Ibid.

113 NA 2001/5/1, G.C.13/56, Cabinet Minutes, 26 May 1970, pp. 1–2, D/T 2001/6/248, S.17238, Ó Nualláin to M. Ó Flathartaigh, 31 July 1970.

114 *Irish Times*, 'Far Reaching Post-Primary Re-organisation Outlined', 12 November 1970.

115 *Irish Times*, ' "Unified" System for Post-Primary Education Planned: Department's Working Document under Study by the Hierarchy', 12 November 1970.

116 *Irish Times*, 'Community Schools Result of Unitary Policy', 12 November 1970.

117 Ibid.

118 Troddyn, 'Editorial', *Studies*, vol. 59, no. 4 (Winter 1970), pp. 341–4.

119 Ibid.

120 Ibid.

121 Ibid.

122 Ibid.

123 *Irish Times*, 'Far Reaching Post-Primary Re-organisation Outlined', 12 November 1970.

124 Hyland and Milne, *Irish Educational Documents 2*, p. 267.

125 *Irish Times*, ' "Unified" System of Post-Primary Education Planned: Department's Working Document under Study by the Hierarchy', 12 November 1970.

126 Ibid.

127 *Dáil Debates*, vol. 249, col. 1613–16, 18 November 1970.

128 *Irish Times*, ' "Unified" System of Post-Primary Education Planned: Department's Working Document under Study by the Hierarchy', 12 November 1970.

129 IVEA, *Congress Report 1971* (Waterford, 1971), pp. 44–55.

130 DDA AB8/B/XV/b/08, *McQuaid Papers*, Minutes of the Irish Hierarchy, *Agreed summary report of meeting with the Department of Education*, 10 December 1970, p. 1.

131 Ibid.

132 Ibid., pp. 1–2, *Appendix II, Growth Centres which the Department regards as having some urgency: Enrolment figures 1969–70*.

133 *Agreed summary report of meeting with the Department of Education*, 10 December 1970, pp. 2–3.

134 Ibid.

135 Ibid., McCarthy, *Decade of Upheaval*, p. 215.

136 DDA AB8/B/XV/b/08, *McQuaid Papers*, *Agreed summary report of meeting with the Department of Education*, 10 December 1970, p. 3.

137 Ibid., p. 4.

138 Ibid., pp. 2–3.

139 Ibid., p. 3.

140 Ibid., p. 4.

141 Ibid.

142 Ibid.

143 IVEA, *Congress Report 1971*, p. 44.

144 Ibid.

145 IVEA, *Observations on the Working Paper entitled Community Schools put before representatives of the Association by the Minister for Education on 14th January 1971*, pp. 1–4.

146 Ibid., p. 4.

147 VTA, *General Secretary's Report 1970–71, Annual Congress 1971* (Dublin, 1971), pp. 38–9.

148 Ibid., McCarthy to Faulkner, December 1970, p. 39.

149 CMCSS, Minute of meeting of the Council with the Episcopal Commission, 18 March 1971, pp. 1–2.

150 Ibid.

151 CMCSS, *Statement issued by the Government Information Bureau on behalf of the Minister for Education*, 13 May 1971.

152 *Dáil Debates*, vol. 253, col. 1964–5, 19 May 1971.

153 Barry, 'Impact of a professional interest group', in Mulcahy and O'Sullivan, *Irish Educational Policy*, p. 146.

154 IVEA, *Congress Report 1971*, p. 55.

155 Ibid.

156 Ibid.

157 Logan, 'Making of a modern union' in Logan, *Teachers' Union*, p. 194.

158 *Church of Ireland Gazette*, 'Archbishop's Statement on Community and Vocational Schools', 21 May 1971, Hyland and Milne, *Irish Educational Documents 2*, p. 268.

159 *Journal of the 34th General Synod of the Church of Ireland, 1972* (Dublin, 1972), p. 104.

160 *Irish Times*, 'Faulkner Says There is No Reversal of Policy on Community Schools', 20 May 1971, J. Whyte, *Church and State in Modern Ireland 1923–70* (Dublin, 1971), p. 392.

161 McCarthy, *Decade of Upheaval*, p. 215.

162 *Irish Times*, 'Changes in Faulkner's Schools Plan: Parents to Have More Influence in Two Areas', 31 July 1971.

163 *Dáil Debates*, vol. 258, col. 2071–3, 17 February 1972.

164 Ibid., col. 2116.

165 Hyland and Milne, *Irish Educational Documents 2*, p. 268.

166 O'Flaherty, *Irish Education*, p. 74.

167 IVEA, *Congress Report 1971*, pp. 44–55.

168 VTA, *General Secretary's Report 1970–71, Annual Congress 1971*, pp. 38–9.

169 *Report of the SEC, 1972, Journal of the 34th General Synod*, p. 128.

170 Ibid.

171 NA D/T 2004/21/95, S.12891H, J.J. Cullen to Lynch, 15 September 1972.

172 Barry, 'Impact of a professional interest group' in Mulcahy and O'Sullivan, *Irish Educational Policy*, p. 146.

173 Randles, *Post-Primary Education*, p. 302.

174 NA D/T 98/6/950, S.18153, C.O.92066/2, *Memorandum for the Government, Ad Hoc Tribunal on Teachers' Salaries, Office of the Minister for Education*, 1 September 1967.

175 Ibid., pp. 5–6.

176 Circular M44/66, Department of Education, October 1966.

177 NA D/T 98/6/950, S.18153, C.O.92066/2, *Memorandum, Ad Hoc Tribunal on Teachers' Salaries*, 1 September 1967.

178 J. Coolahan, *The ASTI and Post-Primary Education in Ireland 1909–84* (Dublin, 1984), p. 274.

179 NA 99/5/1, G.C.12/61, Cabinet Minutes, 19 September 1967, p. 3.

180 *Tribunal on Teachers' Salaries, Report to the Minister for Education* (Dublin, 1968), p. 5.

181 Minutes, CEC, ASTI, 14 October 1967, pp. 1–3.

182 *Tribunal on Teachers' Salaries, Report*, p. 17.

183 Ibid., p. 16.

184 Ibid., p. 9.

185 Ibid., pp. 16–17.

186 Ibid., p. 15.

187 Ibid., pp. 10–14.

188 Ibid., pp. 14–15.

189 INTO, *Annual Report*, CEC 1968–69, Brosnahan to Lenihan, pp. 50–1.

190 McCarthy, *Decade of Upheaval*, p. 208.

191 VTA, *General Secretary's Report 1968–69, Annual Congress 1969*, pp. 1–10.

192 Minutes, CEC, ASTI, I June 1968, p. 1, Coolahan, *The ASTI*, p. 277.

193 McCarthy, *Decade of Upheaval*, pp. 208–9.

194 Ibid., Coolahan, *The ASTI*, p. 280.

195 CMCSS, *Press Statement*, 6 December 1968, p. 2, CCSS, Minutes of Central Executive Committee, 21 November 1968, CHA, Minutes of extraordinary general meeting, 28 November 1968.

196 Minutes, CEC, ASTI, 1 June 1968, pp. 1–2.

197 Coolahan, *The ASTI*, p. 277.

198 Ibid.

199 INTO, *Annual Report*, CEC 1968–69, p. 54.

200 VTA, *General Secretary's Report 1968–69, Annual Congress 1969*, p. 8.

201 Minutes, Standing Committee, ASTI, 26 October 1968, p. 2, Minutes, 16 November 1968, p. 2.

202 Minutes, CEC, ASTI, 18 January 1969, pp. 2–3.

203 Minutes, CEC, ASTI, 25 January 1969, pp. 1–3.

204 Minutes, Standing Committee, ASTI, 16 November 1968, p. 1, CMCSS, *Press Statement*, 6 December 1968, p. 2.

205 *Statement by JMB*, 31 January 1969, INTO, Annual Report, CEC 1968–69, p. 60.

206 NA D/T 2000/6/427, S.18332, *Press Release: ASTI Action Committee*, January 1969.

207 Ibid.

208 McCarthy, *Decade of Upheaval*, p. 212.

209 Randles, *Post-Primary Education*, p. 323.

210 CMCSS, *Press Statement*, 6 December 1968, p. 2.

211 McCarthy, *Decade of Upheaval*, p. 212.

212 Minutes, Standing Committee, ASTI, 17–18 February 1969, pp. 1–2.

213 Minutes, CEC, ASTI, 19 February 1969, pp. 1–3.

214 Ibid., Coolahan, *The ASTI*, pp. 282–5.

215 Minutes, CEC, ASTI, 19 February 1969, pp. 1–3.

216 McCarthy, *Decade of Upheaval*, p. 213.

217 VTA, *General Secretary's Report 1969–70, Annual Congress 1970*, pp. 5–7.

218 INTO, *Annual Report*, CEC 1970–71 (Dublin, 1971), pp. 1–2.

219 VTA, *General Secretary's Report 1969–70, Annual Congress 1970*, pp. 7–8.

220 INTO, *Annual Report*, CEC 1970–71, p. 2.

221 Coolahan, *The ASTI*, p. 288.

222 NA D/T 2001/6/399, S.18332A, *Parliamentary reply by Pádraig Faulkner, Minister for Education*, 5 February 1970.

223 Minutes, Standing Committee, ASTI, 24 September 1969, p. 1, Coolahan, *The ASTI*, p. 289.

224 NA D/T 2000/6/251, *Proposals of the Minister for Education for the implementation of salary increases for teachers with effect from 1ˢᵗ June 1969*, 16 September 1969, pp. 1–3.

225 NA D/T 2001/6/399, S.18332A, *Telegram by Michael Sheedy, President, ASTI, to the Taoiseach*, 6 February 1970.

226 INTO, *Annual Report*, CEC 1970–71, pp. 1–3, VTA, *General Secretary's Report 1969–70, Annual Congress 1970*, p. 18.

227 Minutes, Standing Committee, ASTI, 13 September 1969.

228 Circular M56/70, Department of Education, May 1970.

229 Minutes, CEC, ASTI, 13 June 1970, *Official Programme*, 1970, p. 63.

230 VTA, *General Secretary's Report 1969–70, Annual Congress 1970*, pp. 15–16.

231 Ibid., p. 17.

232 Coolahan, *The ASTI*, pp. 295–7.

233 VTA, *General Secretary's Report 1970–71, Annual Congress 1971, Proposals of the Minister for Education*, 3 July 1970, pp. 42–4.

234 Minutes, Standing Committee, ASTI, 20 July 1970, p. 2.
235 NA D/T 2001/6/399, S.18332A, M. MacMahon to Lynch, 2 November 1970.
236 H.S. Ó Dubhda to MacMahon, 5 November 1970.
237 Minutes, CEC, ASTI, 30 January 1971, pp. 1–4.
238 Minutes, Standing Committee, ASTI, 15 February 1971, pp. 1–2.
239 Minutes, Standing Committee, ASTI, 20 February 1971, pp. 1–2, VTA, *General Secretary's Report 1970–71, Annual Congress 1971*, pp. 11–12.
240 INTO, *Annual Report*, CEC 1970–71, *Proposals of the Minister for Education Relating to Teachers' Salaries and Allowances*, 22 February 1971, pp. 35–7.
241 Minutes, CEC, ASTI, 24 February 1971, pp. 1–5, Minutes, Standing Committee, 3 April 1971, p. 1.
242 Coolahan, *The ASTI*, p. 303.
243 McCarthy, *Decade of Upheaval*, p. 216.
244 *Third Programme, Economic and Social Development 1969–72, laid by the Government before each House of the Oireachtas, March 1969* (Dublin, 1969), p. 193.
245 NA D/T 2001/6/79, S.12891G, P.29/21, *Memorandum for the Government, School Leaving Age, Department of Education*, 13 January 1970, p. 1.
246 Ibid., p. 4.
247 Ibid., p. 1.
248 Ibid., p. 4.
249 Ibid., p. 1.
250 Ibid., Appendix A.
251 Ibid., p. 1.
252 Ibid., Appendix B.
253 Ibid., pp. 1–2.
254 Ibid., Appendix B.
255 Ibid., p. 4.
256 Ibid.
257 Ibid., p. 3.
258 Ibid.
259 Ibid.
260 Ibid., p. 4.
261 NA 2001/5/1, G.C.13/34, Cabinet Minutes, 20 January 1970, p. 3.
262 Coolahan, *Irish Education*, p. 138.
263 NESC, *Educational Expenditure in Ireland*, no. 12 (Dublin, 1975), p. 38.
264 Appendix 1, Table 4, p. 329.
265 Appendix 1, Table 5, p. 330; Figure 1, p. 330.
266 McCarthy, *Decade of Upheaval*, p. 216.
267 NA D/T 2000/6/655, S.18347B, *Higher Education: Statement issued by the Minister for Education on behalf of the Government*, 6 July 1968.
268 Ibid., p. 1.
269 Ibid., p. 2.
270 Ibid., pp. 4–6.

271 Ibid., p. 8.

272 Hyland and Milne, *Irish Educational Documents* 2, pp. 424–5.

273 DDA AB8/B/XVIII/18, *McQuaid Papers, Higher Education: Statement Issued by the Minister for Education on behalf of the Government*, 16 August 1968, pp. 1–3.

274 Ibid., p. 1.

275 Ibid., pp. 1–2.

276 Ibid., pp. 2–3.

277 HEA, *First Report 1968–69, Appendix 2: Address by the Minister for Education, Mr. Brian Lenihan TD, on the occasion of the first meeting of the HEA, 12 September 1968* (Dublin, 1969), pp. 54–7.

278 Interview with James Dukes, 28 April 2003.

279 NA D/T 2001/6/405, S.18346, Ó Raifeartaigh to MacGearailt, 4 March 1970.

280 NA D/T 2001/6/405, S.18346, C.O.1220, *Memorandum for the Government, Proposals for legislation for the establishment on a statutory basis of the HEA, Office of the Minister for Education*, 13 March 1970, pp. 1–3.

281 NA 2001/5/1, G.C.13/52, Cabinet Minutes, 5 May 1970, pp. 1–2.

282 NA D/T 2001/6/405, S.18346, *HEA Bill 1970*, p. 2.

283 Ibid., p. 3.

284 NA D/T 2002/8/381, S.18346, Ó Nualláin to Ó Conaill, 27 July 1971.

285 P. Clancy, 'The evolution of policy in third-level education', in Mulcahy and O'Sullivan, *Irish Educational Policy*, p. 112.

286 Ibid., p. 113.

287 DDA AB8/B/XVIII/18, *McQuaid Papers, Higher Education: Statement by Minister*, 16 August 1968, p. 2.

288 Meenan, 'The University in Dublin', pp. 314–15.

289 NA D/T 2000/6/655, S.18347B, Ó Dálaigh to Ó Dubhda, 5 February 1969.

290 NA D/T 2000/6/655, S.18347B, *The Case for University College Dublin*, p. 15.

291 J.J. Hogan to Lynch, 1 April 1969.

292 NA D/T 2000/6/655, S.18347B, *The Case for University College Dublin*, p. 14.

293 Ibid., pp. 14–19.

294 Lynch to S. Wilmot, 16 January 1969.

295 Ó Raifeartaigh, *Briefing note, Meeting of Taoiseach with NUI Senate deputation on Thursday, 6 February 1969*, pp. 2–3.

296 HEA, *Report to the Minister for Education on University Reorganisation, Appendix III: Proposals (the NUI/TCD Agreement) put forward by the National University of Ireland and Trinity College Dublin* (Dublin, 1972), pp. 83–7.

297 DDA AB8/B/XV/b/07, *McQuaid Papers*, Minutes, General Meeting of the Hierarchy, 22–24 June 1970, p. 5.

298 Ibid., *Appendix III, TRINITY COLLEGE, Statute 287/1956, Statement 25/6/1970*.

299 O'Connor, *A Troubled Sky*, p. 204.

300 HEA, *Report on University Reorganisation*, p. 59.

301 Ibid., pp. 46–7.

302 Clancy, 'Third-level education', in Mulcahy and O'Sullivan, *Irish Educational Policy*, pp. 106–7.

303 NA D/T 99/1/311, S.16735B, Press Release, *Speech by Brian Lenihan TD, Minister for Education, opening this year's Festival of Shannonside, Limerick*, 18 May 1968, pp. 1–2, *Statement by Limerick University Project Committee*, 7 September 1968.

304 NA D/T 99/1/311, S.16735B, Decision slip, *Cruinniú Rialtais*, 12 November 1968.

305 NA D/T 99/1/311, S.16735B, *Speech by Lenihan to the HEA*, November 1968, p. 1.

306 Ibid., p. 2.

307 Ibid., p. 3.

308 Ibid., pp. 2–3.

309 NA D/T 99/1/311, S.16735B, *Memorandum from the Minister for Education, University Education in Limerick, Additional information*, 19 November 1968.

310 NA D/T 99/1/311, S.16735B, Decision slip, *Cruinniú Rialtais, Establishment of (1) institution of higher education at Limerick (2) Institute of Technology and (3) Institute of Education*, 6 December 1968.

311 NA D/T 99/1/311, S.16735B, *Statement issued by the Government Information Bureau on behalf of the Minister for Education*, 12 December 1968.

312 *Irish Independent*, 'Minister's Statement on Limerick Plans', 13 December 1968.

313 *Limerick Leader*, 'Something Better than a University', 14 December 1968.

314 *Irish Times*, 'Limerick Group in Education Talks – No Detail of Institution', 3 January 1969.

315 NA D/T 99/1/311, S.16735B, *Memorandum B, Recommendation of the HEA on the Provision of Third-Level Educational Facilities at Limerick*, 20 March 1969, p. 3.

316 Ibid., p. 4.

317 Ibid.

318 Ibid., p. 6.

319 Ibid., pp. 5–8, Clancy, 'Third-level education', in Mulcahy and O'Sullivan, *Irish Educational Policy*, p. 120.

320 NA D/T 99/1/311, S.16735B, *Memorandum B, Recommendation of the HEA*, p. 8.

321 Ibid.

322 Ibid., p. 10.

323 HEA, *First Report 1968–69*, pp. 35–8.

324 Ibid.

325 NA D/T 2002/8/831, S.18346, C.O.1144, *Memorandum for the Government, First Report from HEA*, 31 March 1969, pp. 1–3.

326 NA D/T 2002/8/831, S.18346, C.O.1144, M. Lyddy to Lenihan, *Summary of main proposals for Higher Education in the Limerick Region emerging from the meeting on 11 April 1969 with the Minister for Education and the Secretary of his Department*, 18 April 1969.

327 Ibid.

328 *Limerick Leader*, 'Something Better than a University', 14 December 1968.

329 NA D/T 99/1/311, S.16735B, *Statement, Limerick University Project Committee*, 16 May 1969.

330 NA D/T 2002/8/831, S.18346, J. Moloney to Faulkner, 8 October 1970, Moloney to Faulkner, 6 November 1970.

331 NA D/T 2004/21/95, S.12891H, *Address by Jack Lynch at the opening of the National Institute of Higher Education, Limerick*, 27 September 1972.

Conclusion

The Irish state's policy towards education in the 1950s was dominated by a conservative consensus shared by politicians, officials and educational authorities. The Department of Education pursued a cautious and tentative approach towards the development of the educational system, while one of its ministers, General Mulcahy, disclaimed all responsibility for policy formulation. The first indications that a younger generation of politicians were seeking to promote a more active approach became apparent in the late 1950s. The department under Jack Lynch adopted a cautious reforming approach in some areas, which delivered incremental changes particularly in primary education. But Lynch was obliged to work within the constraints of the traditional political consensus, which gave a low priority to education.[1] While *Economic Development* underlined that political attitudes towards education were beginning to change, the state made little progress towards the development of a proactive education policy until Seán Lemass's election as Taoiseach in 1959.

Lemass's policy statement on the extension of the school leaving age in October 1959 marked the emergence of a viable government policy for the expansion of the educational system. Lemass adopted the raising of the statutory school leaving age to fifteen years, on the basis of a gradual expansion of the necessary facilities and teaching resources, as a key policy objective for the first time. While he did not prescribe a definite timescale, the government later indicated its intention to raise the school leaving age by 1970. The new policy approach enunciated by Lemass and Hillery in 1959 was the first serious attempt by the Irish state to plan the expansion of post-primary education as a whole. The reforming initiatives introduced by Hillery in primary and post-primary education marked the cautious beginning of a sustained process of state intervention in education. While the changes introduced in his first term were often small-scale, the department under Hillery adopted an activist approach to the resolution of pressing educational problems. But arguably the most significant legacy of Hillery's first period as Minister for Education was not any particular initiative but the evolution of a viable policy by the state for a gradual expansion of the educational system.

The transformation of the educational system, which began in the early 1960s, was driven by the reforming policies adopted by the state. Hillery's policy announcement on 20 May 1963, which saw the initiation of the comprehensive schools scheme and the plan for Regional Technical Colleges, underlined the rapid evolution of the state's educational policy. Hillery's policy statement was the first of the major reforming initiatives which transformed the Irish educational system during the era of expansion. Hillery and Lemass established for the first time a coherent and definite role for the state in directing the expansion of the educational system, paving the way for more radical reforms after the publication of *Investment* in 1965. But Hillery did not simply prepare the way for important policy changes delivered by others; he made a vital contribution to the development of a proactive, reforming policy towards education.

The new policy ideas adopted by politicians and officials were heavily influenced by the OECD, which encouraged the policy changes in various ways. The critical evaluation of technical education and the training of technicians in Ireland by OECD examiners in 1962 gave a strong impetus to the upgrading of vocational and higher technical education. But the OECD's most striking contribution was the proposal by its Directorate of Scientific Affairs for a pilot survey of long-term needs for educational resources in the Republic. This project, which was undertaken by the Irish survey team under the auspices of the OECD and the Department of Education, illuminated the severe deficiencies and inequalities in the educational system. The OECD exerted a profound influence on the transformation of Irish education, especially in the early stages of the process of expansion.

The *Investment in Education* report was a watershed of profound significance in the reform of the Irish educational system. The pilot study provided the statistical data to support and underpin state action, which could address the wide-ranging educational problems identified by the survey team. The report of the survey team also supplied the rationale and the specific policy content for many of the reforms of the period. The department acted decisively to initiate radical reforms in primary and post-primary education, which were inspired by the analysis of *Investment*. George Colley played a leading part in revising the government's policy to incorporate reforming initiatives based on the report. The pilot study paved the way for far-reaching policy changes, which would not have happened otherwise. Moreover following the publication of *Investment*, long-term planning of educational needs became an indispensable element of the government's policy for educational expansion.

The consensus that education was a key factor in national economic development, which was fully accepted by leading politicians and officials in the early 1960s, provided a compelling rationale for the policy changes initiated by the state. The success of the policy of economic development and the achievement of rapid economic expansion, especially in the early 1960s, provided an essential part of the context for educational progress, facilitating the allocation of increased resources to education. But the adoption by the government of the OECD's policy ideas, which emphasised the economic value of education as an investment in human resources, was equally significant in underpinning educational expansion. The *Second Programme for Economic Expansion* identified educational progress as a key national priority, which was essential to future economic development.[2] The aims of economic progress and educational expansion became inextricably linked in the government's project for national development in the 1960s. But the need to sustain economic expansion was not by any means the sole motivation for the government's decision to invest in education. Successive ministers endorsed the principle of equality of educational opportunity for all. Ó Buachalla argued that ministers and officials since the mid-1960s often used the concept of equality of educational opportunity as a general basis for policy without defining what it meant in operational terms.[3] But the department in the 1960s clearly identified equality of educational opportunity with the objective of access to post-primary educational facilities for all children.[4] Colley clarified the official view of equality of educational opportunity in practice when he indicated in 1965 that the government aimed to provide a three-year post-primary course for all pupils. The achievement of wider educational opportunity became a key objective of the state's policy by 1965 and formed an essential element of the rationale for the introduction of free post-primary education.

Donogh O'Malley's dramatic initiative for the introduction of free second-level education was an important landmark in the rapid expansion of the post-primary sector, which identified him more firmly with the reform and expansion of the educational system than any other public figure. O'Malley's flamboyant political style certainly tended to overshadow the real achievements of his predecessors, especially Hillery's.[5] But the transformation of the educational system was not simply the product of free post-primary education: it was an evolving process, which began in the late 1950s and continued throughout the following decade. O'Malley's charismatic style sometimes obscured the considerable continuity between his policy approach and the reforming initiatives pursued by his immediate predecessors. The Minister's dynamic approach greatly extended and deepened the ongoing process of educational reform and expansion. The transformation of the state's policy towards education, which had been initiated by Lemass and Hillery in 1959, reached its fullest extent under O'Malley. O'Malley's term of office saw the full development of a dynamic and ambitious policy for the expansion of the educational sector.

The department under successive ministers sought to develop strands of the educational system which had traditionally been neglected by the state. The reforms initiated by Hillery and Colley were designed to upgrade vocational education through the establishment of a common system of public examinations and a comprehensive curriculum at post-primary level. The foundation of the RTCs and the NIHE in Limerick underlined the commitment made by the government to the expansion of higher technical education by the early 1970s.

The state also gave serious attention to the development of special education for the first time in the 1960s.[6] The department under various ministers began to extend the limited educational facilities available for children suffering from various forms of disability. The department had some success in developing educational facilities for pupils with mental disabilities, but special education remained underdeveloped in other respects, notably provision for the education of physically disabled pupils and pupils with impaired hearing. The delivery of adequate programmes of special education in many areas remained a difficult challenge for the 1970s. Official efforts to develop educational facilities for Traveller children were much more limited and half-hearted: Traveller education was the strand of the educational sector least affected by the policy changes of the 1960s.

The transformation of the educational sector occurred with almost breathtaking speed. The department by the early 1970s was increasingly preoccupied with managing the rapid expansion of the educational system, which had been largely generated and sustained by the state's policies since 1959. The government approved the extension of the statutory school leaving age in 1970, but the decision to delay the implementation of the initiative until 1972 reflected increasing resistance by the Department of Finance to further expensive reforms in education. The success of the state's educational policy created a new series of challenges, notably the escalating costs of new educational services and the considerable discontent among many private educational interests at the department's methods of achieving educational reform. This widespread resentment at the department's approach, which was closely intertwined with opposition to the official policy of rationalisation, led to a full-scale conflict between the state and established educational interests at secondary level in 1969. The ambitious reforming policy pursued by the state since the early 1960s reached its political and fiscal limits by the end of the decade.

The increasing political difficulties and financial constraints encouraged Pádraig Faulkner to adopt a more cautious, low-key approach than his immediate predecessors. The creative policy developments and dramatic ministerial announcements, which had characterised the previous decade, gave way to the more prosaic business of implementing existing commitments and managing the ongoing transformation of the educational system.

Explaining expansion: what changed Irish education?

The transformation of the Irish educational sector was shaped by persistent and far-reaching intervention on the part of the state. The constructive interaction between dynamic ministers, reforming officials and expert advisory groups gave a decisive impetus to the process of educational expansion. The relative influence exerted by key individuals or organisations is sometimes difficult to determine precisely and certainly varied widely between the different sectors of the educational system. There is little doubt that the senior officials of the Department of Education itself exerted a profound influence on the transformation of primary education. Yet it is also evident that many of the reforms initiated by the officials were based on the critical analysis and comprehensive statistical data provided by *Investment*.

The first incremental reforms in primary education were closely linked to the gradual reduction of the pupil-teacher ratio. Lynch initiated the abolition of the marriage ban in 1958 on the advice of the senior officials, who aimed to provide more trained teachers and to improve the pupil-teacher ratio. The department under Lynch took the first modest measures to reduce the pupil-teacher ratio. Hillery sought to alleviate the extensive overcrowding in urban primary schools by authorising prefabricated classrooms, seeking to expand the supply of trained teachers and eventually limiting class sizes by departmental regulation. This attempt to limit class sizes remained a key preoccupation of the department under successive ministers throughout the 1960s, underlining the high priority given by the officials to the gradual improvement of the pupil-teacher ratio. The reorganisation of primary education began in earnest with the amalgamation of small national schools, which was largely inspired by the conclusions of *Investment*. The policy of amalgamation delivered a radical reshaping of the traditional pattern of primary education within a decade of its introduction. The report of the survey team was invaluable in providing the basis for the new policy, but the commitment of the Minister and key officials to amalgamation was crucial in securing its rapid implementation. Colley's steadfast defence of the new policy and his willingness to confront influential opponents of amalgamation publicly underlined the importance of effective ministerial leadership in promoting educational reform.

While amalgamation flowed directly from the analysis of the survey team, other reforms owed more to a general reappraisal of outdated, traditional approaches by ministers and senior officials. The abolition of the Primary Certificate from 1968 was a major policy change, which helped to pave the way for radical changes in the curriculum. The prolonged campaign by the INTO for the abolition of the examination maintained a steady pressure on politicians and officials to change an antiquated system of assessment, but this lobbying alone was insufficient to change the state's approach. It was O'Malley who took the decision to abolish the examination, while the senior officials also favoured a fundamental reappraisal of the state's traditional approach to the assessment of primary pupils. Seán MacGearailt, who viewed the abolition of the examination as a necessary part of a wider process of educational reform, secured the agreement of the managerial authorities to an alternative form of assessment.

The development and implementation of the new curriculum for national schools was the most far-reaching change initiated by the state in primary education in this period. The child-centred approach underlying the new programme, along with its attempt to create an integrated and flexible learning process, marked a radical departure from the rigidity of the previous curriculum. The introduction of the new curriculum in 1971 was carefully planned and implemented by senior officials and inspectors of the department, with little ministerial input in the development of the new programme. Lenihan and Faulkner certainly worked assiduously to promote the acceptance of the new curriculum but it was essentially a project designed and driven forward by the officials. The proactive approach of the INTO accelerated and facilitated important educational reforms, especially the introduction of the new curriculum. But on the whole primary education was an area in which effective ministerial leadership and the input of reforming officials combined successfully with the critical analysis of *Investment*.

The considerable changes in educational policy affecting the Irish language in this period were dictated largely by the distinctive approach of different ministers. Hillery initiated a quiet but far-reaching transformation of the Irish language policy in education, which was reflected in the reform of the system of recruitment for national teachers and in the reappraisal of traditional methods of teaching the national language. The established approach underpinning the language policy in primary education, namely teaching through the medium of Irish from the earliest possible level, was effectively dropped by the department under Hillery with little fanfare and no vocal opposition. Hillery himself played a decisive role in promoting this momentous policy change, which was greeted with serious misgivings by some, but by no means all, of the senior officials. Hillery's reforms diluted the traditional precedence given to Irish in primary education. The Minister also showed no enthusiasm for the more demanding recommendations of the Commission on the Restoration of the Irish Language, taking care to avoid any new commitments to the revival of Irish through the schools. Hillery showed greater scepticism concerning the policy of reviving the Irish language through the schools than either his predecessors or his immediate successor. Certainly Colley adopted a more conventional approach, introducing new methods of language teaching in an effort to reinvigorate the established policy. He shared with most senior officials a firm conviction that the schools should make an important contribution to restoring the national language. The initiatives taken by Colley promoted a process of experimentation in the teaching of oral Irish, which led to the introduction of new Irish language courses in all primary schools based on *Buntús Gaeilge*. The government's policy, which was outlined in its *White Paper on the Restoration of the Irish Language*, placed great emphasis on the development of oral Irish. Hillery and Colley both adhered to this policy, but each Minister interpreted it in a very different fashion, just as they clearly disagreed over the contribution to be made by the educational system to the restoration of Irish. It is evident, however, that both men left a distinctive imprint on the Irish language policy in education, which changed very considerably from the traditional approach of the previous generation.

The expansion of second-level education was shaped particularly by the efforts of successive ministers and officials to establish a form of comprehensive post-primary education which combined the vocational and academic streams in a single system. Hillery's policy statement on 20 May 1963 reflected a new commitment by the state to the introduction of comprehensive education. The initiative marked a fundamental policy change from the practice of successive governments since the foundation of the Irish state. The direct intervention of the national government to establish a new form of post-primary school was unprecedented. The Minister's initiative was based in part on new thinking about second-level education within the department itself, which was illustrated by the *Forecast of Developments* drafted by the senior officials in January 1962 and by the report of the internal committee chaired by Dr. Duggan. The OECD also played a significant role in promoting the policy changes announced by Hillery. The investigation of the training of technicians in Ireland undertaken by OECD examiners in 1962 exposed the considerable deficiencies in vocational and higher technical education.[7] The 'confrontation' between the Minister and the OECD experts in January 1963 influenced Hillery's policy announcement in May. The OECD's strong recommendation for the development of technical education at post-primary and higher level shaped the Minister's proposal for the Regional Technical Colleges. Hillery readily adopted the ideas of the senior officials and the OECD examiners, incorporating them into a wide-ranging new policy initiative. The rapid launch of the comprehensive schools plan was largely due to Lemass's skilful promotion of the initiative within the government. Hillery and the senior officials then pursued the new policy approach skilfully and tenaciously in tortuous negotiations with the Catholic Hierarchy, which reluctantly accepted the establishment of the first comprehensive schools in 1966. The implementation of the comprehensive schools pilot project marked the beginning of a much broader attempt by the state to secure the establishment of a comprehensive system, on the basis of a pooling of resources between secondary and vocational schools.

Colley's appeal for collaboration between secondary school authorities and the VECs in January 1966 made the creation of an integrated post-primary system an essential part of the state's approach to educational reform. Colley's initiative was dictated by the reality that comprehensive schools alone would not deliver the reshaping of post-primary education sought by the Minister and senior officials, as the Catholic Hierarchy would not accept co-educational state schools as a general model for the future. But the process of general rationalisation envisaged by the Development Branch made minimal progress, due to the hostility of the secondary managerial authorities and the ASTI to state intervention in general and the policy of integration in particular. Colley's immediate successors, O'Malley and Lenihan, did not give the same priority to the restructuring of post-primary education and it fell mainly to the officials of the Development Branch to drive forward the policy of rationalisation. The failure of the process of voluntary rationalisation encouraged the officials to consider more formal arrangements for the integration of secondary and vocational education, which came to fruition with the initiative for community schools in 1970. The officials of the Development Branch played the central part in formulating the new initiative. Faulkner was deeply involved in the negotiations with various educational stakeholders concerning the proposal for community schools, but the basic policy approach and indeed the specific concept itself pre-dated his term of office. William Hyland initially raised the idea of the community school during the drafting process for *Investment*, although it did not feature in the report itself. This concept was taken up by the Development Branch, which numbered Hyland as one of its key figures, in the late 1960s as a means of achieving a comprehensive post-primary system, which would break down the barriers between academic and vocational education. O'Connor's controversial contribution to *Studies* in 1968 illustrated the Development Branch's concern to rationalise the traditional network of small secondary and vocational schools, which failed to offer a comprehensive curriculum.

The initiative for community schools was the department's most determined and effective attempt to secure the integration of second-level education. The concept of the community school shared important features of the comprehensive system in Britain and the USA. But the officials of the Development Branch were concerned to adapt the comprehensive model to meet the demands of the Irish educational system, having learned from the failure of their previous efforts to achieve collaboration at post-primary level. The community school was designed to deliver comprehensive education within the framework of an institutional model which would be acceptable to established educational interests. The department's latest initiative was ultimately far more successful and influential than its previous attempts to reshape the post-primary sector. The rapid development of community schools testified to the achievement of the officials in devising a workable new model for the expansion of second-level education and the implementation of a comprehensive curriculum.

The rapid expansion of second-level education in the late 1960s was, however, dictated especially by the introduction of free post-primary education. The implementation of the new schemes for free tuition and free transport delivered a dramatic upsurge in the overall level of participation in post-primary education. The limitations of the initiative should not be overlooked: it did relatively little to encourage low-income families to keep their children in full-time education beyond the school leaving age and tended to reinforce the existing pattern of second-level education, which was characterised by a traditional imbalance favouring secondary schools over the vocational sector. Despite its deficiencies, however, the reform initiated by O'Malley offered a viable means of expanding access to second-level education, which took account of the realities of the Irish educational system. The Minister's policy announcement in September 1966 marked a new departure in the state's policy for educational expansion, although it was consistent with the government's long-term objectives. *Investment* helped to pave the way for the initiative by illuminating the severe social and geographical inequalities in participation at post-primary level. But free second-level education would not have occurred in such a rapid and ambitious fashion but for the crucial intervention of Donogh O'Malley. Although the senior officials were preparing plans for the phased introduction of free post-primary education, O'Malley exerted a decisive influence on the scope and timing of the initiative, so that the reform proved much more radical and far-reaching than the department or indeed the government had initially envisaged. The Minister's unauthorised policy announcement effectively compelled the government to accept the principle of free post-primary education in November 1966, although much difficult negotiation still lay ahead with the Department of Finance concerning specific aspects of the reform. It is evident too that the initiative was possible only because educational expansion was already enshrined as an essential national priority, largely at Lemass's instigation. While the Taoiseach was certainly cautious about the far-reaching nature of O'Malley's initiative, it was Lemass more than any other political figure who created the conditions necessary for the achievement of free post-primary education.

The dramatic impact of O'Malley's initiative for free second-level education was so great that it overshadowed the equally important advances in vocational and higher technical education which occurred during the same period. The department under most ministers made a sustained attempt to extend the scope and raise the status of vocational education. The new direction of the state's policy was underlined by the enactment of legislation in 1962, which provided for an enhanced level of financial support for the VECs. The establishment of a common Intermediate Certificate examination by 1966 and the revision of the Leaving Certificate to incorporate technical subjects from 1969 were important educational reforms, which opened up new opportunities for vocational school pupils. These reforms still did not place vocational schools on an equal level with secondary schools in attracting pupils, not least because they could not transform established public attitudes towards post-primary education. But the department acted effectively to facilitate the full development of the vocational sector, through increased financial support for the VECs and the adoption of significant curriculum reforms. The state's approach was undoubtedly influenced by the critical analysis of the academic bias in Irish education provided by the OECD examiners in 1962. The officials and inspectors of the department also played a leading part in the extension of traditionally academic public examinations to include practical and technical subjects. Perhaps most significantly, reforming ministers such as Hillery and Colley acted decisively to remove the traditional limitations imposed on vocational education by the state and the Catholic Hierarchy for the previous generation.

The most effective intervention made by the state in higher education during this period involved the expansion of higher technical education, which extended educational opportunity and upgraded the status of technical studies within the third-level sector. The foundation of the RTCs was one of the most significant educational advances delivered by the state in the entire period of economic expansion. This advance was due in no small measure to O'Malley's initiative in establishing the Steering Committee on Technical Education and to the influence exerted by the Minister on the state's policy for the expansion of higher technical education. The report of the Steering Committee presented a compelling rationale for the rapid development of the RTCs and provided a detailed educational brief for the new colleges. Leading officials of the Department of Education employed the analysis of the Steering Committee to good effect in making the case that the state should finance the establishment of all the proposed colleges as a matter of urgency. O'Malley himself lobbied the Cabinet tenaciously and successfully to secure its agreement for the establishment of the new technical colleges in most regions of the country. The effective lobbying undertaken by O'Malley and senior officials of his department paved the way for the rapid development of higher technical education and the establishment of a new sector in third-level education by the early 1970s. Indeed O'Malley's influential role in the development of the RTCs was his most enduring contribution to higher education. The upgrading of technical education in this period marked a decisive break with the restrictive and tentative policy of the previous decade, which had neglected technical instruction at best and in some respects actively obstructed its development. The upgrading of higher technical education, especially the creation of a new technological sector within third-level education, was the most radical reform undertaken by the state in the era of educational expansion.

The rapid and successful expansion of technical education at higher level contrasted sharply with the fate of O'Malley's cherished project for the university merger. The proposal for merger was very much a personal initiative promoted by O'Malley himself, which had not been contemplated by previous ministers or most senior officials of the department. The Minister won the support of the government for his proposal, especially by emphasising the financial advantages to the state of a merger between the two universities in Dublin. But the initiative eventually foundered due to the profound scepticism of the university authorities in both Trinity College and UCD. The main result of O'Malley's initiative for merger was the negative outcome of sidelining the Commission on Higher Education, whose lengthy deliberations were largely disregarded by the government. A committee of senior officials established by O'Malley in 1967 was more influential than the Commission in shaping the state's policy for higher education under his successors. The committee presented a critical commentary on the report of the Commission and dismissed several of its most significant recommendations, including the controversial proposal for

New Colleges. The committee's conclusions were generally accepted by successive ministers, with the result that the Commission exerted only a limited influence on the subsequent development of higher education.

The establishment of the HEA in 1968 and the passage of legislation giving statutory recognition to the new Authority in 1971 shaped the structure of third-level education for the following generation. The government provided for the delegation of significant executive functions to the HEA in dealing with the universities and other institutions of higher education, but gave the Authority no executive role with regard to higher technical education, which remained directly under the supervision of the Department of Education. While the HEA had a general advisory role for the entire sector, a binary structure of governance for third-level education was firmly established by the early 1970s. The officials of the department were intent on maintaining their ability to shape and control the development of higher technical education. The binary structure was a product of the conviction among politicians and officials that the state should remain directly responsible for the expansion of technical education.

The HEA played an important part in the expansion of higher education, not least in its recommendations for the establishment of the National Institute of Higher Education in Limerick. O'Malley and Lenihan were concerned to satisfy the political agitation for a new university in Limerick, which was effectively co-ordinated by the Limerick University Project Committee. The committee of senior officials also supported the establishment of a university college in Limerick, provided that the new institution was willing to provide facilities for higher technological training. But the HEA exerted a decisive influence on the role and functions of the new institution of higher education, which was not recognised as a university but enjoyed many of its characteristics, such as the ability to offer degree courses. The Authority provided the blueprint for the creation of a new type of third-level institution, which combined a strong technological orientation with the prestige of more traditional Arts courses. The HEA, which was itself influenced by the example of the Polytechnics in Britain, made an invaluable contribution to the establishment of the NIHE in Limerick and the wider development of technical education at higher level.

The politics of reform: some underlying patterns

The radical reforms of the 1960s could not have been achieved without a dramatic change in political attitudes towards the role of the state in the educational sector. The appointment of dynamic members of Fianna Fáil's younger generation to head the Department of Education certainly increased the political status of the department, which was widely regarded as a political backwater in the 1950s.[8] De Valera began this practice in 1957 with the appointment of Jack Lynch as Minister for Education. But it was Lemass who made the Department of Education an important stage in the ministerial careers of younger Fianna Fáil politicians: Hillery received ministerial office for the first time as Minister for Education, while the department was Colley's first Cabinet portfolio. O'Malley had served as Minister for Health for little more than a year before he was transferred to Education. All three of the ministers appointed by Lemass undertook far-reaching reforming initiatives, which contributed significantly to the transformation of the educational system.

It is apparent, however, that politicians were not forcing unwelcome changes upon a reluctant corps of officials. The reforms would not have happened in such a rapid and far-reaching way without the active collaboration of the Department of Education. Most of the new initiatives could not have been implemented at all but for the essential contribution made by senior officials. The reforming approach adopted by the senior officials marked a radical change of direction. The department had pursued a low-key, tentative approach to the development of educational policy until the late 1950s, restricting its activity mainly to the implementation of existing state policies, such as the revival of the Irish language, and the quiet administration of the segments of the educational system within its remit. But the same department acted by 1972 to establish the central role of the state in the development and implementation of policy across the educational sector. This transformation may be partly explained by the elevation of a new generation of middle-ranking officials, who were discontented with the state's traditional approach, to senior positions within the department. The appointment of Seán O'Connor as head of the Development Branch in 1965 and of Tomás Ó Floinn as an Assistant Secretary in 1967 marked the promotion of officials who were strongly committed to educational reform.[9] But a gradual changing of the guard does not fully explain the sweeping transformation in the department's approach. Dr. Ó Raifeartaigh, who served as Secretary until 1968, and his successor, Seán MacGearailt, were very experienced officials who had held senior positions within the department in the 1950s and remained in office throughout the following decade. But both Ó Raifeartaigh and MacGearailt embraced the new agenda of expansion, reform and rationalisation. MacGearailt was a constant presence throughout the 1960s in negotiations for the implementation of various reforms; he was later singled out by Hillery as a key figure in delivering the most important changes at primary and post-primary level.[10] Ó Raifeartaigh's considerable diplomatic skill and his close connections with McQuaid proved invaluable to various ministers in

negotiating the agreement of the Catholic Hierarchy to reforming initiatives. Ó Raifeartaigh was supportive of the reforms pursued by the government and worked effectively to minimise conflict with the Catholic Bishops
in achieving the implementation of ministerial initiatives. The senior
officials generally favoured more effective state intervention to expand the
educational system by the early 1960s.

The sweeping changes in the educational sector did not, however, all
originate with the Department of Education, its political head or expert
advisory groups. Lemass played a central part in initiating and directing
the radical reform and expansion of Irish education during his term as
Taoiseach. 'Expansion would not have happened except for Lemass', was
Hillery's generous but essentially accurate comment on Lemass's role in
promoting educational reform.[11] The appointment of younger, more
dynamic ministers to the Department of Education formed only a single
aspect of Lemass's substantial influence on the politics of education during
his term as Taoiseach. It was Lemass's interaction with successive reforming ministers which provided much of the momentum for key policy
changes. He not only provided essential support for initiatives proposed by
various ministers, but also acted decisively to facilitate educational reform.
Lemass both shared and helped to foster the growing conviction, which
took hold among Irish political elites in the early 1960s, that education
made an invaluable contribution to economic development. Lemass's vigorous advocacy of long-term educational planning and his decision to give
priority to education in the allocation of scarce national resources created
a favourable political context for the reforms of the period. Lemass made
the development and expansion of the educational system, on the basis of
coherent planning, a key policy priority for the Irish state. His successor,
Jack Lynch, generally maintained Lemass's approach of giving priority to
education in the late 1960s.

The Department of Finance also accepted the case for investment in
education in this period. The officials of the department highlighted in
Economic Development the potential contribution of vocational education
to agricultural training.[12] John McInerney of the department's Economic
Development Branch endorsed the OECD proposal for the pilot study of
long-term educational needs at the Washington conference. Whitaker also
played a significant role in facilitating the rapid launch of the OECD study,
by securing the agreement of the relevant departments to the pilot study.
The senior officials of the department were supportive of educational
expansion as an economic imperative, devoting considerable attention to
education in drafting the *Second Programme for Economic Expansion*. The
Department of Finance certainly gave a far higher priority to educational
expansion in the 1960s than they had at any time during the previous

generation. But there were also definite limits to the department's willingness to support expensive educational initiatives. The Minister for Finance, Jim Ryan, was critical of the proposal for comprehensive schools in 1963 and Hillery needed Lemass's assistance to overcome the department's reservations. More significantly, Whitaker was appalled at O'Malley's policy announcement on free post-primary education in September 1966 and the Department of Finance sought unsuccessfully to modify the proposals or at least delay the introduction of the initiative. Moreover the department's tolerance for costly educational reforms was entirely eroded by 1970, when its officials made a strong case against the early extension of the school leaving age. The Department of Finance became much more critical of further initiatives in education by the early 1970s, especially due to the escalating cost of previous reforms. There is little doubt, however, that senior officials of the department made a significant contribution to the transformation of the state's educational policy in the early 1960s, although they may not have appreciated the results of the new policy by the end of the decade.

The Opposition parties also formed part of the new political consensus, which regarded educational reform as a key element in the economic and social development of the nation. The radical left-wing deputies, Noel Browne and Jack McQuillan, were the most persistent and effective parliamentary critics of the state's minimalist policy in the 1950s: it was their motion on the school leaving age which set the scene for Lemass's intervention to clarify the government's educational policy. The Labour Party was the first of the main political parties to endorse a comprehensive programme of reform for the educational sector, when they launched their policy document *Challenge and Change in Education* in 1963.[13] Labour also proved willing to support controversial reforming policies adopted by the government, notably the amalgamation of small national schools. Fine Gael was less proactive than either the Labour Party or the government for much of the decade, reacting uneasily to some of the policy changes by the state and even opposing the policy of amalgamation. But Fine Gael also adopted a detailed programme for reform in its policy document on education in 1966, presenting its own scheme for free post-primary education.[14] The Fine Gael policy had little influence on the department's plans, but it certainly reinforced the political imperative for the government to support O'Malley's initiative for the transformation of second-level education. The Opposition parties or representatives usually exerted only a marginal influence on the state's policy, although their activity sometimes dictated the timing of ministerial initiatives and usually reinforced the political pressure on the government to pursue wide-ranging educational reforms. Moreover the increased political competition concerning educational reform both reflected greater public interest in education in the 1960s and established the importance of education as a central issue within the political arena.

The transformation of the educational system involved profound changes in the balance of power between the state and the private educational authorities. The churches and private managerial bodies were obliged to adapt to the reforming policies of successive ministers. While no minister and very few officials sought the secularisation of the educational system, the role of the state in the development of the sector was greatly enhanced. The majority of private educational interests had no influence on the policy changes promoted by the Department of Education. The Catholic managerial bodies and the ASTI were particularly discontented at their inability to affect the department's policy of rationalisation and generally opposed the state's agenda in education. The Catholic Hierarchy, which was consulted on most of the reforms, lobbied effectively to maintain the church's substantial influence in the management and ownership of the secondary system. But even the Hierarchy usually had no influence on the formulation of the state's policies in this period and tended to react to ministerial initiatives rather than seeking to develop alternative proposals of its own. Despite its suspicion of many of the specific initiatives proposed by the government, the Hierarchy proved willing to accept sustained and assertive state intervention in education.

It was also apparent, however, that not all private interests pursued an essentially reactive approach to the challenges of educational expansion. The SEC, representing the Protestant churches, took a proactive approach to educational reform and collaborated with the department's attempts to re-organise post-primary education. The SEC was relatively successful in its negotiations with the department in the late 1960s, securing a separate scheme of assistance for Protestant pupils as part of O'Malley's initiative for free second-level education. Likewise the INTO secured the implementation of several long-standing objectives in this period, notably the withdrawal of the marriage ban and the abolition of the Primary Certificate examination. The INTO, which consistently advocated large-scale educational reform, exerted considerable influence on the government's policy in primary education.

It was, however, the proactive reforming approach adopted by the state which marked the most decisive change from the political inertia and conservative policies of the previous generation. Leading politicians and senior officials considered that an innovative educational policy was essential not only to overcome long-standing problems in the educational system but also to create the necessary conditions for continued economic and social progress. The state's approach to education had changed beyond all recognition by the early 1970s and the profound impact of the policy changes would continue to shape the educational system for the following generation. The transformation of the state's educational policy provided the essential impetus for the radical reform and reshaping of the Irish educational sector.

Notes

1 Ó Buachalla, *Education Policy*, p. 70.
2 *Second Programme for Economic Expansion, Part II*, p. 193.
3 Ó Buachalla, *Education Policy*, p. 358.
4 O'Connor, 'Post-primary education', pp. 233–49.
5 Horgan, *Seán Lemass*, p. 293.
6 Coolahan, *Irish Education*, pp. 135–6.
7 OECD, *Training of Technicians in Ireland, OECD Reviews of National Policies for Science and Education* (Paris, 1964), pp. 88–9.
8 Ó Buachalla, '*Investment in Education*', pp. 10–20.
9 O'Connor, *A Troubled Sky*, p. 2, Interview with Dr. Hillery, 25 February 2002.
10 Interview with Dr. Hillery, 25 February 2002.
11 Interview with Dr. Hillery, 25 February 2002.
12 Whitaker, *Economic Development*, pp. 112–13.
13 Labour Party, *Challenge and Change in Education* (Dublin, 1963).
14 Fine Gael, *Policy for a Just Society 3, Education* (Dublin, 1966).

Appendix 1

Educational expenditure by the state

Table 1: Net current expenditure by the Exchequer on primary, post-primary and higher education: 1950–60 (selected years)

Year	Primary education (£)	Secondary education (£)	Vocational education (£)	Universities and colleges (£)	Total (£)
1950–51	6,354,093	1,041,148	696,218	481,724	8,573,183
1954–55	8,154,013	1,678,186	1,012,746	567,492	11,412,437
1956–57	9,054,911	1,811,506	1,104,622	678,547	12,649,586
1957–58	9,110,250	2,304,607	1,128,047	661,180	13,204,084
1958–59	9,178,442	2,184,027	1,241,943	692,180	13,296,592
1959–60	10,258,765	2,483,216	1,364,101	948,560	15,054,642

Source: Committee of Public Accounts, Appropriation Accounts, 1950–51 to 1959–60.

Table 2: Net current expenditure by the Exchequer on primary, post-primary and higher education: 1960–72

Year	Primary education (£)	Secondary education (£)	Vocational education (£)	Universities and colleges (£)	Total (£)
1960–61	10,498,584	2,698,875	1,497,545	984,017	15,679,021
1961–62	11,120,252	2,947,592	1,659,565	1,069,680	16,797,089
1962–63	12,247,928	3,461,272	2,078,228	1,684,380	19,471,808
1963–64	13,686,332	3,691,235	2,146,590	2,374,771	21,898,928
1964–65	16,517,853	5,241,770	2,437,245	3,223,462	27,420,330
1965–66	18,609,690	5,846,209	3,717,991	2,706,738	30,880,628
1966–67	19,335,682	6,746,161	3,605,138	3,364,138	33,051,119
1967–68	20,212,599	10,285,294	4,567,627	3,697,456	38,762,976
1968–69	20,635,273	13,835,555	5,738,856	6,324,251	46,563,935
1969–70	23,903,619	16,720,742	9,546,117	7,721,246	57,891,724
1970–71	27,741,246	19,789,742	10,695,099	8,206,892	66,432,979
1971–72	31,880,044	22,035,008	12,794,214	11,202,935	77,912,201

Source: Committee of Public Accounts, Appropriation Accounts, 1960–61 to 1971–72.

Tables 1 and 2 illustrate the increasing level of current expenditure allocated to the educational system by the central government in this period: these tables do not include capital spending or expenditure by the VECs based on funding from the rates.

Table 3: The expansion of the primary school building programme: 1956–57 to 1964–65

Year (to 31st March)	Number of new schools sanctioned	Grants allocated by state to programme (£)
1956–57	53	1,042,602
1957–58	55	1,096,486
1958–59	81	1,249,998
1959–60	73	1,499,999
1960–61	74	1,600,000
1961–62	104	3,146,320
1962–63	87	2,135,823
1963–64	112	3,098,031
1964–65	154	4,086,352

Source: *Tuarascáil, Táblaí Staitistic, An Roinn Oideachais* 1964–65 (Dublin, 1966), p. 8.

Table 4: Educational expenditure as a proportion of overall government expenditure: 1961–62 to 1971–72

Year	Current educational expenditure (£million)	Current share of all public current expenditure (%)	Capital educational expenditure (£million)	Capital share of all public capital expenditure (%)
1961–62	17.36	9.37	2.15	4.22
1962–63	19.45	9.91	3.06	5.20
1963–64	21.01	9.81	4.32	6.65
1964–65	26.18	10.42	5.62	7.03
1965–66	28.70	10.32	6.91	7.88
1966–67	33.58	11.06	5.66	6.85
1967–68	34.73	10.28	8.77	8.69
1968–69	40.46	10.39	11.59	8.87
1969–70	56.46	12.33	14.16	9.02
1970–71	63.60	11.58	12.93	8.23
1971–72	76.12	11.79	13.46	7.54

Source: National Economic and Social Council, *Educational Expenditure in Ireland*, no. 12 (Dublin, 1975), p. 38.

Table 5: Educational expenditure as a proportion of Gross National Product
(GNP) over a ten-year period: 1961–62 to 1971–72

Year	Percentage of GNP
1961–62	3.05
1962–63	3.26
1963–64	3.45
1964–65	3.85
1965–66	4.09
1966–67	4.34
1967–68	4.38
1968–69	4.64
1969–70	5.53
1970–71	5.39
1971–72	5.58

Source: National Economic and Social Council, *Educational Expenditure in Ireland*, (Dublin,
1975), p. 38.

Tables 4 and 5 display all educational expenditure by the Exchequer over
a ten-year period. The figures for educational expenditure drawn from
NESC are not directly comparable to the amounts recorded by the Public
Accounts Committee, as they are calculated on a different basis, although
both reflect the upward trend in public expenditure on education.

Figure 1 illustrates the doubling of educational expenditure as a proportion of GNP over twelve years between 1961–62 and 1973–74.

Figure 1 The expansion of educational expenditure by the state as a percentage
of GNP between 1961 and 1974

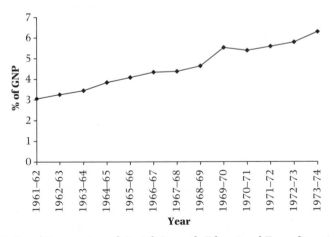

Source: National Economic and Social Council, *Educational Expenditure in Ireland*,
p. 38 (Dublin, 1975).

Appendix 2

Regional inequalities in educational participation at post-primary level

Figure 2 Post-primary school pupils by county, 1962–63

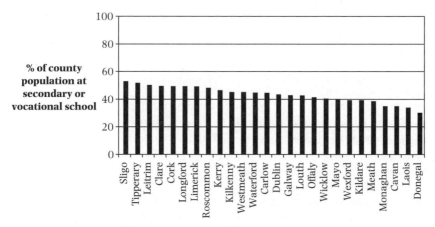

Source: Investment in Education, Part 1, p. 157.

Bibliography

State archives and records

Department of education
Circulars for Primary Schools 1957–72
Circulars for Secondary Schools 1957–72
M-Files 1957–72
Papers relating to the Commission on Higher Education
Progress reports 1957–66

National Archives of Ireland (NA)
Department of the Taoiseach (D/T)
Department of Finance (D/FIN)
Department of Foreign Affairs (DFA)
Minutes of Cabinet Meetings
Minutes of Government Meetings

Reports and official sources

Children and their Primary Schools: *A Report of the Central Advisory Council for Education (England)*, vol. 1 (London, 1966)

Committee of Public Accounts, Appropriation Accounts 1950–72 (Dublin, 1952–75)

Council of Education, *(1) The Function of the Primary School (2) The Curriculum to be Pursued in the Primary School* (Dublin, 1954)

Council of Education, *(2) The Curriculum of the Secondary School* (Dublin, 1962)

Dáil Debates

Department of Education, *County Report for Co. Cavan, Projected Organisation for Post-Primary Education: General Principles*, 1966

Department of Education, *Notes on the Organisation of Secondary Education in a Sample Rural Area*, internal document, 1967

Department of Education, *Structure of the Leaving Certificate Course and Examination, Summary of the Conclusions*, 1967

Department of Education, *Ár ndaltaí uile – All Our Children* (Dublin, 1969)

Department of Education, *Committee Report: Educational Facilities for the Children of Itinerants, Oideas*, no. 5 (Autumn 1970), pp. 44–53

Department of Education, Departmental Committee, *Tuarascáil Shealadoch Ón Choiste a Cuireadh I mbun Scrúdú a Dheánamh ar Oideachas Iarbhunscoile*, 1962

Economic Development (Dublin, 1958)

Education of Children who are Handicapped by Impaired Hearing (Dublin, 1972)

Final Report of the Commission on the Restoration of the Irish Language (Dublin, 1964)

HEA, *First Report 1968–69* (Dublin, 1969)

HEA, *Report to the Minister for Education on University Reorganisation with Special Reference to the Projected Formation of a Single University of Dublin and to the Alternative Solution Put Forward Jointly by the National University of Ireland and Trinity College, Dublin* (Dublin, 1972)

Investment in Education, Report of the Survey Team appointed by the Minister for Education in October 1962 (Dublin, 1965)

NCEA, *First Annual Report 1972–73* (Dublin, 1973)

NESC, *Educational Expenditure in Ireland*, no. 12 (Dublin, 1975)

NIEC, *Comments on Investment in Education* (Dublin, 1966)

OECD, *Reviews of National Policies for Science and Education: Training of Technicians in Ireland* (Paris, 1964)

OECD, *Country Reports: The Mediterranean Regional Project: An Experiment in Planning by Six Countries* (Paris, 1965)

OECD, *Review of National Policies for Education: Ireland* (Paris, 1991)

Report of the Commission on Accommodation Needs of the Constituent Colleges of the National University of Ireland (Dublin, 1959)

Report of the Commission on Itinerancy (Dublin, 1963)

Report of the Commission on Mental Handicap (Dublin, 1965)

Report of the Commission on Higher Education 1960–67, vol. 1 (Dublin, 1967)

Report of the Committee on the Constitution Pr. 9817 (Dublin, 1967)

Second Programme for Economic Expansion, Part I (Dublin, 1963)

Second Programme for Economic Expansion, Part II (Dublin, 1964)

Third Programme, Economic and Social Development 1969–72 (Dublin, 1969)

Seanad Debates

Steering Committee on Technical Education, *Report to the Minister for Education on Regional Technical Colleges, 1967* (Dublin, 1969)

Thom's Directory of Ireland

Tribunal on Teachers' Salaries, Report to the Minister for Education (Dublin, 1968)

Tuarascáil, An Roinn Oideachais, 1957–58 to 1971–72 (Dublin, 1959–74)

White Paper on the Restoration of the Irish Language (Dublin, 1965)

Religious and diocesan archives

Archives of the Irish Christian Brothers, St. Helen's Province, York Rd, Dún Laoghaire

Correspondence of the TBA
Notes and correspondence of the Provincial, St. Helen's Province
Archives of the Irish Christian Brothers, St. Mary's Province, 274 North Circular
Rd, Dublin 1
Minutes and correspondence of the TBA
Minutes and papers relating to the Christian Brothers' Education Committee
Dublin Diocesan Archives (DDA), Archbishop's House, Drumcondra, Dublin 9
Papers of Dr. John Charles McQuaid, Archbishop of Dublin: correspondence and
papers; Minutes of the Irish Hierarchy, 1957–72
Irish Jesuit Archives, Leeson St., Dublin 2
Representative Church Body Library, Braemor Park, Churchtown, Dublin 14
Journal of the Proceedings of the General Synod of the Church of Ireland, ed. J.L.B.
Deane, 1957–72
Church of Ireland Gazette

Archives of teaching unions and managerial associations

ASTI, ASTI House, Winetavern St., Dublin 8
Minutes of Standing Committee and Central Executive Committee 1957–71
Official Programme for Annual Convention, 1957–71
Central Secretariat of Secondary Schools, Emmet House, Dundrum, Dublin 14
CCSS, Minutes of Standing Committee and Central Executive Committee,
correspondence and reports
CMCSS, Minutes, correspondence, reports and statements; CHA, correspon-
dence and statements
INTO, 35 Parnell Square, Dublin 1
Official Programme for Annual Congress, 1957–71
Reports of the Central Executive Committee 1957–71
IVEA, Annual reports 1957–71, National Library of Ireland
TUI, 73 Orwell Rd. Rathgar, Dublin 6
Reports for the Annual Congress of the VTA 1960–71

Publications by political parties and research groups

Fine Gael, *Policy for a Just Society 3, Education* (Dublin, 1966)
Labour Party, *Challenge and Change in Education* (Dublin, 1963)
Tuairim, *University College Dublin and the Future: A Memorandum from a Research
Group of Tuairim, Dublin Branch, on the Report of the Commission on Accommoda-
tion Needs of the Constituent Colleges of the National University of Ireland* (Dublin,
1960)
Tuairim, *Educating Towards A United Europe* (Dublin, 1961)
Tuairim, *Irish Education* (London, 1962)

University archives and libraries

Archives Department, UCD (UCDA)
Cearbhall Ó Dálaigh Papers (P51)

Fianna Fáil Papers, Minutes of the Parliamentary Party (P176)
General Richard Mulcahy Papers (P7/C/152, P7/C/154)

Newspapers and journals

Administration
Belfast Telegraph
Clonmel Nationalist and Munster Advertiser
Evening Press
Gairm
Hibernia
Irish Educational Studies
Irish Independent
Irish Press
Irish Times
Limerick Leader
Oideas
Roscommon Herald
Secondary Teacher
Studies
Studies in Education
Sunday Independent
Sunday Press

Secondary works

Akenson, Donald H., *The Irish Education Experiment: The National System of Education in the Nineteenth Century* (London, 1970)

Akenson, Donald H., *A Mirror to Kathleen's Face* (Montreal and London, 1975)

Barrington, Thomas J., 'Whatever happened to Irish government?', in F. Litton (ed.), *Unequal Achievement: The Irish Experience 1957–82*, (Dublin, 1982), pp. 89–110

Barry, David, 'The involvement and impact of a professional interest group', in D.G. Mulcahy and Denis O'Sullivan (eds), *Irish Educational Policy: Process and Substance*, (Dublin, 1989), pp. 133–62

Bhreathnach, Aoife, *Becoming Conspicuous: Irish Travellers, Society and the State 1922–70* (Dublin, 2006)

Bonel-Elliott, Imelda, 'La Politique de l'enseignement du second degré en république d'Irlande 1963–93' (Ph.D thesis, Sorbonne, 1994)

Bonel-Elliott, Imelda, 'The role of the Duggan report (1962) in the reform of the Irish education system', *Administration*, vol. 44, no. 3 (Autumn 1996), pp. 42–60

Browne, Noel, *Against the Tide* (Dublin, 1986)

Buckley, Denis, 'Secondary teacher (2)', *Studies*, vol. 57, no. 3 (Autumn 1968), pp. 296–304

Chubb, Basil, 'The university merger', *Studies*, vol. 56, no. 2 (Summer 1967), pp. 130–7

Clancy, Patrick, 'The evolution of policy in third-level education', in D.G. Mulcahy and Denis O'Sullivan (eds), *Irish Educational Policy: Process and Substance*, (Dublin, 1989), pp. 99–132

Clancy, Patrick, 'Investment in Education: the equality perspective – progress and possibilities', *Administration*, vol. 44, no. 3 (Autumn 1996), pp. 28–41

Coolahan, John, *Irish Education: Its History and Structure* (Dublin, 1981)

Coolahan, John, *The ASTI and Post-Primary Education in Ireland 1909–84* (Dublin, 1984)

Coolahan, John, 'Educational policy for national schools 1960–1985', in D.G. Mulcahy and Denis O'Sullivan (eds), *Irish Educational Policy: Process and Substance*, (Dublin, 1989), pp. 27–75

Coolahan, John, 'Dr. P.J. Hillery – Minister for Education: 1959–1965', *Journal for ASTI Convention*, Easter 1990, pp. 15–19

Cooney, John, *The Crozier and the Dáil: Church and State 1922–1986* (Cork, 1986)

Cooney, John, *John Charles McQuaid: Ruler of Catholic Ireland* (Dublin, 1999)

De Buitléar, Séamus, 'Curaclam Nua le hAghaidh na Bunscoile', *Oideas*, no. 3 (Autumn 1969), pp. 4–12

Donoghue, Denis, 'Comment', *Studies*, vol. 56, no. 2 (Summer 1967), pp. 160–4

Donoghue, Denis, 'University professor', *Studies*, vol. 57, no. 3 (Autumn 1968), pp. 284–8

Doyle, Eileen, *Leading the Way: Managing Voluntary Secondary Schools* (Dublin, 2000)

Executive of the TBA, 'Teaching Brothers', *Studies*, vol. 57, no. 3 (Autumn 1968), pp. 274–83

Foster, Roy, *Modern Ireland 1600–1972* (Penguin, 1988)

Garvin, Thomas, *Preventing the Future: Why was Ireland so Poor for so Long?* (Dublin, 2004)

Horgan, John, 'Educational policy and public interest', *Secondary Teacher*, vol. 9, no. 1 (Spring 1980), pp. 9–10

Horgan, John, *Seán Lemass: The Enigmatic Patriot* (Dublin, 1997)

Hyland, Áine, 'The curriculum of vocational education 1930–66', in John Logan (ed.), *Teachers' Union: The TUI and its Forerunners in Irish Education 1899–1994* (Dublin, 1999), pp. 131–56

Hyland, Áine and Milne, Kenneth (eds.), *Irish Educational Documents*, vol. 2 (Dublin, 1992)

Jones, Valerie, 'Coláiste Moibhí: the last Preparatory College', *Irish Educational Studies*, vol. 15 (1996), pp. 101–11

Lee, Joseph, *Ireland 1912–85: Politics and Society* (Cambridge, 1989)

Lee, Joseph and Ó Tuathaigh, Gearóid, *The Age of de Valera* (Dublin, 1982)

Logan, John, 'All the children: the vocational school and educational reform', in John Logan (ed.), *Teachers' Union: The TUI and its Forerunners 1899–1994*, (Dublin, 1999), pp. 276–303

Logan, John, 'The making of a modern union: the Vocational Teachers' Association 1954–1973', in John Logan (ed.), *Teachers' Union: The TUI and its Forerunners 1899–1994*, (Dublin, 1999), pp. 157–203

Lyons, F.S.L., *Ireland since the Famine* (London, 1973)

Macnamara, John, *Bilingualism and Primary Education: A Study of the Irish Experience* (Edinburgh, 1966)

MacHale, J.P., 'The university merger', *Studies*, vol. 56, no. 2 (Summer 1967), pp. 122–9

McCarthy, Charles, *The Distasteful Challenge* (Dublin, 1968)

McCarthy, Charles, 'Vocational teachers', *Studies*, vol. 57, no. 3 (Autumn 1968), pp. 270–3

McCarthy, Charles, *The Decade of Upheaval: Irish Trade Unions in the Nineteen Sixties* (Dublin, 1973)

McDonagh, Kathleen (ed.), *Reports on the Draft Curriculum for Primary Schools* (Dublin, 1969)

McElligott, T.J., *Education in Ireland* (Dublin, 1966)

Meenan, James, 'The University in Dublin', *Studies*, vol. 57, no. 3 (Autumn 1968), pp. 314–20

Milne, Kenneth, 'A Church of Ireland view', *Studies*, vol. 57, no. 3 (Autumn 1968), pp. 261–9

Milne, Kenneth, 'The role of the Protestant school', *Studies in Education*, vol. 11, no. 1 (Spring 1995), pp. 14–22

Moody, T.W., 'Comment', *Studies*, vol. 56, no. 2 (Summer 1967), pp. 173–5

Murphy, John, A., *Ireland in the Twentieth Century* (Dublin, 1975)

Ó Buachalla, Séamas, *Education Policy in Twentieth Century Ireland* (Dublin, 1988)

Ó Buachalla, Séamas, '*Investment in Education*: context, content and impact', *Administration*, vol. 44, no. 3 (Autumn 1996), pp. 10–20

Ó Ceallaigh, Tadhg, *Coláiste Phádraig: St. Patrick's College, Centenary Booklet, 1875–1975* (Dublin, 1975)

O'Connell, T.J., *A History of the INTO 1868–1968* (Dublin, 1969)

O'Connor, Seán, 'Post-primary education now and in the future', *Studies*, vol. 57, no. 3 (Autumn 1968), pp. 233–49

O'Connor, Seán, *A Troubled Sky: Reflections on the Irish Education Scene 1957–68* (Dublin, 1986)

Ó Cuilleanáin, T.A., 'Special education in Ireland', *Oideas*, no. 1 (Autumn 1968), pp. 5–17

O'Donoghue, Martin, 'Investment in Education: the economist's view – great change, little change', *Administration*, vol. 44, no. 3 (Autumn 1996), pp. 21–7

O'Flaherty, Louis, *Management and Control in Irish Education: The Post-Primary Experience* (Dublin, 1992)

O'Malley, Donogh, 'University education in Dublin: Statement of Minister for Education – 18 April 1967', *Studies*, vol. 56, no. 2 (Summer 1967), pp. 113–21

O'Meara, John, *Reform in Education* (Dublin, 1958)

O'Raifeartaigh, Tarlach, 'Some impressions of education in the USA', *Studies*, vol. 50, no. 1 (Spring 1961), pp. 57–74

O'Sullivan, Denis, *Cultural Politics and Irish Education since the 1950s* (Dublin, 2005)

Parkes, Susan, *Kildare Place: A History of the Church of Ireland Training College 1811–1969* (Dublin, 1983)

Randles, Eileen, *Post-Primary Education in Ireland 1957–70* (Dublin, 1975)

Troddyn, Peter, 'Editorial', *Studies*, vol. 57, no. 3 (Autumn 1968), pp. 226–32

Troddyn, Peter, 'Editorial', *Studies*, vol. 59, no. 4 (Winter 1970), pp. 337–76

Tussing, Dale, *Irish Educational Expenditure: Past, Present and Future* (Dublin, 1978)

Whyte, J.H., *Church and State in Modern Ireland 1923–70* (Dublin, 1971)

Interviews or correspondence

Professor John Coolahan
Mr. Barry Desmond
Mr. James Dukes
Dr. Garret FitzGerald
Dr. Patrick Hillery
Professor Áine Hyland
Mr. Thomas Leahy
Dr. Séamus Ó Buachalla
Mr. Tony Ó Dálaigh
Professor Martin O'Donoghue

Index